A word from the readers, without whom this book would certainly have never happened –

*"Happy New Year, Girlfriend! I am really hoping that this year you decide to write a book. I love your articles and I think a book is forthcoming. You make me feel the sentiments, the smells and the warmest of whatever you are writing about. Your column is the first thing I read from the Soledad Bee."*

- Angie

*"If I were to buy a house, I would use your services. I enjoyed reading your recent column. You have an unusual talent with words: clear, distinct, logical, informative, sensitive, useful, reassuring all come to mind. Did you learn your language skills all in the Homeland? I learned mine in the Colonies, and I have a long, long way to go to match yours. I'm not going to even try. I kant evan spel."*

- Bud

*"Lucy Lucy Lucy. I read your column. From the bottom of my heart, thank you so very much. Your words inspired more than I could imagine. We had three brand new jackets delivered this morning to our office because of your story. I have never before felt the Christmas Spirit as I have this year."*

- S

2013

To Teri

# WINDOW ON THE WORLD

---

LUCY MASON JENSEN

Love, Lucy

INFINITY PUBLISHING

ISBN 978-0-7414-7988-4 Paperback
ISBN 978-0-7414-7989-1 eBook
Library of Congress Control Number: 2012916808

Printed in the United States of America



Published December 2012

INFINITY PUBLISHING

Toll-free (877) BUY BOOK
Local Phone (610) 941-9999
Fax (610) 941-9959
Info@buybooksontheweb.com
www.buybooksontheweb.com

# THANKS

When our local librarian at the Soledad library, Angie Lopez, sent me her encouraging email, in the New Year of 2007, on the topic of compiling my various newspaper columns into a book, she sowed a seed in my mind, which grew over time – a long period of time – and culminated in the publication of this, my first book. Five years past due – for that I'm sorry, Angie.

At the time, I promised Angie that I *would* publish a book of my columns and pledged to have my first book signing at her library. Sadly, Angie has already passed on; but I will make good on my promise and do the book signing in her honor at her library. I do thank her, through the ether, for her all of her encouragement along the way, both before and after she passed.

Thanks also to all who supported me on my journey towards publication – to Sandy and John, who bought me my first laptop that held the contents of the entire book from start to finish. To my friends in the newspaper world, who edited and encouraged me along the way – you know who you are. To my faithful, weekly readers, who told folks that they felt that they knew me through my stories, even though we had never actually met! And, of course, to my wonderful, crazy family and friends – all of you, two and four-legged – near and far and, for sure, in other spheres. Without you, the material would never have been so forthcoming or diverse.

Love you all,

***Lucy***

# CONTENTS

# FAMILY

# A LITTLE OF WHAT YOU FANCY; OR LIFE IS SHORT

Granny used to say that "a little of what you fancy does you good, dear", and I personally like to live by that maxim in my life, wherever possible. If I want a small piece of chocolate or even that large slice of cheesecake which has my name on it; I think that I should be able to indulge myself; just not every day. If I want to take a trip, I like to try and find a way to do it. A little of what you fancy will, ultimately, give you a better life; or that's my opinion anyway.

I try to instill the same self-indulgent values in my daughter, 'cos life is too short to do without much of what we fancy, for heaven's sakes. Shouldn't we try and enjoy ourselves just a little bit more than we do in the blah-blah same ol' of every day life; especially during summer vacation, when the schedules are a little off, the days a little longer and the credit cards not so tight with the threat of the holiday shopping onslaught?

It's the middle of the long hot summer and, rich though we're definitely not, for the past few days my daughter has been out there lording it with the horsy gals. She's been clipping around with the ranchers' daughters; the Princess Rodeos, the lucky ones, in her book, who mostly get to eat, sleep and breathe horses in their regular lives. Her one unique horse experience in life was, up until this week, sitting on a Shetland pony in the fair, and that was a very long time ago. But this time, she is signed up for 2 weeks of horse riding camp and, boy, is she happy!

Though we do live out in the country, the closest thing we have to a horse is my old wooden rocking horse which decorates our dining room. "Why don't you get a horse?" people ask when they find out you've got more than a patch of scrub to feed the blessed thing. My response is pretty standard ..."That would be like having another teenager living at home," (and we're really quite happy we don't have those around at the moment, thank you very much!) But I do confess that I deeply admire the majesty of the horse, and especially in some one else's back yard, teenager or not.

My daughter has wanted to learn how to ride for a long time now and I've had so many good excuses, over time, not to go down that road. The first being I'm very afraid of the power of genetics. I was a self-confessed horse maniac when I was a little girl. I did not own a horse of my own, but went riding every Sunday, (and in my mind every night, when my rocking horse –the same Moonshine who now lives with us– would magically come alive and gallop over the hills and dales with me like Black Beauty). In those days, if I heard that a distant friend had a horse, all of a sudden we weren't "just friends", we were the "bestest friends in the whole wide world" and I would somehow, miraculously, manage to manipulate my determined little body over to her house and onto her horse. I would read books about riding, draw pictures of horses, write stories about the beasts … you get the picture. Mother was always cautious, but tolerant. "Don't turn your back on the brutes," she would warn me, (not much of a horse lover herself). And then she'd drive me to riding lessons every week and sometimes twice a week, because she was an awesome mother and I was horribly spoilt. I had the boots, the hat, the jodhpurs, the crop; I was the total horsy gal. I do believe mother was quite relieved, however, when I became a teenager, we moved to the big city and I began chasing other things around the place rather than horses. Always something, isn't there, for parents to stress about!

My daughter's first day at camp presented her with a real life tester. Firstly she was nipped in the chest by a not-so-friendly pony, before she had even had the chance to sit on his back. Real tears in front of her peers ensued. "Oh dear," I thought. "This could be the beginning of the end of her horse passion." Nope. She was riding within the hour. Next there was a death in the family, when the young campers endured witnessing a horse getting very sick and dying, literally before their very eyes. A huge life lesson there! "Have you had enough yet, dear?" I ventured. Nope. She wanted more; she wanted to stay over at camp for the sleepover with the other horse maniacs. Reining my self and my cautions in, no pun intended, I resolved, at that point, to support her passion finally; let her love it. Let her ride, if she is so inclined, let her whole-heartedly embrace something which is so good and wholesome, that it makes her hug herself with excitement and look forward to tomorrow. Loving something that much cannot be so bad, especially when you're nine years old and feeling the wind in your hair!

The weekend arrives and, all of a sudden, there's a different child in the house. Gone is the girl who is crazy for baseball, soccer, bike riding and all those other passions which were so the beginning of the summer! Now she's a horse rider. I'm having flash-backs with all this talk about tack, bits, saddles, horns, trotting .... And I'm realizing that something's coming my way in the form of me 30 something years ago. That's a pretty scary encounter for most people, but especially in the space of yesterday to today!

So here we are – another week to go in the land of equine experience and life's little tests. Baby goats were born today, which softened the blow somewhat of the horse dying a few days ago. It's probably, all of it, something solid for the memory banks and that is more than okay. In a week of horse camp, they get to see, up close and personal, the inevitable circle of life.

When you look back on your summers years ago, what gives you that warm and fuzzy feeling? Maybe it was the first time you slept over at camp and giggled around a camp fire; maybe it was the first time you found a passion and you held it really close. Perhaps it was the day you realized that you didn't need your parents around you all the time for you to feel totally safe and fine with the world.

Whatever you're doing for your little miracles this summer, add a little touch of special to it and hope that they hold it tight. Can't recreate the memories, now can we, if they get all muddied up along the way? We've got to let them evolve and blossom in the here and now; we've got to let them give it their all. There's no time like the present. It becomes the past way too quickly.

**Lucy has always adored horses. Her daughter Francoise is by far the superior rider.**

# DEATH, DIVORCE AND MOVING HOUSE

The words death and divorce will generally get a reader's attention; moving house not so much. But, did you know that these are alleged to be the top three things that can cause you major stress, ill health, and even, possibly death? When I read that little factoid, the first two did not surprise me one bit, but the third gave me some food for thought, which took me back to my last moving house experience and just how many grey hairs I gained from the exercise, (plus my resolve – and the resolve of those around me – to never, I say never, repeat the experience again. My husband and I have an agreement – already – that if we split, we will split the house in half and share it. He can have the kitchen; I take the lounging tub. We hated moving that much!)

We chose to move house at a really unbelievably stressful time in our lives, in any case. Having happily lived together for quite some time in unwedded bliss, we opted to get married, almost simultaneously with the realization that we needed to move house. Not content with fleeing the state quietly on our twosome and finding the chapel of 'Elvis in Vegas' for our eternal commitments, we had to invite the whole darn family; that meant not just the good people of Watsonville, the Washingtons and Oregon, but also the British contingent. The ever-so-smart plan was to move house in July and get married in August. Ha! If ever you think that that might be a good idea, please use the benefit of my many stress lines and eternally grey patches of hair to tell you that you couldn't have a worse idea if you tried. This is what happens when you try to move house whilst living under the most unbelievable tornado of a deadline:-

1. You plan to pack the garage that weekend. The caterer calls and wants to meet you at the "site" to discuss set-up arrangements. The garage stays unpacked.
2. You save all the boxes from work, planning to pack two boxes a night to be on schedule. The kids have a bonfire and burn all the boxes.

3. You plan to take all the pictures down from the walls and patch the walls. (You will need that deposit with all the wedding bills you are accumulating). Your sweet teenage son gets arrested and you have to go and bail him out.
4. You totally intend to pack up the garage, marking all the boxes with anal concern, plus give the garage a good clean, (again to make sure you get that deposit back). Child number two takes this weekend to announce that he needs to move back home and where has his bedroom gone anyway? Plus he needs boxes to bring all his stuff back to your home.
5. You need to spend that weekend taking all the items down from the porch and packing them away in the new boxes that you have brought from work. You even have a marker pen that works. The DJ calls and wants to meet you out at the 'site' to discuss the music, location of the DJ equipment and so on. The magic marker disappears. It is later found without its top and has to be thrown away.
6. You have a new plan which means that you have to pack 10 boxes a night to get back on schedule. Your in-laws announce that they need to move in with you. They can no longer live at the brother's house, while they wait for their home to be finished. You contact the landlord who tells you that your folks can't move in; there are too many people on the one septic tank already and they don't even know about the return of child number two. You have to go and deal with the brother and the in-laws' living arrangements. You're already a week behind with your 10 box plan.
7. The caterer calls. The price per plate just went up due to the cost of dish liquid or some other such trivia. Plus they need to meet you out at the "site" to check that the dishes match the color of the ocean appropriately.
8. All of a sudden, all kinds of special friends and family members come out of the woodwork to announce that they have not yet received their wedding invitation.
9. You call the caterer. The price per plate just went up due to the lack of warning about untold guests.
10. You are now needing to pack 12 boxes per night to be on schedule.

And so it went on, until we finally tied the knot on a chilly foggy August morning in front of too many of our very bestest friends and relatives in the whole wide world. We had moved house about two weeks before and were still suffering sore backs, torn nails and the deep furrows of a highly stressful experience. If we would have had time and money for a honeymoon, we would have slept the entire time amidst piles of unpacked boxes.

We didn't get all of our deposit back; the cost per plate continued to rise; we still have stuff in boxes – not all of them marked – and we survived to tell the tale; in fact we are still married even. The moral of this story is that if you are planning on moving house; do not underestimate the overwhelming impact this seemingly slight life-event will have on yourself and your family. It does take a village to pack up a life and move it on to another village. Do not imagine that you can combine such a life-heaver with any other kind of life-heaver and get through the experience unscathed.

**Lucy hasn't moved house since and is not planning to.**

# DROPPING EGGS

I've been feeling recently that I am more of an egg juggler in a circus than a real estate professional; and that, with the yolky mess I'm seeing all around my feet, I'm likely to get fired from the traveling show at any minute.

It's the beginning of the long, hot, summer vacation for all of our children; the time when parents sigh and study the many, many days, months even, on the calendar, before their little blessings will return to the safety of their teachers and their 8-3 mandatory attendance away from the enticements of friends, freedom and driving their parents potty. This is only the second week of school vacation and already I'm longing for August and those sweet, sweet words 'they're going back to school'. Not that I don't think my darling deserves some rest and relaxation; she absolutely does, and I wish that I could 'R and R' for 10 weeks along with her; but she's on holiday, I am not; and therein lies the challenge.

"Mum, can you pick me up at 11, take me home, then go and pick up Maritza, then take us to Brit's house, then take us home again and then, Mum, I really need new shoes and can we please go and see a movie...' and she really can say all of that in one sentence without punctuation, or really even taking a breath.

Mix and match that 'new-found' summer challenge for us parents with the annual visit of various members of my family and you can see why I'm knee deep in broken eggs that I keep trying to juggle, managing to drop way more than I catch.

Normally I would take darling child on vacation to England this time of year; a break for us both; time away to split up the thick wad of vacation time a bit for her and equally get me away from real estate and my regular life. This year is not holiday time for me, but at the same time it's not really a regular work time either; though it should be. Foolishly, I had thought that by not going on our annual trip to the old country I would just be able to focus on my work. I had discounted the presence of the other people in my midst who might need me to try and juggle my needs with their more pressing needs and there you have it; broken eggs and no one's scrambling them or doing anything really useful or salvageable.

So what do we do with all this juggling? How do the busy people of the world manage to hold it all together without losing our tempers, our families or our jobs? I've decided that we take mini-trips to try and appease all concerned. We break up the weeks with some pleasure; some pain. We work two days and play two days, if at all possible, and try to add the rest of the work back in when the people concerned are either sleeping or relaxing.

This experiment was recently tested and proven a fair success. While my father was staying from England, my daughter, father and I went over to Carmel for a couple of nights and stayed in a nice bed and breakfast in the heart of the village. Spending time in Carmel is about as foreign as going to the Bahamas, if you live in Soledad, so it was quite a little holiday for all. We day-tripped to Monterey, rented bikes, played some tennis and ate on the wharf. We visited the local shops and aided the economy somewhat. We enjoyed the white sand beach of Carmel, did some people watching and enjoyed good food in the restaurants. In short, we traveled less than an hour, but had a mini-break and felt duly refreshed when we got back home again. Never mind that the lap top and the cell phone were never too far away. When you are out cycling, your extended absence voicemail can always say 'I'm in a meeting right now and I'll call you back this afternoon,' and no one will be any the worse for not knowing exactly what kind of meeting you are in. My daughter was happy; my father enjoyed his time over there and I did not go out of business just because I slept some where else and ate in different restaurants. I even felt a little relaxed myself, away from the washing machine, the home phone and the bills; not to mention the dishes.

If it's school vacation time in your home and it's stressing you out and making you juggle and break all the eggs, I recommend the mini-break to satisfy all the appetites. Kids are so flexible that if you take a tent to the local camp ground they will probably thank you ten-fold for their lovely vacation and write it up as the high point of their long hot summer.

Mini trips; the key to my sanity this summer, I'm thinking. With 8 more weeks of free time for our little blessings still to go; where shall we go next?

**Lucy is a local circus performer.**
**What would you recommend as the key**
**to holding it all together?**

# EVERYTHING YOU WANT TO KNOW WILL BE IN MY OBITUARY

An old friend passed away this week. I say "old" and "friend", truly for want of better words. He was a person I had a lot of respect for years ago; we had a mutual understanding at a different time and place in life, when mutual understanding and some completely silent but understood exchange was necessary. He needed a little help from me at the time which I was in the position to afford. In return, he rewarded me with the most divine pair of deerskin boots ever known to clip clop over land, (he was the owner of a shoe shop), which I still have and which still give me pleasure. His family also gave me many a meal and whatever shelter I needed at any times that I needed them. You don't forget things like that; however far you have moved away from the times and places that demanded such things.

He was not old at all when he died, this man whom I respected, and I had not really seen him for some years, though, ironically I did catch sight of him in a wheelchair at a recent event and I was so taken aback by his decline that I could not say hello even. However sad I felt that he had left the planet and left it prematurely in my opinion, it did give me great pleasure to read his obituary. That may sound strange to some; but I have come to realize that the more I read and even, on occasion, write obituaries, the more obvious it becomes that, very often, we do not know the true metal of a man or woman until we see their biography in black and white. I had no idea, for example that my old friend was a navy man. I saw the stars and stripes above his name in the paper and wondered how he had such a complete life before the life that I met him in; and how did he never mention to me, during our many conversations, the years that he had served his country, the foreign lands and peoples he had seen? Maybe we just didn't have enough time.

My father told me recently that he wanted to write his autobiography of sorts. He wanted to put down as much as he could remember in some kind of coherency; a record for our family, "for you especially," he said talking to his granddaughter.

She doesn't realize it now but she will cherish the gift later on in life, if he follows through. Father is a walking history book; never mind the fact that he is, actually, a Doctor of history. He was born in the roaring 20's in England at the tail end of the 1st World War. He nearly lost his leg when he was run over as a boy and spent many years in rehabilitation. He was sent away to the countryside during the 2nd World War; and didn't see much of his family at all during his youth, as far as I can make out, except for his sister. His family had staff and he was pretty removed from his parents throughout his life. His detailed story – not my casual pointers- would most likely reveal more than I ever could imagine, just knowing him the flipside of the 1960's when we lived in relative calm and peace, as family units together. The complete story would most likely make me more kindly towards him when he exhibits signs of insecurity or what might be termed a "depression attitude". My mother always said that he didn't get enough cuddles from his mother as a child, and she was probably right. There is no doubt that his generation had it really tough. Just living through a world war must have given the people invisible battle scars that my generation cannot possibly imagine. You look at our youth of today and wonder how they would manage with even a modicum of any of that.

I look forward to my father's story and will encourage its completion; not only to know him a little better myself and be more prepared for the ultimate obituary, but to pass it along for the generations to come and not bury a wonderful rich tale in the sands of time. There have been too many people in recent years whose final biography I have read and said to myself, "I knew them, but I really didn't know them at all; and now it's too late." I have been trying to piece my mother's story together for years and have felt her nudge me every now and then when my poetic license gets the better of me and wanders into untrue waters. I don't know necessarily when I'm crossing the threshold, but there was just so much left unsaid and so many unchartered waters in her tale, that the story-teller is forced to fill in the gaps. I'm hoping that my father does not leave the door open for vacuous gaps to be filled.

Be kind to your family and the generation to come. Even if you are not a writer, write it down. Use bullets, if you need to, or find a ghost writer, but get it out of your brain and your heart and onto something indelible. Time is of the essence they say and none of us knows when that time will be up. Take a leaf out of my old friend's book and make a mark, however slight. Leave something good for the obituary and at least a pair of deerskin boots for those who made a difference to you.

**Lucy is a daily reader of the obituary column in the paper.**

# LIZARD ON A HOT TIN ROOF

I feel as stretched as a lizard pinned down on a hot tin roof right about now; and if that doesn't make any sense then neither does my life. Sometimes you feel so immensely overwhelmed with life that you want to run and hide in a dark room with your hands over your ears to keep out the noise. That does not work well when you have a house full of relatives, a family that expects your attendance at regular events such as meals and laundry, and a job that keeps on sucking your blood most parts of most days.

Watching the lizard cavort across the logs, fall brutally between two sticks and then get itself just a little stuck between two timbers, when it tried to rescue itself, mirrored how I'm feeling these days. I keep trying to get ahead, I keep trying to climb the Mount Everest of my own existence, but the harder I try, the quicker I fall back down again and get squashed and bruised between at least two of the sticks, which are somehow set up to trip me.

It's the modern way; so they say. We try and we juggle and we sometimes fail miserably, we do. So what can we do? We cannot cease to exist. We cannot really hide in a dark room for very long; regardless of the known benefits for the universe to stay firmly away from pre-menopausal women, (sometimes we need to be locked in dark rooms.) We have to believe that the morrow will be somewhat improved; that there will not be two escrows that fall out with the drama of crashing shooting stars every single day. We have to soldier on and weather the storm. We must see the bright side of each day; not knowing how many of those things we have left to squander. Here is my latest, brightest compilation on that particular melting pot of ideas:-

1. Hug and stroke dogs at least four times a day; more if you have the time. They make you feel like you rock, you totally rock; and when they are making you feel that way, they feel that way too. Nothing has that same ability. Cats are good too, except that most of them will get quickly bored of all the attention.

2. Eat chocolate. It is the simplest most divine pleasure; as close to god, just about, as you can arrive, in one second. You don't have to eat a lot; just a snickle on the end of the tongue and see how long it can last.
3. Drink wine. It is another of the most divine pleasures in life. It has to have been created in heaven – wherever that is – by some really old souls who knew what the rest of us needed. Don't waste your time on cheap wine; life is so definitely too short.
4. Exercise. It is such a gift. You don't have to be a major athlete to do it, just get a pair of well-fitting sneakers on your peepers and go and do something. Even if it's only fake karate or pseudo ballroom-dancing in your living room while you watch 'Ellen', it's so very important for your body's blood flow and your sense of well-being. It can also keep you away from needing the dark room as much as you possibly do.
5. Don't over-book. Life is one day after another. There will be 365 days to the year and you do not need to fill each one chock-a-block with something to do. Cherish the days of nothing and take your gift to heart; you may not have another one for a week or so. Do the same thing for your children. Every minute of their existence does not have to be filled with something scintillating which makes them a sure bet for Harvard or Stanford. Really, truly. Sometimes it's okay to let them play XBOX or chat to their friends on 'Facebook'. Remember what you forbid them to do, they will just do at some one else's house.
6. Give yourself a daily time out. That requires a few minutes of nothing each day when you sit and look at the birds, the sky, the mountain; whatever toots your horn, a time when you do not check email or talk on the phone, and you definitely don't speak to other people. You cleanse your psyche; a colonic for the soul. Some other people might also call it praying.
7. Try to laugh more than you do. Whether it's watching a season re-run of 'The Office', or just chatting with your young one – they've always got something funny to say. Stretch the laughter lines of your face; and put one more character line around the eyes, why doncha? I'm a firm

believer in the powerful release of laughter; cough up the tension, get it out. Follow the example of the children; they can teach the adults a thing or two about laughing. They do it, consistently, much more than we do.

8. Find a fabulous book you can't put down and feed your brain some mind candy. It's a vacation for the mind truly to go somewhere you were definitely not planning to go that day. If you can't afford to buy a book, the library is full of wonderful choices; all free.
9. Plan something fun for somewhere down the road; but not so down the road that you feel doubtful you will ever make it. If you can't plan a vacation, plan a mini visit somewhere; even a day out somewhere fabulous, or preferably a night too, which will give you the makeover you need and help you with that stretched out feeling. The world will not close down if you take a day off; you will not be fired from your job, or have clients banging down your door to cancel contracts. No; it is for the betterment of all and we have to allow ourselves to be a little more healthy-minded than perhaps we have become in this rigorous planet of land mines across which we tread.

If you too are feeling like a lizard on a hot tin roof and you've fallen off the burning roof into the wood pile and feel like you can't get out, then know this; you are not alone. There are too many of us feeling this way and it needs to stop. If you can't get hold of me one day, don't worry; I'm either in a dark room with my hands over my ears or I'm taking the day off. Don't laugh; it might happen!

**Lucy is a sometime juggler in the circus of life.**

# MOTHERS AND DAUGHTERS

Several years ago, I wrote a column in the Salinas paper on the subject of mothers and daughters. I recall being amazed at not only how many people still read papers, but also the power of such simple subject matter to touch people's hearts so intensely. It's a pretty fundamental thing; if you are a daughter, then some one, somewhere is your mother. The complexity of the relationship, however, in many cases, transcends life and time. The older I get, the more I appreciate that.

I lost my mother to another planet over a decade ago – 9 am on November 9$^{th}$, 2000 to be precise, if you're clock watching, as I find myself doing increasingly, the older I get. I was privileged enough to be able to watch her leave us and I have never tired of recalling those last few precious minutes, when she proceeded to leave one world and enter the next; as if that was ever a vision I could lose over time. My anxieties not to let her go; and yet her pressing need to leave. The battle of the wills between the mother and her child still waging war to the very last breath. The magic and the agony of the end of life contrasting deeply with someone's faith in an after life and their willingness to embrace it.

She had planned her departure. I had known she was leaving. She waited for me to arrive at her home in England from my home in America, she had given us some time to catch up on a few things, clear up a few issues, pack up her clothes, say her goodbyes to others and even buy and wrap her Christmas presents, and then she had left our world; her last gift to me being that her final human breath was taken in my arms. I am glad that I struggled through the 'Lords Prayer', as she slipped away on her journey with a pocket full of faith; and the last words she heard were my words, that surely comforted her, as she quietly left the room, rosary in hand.

I see my life now as separated by a deep line in the sands, which has been permanently marked in the tides of my existence. There is life before my mother died and life after; different planets where I am also a different person.

"The apple doesn't fall too far from the tree!" I tell my daughter, when she is disliking me most especially and I feel like pushing her opinion of me to the edge of her tolerance. After my mother left, I realized that I carried even more of her with me than I had before. Part of her did stay with me after all, I came to see, and blossomed inside me, the more we lived together. She became a branch on my tree. I became a branch on hers. It has been a most satisfying and symbiotic relationship ever since. Though my daughter most resembles my mother's mother – a woman she never met – we are all there together, branches on each other's trees with the roots stretching out to eternity.

After Mum left, I found gifts of her in myself that I never thought I possessed. I came to appreciate things that she had loved and I hadn't really noticed until she was no longer around. I'll talk to her about things that happen and feel a calmness spread throughout my aura in her response to me. Sometimes, when I am stressed or unhappy, a warmth will radiate through me which I take to be my mothers arms wrapped tightly around my ageing body and her whispered words I recall from years ago, "No matter how old you are, you'll always be my baby."

I have learned to open my eyes more now she is gone. Maybe those gifts were there all along, but I like to think not. I like to think that she has arranged them just for me; an ongoing buffet of offerings to delight, surprise and make me smile – sometimes when I am awake, and sometimes in sleep. If she can't send me the chatty letters like she used to with all her news in scratchy hand, or make that late night phone call when she knew my dad was in bed, and I was at work and would pick up for a good chat; she sends me other messages. Now I'm able to better tune in, I see things all the time. That swooping hawk over the lush valley has her vision. The road runner on the post in my yard has her agility. That divine rose over there with the sweetest aroma would have her clipping several for a posy on her table. I pick them for her. There she is again! The cormorant diving into the bay – her favorite bird – he's performing just for me. That poem she loved – falls open into my hand, as I browse in my book shelf. She wants me to re-read it and, in the re-reading, learn something new. I open the dust cover of a book and see her name in her hand – sometimes with a date next to it, which I love. A post card she wrote years ago becomes a gift I had forgotten in the deep recesses of a dusty box. So many years later, it can still draw a tear. That random penny we picked up from the ground - 1933 – the year she was born. The crazy diamond planet that lights up the night sky. She was a crazy diamond. There are so many gifts if you open your eyes to see.

If you are aching inside to see a loved one again; look around you and you just may find that they have been there all the time.

Another Mother's Day is here and gone. A lot of talk about mothers, a lot of gifts, of cherishing and showing them how much you care. I look at my mother, as she treks around the universe, inside of me and beyond. I know she is very, very close – I can feel her most days and I can see her inside not only myself but my daughter too. She transcends the generations. I cannot actually touch her, but closing my eyes I can too touch her and smell her fragrance on the air. I see her hands, her neck. I hear her voice, her laughter. She is real, she is present; I know she'll always be so and that is everything to me. The comfort I take from that knowledge softens all the other sad feelings I carry with me throughout life, when the universe takes your beloved out of your line of vision and situates her elsewhere.

For those of you who just celebrated Mother's Day with your mother; if you got to love on her and hold her in the here and now, you are the lucky ones. For those of us who have to close our eyes to touch and inhale deeply on the ether to sense, I hope you saw the full moon recently that I feasted on with my eyes and the face I saw within. I hope you felt the rays of warmth on your soul this Mother's Day and the sound of familiar laughter which came from just around the corner, a mere step from where you are now. If you did not, trust me it's there. You just have to open up your heart to hear.

**Lucy's Mother, Una Bagnall Benedicta Theodora Mason,**
**will always live inside of her.**
**May 27, 1933 – November 9, 2000**.

# MY BIRTH MONTH

I have decided to enjoy a birth-month this year, in lieu of simply a Birth Day. I think I have earned it. In our family, there are just so many birthdays in September, we might as well dedicate the entire month to our clan and be done with it. If we didn't all live the world over, we would get together for sure and have a big ol' shin-dig with mounds of food and wine, lots of opinions, an enormous cake and a gazillion candles. In fact, the entire month should just be dedicated to me and mine.

If my Myrtie were still here, my gorgeous, elegant grandma, we'd need a bunch of candles this year, since she would have just celebrated her ninety something birthday and the mind just boggles at that achievement. And so the birthday whirl spins on. My daughter celebrates her birthday two days before me, my sister is the same day as me, various friends and family share days around our days and so it goes on. The month is completely nuts if, like me, you try and at least keep up with a phone call or a card. My mother always said there was something magic about September – maybe because she seemed to spend a lot of time that month rich with all the life around her or glowing with pregnancy herself.

I am not far away from being a half century old, I realize, as I ponder my birth month and what I would like to do to make it particularly special this year. After the year that I have had thus far, I have decided to never complain about getting old; it just means that – totally cool and awesome thing - I am still here, really pure and simple. Now that I am bald, and not attractively so, with few eyelashes to boast and not much in the way of eyebrows either, ageing has become a thing that other folks can get concerned with, but definitely not me. I flick swiftly through the shampoo ads in the 'Over 40's' magazine, the anti-ageing creams, the glossy black mascara commercials; none of those are any good for me at the moment, though I do hope they will be one day, when I need a little black on my lash or a rich and smooth conditioner on a lock or two. Now if they could come up with a full-body, magic healing potion or a cure for cancer, we'd really be talking - but your paradigms can shift, when life stuff happens to you and some how everything gets tilted a little differently from where it was before. Maybe I'll never care about ageing lines or the rich luster of my beautiful hair ever again. I'll just care that I am well again and alive for the here and now. I'll go back to basics and be a better person for it. Not surprisingly, I no longer view things in quite the same way as I did before April 30, 2010 of this long, long year, which is still going.

My Grandma - always Myrtle to us - had a feeling that the life race was a quick one, even if you outlived all your husbands and siblings and, at the very end, you were ready to go join them all again; as she most certainly was. She remained cheerful, optimistic and a pleasure to be around to the very end of her long and interesting life. She was a ray of sunshine that consistently lit up the room – either that or no one was going to get to see her that day. Those seemed to be her unwritten rules. She would be private with her suffering or her grief, if that was going to be her day. However, when she presented herself to the world, it was fully and immaculately dressed and coiffed with pearls, make up and all. There was simply no other way to do it. She prided herself on sharing Princess Diana's hairdresser – which she did right up until the end – and consistently glided like a Princess herself, even when she wasn't feeling much like a swan. She had a way of making everyone feel special from the postman to the waitress to her very own grandchildren. Once encountered, she was never forgotten. Her unique way of conducting her life gave me a life lesson over the years of the highest order, that I didn't realize had gone so deep, until life started doling out some different lessons for me all by itself.

I realize now that Myrtle suffered quite seriously for quite some time with osteoporosis, but we did not hear her complain. She must have been lonely, losing the husbands she loved and all her darling sisters over the course of time; but she never mentioned it; only that she missed them, not that she was lonely without them. She must have worried about how she was going to manage all by herself in her apartment, but there was never a pity party for us to show up to, or a reason for us to think that she hadn't got it all planned out. She never allowed anyone to feel sorry for her in any way and therein lies a big clue to making yourself a pleasure to be around – something that is so important and intrinsic in life that many of us forget; especially when we are suffering something that we feel we shouldn't be.

Myrtle was always delighted to hear from me when I called her on a Sunday morning, which I did every week. I'd ask her how she was feeling and she would tell me that she was all the better for talking to me and that I had made her day, her weekend, her life – yet again. She never mentioned her aching bones or the fact that, maybe even that day, she hadn't wanted to get out of bed, let alone eat a meal. I always left the call feeling more cheered than when I entered it. I thought about Myrtie on the anniversary of what would have been her birthday this week and how many gifts she gave us all. Not just the elegant stone bench I attach to her memory every time I'm in my back yard or the lovely, timeless photos I have of her, a moment in time from her glamorous youth, but the simple things I should have realized I'd taken from her sooner than I did. The grace you need when you get dealt a tough hand, the struggles no one truly wants to hear about when you are frightened or in pain, where you can hide your fears so no one can see, and, ultimately, how the scars we carry with us down the road are just the fault lines that make us human and worth knowing in life.

As we celebrate a bunch of birthdays in our family – from the sweet sixteen's of my daughter (and how did that happen I wonder?) - to the 94$^{th}$ birthday of my dear and five year never-really-gone Myrtie – and all of us in between – I do need to look at another birthday for my old bald self and examine how much I have learned this year and how much still needs to be gleaned, until I can walk and talk with the grace of my Myrtie and all those lessons I should have picked up earlier. In that regard, I guess I am still pretty young. She taught me that, when we know better, we can do better and I do think that is one of the wonderful things about getting older. You cannot look like the sixteen year old and carry the knowledge of an octogenarian. As with everything in life, there is a price to pay. I've paid the price a little bit this year, I think, and will come out of my birth month, I do hope, a little richer in the compassion and humility departments.

My birthday wish, if I get one, is that my Myrtie will think to drop a little birthday sprinkle on my lot and hand me down some of her innate grace and style under fire. Then, maybe, I will be able to glide a little more impressively into my next year of life with better health, more wisdom and perhaps even an additional eyelash or two to put the icing on my cake.

**Lucy thinks that maybe a birth month should be mandatory when we hit middle age? This column is dedicated to my darling Myrtie and all the love she gave.**

# NEVER TOO OLD

You are never too old for most things; I have found in all my maturity. The older you get, the more you can sharpen your people skills, work on your patience, enhance your sense of humor and, ultimately, become more yourself. I like ageing, I have noticed. If you get over the laughter lines, the crow mouth, the leathery skin, old lady hands and all those terrific gifts that walk along hand-in-hand with a few decades of existence on the planet, then you've got it made.

In early life, I recall, you struggle much of the time with yourself. You struggle also with work, money, relationships, family; and then again, mostly with yourself. You are on a journey and you keep tripping up along the way. In my fourth decade, I may still have struggles of all kinds. I may not always have the bank accounts I think I deserve or the super sweet reciprocal bond with my tween girl I know I've earned; but I can say that I struggle much, much less with myself.

I also struggle less with friends. It gets really simple the older we get; either we really like each other or we really don't. There is no footsy on the playground; the best friend forever one minute and the worst enemy the next. I watch from a distance the shenanigans of my daughter and her friends and the cold mist of memory comes washing back over me. You don't forget those times. Remember when your "BFF" at the time ignored you as she walked by with her books high on her chest and her new "BFF" of the moment sidled up right beside her? (Ouch; that searing pain in the chest!) Remember when this new-found-best-friend-forever relationship lasted more than a few days and you thought that you really were forever out in the cold and alone; exiled permanently from 'BFF' status? Remember when you did something really howling like try to snatch another girl's boyfriend and got caught? It was like spending the night in a deep freeze and, along with that, the agonizing suffering of wishing you could turn back time and make everything turn out differently. The painful tears, the wishing you could move the clock back to yesterday and have a chance to make it better again. All of those things come back to me in a minute when I witness the games that the young things play, and I reassure myself that, in my old age, I'm totally over all of that. Either we are friends or we are not, in my world these days; we do not have to play footsie, or pretend we don't like some one when we really, really do. That is such a relief.

What is good too is when you discover that, though you are obviously too old for friend games, you are not too old to make another friend; that, in all your eccentricities, some one else can bother to meet you half-way and say, 'boy I'm glad we met!" That can be so refreshing after a long time out in the cold.

I left good friends in England when I left the country twenty something years ago, and we still stay in touch by email or phone. Sometimes I even get to see them; but it can never be what it was way back when, because geography steps in. The friendship takes on another life of its own. "You left," one of them told me, "And we had to move on." And they did. But I have learned that emotional capacity does not dissolve with time. One of my oldest friends has the ability to communicate with me through the ether. Sometimes I just feel that she needs me, though she's struggling too much with too many things to tell me that directly. I contact her and I am never wrong. It's just how it is and we both accept that. Though I lost a dear friend years ago – she died at the age of 40 from an asthma attack - I still count her as a dear friend; death does not alter that. And I can still approach a new friend and hope that we can hold each other dear for a period in this passage of time. That is such a gift; stepping into some one else's life, making a connection, trying to make a little difference along the way, and ultimately creating richness for both lives.

One's intrinsic empathy can improve also as we age. If you have traveled down difficult pathways in life; through death, divorce, loss of many kinds, then you can instantly empathize when another human being is traversing the same terrain. We are human beings; we have the ability to feel for one another, if we choose to exercise that ability. I am always instantly drawn to some one who is going through some of life's great testers, as I did years ago, and will again, for sure.

My "new friend" is suffering some of those same life challenges, as we speak, and I have tried to give her some comfort, some reassurance that things do and will get better. One day, she will not wake up every single, monotonous day with a heavy cloud of doom covering her eyes. One day, she will be able to pick her self esteem up from the floor and see life from a different aspect; step out tall into the world, breathe without restriction and feel the fruits of freedom all around her. Some of the best gifts we can share are the gifts of experience; and it is within all of our capabilities to be open to giving back all we have absorbed over our lifetimes thus far.

Thankfully for my new friend and I, there is no footsie on the playground. She can have all the other friends that she wants and me too. She will not ignore me with her books high on her chest when she sees me on the street with some one else. She will not snuggle closer with her "BFF" just to cause me pain. We will be able to enjoy and exchange as free people in the free world. She'll give me things and I will give them right back. There are so many wonderful things about ageing.

**Lucy is a some time new, some time old and an always-and-forever friend.**

# REASONS TO BE CHEERFUL

We've had yet another visitor in our house the last few days, and again not the invited kind. Never mind the wrapping and the packing, the baking, bell-ringing and card writing. Just when you thought we've got more than enough stuff going on to fill the coffers of one family, along comes an intruder to burst our little bubble and take us over the edge; and this time, the visitor wasn't even one of mine.

No real way to sugarcoat this one. My baby sister has breast cancer. She lives in Turkey, but she does not currently have a visa to get home where she wants to be and she is stuck in London where she doesn't want to be. She's got more than enough unwelcome visitors in her life right now, poor baby, to keep her stress levels high; just when she really needs to take the time out to chill and to heal. And now the visitors have moved into my home, and I'm there with her, feasting on her anxieties with my own. All seems a bit much really.

My cell phone rings: 'Where are you going?" It was my other sister, who seldom rings me, let along at 7.50 on a Monday morning. Somebody must have died, or she's getting remarried, I think. "Call me back when you're done with your meeting", she tells me. "Never mind how late." Well, now I'm really suspicious. First she calls at all and then she's prepared to have her beauty sleep crushed by my return call, at any time of the night? Something really dodgy is going on over there in the land of Britsy. And sure enough, my sniffing beacon of a nose wasn't wrong. Our baby sis had been diagnosed with the cancer, whipped into the hospital and was already out of the hospital with said nasty mass removed. Talk about be blown over by the Soledad wind! That was the very last thing I would have imagined hearing, and I don't imagine it was top of her list either.

As happens when a tornado crashes through your home and you're left standing, bemused, in all the rubble, life's edges get a little blurry. You don't remember what people told you that day, you forget why you walked into that room and to do what. Today's not going so well and tomorrow is looking pretty cruddy also. All of a sudden, my Carpenter's Christmas music just sounds really depressing, not festive at all. Chocolate doesn't taste so good. I don't want to go Christmas shopping and I sure as heck do not want anyone to try and cheer me up. These things happen to a person when you hear something really horrible about some one you really love and there isn't a darn thing you can do to fix it.

I had to do something though, or I would fall over and drown in my own dark cavern of misery and never re-emerge. So I started out by trying to say nice things to the people around me. That worked; sort of. Then I baked some brownies – always good, can't go wrong with chocolate. Then I lit a candle and thought about my Mum and how she would have reacted to such foul news. Bad move; feeling depressed again. Stop that. I then proceeded to pick up my cat and feel his loving, purring warmth penetrate my inner being. Felt good for a second and then he wanted to get down, claws and all. Spoke to husband; he's got a good pair of ears. But then he was saddened by the news too, so that wasn't too helpful. None of these heart-warming techniques was really working inside my house, the inner world of my daily life; so I stepped outside to look at the world beyond mine. There my own personal healing began.

Firstly, I watched the green-striped humming birds swatting at each other, as they tried to be the only one poking at the nectar; that was amusing. Then I watched the swirling greys and blacks of the storm clouds cascade heavily across the Santa Lucia Mountains and drench the mountains of Big Sur, which I love with certain passion. That gave me a happy whoosh; because maybe I can, perhaps, go back to that place quite soon and feel the way I love to feel when I am over there. I then proceeded to admire my Princess Diana Roses, still resplendent in their pinks, yellows and whites and it's already the middle of winter; a gift in itself. I looked around at all these mini-miracles and thought to myself, '*guys, how about a miracle for my sis?*' I talked to my Mum inside my mind and said to her: show me what you can do from wherever you are. A patch of blue broke through the swirling storm furrows and I felt better about the prognosis already.

Still in the mode of staying outside of myself, I put on my red and white Santa hat and trotted down to the local Post Office to ring the bell for the Salvation Army. That's the spirit; do nice things for other people - that's sure to help the gloomies. First I was disappointed, as one of our elected officials decided to ignore me, as he walked by. He didn't even put a dollar in my kettle, (a poor move, politically!) Not a good start. Then, friends came by and chatted, I waved the royal wave, as familiar locals drove by, and I smiled as the children reached on tiptoes to put pennies in the slot. '*Thank you and Merry Christmas*', I tried to say to everyone who was in the giving mode. Even though I wasn't feeling very merry. "*Look, Mommy, it's Santa Claus!*" one little girl exclaimed, as she pointed at me and hopped happily along the sidewalk. Well, I was hardly your run-of-the-mill Santa standing there, but I'll take the good intention and hope that goodwill is contagious.

We could use some of that in our family this year, as my sis starts several months of unpleasant treatment and begins her journey forward towards an uncertain future. I shall continue to try and do good works and be a little nicer; that will be my own personal contribution to the mess. Perhaps what goes around will come back and be there for our family in the coming months. Good will to y'all too.

**Lucy's sister Rosie got through that particular battle with her usual amazing spirit and wonderful humor. There's a lesson there.**

# REVERSING THE ROLE

When we're young, our parents are our all. In our naïve little minds, they will always be there to hold, protect, pay the bills and fix broken things, including our cars and our hearts. What happens to us, the "children" in middle age, is that the roles begin to reverse; sometimes quiet and subtly; sometimes like a freight train cascading down a mountain side with no brakes.

When my mother became terminally ill, I still believed, somehow, that she would rise up from her bed one day full of beans and say, as she had always used to, "what would you like to eat, darling?" or "Do you have any laundry that needs doing?" She was the quintessential mother and could not help herself. We were her babies and she loved to baby us, no matter how old we were.

When she was no longer able to do that, it was deeply disappointing for all of us; the end of an era, the end of so many things, in fact. When her life on earth was so obviously almost to an end, our roles became eternally reversed. I fixed her things to eat and helped her to do the most necessary functions she could no longer manage by herself. I read to her as she had to me for so many years and repeated over and over the poems she liked best; as she had repeated, so many years ago, my favorite stories over and over 'til she could tell them by heart. When her eyes were closing for the last time, I stroked her brow, as she had mine when I was sick in bed with a fever; and there you have it, the ultimate role reversal.

My father recently had a knee replacement and I had nightmares about the implications of this surgery; necessary though it was. Your knee is part of your leg which is what you need to walk with. If you are unable to walk anymore, your life as you know it will change for good. My father lives by himself and I couldn't imagine him not being able to stroll in the park or down to the shops. It was scary for all of us, but mostly for him.

"It's not too bad today," he would say. "Can't think why I should have this stupid operation when I feel this good."

"No, it's no use," he would say the next day. "If I can't walk in the park without pain, then I'm just going to have to get the wretched thing done." And so this worn out knee took on a life of its own; a new person living in the house that sometimes behaved itself and sometimes most definitely did not. The topic of independence became the elephant in the room of all of our existence. My sisters and I live all over the world; thousands of miles away from father. If his new knee didn't work out, what would that mean for him and for us? It's not a subject you can approach without sounding like you're trying to take over his life and his decisions already before he is ready for you to do so; but in a sense you have to help him take care of himself. It's time. He's taken care of you all his adult life; it's now your turn.

In one of his fluctuating moments of doubt and indecision, I told him that it was his decision to make, but for the sake of the quality of life, he should probably get it done, ("in my opinion", I noted, as an afterthought). My daughter wrote him a letter that he took to heart; "you need to get better, so that you can be happy," she wrote and, ultimately, he knew that that was the heart of the matter and the reason for all of this.

And so we have it. Those of us with loving, caring children can only hope that they grow up to be loving, caring adults who will cherish us the way we have always cherished them; who will help us make decisions that we have a hard time making ourselves and stroke our brow when it's our time to go. The circle of life goes on; the hand that feeds the hand feeds the hand; ultimately it's what good family is all about.

My father had a very successful knee replacement operation recently and is already making his travel plans for the spring; ready to move on with his new lease of life on his brand new knee, all at the age of 76.

**Lucy is so fortunate to have such a happy healthy father.**

# TECHNO BABIES

I distinctly remember being totally impressed, circa. 1975, by the inaugural visit of the electronic calculator to our classroom.

"This does not mean that you do not have to learn how to add and subtract," our teacher said primly, to some resounding "boos" from the raucous young audience, "On the contrary. But it does mean that you will be able to very quickly verify your work and check formulas. This is an important development for the future," she said with confidence. Little did I know back then that that would be the beginning of a life-long techno journey for myself; mostly a struggle, in all truth, to accept all that I could never know, because my brain just doesn't seem to work that way. Though I resisted that scary machine back then, just as I later resisted the electric typewriter – with my father insisting that I take typing classes, because "you have to be able to type to do just about any job" – I have gradually, over the years, adapted to living with machinery, some easier to operate than others, and even, on occasion, welcomed the odd machine into my home and co-existed with it in a semi-cheery way.

I love my personal computer – as long as it is behaving itself and not refusing to shut down or refusing to save. I like to use my email, save word documents and even download and mess with the odd photo. That is about the extent of my tech-expertise. Beyond that; I panic. During a recent argument with my machine over its refusal to close out its anti-virus or shut down how it was supposed to, I realized, once again, what a techie-dumbo I still am, years away from my first encounter with the electronic calculator or even my first pc.

"You are trying to shut down with things still open," my semi-techie sister pointed out. "It has got stuck." She closed me out, as it were, one window at a time, and all was quickly well again in my tech-world to my greatest relief.

"It needs de-fragging," said my brother-in-law; I assume discussing some serious computer surgery that the machine was now in desperate need of, as he tapped around in untrodden pastures of hard and soft drives.

"Oh great," I sighed, as I tried to download some photos, after all these many computer operations were dealt with by various different semi-tech folks who paraded through my office, which was also temporarily masquerading itself as a visitor's room. "It's broken again!" Somehow my camera was now refusing to have a conversation with the now unstuck, de-fragged machine. The techie clan gathered quickly to my side to point out, with a bit of a snorting scorn they probably couldn't help, that the camera cable was actually unplugged.

"Whoever wants to use my computer, please make sure to leave it as you find it!" I squawked to anyone who was still in the vicinity. Deep down, I was a little mortified that I remain still so deeply tech-stupid that I cannot even recognize when there is an unplugged cable.

And there's probably little hope for me now. I will always choose simplicity in any type of machine, I want as few buttons on my camera as feasibly possible, I have never been able to program a VCR, ( and now they're obsolete), and I have decided that most Sony machines were made by male engineers for male engineers and should be strictly avoided; (the case in point being why I gave my very expensive Sony video/camera to my son after it had sat for two years in the closet and I still needed the instructions to even just turn it on!)

Recently my daughter reached the pinnacle of her money-saving goals in life, and had saved up enough cash to purchase her very own lap top. Once she had secured all the various boxes and disks and cables that one needs when one buys one of those super-tech items - (don't believe the sales price on the circular; it adds up to way more than that) - we drove home and I stressed who the heck was going to put together these pieces of modern wonder without the whole chabang at least blowing up. I shouldn't have worried. By the time we got home, my daughter and her friend had pretty much got everything ready to go, except for the router – whatever that is - which she explained she would need to set up when we got home. As I watched her cruising around this fine machine, with all its bells and whistles, now successfully installed and running its various programs, I realized that the tech generation, i.e. people way younger than me, is completely at home with machinery of all kinds. They have been raised on it, from x-boxes to cell phones to computers. My generation had to learn all of it later on in life; and some of us will never really get there. We went to school with paper and pens. We used notebooks, we got carpal tunnel syndrome – some of us - from all the handwriting, and learned to count in our heads – some of us. We put records on the record players and we recorded music on tape cassettes. We used regular film in easy, back-opening cameras and processed our films at the drug store. This generation has spell-check, digital everything, "PSP" machines, photo phones, email phones and quick and instantaneous everything in their fast lives.

I try to keep up, really I do, while endeavoring to keep it all as simple as possible. Why should I learn how to put music on my IPOD when my daughter gets a kick out of me not knowing and totally handles all of it for me? So take only what you absolutely need from this modern day life and leave the rest for the techno kids. If I really tried to get my head around the latest gadget, I'd get with the program, pass the test in my own mind at least and already be technologically obsolete by breakfast time.

**Lucy is a proud non-techie. What do your kids teach you every day?**

# THE WAITING ROOM

I recall very clearly a wonderful play I saw recently at the Western Stage in Salinas. “The Waiting Room” was an interesting study of very different characters meeting over time in a doctor’s waiting room; the evolution of their characters and how they ultimately assist in changing one another’s lives. The play was so much more than that of course; but the waiting room topic did bring to mind my own family and how, on occasion, we meet in “rooms” all over the world and, sometimes, tiptoe around each other like strangers waiting for our appointments; other times behaving as if what we know is actually not so and walking around the elephant in the room, as it were, to avoid the enormity of the reality we do not wish to face.

The play came back to me again this vacation as my family gathered in Turkey, the home of my younger sister; and we spent time together, tiptoeing around the subject of my sister’s illness. We all sat in the waiting room of our lives, awaiting the results of the latest shadow on her chest, whilst still feasting on the togetherness, drinking in the sunlight and the delightful atmosphere, playing competitive word games as if our very lives depended on them and watching the hot red sun dip down over the craggy mountain tips near the bay. A mixed, contrasting fiesta of strange, sad thoughts in a very beautiful place.

Family is funny. You know each other and, hopefully, understand one another more than most other people can ever hope, or, indeed, want to. You care very often too much for your family members and you always want to fix things to make them better. In Turkey, I watched my father at times silently watching my sister and the unwritten agony was written all over his face. Occasionally, it became so bad he would twitch.

My sister is a free spirit and lives her life as if there is no tomorrow. She refuses to live beneath the cancer shadow and has not changed her ways one bit since her diagnosis. She has no children; she can live pretty much for herself. My father aches for her to pursue a healthier, more holistic existence; to at least cut back on her lifestyle just a tiny little bit to allow her body to heal properly, to give herself more of a fighting chance at a longer life. She has no interest in that. She's a grown woman; she's his youngest child. And so you have it; the large, unspeakable subject; the rhino in the room of our family.

I have to hand it to her. Her outlook and attitude is tremendous, infectious even. We all know about the things that we should and shouldn't do. We know we shouldn't eat French fries, but we do and we delight whole-heartedly in the naughtiness until the pleasure is over and we have heart burn and the feeling that we just gained three pounds. We'll even top that with a large vanilla shake and super-sized onion ring, knowing that the fat and cholesterol contained within could lead to certain death. We know we should exercise more and stress less. Do we? Most of the time we don't. Do we live our lives as if there were no tomorrow? Seldom. Do we delight in every sunrise and feast in every sunset? Only when, by chance, they cross our paths. Live like we are dying? Do we? My sister does.

During our visit to her home over seas, in the most foreign of countries, I elected to love my sister with all I have and to say nothing to her of the dinosaur that was breeding in our family's waiting room and the time that was swiftly passing until her next doctor visit. In typical family style, she thanked me for it without a word. We were relaxed together; we talked; we shared. We did share concern over our father and his concern for her; we didn't examine the whole entire subject. She knows, I know; it is enough.

As we were saying our goodbyes, we held each other by the elbows and looked a little deeper than usual. We knew what we were saying. We were saying everything and nothing at all. She loves her life; however much she has left of it and that is her prerogative which she intends to exercise. From the sidelines of my own life and our family, I can only show I care and listen to whatever needs to be heard; if and when it arrives. Other than that, I need to remain quiet; as I endeavor to do; for as long as we all have. Some things, in the enormity of it all, are just better left unsaid. Saying nothing says everything.

**Lucy's sister Rosie is still enjoying her life in Turkey and the many other places she travels.**

# TIME – CLOCK OF THE HEART

Without my daily calendar of times and obligations, I am lost. There is something about writing a list, and then checking the things off, that works well with the human psyche and keeps everything even, like the systematic tick tock of the mantelpiece clock. Never mind that I can now put everything inside my fancy-smancy phone to ping me when I need it to, or even synch my home calendar with my phone calendar, so you'd think Big Ben were chiming in the midst of my life, when it was just time to pick up the dry cleaning. But no, that doesn't work well for me, plus I don't have the necessary vacant days to learn how to program these machines to do these amazing things. Just give me a piece of paper, a pen and a few lines – they don't even have to be straight ones. If you give me that, I can assemble some type of order into my day, and at the end of it, be able to look at the check marks and feel some sort of satisfaction at a job mostly somewhat done, with plenty of blank lines and occupation left for tomorrow, not to mention the day after.

Sometimes – if the truth were really known - I even add the items I have already completed which are not on the list, just so that I can check them off. I'm sure there is a disease called just that. But over the years I have learned the importance of time maintenance and good time-keeping. The older you get, the more you realize that you don't get yesterday back to do over. Lose her and she's gone. The years start to move more quickly all of a sudden, like a bad joke that's got out of control, and somehow, almost consistently, there is never enough time in the day to do all the tasks on your daily list, let alone the things you'd really like to do.

I hate to be late these days, as if I were chasing time. Never used to bother me! I don't like to keep others waiting and I certainly don't like myself to be kept in a time vacuum when I could be busy doing something else. I always have something to read with me just in case. Don't want to waste any time! I look at myself once in a while, as I pass quickly by a mirror, and note my face has some how taken on some of the scars of time, the deep lines of weathering and stress, combined with living in a sunny clime and forgetting to put on sun block. Can't find that 18 year old fresh face again either! Don't even know if I'd want to if I could. That face was way too trusting and innocent. She hadn't gone around the block enough to be able to tell where the real road blocks were, or who to trust and who to leave behind along the way. She learned through the cross country course, also known as time, and hence the lines and troughs, also known perhaps as character, became entrenched and forever.

But time can stop once in a while if you give her the chance. I stopped her for a while, amidst all the turmoil that was going on this week, and forced myself back to the time when I was the same age as my daughter. And how old was my mother then? I asked myself. We have mirrored each other a lot over the years. This time I had to find a photo of her and see us both side by side, just a few decades apart. Ah there she is. I find a photo of her when she was my age. I'm desperately seeking her face in the shadow of the photo, and equally my own, and wondering if our lines were similarly deep – she from where she was and me now. I take myself back in my mind to when I had my first significant boy in my life who I liked and how my mother responded to me over this thing that was the most enormous fixation for me ever at that vital time in my existence. Was she excited for me, was she afraid? Did she want to wrap me up in a large bubble and keep all the wolves at bay? Yes, I think it was all of those things – plus her mother wolf's fury when he hurt me badly and dumped me on the side of the road. To defend and eternally protect her cub to the death is every mother's instinct; but time and the growing people themselves tell us that that is not how life goes, and we have to unwrap our arms eventually and let our cubs venture out without us. They may get hurt, they will most likely not always be well fed and certainly not happy, but we have to let them go and we have to be happy for them that they are ready to leave.

Mother Time has been nudging me quite a bit this week, as we have encountered new and wonderful things in our household. Quite normal things, under a regular family microscope, and definitely in the realm of the evolving teenager; but for me it has been an interesting journey back to times of black and white photos, thirty years into the past of when she was here and I was there. Play me a few songs from that time and I'd be back there entirely, the moods, spots and all. I treated my mother with the same disinterest as my daughter can sometimes treat me now. Thirty years on, I know the ravages of time and how cruel regret can be when the space at your table, not to mention the one in your heart, is large and irreplaceable.

My mother wouldn't have had it any other way; she would have expected that our dynamic would naturally alter over the years as I urged to flee the nest more and more, and as far away as possible; and, like a good mother, she had to let me. Now I wish some times I could crawl back, if only for a few minutes. I'd like to go back now and revisit the scene together when she was my age and I was my daughter's. We'd have a good laugh, she would commiserate a little, and then she would remind me of the umbilical bond that can transcend all. We'd talk about that, also our telepathy through life to death and out the other side. Then I would feel reinvigorated and ready, once more, for the challenge that lay before me in my lap of motherhood – my main life job to help my teenager move forward from her childhood and develop into a positively-contributing human being who has the ability and sanity necessary to function in the toils of daily life – without her mother being constantly close by, ready to deliver lunch money or drop off the missing book. It's a big job. It's an underestimated obligation we should take on tirelessly, if we bring life into the world.

If I were back in the nest with my mother, instead of her out there somewhere and me right here, she'd tell me that I have evolved over time into a fair parent. I have stumbled and fallen, but I'm still sticking with my job and I'm doing okay. She'd also note that our lines are pretty much on par with one another in the larger scheme of things, and that those are lines we earned and should be proud of. She'd tell me these things and then we'd compare lists. Her list would be a lot of almost illegible chicken scratching on a recycled post card; mine would be a piece of lined paper with check marks to the side. She'd have a lot of movies and art galleries on her list, not to mention shopping for the evening's dinner; mine would be bank tasks and real estate obligations. All things to ponder when mother time sends you a curve ball and sends you back to when she was here and you were there; and it all looks different, but somehow similar! I had better start making my list for tomorrow; it helps me feel as if tomorrow is somewhat under control before she has even begun.

**Lucy has all the techno gadgets, but still loves an old-fashioned pen and paper.**

# WATCHING YOUR TONGUE

I have heard that we should pick the pieces out from our parents that we would like to emulate, and dispose of the rest; the idea being that, since no one is perfect, as we develop over time as people, we should strive to not allow any less than attractive genes to seep into our characters. It's a concept. My mother had a wicked tongue when she wanted to; mostly when she was frustrated, displeased, tired or ill. She could cut you to a quick with a glance or a word. That's a part of the gene pool I could really do without. I've known it forever, but fighting it is a whole other thing.

I recall many moons ago that mother criticized something I had written for school. I was a high-strung teenager. I immediately stopped showing her examples of my writing, which had prior to that been my pride and joy. Heck, I was lousy at math and geography; I might as well coo over my fair attempt at the written word. In fact, after she somewhat ridiculed the piece – which I recall took on an uncanny resemblance to the Welsh poet Dylan Thomas – I was 15 at the time and studying the poet – my creative juices went into hibernation and I became a closet writer.

I would no longer leave out examples of my work for any curious passers-by to peruse. I would no longer show any highly graded pieces to mother or tell her of my achievements. She had no idea what she had done, I'm sure, or she would have been mortified. She had no clue of what criticism can do; I believe she thought it would do the opposite. That quality has always been something I have consciously tried to avoid; but genes are darn strong things; I'm here to tell you. They can creep up on you when you least expect them to.

"You did the laundry, cleaned the yard, the kitchen *and* made dinner!" I said astounded to my husband, when I returned home one day from doing an open house. I even thanked him.

"Yeh," he gruffed, "I didn't want to hear about it." I stopped to think about what that meant, and then thought it better that I simply asked; since, as we know, men and women can have their brains on very different hemispheres much of the time and I thought it highly possible I had missed something here.

"You make me feel sometimes that I don't pull my weight around here, "he went on in uncanny communicative mode. (This feeling must have been festering for a while and was over-ripe and ready to break out of its pod!) Ah, now I got it! The critical gene had seeped in through the cracks of my make-up and was making hay in my household.

I now recalled the snippy remark I had made earlier that I wasn't the only person who knew their way to the washing machine; the only one who could navigate the "long" journey down to the grocery store for the necessities and the one who watched for the vital gauge on the milk carton which meant, "jump in the car, girlfriend! The family is nearly out of the white stuff!" When you get tired, you can get resentful; we all do. Some of us just have to watch the viper tongue from unleashing on the undeserving.

I am now in "Critical Rehab." It has been nearly 7 days since my last critical remark and I feel lighter somehow, relieved of a burden. No one enjoys that feeling when they have just made a really cruddy observation and caused hurt to another person. I see my daughter's face sometimes when she is looking for endorsement and I give her a fistful of onions. I am nipping that nasty seeping gene in the bud; I tell you! If I can't say something nice, or at least encouraging, I won't say anything at all. I will walk away with my tongue between my teeth and spare everyone my cutting edge; uncharacteristic, I know!

Sometimes in the hectic stew of our busy lives, we forget where we came from and how we got there. My darling ma, bless her, did not have the benefit that I had of observing the gene pool at work and having the opportunity to try to make a change for the future. Her own mother was a sweet darling with a good word for everyone. (Her father not so much!) That must have been where she got the critical gene from and unwittingly passed it down without giving it another thought.

But I'm stopping it right here at the doorway of my family; and hoping that I've caught it just in time. Like a terminal disease, we hope that the last case died with the generation that came before. I'm a work in progress, that I do know; and I shall probably be watching my tongue with vigilance for the rest of my life.

**Lucy can be a sharp-tongued viper,**
**but she still works at not being so.**

# WITH EVERY SEASON

My mother used to say that autumn was her favorite time. She would recall the lovely changing colors, the wonderful feeling of carrying and delivering babies that time of the year – which she did twice, to my certain knowledge. She also despised winter; so autumn was a tricky and often brief, transitional period for her, never really knowing which way it was going to go; either forward to winter and despair, or back to summer and delight. That is one of the great unknowns; whether autumn is going to accelerate onwards to winter, or take a swift reverse gear and become summer once again, especially in England.

I myself recall the Indian summers when I was away at school in Saffron Walden, Essex, and we would be wearing our mandatory, thick, winter green uniform and sweating under a September blaze; or trying to play hockey in full gear with the sweat dripping and our hockey coach yelling at us to run just that little bit faster down the bone dry hockey field. I do remember those days when I questioned the seasons and our expectations of them. But mostly I loved the autumn with her long afternoon shadows and crisp early morning promise of the long winter sleep ahead. We were, mostly, still eating ice cream and playing tennis, when we weren't supposed to be – also crunching wonderful fall leaves under foot and living eye to eye with the wiles of Mother Nature.

Now, in this part of the world, we don't see much by way of fall colors or the changing of the seasons. If I didn't have the grapes to watch, I'd be lulled into thinking that just about every season was a summer one. Though my dog Baxter and I loathe the bird cannons at this time of year, (we are both deathly afraid of the bangs), those noisy instruments, which pretty unsuccessfully try and ward the marauding flocks of birds away from the ripening vines, they do herald a turn in our seasons. They signal the time when we will soon be seeing huge trailers being dragged alongside the vineyards ready for their loads of fruit, when we will be kept awake at night with the picking machines doing their seasonal job.

They remind us that Halloween will soon be here, followed shortly by Thanksgiving and then Christmas and the end of another year.

How can we already be looking at the last quarter of this year? Our ripe tomatoes and ripening apples should give me the 'hello' that I am looking for, but I still cannot believe the swift cantering of time. It has been almost a year since my last chemo. (I see my daughter's eyes roll. "Oh no, not more talk of breast cancer!") No, my lovely, no talk of cancer, only of recovery and looking forward! My lovely nurse Rhonda told me that it would take a year until I recovered from the effects of the chemotherapy and she was exactly right. I could not believe, at the time, that it would take that long, but, honestly, it did. People ask me how I'm doing and I reply that, mostly, I don't have time to think about it, which is probably the best recipe for recovery in anyone's book. If I were to sit in my chair and watch my tomatoes redden, I would almost certainly have sent myself mad with all the dreadful things I could imagine that might be going on in my body. But no; as soon as I was able, I was up and about, back to work, driving, traveling, doing, seeing and, simply, being. I have already accomplished two items on my bucket list, I most likely would be still compiling if things had been otherwise. And now in the third quarter of this year I am here to say that our fall this year is an extraordinarily beautiful season. It is unpredictable, just like life itself. It can still have its summer fog and its winter cooling. It can blaze like high summer or storm like January. We just never know what we are going to get. But with that unpredictability comes a certain gratitude for the gifts of each day and the spread we get to enjoy, no matter the season. When you have felt clouds inside your heart, you are happy for any season. They herald a new day; one where you are still alive.

And I won't mind when we pass into the winter season with her swift blanket of darkness and cooling airs, along with her kind buckets of rain for the parched ground. We will welcome that time just as we welcomed this, knowing that the only guarantee in life is change itself and that, always, change it will.

Before we know it, the twinkle-twinkle will be on the homes and the shops will be full of glitter. Then we will be looking forward again, around the corner of that particular season, to another year full to the brim of opportunity, adventure and surprise. With every season there is a pleasurable anticipation attached to it. I know that now. It is very simple. It means that I am still here.

**Lucy tries to be an eternal opportunist.**

# THE HEARTH OF HOME

# A WEEK OF APPLES

This week I sound a bit like that lovely, classic book 'Cider With Rosie'. "Apple this, Apple that, Apple the other" and, true to say, we do have a fair crop of Golden Delicious and Fuji's out front on our homegrown trees this year; but then this would be a gardening column not a life column, and I'd for sure lose some readers. No, no happy apple story here folks. I have had a week of dealing with the mega "Apple" corporation, apple with the Capital "A", yes that apple. That would be that supersonic band of geniuses who have enthralled the world over the past few years and given the other bad boy, Microsoft, a run for their money in more ways than one. Yeh, those guys!

For those of you who know me, you know I'm much more at home with a pen and paper, a diary full of gloop, bits of paper here and there and maybe a laptop for putting it altogether, because I have to. I am not what they call a 'Techie', not even remotely tech-savvy if I'm honest. I have probably mentioned this before. However, in my line of work, you do have to be pretty much "on it" 24 hours of every blessed day. If you don't have the latest tech gadget, your nearest and dearest competition will definitely have it and you will be left behind in the dirt, as it were, with your pieces of paper and your diary scribbles, just like Grandma sitting in the rocking chair of progress.

It had come time to get one of those super brain phones, the ones that can do everything practically, except for pick up your dry cleaning and raise your teenagers. Much as I had become attached to my little friendly number and its quaint way of refusing to quit working even when I trod on it, it could not check my email for me and had therefore, sadly, become redundant in its own time. I did not approach this acceptance lightly. Last year at the annual California Association of REALTOR meetings, I had touched one of the mega monsters, even attended a class about becoming an owner of one. In short, I had done just about everything except for purchase the wretched thing. No, I wasn't quite ready for that kind of responsibility I told myself, so I walked away with my faithful little black leather-cladded friend for a few more months of togetherness.

Finally the reality was clonking me in the head. My lap top with its so-called "wireless" adaptor was temperamental at best. Sometimes it didn't have enough of a signal; other times its slowness drove me to distraction. No, that was not a marriage with any longevity. I needed one of those mega things. Would it be a "Blackberry"? I loved the name at least and had seen business people out and about with those things. My sister even possessed a handy-dandy little holster for hers and slapped it out even while on vacation. How about a 'Treo'? What about an IPHONE – the latest and greatest? I could really shock everyone with getting something so trendy and fashionable my daughter could taste it! No, it would definitely have to be a Blackberry – the commercials told me so. And so went another few months of indecision on that little cornucopia of mega machine choices.

"I need one of those Black Berry things." I told husband, knowingly directing him towards my birthday present, (he was at a loose end. You can always tell.)

"A Black Berry? That is so last year! You need an IPHONE," he snorted. What do I know? So an IPHONE it was. How hard could it be? I had an IPOD which my daughter masterfully dealt with whenever it needed dealing with. The IPHONE would be the same way, I was sure of it; just a different word after the I-.

Sure enough, for my birthday I received an IPHONE, (I did spare a thought for my mother who could only ever deal with attached cords, not even the cordless things. She would be turning now, if she had a grave to turn in.) "Wow! That is quite a machine", we all exclaimed, except for my daughter who was furious that, yet again, I received the very thing that she wanted most in the whole wide world.

The instructions were simple for such a clever machine. You go onto ITUNES and get activated online. Well, that is great, isn't it? You don't have to sit on the phone for hours and wait for A Phone Company to find the time to help you! Well, it would be great if it worked, which it didn't for us for a few days. "Mine's broke," I exclaimed during the millionth time of trying to get activated. Then, all of a sudden, it worked and I almost cried with pride at my accomplishment. My husband was also quite impressed.

I checked that this mega machine would both receive and send calls and off I went out into the big wide world. Just shy of leaving town, the phone crashed right in the middle of a call. "No SIM" it told me, with no further explanation. There was no earth to planet contact via '611', no nothing. We had no phone, pure and simple. It was just me and my car. My mother would have chuckled. The world was looking for Lucy; but guess what? For several hours Lucy had no phone and could nowhere be found. I finally went over to the A Phone Store in deepest distress. "I have to have my phone working!" I stressed. "That is my lifeline, my business, my everything!"

"Sorry," they said and they were. "We can't do anything at the store. You have to go back to ITUNES on your computer and reactivate with a new SIM card." Oh dear. The mega machines have taken away the art of customer service. If you can't do it online, you can't do it. I did have to feel rather for the store staff who would have loved to have helped an obviously distressed and non-techie human being, but their hands were tied. After stealing my husband's reliable leather-cladded relative to my former friend, I called up everyone I thought I knew would be calling me to advise them I wasn't dead in a ditch somewhere, and then rushed home to communicate with ITUNES - again. Fortunately for Mr. Apple, or whoever might be on the customer service desk that particular night, the activation was a successful one and I have since begun a new and cautious relationship with something that is way smarter than me.

What will they think of next? You do have to wonder. Now I have stepped inside the tech ring, there is probably no stepping out, but it is a curious world and not one I tread in lightly. My faithful old leather friend is still sitting on the side smiling up at me and saying, "I'm here for you babe, if you need me!" The way my luck goes with *Apple*, apples, a whole orchard of the blessed things, I may just.

**Lucy is a new owner of a fine IPHONE. These things are amazing when they work! Just ask my daughter.**

# BE LIKE A DUCK

"Be like a duck. Calm on the surface, but paddling like the dickens underneath."

- Michael Caine

I read this quote in my day planner and it kept coming back to me that now really ***is*** the time to stay calm, no matter what. The time for panic is never. Stay cool above all else, but be working like crazy, underneath your calm exterior, to keep your head above the water and your psyche intact. Everything and everyone around you depends on it.

Stress is a very powerful thing. If you let it, it will suck you in and spit you out, leaving what remains of your regular daily life in tatters. With our world in endless financial turmoil currently, stress is rampant. Ask anyone. Anyone you talk to has worries about their work and whether it will dry up; or if they will become another statistic of layoffs coming down the pipeline. Just around the corner, many fear, may possibly lie the prospect of their plateaux further shifting with the change of their family's financial wind. It could come as soon as today. And I'm not just talking about people's retirement funds. Folks ponder the death of their type of business or service and begin to research diversifying their business model, no bad thing. Human beings should always be reinventing themselves and evolving, during the inevitability of changing times that invariably circle around and surprise us, for no good reason. Change shouldn't surprise us; it's a fact of life. But ask anyone if they are worried about work or money right now and most honest people are.

"I can't read the papers at all at the moment," I heard one lady comment to another in the coffee shop. (She was buying a small, cheap drink, by the way.) "Can't watch the news either! Makes for a very peaceful time, living in oblivion!"

"Yeh, but just because you put your head in the sand doesn't mean it isn't happening," her companion commented. "Isn't it worse to know it is actually happening all around you, but not to know exactly what?" The other lady had a different opinion on the matter. I pondered this discussion, as I casually eavesdropped on their conversation. Personally, I think it is always better to be informed, but to know, equally, that history is in the eyes of the beholder and that a presentation of a piece of national "history", as it were, does not necessarily reflect the happenings in our local area. America is a huge and diverse land mass. I know that when I watch so-called national real estate talk shows from the East Coast; they do not particularly relate to real estate in Monterey County and their arguments are to be taken in a more general nature. So you take what you need from the news, you cast your eyes briefly over the articles which cause you pain and you enjoy the local good news stories, the snippets about the youth sports achievements, the weddings and the winning ways of local people. That is what our local papers should focus on! Leave the grime and murk of modern day politics to the instantaneous nature of the internet! It's quite a movement I realize – the good news seekers - and so it should be. Another good reason that local papers will survive this difficult downturn in their industry; the 'Good News Network' will out! These optimistic folks will dig out more good news stories about our local people, find more businesses to use their pages as an advertising vehicle and they will ultimately emerge through the desolate tunnel with a stronger business model - maybe a tighter connection to the internet - but still with plenty of black ink to go around. They will seek out the good news and they will print it. Sure, you still need the local crime reports and the real estate sales – the local people want those too, but they don't need to read about Washington's latest-greatest idea in your paper, unless they want to – and they can probably find the absolute to-the-minute-latest on line, so why even go there?

I may be the growing minority, especially among the younger folks, but I do not want to lie in bed on a Saturday morning with my pot of coffee and my computer, as I click through the online pages and try to find something interesting to read on the screen. I want my paper. I want to flick and glance, save for later, clip to send to my father or post up on the fridge. My paper is my own personal slice of peace and quiet that I pay a few cents for and treasure as my own precious chunk of down time each day. Just forget to deliver my paper and you will hear from me, I can tell you! Me and many households just like me. Local news is a compilation, a collage of images from your local community pieced together to entertain, inform and divert. Send something to the paper and they will print it; be a part of the good news movement and keep the chain going. Think about that and share it with our young people. They like to see themselves in print also – it has a permanency about it you can't find on a computer screen.

Be like a duck. Stay calm, but paddle like mad through these crazy days to make it successfully through today, into tomorrow and onto the next day. Build your reserves, conserve where you can and tell the good news police that better days are coming. It's just one or two positive observations away.

**Lucy is a local worker bee, trying to stay calm and paddle through the madness.**

# CHANGING MY NATION

Even though I had lived over here for 18 years as an "alien" – a resident alien - without even the slightest trace of a green skin or space ship to my name, (whoever made up that wretched alien title was obviously not one); it was later rather than sooner that I was able to acknowledge that I felt more at home in my adopted country than my native one.

It was later still that I was woman enough to face the fact that I was never going "home", except to visit; my adopted country had become my home for always. The strangest thing, trust me, is to go "home" and feel a bit of a stranger in your own land; but it happens more often than not to those of us transplants who sound a little different, are a little different and choose to nest elsewhere than the god given path we were thrown at birth.

Giving up my "citizenship" was a whole other thing. You can take the gal away from the Brits, but never the Brit away from the gal; that much is a for sure. As long as I shall live, I'm sure I'll say "garidge" instead of "ga-raage". It will always be "barth time" in my house, and the "grarse" will always be a little greener after husband has watered it. Some things are too deeply rooted to get misplaced along the road of life.

When I came to realize that I could become American without losing my British, vistas opened up that I had never before imagined. "Hooray, "I exclaimed to just myself, (and now, what American would ever say that?) "So now I could get my own vote and stop stealing my husband's; continue to choose which line to travel through at immigration and still get to pay all these lovely taxes to the Americans! Now isn't that a great deal? (And that is the same in any language).

"Oh! You're not a citizen?" the nice living trust attorney queried, as I was trying to get my affairs in order at the ripe old age of 40. "That will make a difference in how your estate would be taxed, should your husband die first." What? I pay bountiful taxes just like the next American, and yet my estate would be handled differently because of my green-headed status? In some circles, that could be viewed as a type of preferential treatment the lawyers would love to get their hands on; but in my world, it just made the vista a little clearer that I needed to get my act together and pledge my allegiance where it had been for some time. To coin an age-old adage, "home is where the heart is" and it just seems to become more so as time goes by.

And so began the journey towards placing my hand on my heart and swearing allegiance to another flag other than the one I was born under. Anyone who has ventured forth towards the daunting N-400 naturalization application process will know that the paperwork can scare you off at first base and make you quickly acquiesce that a lifetime of alien status is really not that bad after all, never mind the name.

It is simply inconceivable that, for this application, you should have to be able to track down the names of some of your long gone relatives, their places of birth and so on; but you do. Let's hope the details of that search are not part of the interview, since they may have got a little churned on the way. I scanned back in my mind to my great grandfather Samuel Bagnall Baxter, a smoking drinking coal mining gentleman by habit and by trade and wondered whether perhaps he could possibly be a distant kin to the notorious Dick Turpin, a highway robbing horseman of mythical proportions who was hung at the stake a very long time ago. It was a reach, but maybe the FBI was just about to uncover this piece of trivial connection, advise me of that fact and banish me from their midst. (Having a bad relative like that could really soil the cleanliness of my application and the success of my quest! I've never even had a speeding ticket, for crying out loud!) Gosh, your mind goes to funny places when you're trying to change something really fundamental in your life such as your nationality.

In the fingerprinting office, the nice federal lady advised me that their new "Homeland Security" machines were extremely sensitive and that I'd better try not to breathe while I was in the process of being scanned. "Oh!" she exclaimed, as I hovered, puce in the face from lack of oxygen, "you have worn out the prints on your thumb! They won't accept this." "Won't accept my fingerprints?" I choked, once I had started breathing again. "How could I possibly wear out my fingerprints?" Then ensued several days of toxic stress, as I wondered whether my quest for citizenship could really be thrown out, based on the fact I had no discernible fingerprints and therefore did not really exist. Could you get a fingertip transplant? I wondered. Let's face it, they can transplant everything else. Could my fingerprints really have worn out from all my hard work? (Bet Samuel Bagnall Baxter still had his fingerprints into his nineties and he really knew what hard work was!)

The finger print exam went through without a glitch, apparently; or, at least, I wasn't penalized as I came through the gate. After that obstacle course, came the time to prepare for the 2 hour US History and Civics testing affair in San Jose. "Do not arrive early," the official notification read. "Do not arrive late." Only aliens could really imagine that anyone traveling up in the San Jo traffic is going to arrive exactly on time!

"Which country did we fight during the Revolutionary War?" the question glared at me from the page. "Oh, er, England," I respond, guilty as charged. "Duh", one might add, except that then I would definitely be penalized. And so I abandon the country which got slaughtered in the war, way back when, for the home turf of their victors – I went over to the other side, as it were, sporting a passport for each one in my hot little hand.

And what would Samuel B. Baxter have to say about all that? "Ey oop lass," he'd say, (to translate into another form of English: "you go girl!") which, in all languages, must mean … "live for today, for heaven's sakes. Tomorrow is a gawd only knows what waiting to happen!"

So that's what I'll do. Who knows; perhaps the lack of fingerprints is a minor issue in the larger scheme of things and I may end up as the first female alien president after all.

**Lucy is a Brit transplant; also known as a dual national.**

# EVERYTHING YOU KNOW

The older the get; the more you feel as if you know almost everything. Once in a while, a reminder will come along and hit you upside the head, reminding you that, old though you may be, you know very little and, for sure, you will never know everything. I had one of those reminders recently and, from now on, I shall always and forever know, that I do not and cannot know everything.

I had had a feeling of foreboding that week. I felt that I was carrying the troubles of the world in a large, heavy sack on my back and it was making me as bent-over and heavy of heart as the grim reaper. I couldn't figure it out. A small earthquake removed the sack from my back and the grim position from my psyche. "Oh that was it!" I said to myself. The pressures of the earth and the atmosphere were just weighing me down. "A quick movement of the plates and I'm all better now!" My husband had strangely felt the same and yet the build up of the earth's crust had never bothered him before. We should have known that something was up. We didn't.

"Not so fast, Mary Jane!" Something was to happen later in the week to make us wonder if, in fact, our feelings of foreboding were for something much worse than our sober ponderings about the property market or the fact that we really didn't feel like going to work that day. Sometimes, something happens in life to make you stand up, pay attention and re-evaluate where you were before the something happened.

It was a fair Sunday morning up in Riverview Estates. Not too much wind, a little sun; your usual early Sunday. Neighbors were out in their yards, the noise of lawn mowers high on the wind. My husband chugged off down on the property on his golf cart, as he is wont to do once in a while, ploughing his way through the dry grass as he went. After he returned home, I noticed a little smoke over on the neighboring property and some furtive movements of our neighbor who was working on his new home construction project. I wondered if the neighbor was doing a small controlled burn. As I focused again, I realized that the grass was on fire. Quietly, furtively and very close to the ground, the smoldering grew to hungry flames and began to lick across the land, strangely in two directions at the same time.

We called the emergency services; that number that is engrained in your brain but you hope you never have to use. My husband ran around the front of the house where the hoses were and ran back to the scene hoses in hand, falling down a hole and twisting his ankle in the process. At this point, neighbors appeared from their yards and began to help. From a small smolder, in just a few minutes, we had a full blown fire in progress, whipping up and heading for our neighbor's home and our back gate. The Sheriff's Department was swiftly on scene, closely followed by the Soledad Fire Department, (in only 7 minutes, I might add.) I stood guard by my back gate watching the ground turn to black and the fire willfully eat up the land.

"Should I tell everyone to evacuate my house?" I wondered. My sister was resting inside; my daughter was playing with her friend in her room. We had animals, documents, pictures, you name it – a lifetime of things to gather up if this was going to get out of control and we needed to evacuate. At times like this, the mind runs wild with the wind, and, in this case, the fire.

"Don't worry; they'll put it out," the nice Sheriff assured me, as we stood at the fence and he endeavored to calm me down and I stressed, deep in shock. And put it out they did. The CDF crew arrived and finished up, making sure that all the hot spots were out and everything was secure. They also researched the source and agreed that a spark from my husband's golf cart had ignited the fire. They were thorough, but kind; real professionals.

Once everyone had left, my husband stumbled in, covered in dirt and soot with his swollen ankle. We were both reeling with what could have happened; it stayed with us for days. We were poorly prepared for what had happened and nature had taught us a worthy lesson. We will not be so ill-prepared again. The 'what ifs' of the day kept the adrenalin rushing and awful thoughts cascading through the mind, from the day into the night. You don't sleep much after an experience like that.

We learned a lot that day. We are now devising a fire plan. We are going to situate hoses attached to faucets on all sides of our property lines. We are going to buy and learn how to use fire extinguishers. We are also going to have our golf cart majorly over-hauled and not drive it through dry grass.

Except for my husband's injured ankle, no one got hurt last Sunday and no one's property was ultimately damaged. We learned, hands on, that fire can be a cruel and unforgiving thing. We have had little rain this year and it is phenomenal how quickly a tiny smolder can whip into a blaze. Lives can be forever altered in a moment. Let our story be a wake up call for those who think they know everything and, in a nano-second, realize that they know nothing at all.

**Lucy was once a property owner with a charred back yard. We're always learning, aren't we!**

# FINDING OUR WAY BACK

I think we lost our way some how through the boom years. Real estate values were appreciating by the minute, purchase offers were coming in over the asking price; there was an unprecedented frenzy of buying that permeated our world back then. You would no sooner list a house than be able to list its twin even higher. Those who already owned real estate found pleasure in their version of the American dream. They had "money" in their home, "value" in their nest egg. They could use up some of that value in that brand new Cadillac they had been coveting, because the "value" would continue to go up; everyone said so, so why not. There were people out there everywhere touting the innocent to do such a thing and making the process stress free and seemingly without consequence.

Fortunately for me, I had made my poor financial decisions earlier on in life, well before I was sensible and stable enough to even think about purchasing real estate. By the time I purchased my first stack of bricks and mortar – or in my case stucco – I had already, a few years earlier, driven myself into the ground with horrible credit card debt, a car payment I couldn't afford and various other financial misdemeanors.

When I signed on the dotted line of my first house, in fact the one I am still living in, I knew I had signed up for a payment I could afford, I had plans to live in the house for a very long time, if not forever; and my only long term scheme was to make the house more and more perfect in my own mind's eye for our quality of life to get better and better. I still feel that way. I knew that if I took a chunk of cash out, and that would have been so simple in the crazy-easy years of cash out refinance, I also knew that I would have to pay the cash back. It was not free money; nothing that is worth having is ever free, we know that. The easy money would make my payments larger, however I looked at it, and that would not be a manageable situation for me. I knew it back then and I stayed with the program. I still know it.

Not to make light of others' tough times and bad situations, but I think that a lot of what we experience in the difficult market of foreclosures and upside down equities forces us all to get back to basics. Back then, we were living on credit and borrowed time in our lovely America. We were borrowing, not to pay back that month, but to stretch on for as long as possible. Debt until death us do part; if necessary. We didn't care if the interest payments outweighed any common sense we might have had, we would simply apply for an extra card and slam our superfluous needs on that one just for the heck of it.

I was so surprised, when I moved to this country, how the ease of credit could really get you into trouble and quickly. Once I applied for and received a Sears card, some how Mervyns got my name, then Macys and Home Depot. Soon I could be shopping freely without a penny to my name, nor any intent to pay it back. We all got ourselves in a lot of trouble there. I don't know about you, but I seriously think about credit cards now, I turn them down regularly and I desperately try to pay off balances as soon as I possibly can.

We watch inflation now too, knowing that it has to be coming our way very soon. We have started to grow more of our own vegetables and fruits at home in the lofty goal to be a bit more self-sufficient. This "green" outlook is quite pervasive, I understand. From those of us who are thinking inflation to those of us who are trying to be more organic in our lives, it cannot be a bad thing at all. I find myself looking at the price of milk, the price of bread and the price of gas especially. I've heard horror stories of the 80's and the obscene inflation people suffered. We should all have fears in that regard.

I try and save more these days. Rainy day funds are essential; much more important than that new big screen or the new truck we'd really like. You've always got to be prepared for the worst, as many have obviously not been. We had all got out of the habit of putting our money by, secure in the knowledge that if we got laid off, if we were sick and couldn't work, if – and who knows really what can and does happen – we would have reserves set aside for just that purpose. Too many people relied on their cash cow of a house to help them out during the tough times – either the refinance or the home equity loan – and, as many now know, those perceived or imaginary monies are now gone. People had retirement in the stock market, and, for a lot of people, that whimpered down to near nothing also. What happened to putting money in good old fashioned banks and solidly insured saving accounts? We got away from that too.

With all the gloom and doom of credit crunches and falling markets, knowledge is power and many of us have gained a lot of that these past years. Many of us will pick ourselves up from where we find ourselves after a bad hand and say, 'well, I won't do that again!" If you suffered from any of the above, ask yourself, 'did I learn something from that?" And if you did, you now have the tools to work towards not going there again. You'll eventually find your way back to a more manageable life. You'll gain back some footing in the form of savings or security and, ultimately, you'll get back your peace and move forwards in the direction of a more solid and secure future.

**Lucy has been there, done that.**

# GOOD NEIGHBORS

Neighbors are like family; real brief, you don't get to chose them. In an ideal world, your REALTOR will interview potential candidates to be your neighbors and make sure, before there's a contract in sight, that there's a good fit; matching children, things in common, shared animal noises. An offer will not be presented on a house, until the potential neighbors have had time to go out and play together, see if there is a chance that they may not get along; under which circumstance the deal can definitely not go through. In fantasy land, all your neighbors become your friends – under pinky-gold hued lighting and rolling green meadows, you get together for dinners and holidays, your children are in and out of each other's houses like siblings, you watch their animals while they are away and still love them when they return. In short, they become an intrinsic part of your life, your best of friends.

In reality, you can get the good ones and the not so good, like the world itself. One home can mess it up for the rest of you. As a REALTOR, we talk about "neighborhood" a lot; location, location and all. You can have a perfectly lovely street; then the house that is the bomb site with the run-down cars every which way and the dead grass; the house where the music booms every night and the voices are often screeching and not very kind, the house where the kids are headed for juvenile hall and the adults are even scarier. You'll get the ones who speak to you with bad language and make your children cry; you'll get the ones designated for the asylum and the lock down. We all get the house which will bring down the local property values, even just with their rotten personalities, and quash the peace and quiet of other's lives, the one that is the thorn everyone's side, the one home whose occupants never move, no matter how hard you pray. We all have them.

Small town life is no different from the big city, except in the city you don't even have to bother to be polite; you can all just get on with your lives and ignore each other for years on end; you don't even have to bother to mildly dislike one another. In London, England, for instance, we never met some of our neighbors, even after 20 something years of residing in the same house on the same street in close proximity to one another. We'd rush into our triple-locked, alarm-zoned houses, making sure that no one was following us and barricade ourselves in from the world outside. In big towns, you get to the stage where you're even suspicious of the phone ringing. ("Ha! I know their game! They're calling to see if anyone's home. They're stalking out our property as a potential robbery victim, waiting for us to leave, so they can enter!") In small towns, if you ignore your neighbor, the reason is that you're probably mad at them; and, hopefully, that won't last. If it does, they surely weren't worth bothering with in the first place.

I am lucky to be blessed with some really super neighbors. Over time, many of us have become friends; we watch each other's backs, use each other's tools, walk each other's dogs. In short, we're family, we really are. We'll pick up each other's kids from the YMCA, clean each other's cat boxes, lend each other stuff, eat each other's food and drink each other's wine. Coming from the big city, I think that I have received a very rare gift in living where I do. I give and I receive. In the utopia I call my home, we have, what I firmly believe is what you would call, neighborhood.

In small towns, we pay attention more to 'what's happenin' in the microcosm of our close-knit community than the greater world outside. In some ways it is of more consequence to us who is elected onto the city council than who becomes president. We feast on the local news, we talk the local politics; in a very short period of time we can find ourselves invested deeply into our surroundings and it can very soon feel like a home we will never leave, except for feet first. Some people I know await the Soledad City Council elections as eagerly as they anticipate the holiday season!

"South County is growing too fast," I heard an old folk say not so long ago. He was bemoaning the potential loss of the cores of the old towns, the hearts of the antique past. The fear in his voice spoke of the realities of shopping malls becoming the center of town and downtowns fading away behind closed frontages and declining traffic. "Soon there'll be none of the original people left," he gloomed. The 'original people' may pass on to another world, as is nature's way; but many of them will have trail-blazed a heck of a history and left a finer town behind for the rest of us to enjoy, because of their investment. Many of them have will also have left super genetic characters in their places to continue their legacy, their homestead and their family name.

For us 'new folk', those of us not fortunate enough to have been born here and had families here before us to receive us and raise us in the South County way, true, we have a bit of catching up to do; but fresh blood can be pretty energizing for an established community. It can irritate and it can char the old establishment; but it can also go a long way to making a difference. Us 'newbies' can simply apologize for our lateness in arriving and get on with the work that needs to be done. If you want to see something done in a small town, it is surprisingly easy to effect change; you show up and you get involved; it's pretty much as simple as that. Most of the time you will be very well received! I am living proof and I thank those of you 'oldies' who made me feel so very welcome over the past few years and who got me to the place where I feel not only like a neighbor, but also such a very good friend.

**Lucy has lived in Soledad for so long that she is almost considered a native.**

# IT DOES TAKE A VILLAGE

Real estate is not about houses, it's about people. The more I work in it, the more I appreciate the fact. That is why the property world is a local world, one where preferably you live and work close to your home, where you are an expert in your field that crosses over a few miles, not a few counties, where the postmaster knows you and asks you about the market and where you will cross paths with former clients, now friends, at the ball game or in the store. That is community for you and it is a very special gift that we residents of small towns enjoy and some of us appreciate.

Ask anyone who is revered in any given community and they will say that they didn't get up there alone. Most will say that there was a whole village of good people lifting them up on their shoulders and pushing them to reach higher and get to the top. Most people have good intentions that way. (There are a few sour ones along the way and they wouldn't be holding anyone up anyway, they'd be trying to pull them down – we all know those types!) However, what I have learned to love about small communities, among many other things, are the home-town festivals and events they host for their townspeople throughout the year. In small towns there are few paid personnel to bring forth these things – just a host of hard-working volunteers who believe in the importance of celebration and community enough to give up their treasured home lives and hobbies and share something special with their fellow citizens.

The Soledad-Mission Chamber of Commerce is one of those bands of volunteers who bring more to Soledad than most people know. One of their annual events is the Annual Awards Banquet, which is hosted for the benefit of the town. It's the forum where the Citizen and Business of the year and Friend of the Chamber are honored, and where also the community is able to come together to celebrate the winners among other organizations and businesses. It is quite a labor of love or insanity putting the whole thing together, but the people expect it every year and so it is done – every year. There is a small committee of board and chamber members who congregate regularly to go through the myriad of tasks it takes to host a bash of this ilk. From sponsors to letters to food to flowers to awards, tickets, silent auctions, caterers, servers, decorators, hosts, lighting, sound, tables, and invitations – the list goes on and on and, don't forget, these are only volunteers we are talking about here. Some how the volunteers pull it off and the people have a good time, but the small group gets a little greyer with the experience every year and wonders, again, the next time it comes around, if it's really all worth it.

"It'll be alright on the night," they say, and it generally is, give or take the odd complainer who never shows up to help, regardless of grouching, or the mispronounced name or forgotten dignitary we all stumble upon once in a while. It is all forgiven in the euphoria of the evening and the celebration of those honored citizens in our village who stepped up to the plate over a period of time and made our community a wonderful place to live and work.

To this year's recipients, we salute you all and thank you for the work you continue to do to make our town a better place. I'm sure our recipients would all say that they didn't do it alone – I'm sure they would say that they were always standing on multitudes of strong shoulders, members of the same village who know what it takes to make good things happen and reach every time for the stars to achieve what can only be deemed a huge success for us all.

**Lucy was the Chamber President 2009-2010 and proud recipient of the 2011 Citizen of the Year for Soledad.**

# LOOK IN THE MIRROR

The lady came frantically into my office clasping a pile of paper. I had not seen her before.

"I need to talk to some one I can trust," she said. Since she had never seen me before – nor anyone in my office that I know of - I imagine she took our established storefront as a sign of reliability, and hoped for the best. "This guy says that he can help save my house," she went on. "If we pay him $300 and sign these papers, he says he will be able to stop the foreclosure." I looked at the paperwork. A person with a local address was trying to encourage this lady to sign over a grant deed to her home plus a power of attorney – pretty big stuff. The papers had been partially completed with misspelled words. I asked her a few questions and established that her house had already gone back to the bank; she was in the process of cash for key negotiations with an agent from the bank. Even if that was the process to try and work out a modification with her lender, there was no possible way that this character could help her foreclosure go away; she no longer had any rights to the property. She would pay him the $300 and he would vanish into the muck from where he had just come. She did seem a little surprised when I told her that the only business able to work with her on saving a home from foreclosure would be the lender or lien holder on the home. These papers had no legal meaning anyway since she was no longer the legal owner of the house. She was glad she had come to visit with a room full of strangers to find out a simple truth – the world is full of scam artists seeking the innocent, the trusting and those a little down on their luck.

Nearly an hour later, I get another call. "I don't know you, but I read your column," the lady said, "so I feel I know you. My daughter is losing her home and she has been contacted by an attorney group out of Florida, who claim to be able to help her modify her loan if she pays them $2600. I don't want to pay the money, but I'll do it if it will work." Here we go again, I thought. These scams are more widespread than I thought.

Luckily, the California Department of Real Estate is all over this; in fact they are doing little else right now except for going after scam artists and companies that claim they can modify loans for you or save your home with just the writing of a check. After I had discussed with an investigator from the department the first case in the story, he thanked me for bothering. “You guys have to keep reporting this stuff to us,” he stressed, “then we can do something about it. Keep my phone number, call me!” And I will. I now have him on speed dial.

The figures are astonishing. If you have a bona fide loan modification business, then you have to register with the Department of Real Estate in Sacramento. The number of registered loan modification business is horribly low in our state - around 20 in fact - and the number of advertised businesses amazingly high – in the 100’s – and those are just the businesses that give themselves a name. Who knows how many so-called ‘businesses’ are out there with a stack of grant deeds and powers of attorney ready to take your money and disappear into the night? There are ways to check on any one’s authenticity in this matter through the Department of Real Estate, and it is important that we all make sure we do.

During tough times, desperate people sometimes do desperate things. The sly prey on the weak, the weak hope for a miracle and trust in the sly - it is the fable of the hare and the fox all over again. It eats me up when I see wolves coming out of the fabric of our industry again and hurting folk who are down on their luck and continuing to dig our business deeper into the trenches of slime. I vow to report every one of those scoundrels that I come across and spread the word to as many as possible that they need to do the same.

When you haven’t made a payment on your home in a while, there is not a magic wand that will fix everything for you and make the legal ramifications of defaulting on your mortgage go away. You cannot just write a check to some one and the problem will disappear; unless of course you pay your past due in full to your lender! You will have to talk to your lender and try to work out a solution to the problem with the entity that holds the note on your home and the people entrusted by that lien holder to try and keep you in your home and money coming in for your house payment - they are really the ones who can truly help you. Please do not fall prey to the scams out there, the magicians and the fairies waiting out there in the dark; those who will promise you a miracle, take and cash your check, then evaporate with all your hopes and money with them.

There are many honest people in our community who will give you a straight answer, help guide you along a straight path to a solution and not take a dime for their trouble. A few of us even write columns about such a thing. For those of us tasked with trying to steer the confused through these troubled times in our tricky business, task yourself with turning the tricksters in. A quick call to the Department of Real Estate in Sacramento can cascade quite easily into a full blown investigation followed by arrest and prosecution. These are real crimes we're talking about.

On a similar note, please do the same with the gangsters that are ruining neighborhoods and destroying families in our small towns. If everyone was to turn in the bad penny in their circle of acquaintance, perhaps we could spend more time and resources on building up our schools and not desperately trying to keep our children out of the gangs and afraid to be living in the playgrounds of their own childhoods. The negative gets all the publicity and the positive takes a back seat. Stand up, have a voice – turn them in. Look in the mirror – are you proud of what you did today? Does your child look at you and like you for who you are and what you stand for? Speak up, make a difference – stop the bad. We are all counting on you.

**Lucy is frequently saddened by the bad behavior she encounters in her industry.**

# MAD DOGS AND ENGLISHMEN

I never really understood what my grandmother meant when she would say that the weather was good only for "mad dogs and Englishmen"; and since the weather was seldom any good in England, however you looked at it; I always thought that it described rainy days when the stoic Brits would continue to go about their business, always needing an umbrella and rubber boots, and sometimes even a boat. The dogs would be out in it and the English too; as you would if you didn't have the choice.

However, when I was down in the depths of San Lucas in 117 degrees the other day, just me and the rattle snakes, the phrase came back to me and, this time, adopted a more universal significance. Being in San Lucas in high summer can only be for the insane, I concluded. Change the mad dogs and Englishmen vernacular to read rattle snakes and people who don't know better; and that would be me.

The tremendous heat wave we've been suffering these last several days in our state has made everyone a bit "koo-koo", for sure; or even borderline insane. As my family and I huddled in a dark house, almost motionless, beside a fan whirring on high in the middle of the day, sucking on ice pops, I thanked the powers that be that we don't have many days like this; because, in this type of heat, the human race is good for absolutely nothing. The yard work doesn't get done, the chores are laughed at, the only nutrition that is even remotely interesting is cold beers and frozen treats. It's the time of year when I wish my husband had finally installed the air-conditioning in our home, that we've been discussing for the last five years, or even just the attic fan that I've been on about for just about ever. The curtains remain drawn, the cat gasps in the shade and a lot of television gets watched, mostly about the weather. A pretty darn useless existence, wouldn't you agree.

No matter how many people are dying elsewhere and wars raging the world over; at such times, the local weather becomes the main topic of conversation. I talk to my father in the UK where they have also been suffering with intense heat this summer and we compare temperature stories, regardless of any other more significant dramas going on in our lives.

"Ooh," I say, dramatically, "yesterday it was 117 down in San Lucas and 110 in Soledad and they say it's going to continue through the week." He gives me a little gasp of sympathy and then embarks on his own war of the weather story, as reported from his neck of the woods.

"Think cold," I said to my daughter as we experienced serious overheating in Turkey this summer. We were walking along a pathway with the sun full on us in the middle of the day; again, only the mad dogs and English people were around. We were actually on our way to lie in the cool, clear waters of the Mediterranean, so there was a method to our madness; but it did involve a 15 minute stroll along this baking path before we arrived in heaven.

"Let's pretend that it's so cold we need our coats on," I said. "We are so freezing that we can hardly feel our hands or toes. We wish that we had brought along our hats and scarves as well.." and so we played the cold game all the way along the pathway that was probably steaming at around 120 degrees that day.

Weather is pretty exciting altogether, and we are normally so spoiled in our neck of the woods that we seldom have to comment on it, except to say how little or how much rain we are getting in any particular year. I remember John Steinbeck hitting it on the nail when he said that during the dry years they forgot about the wet years and vice versa; it was always that way. So it is with the sizzling summer of 2006. We have already forgotten about the soaking winter of 2006 and the levee banks bursting. We are, in the here and now, focusing on keeping our people alive in our state, taking care of our elderly, minimizing damage to our crops and not bursting the state's power bubble. Our winter is only a few short months away and, by then, this blistering heat will just be a distant memory. Then we'll be watching the rain gauges and the storms. Our cracked dirt and yellow hills will be just a faraway blip in the canvas of our lives and we'll have found another aspect of the weather to discuss, maybe even an earthquake or two. One thing is for sure; the weather will always be a foremost topic of conversation; an uncontrollable, which holds us at bay and keeps us guessing; a power we're forced to respect. When we're complaining about the wet year, we'll have forgotten about the dry year; and it'll always be like that. Mad dogs and Englishmen, rattle snakes and the insane; we're basically all out of the same mold.

**Lucy is so happy to live where she does;
the best climate in the whole world.**

# MY FIRST – AND POSSIBLY LAST – HOME

In these times of financial uncertainty, among so many things; it is sometimes important to look back and see how far we have come in this strange world that we find ourselves inhabiting.

Thinking about my home and how much I love it – strangely the first home I have ever purchased - sometimes I could put my arms around the blessed thing and hold her as tight as I can, if that were indeed possible outside of my mind. I don't really care how much she has appreciated in the last five years, except on paper. I don't want to live anywhere else. I don't want to know how much money I can borrow against her, except on paper. (I'm okay with the payments we have right now and I don't have any pushing urge to increase them). My home is truly my castle; my sanctuary, my pot of gold at the end of my long climb up the rainbow to who knows what. Every day I look at her and say to myself; 'how the heck did I get so lucky?" I think that many of us forget this simple fact during trying times of tough selling markets and relative insecurity. I recently took a trip down memory lane and made myself recall things I had put away for a rainy day in my efforts to get a hold of the American dream and hold her tight. It's a therapeutic exercise which I recommend to all of you.

I immigrated to the US in 1988, the lucky benefactor of one of 10,000 treasured immigration visas; the only thing of any worth I've ever won, though I didn't realize its true value at the time. I was youngish and foolish with nothing to lose. I was renting my apartment in London at the time, had a cruddy old car and a reasonable job in international shipping. I was given my "golden ticket" – one of 10,000 out of the 3 million applicants - and then had 3 months to leave my homeland and get my visa stamped on American soil. The plan was to taste America, as it were, check out the dream and then return home. The visa was cool, because it gave you the right to live and work over there, important as a relatively poor individual. I had absolutely no clue what I was really doing and what I would find where I got there. We went in search of the dream; the one we'd seen on 'American Graffiti' and other cult movies. The dream was, unsurprisingly, evasive.

4 months later, I was a resident of a converted van and living unemployed on the streets of New Orleans in the deep, dark South in the depths of the unreasonable recession of the early 90's. If I remember rightly, it was also at the time that New Orleans was the murder capital of the country and definitely not a place a young Britsy should be sleeping on its streets. The plan had gone just a tad sour, to put it lightly. From silver-spooned University graduate to homeless immigrant in the South; it was an interesting exercise in humility. But, it also taught me some valuable skills I would never have attained without going through it. I did learn a couple of really important things; firstly, people are basically good and kind. Secondly, America is a land of opportunity; you just have to reach out and grab it, and try to be smart along the way.

Once I'd got a couple of restaurant jobs under my belt, I started to climb up the food chain and I gradually went from a van to a trailer on the bayou. I learned that you really don't need furniture if you have a real roof over your head. A shower rates really high on the priority chain too. When I eventually evolved from a mattress on the floor to an actual bed some years down the road, I thought that manna had fallen from heaven. This could never be actually something that any sane human being would plan.

Home ownership had so far evaded me. I had friends and family members who had gone there and had therefore guaranteed themselves a chair at the table of civilized humanity. I struggled so long just to have a roof over my head that I thought that owning a home was something I could appreciate for others and never, ever taste for my wee dumb self. The concept never even knocked at my door until I received the promise of a gift from my dying mother. I knew that I loved living in California; I just never knew how much I wanted to stay there.

"I'm going to give you a little money," Mum told me, wretched with bone cancer and tired of her existence on this planet. "And what will you do with it?" she asked me in her whimsical way. I surprised the both of us by saying that I wanted to, finally, buy a house in America. I really did want to have my own walls around me; my own soil; a slice of my own personal heaven to embrace and nurture for future years. I didn't want to be a traveler anymore; I didn't want to live out of a van in nomadic ignorance, or in some one else's space, where they checked if I hung objects on their cherished porch or had my relatives to stay for more than a week. I wanted my own front door; something to cherish; triumph as it were, for all I had strived for and something that I had, ultimately, achieved.

This slice of the American dream came to me in the bittersweet months after my Mother left us for a planet where she felt no pain and no pain could find her. She knew where we were going with her kind gift and that made everything that came after just a little sweeter. My new life, my arrival in the human race, arrived as a home on land in the kindest, nicest village anyone could wish for. Without realizing it at the time, I had arrived in my forever home. The journey, thus far, had been a long one, with big old rocks to trip me up, not to mention oodles of my own foolishness that almost caused an avalanche. But the views on the way were ones I wouldn't have traded for the world. And when I look at my lovely home in Soledad and say, "how the heck did I get here?" the question is really a rhetorical one and, in the depths of my heart, I know it all. The destination is sweeter because of the journey.

**Lucy looks at her home every day and says "how lucky am I!"**

# PUTTING LIFE IN PERSPECTIVE

It was a regular day in August – warm, windy and as normal as could be. I received a call that there was a fire burning behind my office in the Gabilan Plaza. I stepped outside and witnessed a black rage of smoke issuing upwards in an aggressive plume. 'They'll get it,' I assured myself and hustled back into work. After all, I had paperwork to do and contracts to process. "It's moving quickly!" I get another call. "It's out of control!" I stepped outside again. Sure enough, from the column of black smoke I had seen just a little while ago, now there were angry red and blue flames gouging the hillside behind the school. I watched in disbelief for a few seconds more and went back to work.

"You need to leave at once," my husband said, an air of tension and concern in his voice. "They've closed Metz Road; we can't get home. Frou and I are at Sandy's right now". That was all I needed. My babies – my dogs and cats – were at the house and I needed to get home to them; it was as simple as that. By now, they were probably smelling the smoke and sensing the danger. They were most likely afraid and wondering where we were.

Driving along Metz Road, the hills were now being consumed by a full-blown, raging inferno, such as I have never seen before, except on the news and in movies. The mild puff of smoke from earlier had transformed into a greedy monster which was eating up our hillsides like it was nothing and heading hungrily towards our homes. Folks were lined up along the roads taking pictures of the fire, unable to take their eyes off it for a second. It was like an insane, dark circus; a nightmare. Water tankers swooped overhead as the daylight begun to quickly fade before our eyes. The feeling of powerlessness was immense. Cars crawled along the road, eyes on the amazing theatricals. I smacked my steering wheel in sheer frustration and cussed. "Come on people it's not a circus," I snarled. "That is my life that is burning right there"; and it was. I wasn't going to Sandy's; I was going to go home while I still could and I was going to rescue my babies. Knowing my husband would never put his stamp of approval on that little solo venture, I just went on. Surely they would let me through; I only lived right there. I could see our subdivision from the road. At the crossroads to 146, the CHP had the road blocked off. I purposefully parked the car and walked over to them. "I only live right there, officer. I need to go and get my animals," I urged kindly. "Sorry, lady. Can't let you through," said the man in uniform. Others were trying to get to their homes too. I could see mine; it was right there. My babies were right there. He wasn't letting any of us through. I whipped the car around and wondered if I should just zoom back around, jump on the freeway and come in the back way through Greenfield and onto Metz. Valuable time was being lost. My son with the Greenfield Police told me that Metz Road was still open that end, but I had better hurry. At times like this you have to try and keep a cool head, against the odds. The skies burned red-black and I knew at the time that that had to be the color of fear, however boldly I tried to carry myself. It was an unspeakable surreality. I kept wanting to wake up.

I decided against the solo option and met my husband and daughter back at my office and we decided to park one of the vehicles in town and travel together in the other. At least, that way, we'd all be together and our fears could be shared ones; our plans the sum total of multi- minds thinking together. We zoomed along the freeway towards Greenfield, unable to take our eyes off the licking red flames on the other side of the valley above our home. We had to get home; we just had to. "What if Metz is closed that way too?" my husband was voicing my fears too. That was unthinkable. There is no deeper fear that the one that you may not be able to get home until it is too late. At every corner, he vocalized his fear that there was going to be a roadblock to stop us. At each corner, there was not. We kept driving. We got to our gate. All was intact.

The euphoria you feel, when you have been craving the untouched ground of your home and imagining that it will be denied to you and then you realize that the barricade had actually been an imaginary one, is indescribable unless you have actually tasted it. We had that feeling as we came through the gate and nobody at that point could tell us that we couldn't go home. I could have kissed the ground. Sometimes in life you are reminded of the very fundamentals of your existence. The survival of your home is one of them. Never mind the eerie skies and the pungent smell of danger all around; it was a blissful moment, if even just for the moment.

I am always happy to see my babies, just as they are happy to see me, every time I appear. This time was especially dear. We were truly home, they were okay, we would all be together and that was really the only thing that mattered. Again, the fundamentals of life. But we didn't have time to waste. We had no power. The way the fire was raging towards us we had little time to stop and think clearly. We needed to find our flash lights and our bags. We needed to pack everything into our VW van that we really could not bear to live without. For me that is a lot. I have all my mother's drawings and art works on my walls, I have irreplaceable family photos, I have pieces of our lives plastered all over. Where to start? You start from the beginning; that's what you do when your brain is all over the place and the light switch is not doing anything to help you find some order from the chaos.

"What do I pack, Mum?" my teenager asks. "You pack as if you're never going to be able to come home again," I told her. "All your favorite things." I looked at my amazing collection of shoes and bags. Couldn't take them all, couldn't even take a handful. All you only really need is one of each; the rest can be replaced. I came to see that as a theme, as I packed pictures and jewelry, sentimental items, basic clothing and sensible items like the dogs' leash and water bowl. After all, none of the 'stuff' really matters. A house has insurance; it can be replaced. Pairs of shoes? I can buy more; love to buy more. The stuff inside my house? A lot I would really miss a lot. But not to be able to rescue my babies? That would crucify me for the rest of my life.

We did not have to evacuate that night or the following night; though we were on fire watch through the dark hours, scouring the tenacious glow of the burning brush over the canyon and biting nails, as the fire continued to rage and then cheekily jumped the highway 146, a skip from our homes. Just a whip around the back of the vineyard and the inferno would be on our doorsteps; we knew that for sure. Our van was packed and ready, nose forwards. We had clothes, we had toothbrushes, we had a few of our favorite things and we had our babies. Our dog Baxter sat in the back seat of the van and wouldn't move for two nights straight. It was as if he knew that there was trouble afloat and, if we were going, he wasn't going to be left behind.

We have had a close call with Mother Nature and her raging son Mr. Fire these past few days. We put our lives in perspective and we learned how to pack up our lives in 10 minutes. In retrospect, there are things I would do differently. I would have a list, a plan and a more methodical system of packing up. Other things I would do just the same. I would make sure the whole family is together and that we made it home to rescue the babies. Sometimes in life you are reminded that the very basic things mean the very most. Many of us residents of the Gabilan Hills of Soledad got that message this week. We are now so very grateful that we are all able to go back home and look at our black scarred hills as just a memory and a lesson of what can and does happen in a second to any of us.

More thanks than I can say go to our firefighters, the state over, who came to help during our time of need. Seeing fire trucks from every corner of our state and the amazing work of the crews on and over the hills made me so very proud to live in our wonderful state, never mind the sometimes erratic wiles of Mother Nature and her son, Mr. Fire.

**That was the week Lucy was a near evacuee.**

# THE COYOTES AND THE TRAIN

There's something about a 'white night'; a night when you hardly sleep a wink, which situates you in life; grounds you, as it were; makes you really think about who you are and where you're going in this world. As I lay awake in the pitch black of night listening to the train hurtling down towards Los Angeles and the coyotes howling to the sound of its horn; I realized that this was a pretty common sequel in my home and its surroundings. When the train howls, a minute later so do the coyotes. They know that they're home when they hear the train coming, so they yelp with joy; or at least that was my 3am conclusion. I wondered if I could test my theory for the 4.31 northbound freight; but blearily failed to follow through.

When the earth shakes as it did the other night, I feel sea sick for a while; then I feel small and insignificant, as we all should when Teutonic plates on the earth shift and we are reminded, once again, that we are nothing, we are dust; we are nothing. I am also reminded, when I feel the shudder, that I am home; this is the place I have chosen and, shaking or not, I am always so glad that I do not live in tornado country anymore when we lived under the gloomy threat of "tornado watch" for hours, sometimes days at a time. "You are under a tornado watch," the steely newscaster would say sternly. "This is not a test. Take cover immediately." I recall driving across Baton Rouge under a tornado watch one day and wondering where all the people had gone. I had not taken the gloomy newscaster seriously and was lucky to be able to see another day and tell this story. The people in the nearby trailer park were not so fortunate. Give me an earthquake any day; you never know when they are going to show up and put you in your place. Never mind, we are practically on the San Andreas Fault, and quite often, a good slammer in the Pinnacles can feel as if a big truck had just driven into my house. This is my palace, my pride and joy; and I shall defend it to the last; stucco cracks and all.

"God, it's so cold here!" my visiting sister remarked with dripping red nose and thick woolly hat. "Do you have any thick sweaters and long socks I can borrow? You people don't heat your houses!" I provide as a dutiful sister should and didn't even answer back.

"It's so much warmer in Washington," she went on, as if I were personally responsible for the weather being so uncannily chill in these parts. "They already have blossom on their trees." And so I defend my casa, my land, my territory as if my very life depended on it. Not that I really need to. Everyone knows that California is the center of the universe; the most desirable place to live on the entire planet. Maybe that's why people like to find fault with it.

"It's so windy where you live!" visiting Brits have exclaimed, when they've stayed with us in the summer time. They equally fail to acknowledge the delightful wide starry nights, the clear blue daytime skies and the hour upon hour of sunshine. Most of their days are slate grey; how would they know what's good?

"Oh yes; it is, isn't it! We love it," we gush accordingly, getting ready to defend to the death our lovely wind. "No bugs, no humidity, everything lovely and clean and bright. Aren't we lucky?" And we do love it. It takes down the heat in high summer and blows away any pesky bugs we wouldn't want visiting us. Any mosquito in these parts has severely lost its way and soon gets puffed on out of here. Having suffered the sweltering humidity and buggy environs of a Washington DC summer in my past, or an even steamier Louisiana stifler, I'd take a gust of our wind any time; along with a grounding old-fashioned earth movement for good measure.

I guess we should thank our lucky stars that our visitors can find fault with our paradise; so that they ultimately leave again and go back to their lovely sultry temperatures with swamp coolers and flying cockroaches. Otherwise we'd be in a heck of a pickle; with all these visitors coming to see us and never leaving! I'd better start complaining about the wind myself, come to think of it; just to be sure that everyone knows this place is no more perfect than any other and schleps on back to the burg from whence they came. We have a bit of wind; sure. We have some sun and boy, oh boy, this year it looks as if we may have a dusting of snow on our mountains, burst pipes and more. Better move to Colorado, people and learn some snow-ploughing skills! Who knows what will await us next? But this I know. Come March or April and the last of the winter rains; I shall be glad of that. I shall be ready to swoon with the hug of summer, drink up my huge twinkling skies, move with the ground and embrace, with a big loving smile, my lovely, lovely wind.

**Lucy adores her home in the sunny, windy Salinas Valley.**

# THE PLACE INSIDE

There is a place that cannot be touched by recession, unemployment or the whims of the stock market. It is a quiet place where only the invited can go. It's a place where the uninvited may only hover by the door. Those who have no real concept of what this place might be can only dream that they will be able to go there some time in their lifetime; but they remain unsure as how to get there or if a map even exists to show the way. It's not a place for the young or the seeking, the tormented or the hypocrite. It's an island that either resides within you or it does not. You cannot find it in a church or in a bank account; you can only find it deep, deep within yourself. That place is called inner peace and it's a rare jewel in the midst of the raging sea – it can be yours forever, if you have it, and you can hold on to it.

I have come to treasure my gift, my inner peace, in the early morning light, as the night blanket of fog lifts from the Salinas River and reminds the birds to get up and go drink from that curling whisper of life that moves soothingly south to north. My peace is the snow capped peaks above the Arroyo Seco Valley that remind me of the turmoil of last summer's fires and how grateful we are that they are past and we are still here. From the burning fury to the sublime white; it was a journey for those crests, for sure. My gift is the curl of delicious coffee aroma as the early light changes over the lip of my cup and the tiny moving dots of traveling car lights along the freeway call mankind to service and herald the beckoning of an awakening universe. It's our early bug-eating, chirping bird friend called Floyd who sits on the stick and peruses his universe. He watches us and we watch him and it is magic. It's also his son Floyd Junior with his punk hair cut and sprightly ways, who was almost certainly born and raised under our roof and is already learning the ropes and keeping the bugs from the rafters like a good bird we plan to keep around. Our sanctuary is our bumper crop of lemons or apples, our humming birds in the winter time drinking from our orange flowers and the smile that a sunflower can bring on a cloudy day. It is the call of the coyote and the swoop of the hawk as they dance together, but not, over the green and majestic hills below. It is the very simple things – and very often the free things - in life that can give you the most peace. It is the summation of priceless gifts you have earned but never bought. I couldn't have told you that when I was young, but I can tell you now. My dogs scratching their backs in delight and rolling around on hot tiles in the sun, so happy with their lot; now that is inner peace and tranquility at its best.

I look around me at all the torment in our world, both close to home and far away. I watch a dear friend of mine tormented with anguish in her life, not knowing where to turn or who to turn with. I worry for her and I can't see how and when she will find her peace. Every now and then she will seize a snippet of it and I think she may have ultimately found her way; then I watch her cascading downwards towards danger once more and I know there is a huge gap inside of her, not a sliver of peace to be found. Then I worry some more and hope again that some day soon she will find her own illusive pot of peace at the end of a very long rainbow.

I hear the horror stories every day in my line of work of people not being able to make their house payments and facing the torture of having to tell their children that the home they thought was the center of their world is no longer going to be their sanctuary. They will have to be moving on down the road away from their friends and the walls they know to the uncertain and frightening reality of places and people they do not. Such a lack of peace you would not wish on anyone, let alone our youth.

I know of people who are having a hard time finding work, paying bills, staying afloat – the fundamentals of life will take the peace out of you in an instant if you let them.

So what can you do when the storm is raging around your inner island, when money is short, uncertainty is rife and today is pretty tricky with no guarantees for tomorrow either? I would counsel a step back inside yourself. Take some quiet time away from the turmoil of day to day living and examine yourself and how you live your life, as if you were a stranger on the street. I would ask you to write down the things that are certain today in your world that you know of – your health, your loves, your inner guidance – and I would ask that you hold on very tightly to those things. Then address the items that are less certain – the possibility of less work, the threat of a change in life style, the prospect of losing a home and look at how you might mitigate those items if in fact you were faced with the prospect. There are few things more frightening for a human than a shift in our status quo. Examine the choices you make, where could you make some changes, how could you begin to build a nest egg, a rainy day fund? Make your mind up, write down the plan and set about working the plan. You might never need it, but too many of us have these past few challenging years and, in the present economic climate, the odds are rather stacked against you. With all of these life preparations in place, your inner peace will be a guarded sanctuary, a secret garden you can unlock and revisit in the early dawn with your cup or coffee, or whenever you darn well please, once you have sowed the seeds that needed sowing and watered the areas that needed care. Do what you need to do and you will not need to track it down, the peace that follows will find you.

**Lucy tries to be guardian of her 'I.P.'**

## 'TIL DEATH OR IRRITATION US DO PART

"Good Morning, Darling". (Hark! I hear a bird sing!)
"Good morning, darling. Care for some coffee?"
"Thank you darling. How kind! Would you like the daily paper with that?"
"Oh yes, please! I think it's going to be a lovely day!"
"Oh yes, looks that way!"

And so the day can begin between two people who have been married for almost ten years or so. You can be so sweetly civil so easily at the break of dawn, when there has been nothing yet to blacken your day or taint your waking hours with any shadow of fury or irritation even. Some days, before the day has really begun, you can almost feel as if you were young again and in love. You can feel that the world is at your finger tips and retirement is really only a skip and a jump away, ("retirement" being a day without mounds of stress, a day when you can read the paper with a cup of coffee in peace and leisure, a day when a book outside in the sun might not be completely out of the question.)

However, that is not the case most days. Most days we are racing against the clock and there is not a smidge of romance to be found. *Darling* is saying "good morning darling," as he rushes to get the child up, the cat out, the dogs out and the show on the road, before the show gets a tardy slip and a cancellation notice before its next performance. *Darling* is also saying, "Hurry up with my coffee, woncha, before I am forced to drive on that freaking freeway with no caffeine in my veins, amongst other psycho commuters who are also late and lacking in caffeine, driving wildly whilst applying their make up and fixing the cornflakes in their teeth and hence tumbling – all of them- towards a recipe for disaster". That is what *Darling* is really saying when he is reaching for the coffee pot that has no coffee in it yet and looking at the clock at the same time, while tearing up the house, looking for his cell phone.

Real life is not romantic. Most Super-women know that and their men-partners get there in their own time. You can only go along with what you have to work with on any given day. Ordinarily my husband and I steal a weekend away in December or January to revisit our marriage, have a conversation and see if we would like to renew the option for the coming year. I am only half joking. With kids, animals, houses and work up the ying-yang, the husband-wife stuff takes a dusty back seat to all of the above. Whether we are ultimately the core of our direct family's universe or not; we are required to need not of each other, to carry on carrying on and to be a team, no matter what. That is the case with most marriages, I have discovered. Most years we remember that we need to check in, regroup and check that the team is still intact. This year we missed that. Why? We couldn't make the time. (And what would happen if we found that we could not keep on keeping on? The team would break down and everyone would be surprised, right? We would then say that we should have made the time.)

"You need to write about me," my husband states sulkily. "You never write about me anymore." (If you've read any of my stuff over the years, you'll understand why I pick my battles. The last time I wrote about 'Saving my marriage one lunch at a time," family members arrived by the droves for interventions and we even had my mother-in-law move in for a time!) OK, truth be told, it may be time for a comment or two and I'll take the ma-in-law visit at this time; my house is completely filthy.

Marriage is a tough bag. Even with a semi-saint for a husband, as I have been blessed with the second time around, they can still make you grind your teeth at the end of a hard day. The day can start out with 'darling, would you like some strychnine in your coffee?' and end with 'darling, drink up quickly, there's strychnine in your coffee I'd like you to absorb', without the blink of an eye. Your dream-boat dude can become some one you'd like to relegate to a dog bed in the garage in the space of a few short hours, just because life had sat on your shoulders throughout the course of the day and you couldn't dump it off and get some space to look around at all you had to be so very grateful for.

Ten years married and, if we make it 'til the something of August, that will be what we're looking at! May the fireworks crack and the heavens hum! 10 years? That has to be at least a granite anniversary monument and a medal for us both! Never mind that I still keep him guessing, since he has no memory for dates. He'll look at the calendar and see no wedding anniversary engraved on the month of August calendar, though he'll see his great aunt's birthday and his appointment with the dentist. 10 years wed – I just don't think he should need reminding of the actual day. With couples struggling to get from the early morning banter through to the 'boy, you're annoying', at the end of the day, I shall expect at least a medal some day in August, if I make it to that gigantic 10 year mark. Plus I shall expect him to remember the actual day and mark it with something huge. That's just what happens when you've been together a long time.

**Lucy is a sometime wife and mother,**
**also a part-time Superwoman.**
**Would us modern gals have it any other way?**

# WAKE UP CALLS

The death of a man this week that I didn't know – my age – who was taken from his family and friends in a tragic accident made me mull over his obituary and reconsider my own daily whinings that I am not proud of at all. It is important to do that once in a while, though we seldom take the time out of our busy days to do so. Sadly it is often a wake up call like a swift and searing tragedy that makes us stop and think and muse as I did this week on the many, many reasons to be cheerful - if we are alive, seemingly healthy, employed, surrounded by good people and not neck-deep in debt.

At a time of uncertainty in our nation – both internationally and economically – there is a lot to be said for the confidence of the people as a whole, millions though we are. Confidence counts for a lot, ask the analysts. I often wonder if we do not bring a lot of self-prophesying doom and gloom upon ourselves. The media with their choice for bad news selling papers and building ratings has to take some of the blame, in addition. Good news is mostly tedious, after all. But with all of that said, I have so many reasons to thank my personal lucky stars for so many things, after my mullings of this week, that I consider this a good news letter, (lest I not have many more days to count my stars and relay my good fortune. You just never know.) That guy, my age, in the paper this week reminded me that you just never do know when today is going to be your last. So here are my reasons to be cheerful for the week. Writing things down often makes them so. Try it, you may find you get to the same place I did.

1. I live in one of the most beautiful places in the entire world. I am qualified to say so. If you have ever suffered a slate-grey London winter, or summer even, with terminal rain falling and the kind of flat grey sky that never ends, you know what I'm saying. It has to be one of the most depressing things on the planet. If you've ever been in a Louisiana or Maryland summer and wondered when it would, please, all end, you truly know what I'm saying. I

don't even want to hear it about the wind we boast here during the summertime. If you have been living in temps over the boiling mark this week, you are kind and appreciative about our wind. My relatives from Watsonville take note.

2. Myself and my family have good health – huge reasons to be cheerful! No matter that my husband suffers from severe allergies and I myself have developed a rare and extreme case of premenopausal disorder, which can impact a person and her family in a rotten way certain times of the month, we are alive. We have all our limbs and most of our faculties most of the time. We keep a guarded eye on the horizon for those in our family not afflicted with such meager complaints as ours, but other, larger issues; and we hope for the best. That is all you can do. There are no guarantees in life of a long life. You can only make a good one of each passing day and hope for another.
3. I have work and I can feed my child and my animals, though my husband is the cook in our house and he mostly feeds me. Life has not always been so kind to me. I recall having two waitressing jobs and no home at one time. I was hungry sometimes too – there is no worse feeling, trust me. Though sometimes these days I long for a weekend off, or a chance to just be me without said 'Smart' phone attached to my head, there are so many people out there without regular work, who stress and struggle to put food on their tables during these uncertain times. The more work I have, the more grateful I should be. I should never forget the days that I lived in more humble circumstances and worried about gleaning food to put in my mouth that day, let alone clean clothes on my back. Remind me of that, please.
4. I have good family who love me most of the time – that is so huge – and something that many of us take so entirely for granted, unless a member is taken from us. I have family here, I have family over seas - I have a whole world of family and a complete foundation of caring people who wish the best for me. That is the premier foundation for a civilized human being and I have a responsibility to be so because of it.

5. I have a 'normal' daughter. There are so many families suffering the destructive animals of gang violence, poverty, violence, drugs, alcohol – so many challenges which present themselves in modern day life and permeate a normal, comfortable development of growing minds. My daughter may roll her eyes at me and snarl when I tell her to clean her room, but I do know that she truly loves me deeply to the core – I am confident in that – she knows that I would do anything for her and vice versa. I try to raise her to be able to look back at her childhood with wonder, the way I am now able to look back at mine – and be able to say, as my mother did, looking back at her life before she died, "I had a really good time". I try to embrace her friends too in the same way. If they like to make my home their home, for whatever brief period of time, they are welcome to. 'Mi casa es su casa,' should be the maxim for those of us fortunate enough to provide a safe and comfortable environment for developing minds needing a harbor from the world. I had friends' parents who did that for me also years ago and I still look back with pleasure and happiness at the opportunities and happiness afforded to me decades ago.
6. I have a good partner. We are a team. Whatever I need, he can supply and I return the favor when I can. We have different skills and qualities – we put it together every day and make it work. With love and respect, a lot can be conquered and achieved. That is a life lesson. It has not always been easy, but we have persevered and reached a level playing field of mutual understanding and adoration. We both came from more difficult places and our education along the way gave us the experience to do better the next time around. A good marriage, a solid core for our children; multiple reasons to be cheerful.

If you are having a hard time with the current events in the world and your community, stop a minute and think about things that you do have control over. Write down in black and white and reflect on them. It there's not much there, write down the things you'd like to see on the list and make them a goal and a bright light to strive for. Make them so. For those of you struggling as I did years ago, things can change if you want them to enough. I am living proof of that and I thank my lucky stars for it every day.

**Lucy is a firm optimist.**

# WE STILL WOULD

Remember when a trip to the store meant a diaper bag,
6 teenagers and Vandura to carry us all?
Remember when we'd stay at the freeway motel
Just to have some quiet time together,
And we still would.

Remember how we'd make cards for anniversaries
Of our meeting,
You'd bring home flowers.
I'd write the odd poem.
And we still do.

Remember how we'd look for each other around the home
We'd seek and we'd call 'til we'd find.
And we still do.

Remember our wedding and
How we wanted everyone to come
Who wanted to come.
We gave vows to our children and each other
In front of our families and the ocean.

It was everything.

Remember how we worried about the
Plate cost, then sold the classic car.
We still would.

Remember how we believed in the fairies?
And we still do.
Pennies, hummers, Lucia lamps, frogs and all.

There are so many remembers of the many years married
That we share.

You have given me so many reasons to be happy; so much cause to thank my lucky stars the day I became your ad lady – thank you Barbara - and life took on a new bloom.

She has never stopped blossoming.
To borrow our wedding song, we "let it grow",
And it did.

Would we do it all again?
I'd like to think that we would.

**From Lucy to Mike on the event of our 10th Wedding Anniversary**

# WISHFUL THINKING

With the shorter days and the increased dark time comes the tendency to do a little less and think and ponder a little more, I've found. Being English, we are accustomed to hunkering down in the winter time and closeting ourselves firmly in our centrally heated, cozy homes away from the elements. It could explain somewhat the huge spike in births nine months on from the severe winter months; another story completely.

However, I found myself thinking recently, in the early twilight of a cooling fall evening, about regret and what a searing and lingering state that can be.

I was born on the East Coast of England in a small fishermen's town at the end of the railway line; and the end of all other lines too; since, if you drove all the way through and out the other end, you would drive into the sea, (a lone bank robber from out of town discovered that one time!) We lived in a tiny brick cottage below sea level, which meant that damp was a constant problem. We had three bedrooms, 1 bath, a tiny kitchen and open plan living/dining room with a small back yard and coal bunker for the tiny fireplace. I thought this house was the most incredible palace. It was just a skip away from our stony beach and icy green North Sea; but in those days I wasn't choosy about my water. I just plunged into it anyway and held my breath until I could stand the cold. We had a sea peak from my parent's room where I could stand on my tiptoes and watch the waves crashing to the shore. It always made me feel really, really good and safe, as I scanned the white horses cresting on the horizon and imagined I was on a shipwreck way out in the deep, looking back at the sanctuary of shore and this little girl peeking out of the window at me.

Our cottage was our safe house, our nest, our port out of the storm. Once we moved our primary residence to the city of London, our cottage took on a different role, but a significant one all the same. Every weekend, we would travel down there away from the smoke and delight at the freshness of the air, the call of the sea birds, the phenomenal power of the ocean all over again. Every vacation we would be there with our friends, spending week after week riding bikes, walking dogs, swimming, playing; it was a child's heaven. No crime, no violence. Our parents could open up the doors and let us go. They never locked their doors anyway; not to their homes or cars. It was a utopian childhood existence.

As we grew up and edged away from our parents, as you do, we only wanted to go to the cottage with our friends, not our families. Lives got busy in the big city and the coast had less of a draw in our teen years. My parents started to go less in addition, and the cottage took on an air of damp neglect; as if the life that was once there had departed.

"Are you going to the cottage next weekend? No, okay, great. I'm going to go down with some friends." As a self-centered teenager at the time, I did not appreciate the huge impact that this natural breakaway behavior had on our mother. As we relinquished our childhood leanings on our parents, so our parents suffered from the separation and tried to prepare themselves, in a sense, for the rest of their lives without us. We didn't notice it one bit. At the time I saw my mother's fading passion for our holiday home as a bit of a blessing; selfishly, it meant that the cottage was more available for me and my friends. What it really meant was that if we could not go to our haven as a family, she didn't want to go at all. Once we were grown up and not needing her so much, the place had lost its luster.

I was devastated when my parents informed me that the cottage was being sold. The damp was eating up the walls and the home was taking on the look of a place which had seen better days and more consistent love. They sold the cottage at the bottom of the market for a pittance. I was already living in America and could do nothing about it. I remember wishing I were rich and could buy the cottage for myself. I remember the taste of sadness I had, knowing that I would always miss it and the feeling I had when I was there. The home was sold for a song and I suffered searing regret at the time, which lingered over the years until today, if I am honest.

Truthfully, I have suffered that loss ever since. When I think of my childhood, that place is it. When I think of my real home; my real home is there. I travel back to the village whenever I am in England and still manage to see in the bakery or the fish and chip shop old family friends and people who took care of me when

I was a baby. Not bad for a village which our family officially left nearly two decades ago.

Years later, when I'd visit the town – the place I consider my English home - I would always peek through the windows of my cottage – as I still saw it still – and look at my old furniture, which was sold along with the home and imagine us all in there again. It gave me some comfort to know that the house looked loved and well lived in. I still wonder, if I came into some serious money, whether I might try and own a small piece of soil there once again; a place where I could again steal my sea peek and inhale the unique hearty salty swale. It's probably just wishful thinking. Who, in the modern world, has funds to own second homes these days? But the wistful and the wishful thoughts cost nothing. I can still go there and pretend to myself that the cottage is still mine and everything is as it was.

When I was ill, I would make myself go for walks in my mind to escape my insufferable situation. My childhood town was the place I chose to walk around – to the baker's shop and the sweet shop, the beach, the Marshes, the sea wall, the boating pond and the Martello Tower. I walked around that town for hour upon hour in my mind and I never got tired of it. It took me through some very dark days and back out to the light – as should all places that carry wonderful memories.

It has been a source of lasting and searing regret that I could not somehow keep my childhood home in our family for our children and children's children to be able to have a taste of all I delighted in so many years ago. My husband knows this story well and told me recently that we should start a cottage fund and try to work our way towards replacing our cottage; putting the missing piece back in the family map as it were. It may well be a pipe dream, but just the thought of it made me start a pipe dream fund and feel so much better about something that happened so many years ago and has caused me pain ever since. Who knows; maybe if we work hard enough at it, and lady luck fills our sails with her good will, our dream will come true.

**Lucy still loves to go back and visit the seaside town of her childhood. Some memories just get warmer.**

# WITH LOVE, LIBERTY AND HAPPINESS FOR ALL

I've come a long way in the few short years since I became a US citizen. During this time, I feel that I have grown and flourished beneath the protective cover of my adopted flag. Let's face it; it took me the best part of two decades to get to the stage when I could make the time to obtain all the many forms, fill out the very many said forms, ( and uncover vital information such as the marriage certificate of my grandparents way back when at the turn of the century in the city of Nottingham, England), pay my $400 for my application, (no checks accepted), study for my test, fill out just a bit more paperwork, go to the immigration building in San Ho for my test, (where I nervously proceeded to lose the entire contents of my purse in the security machine); and so it went on.

Had they asked me for at least the blood of my first born in order to achieve this valuable status, I would not have been surprised. Anyone who is venturing forth into the world of citizenship knows what I'm talking about, and I take my hat off to you for following me and many others in our footsteps and stepping up to the plate. But it should be difficult to achieve this; don't you think? It's a great honor to be an accepted and permanent member of the greatest country in the free world, I believe; and we should all have to pass the very rigid test to get there. Much as I don't like to study much these days, I thought it important that I should know how many presidents this fair land has had in its relatively short record, the history of the birth of the constitution, the systems of government et al. I realized, going through the process, that native born people don't always know this stuff, so I felt really quite superior and important to just myself.

I do not think that we should have an easy passage to have the rights to live and work for always in this land; I think I said that already, but it's important. Though I had a super, permanent 'Alien Visa' or 'green card', (which is actually blue), prior to my super sweet US Naturalization status, I always knew, at the back of my mind, that if I turned into an axe-wielding murderer or suddenly took up drug dealing as an occupation, I could swiftly be shipped back to my homeland for always with my tail between my legs. Once I was naturalized, they had me for always, warts and all. There was something really special about that. (Let's face it; if I have to go to jail I'd rather take the Beverly Hills one over the one situated anywhere in the vicinity of the English winter!) It also came to me that, in embracing the country whole-heartedly, I was also given the privilege of a voice; I could vote. Since I received that enormous voice, I have used it; boy, have I! I have read up on all the issues, I have studied each big and small election and I have used my right as a citizen to add my opinion – like it or not - to the melting pot of the free world. There is no greater honor; in my opinion, again, and I challenge all of you who do not hold that privilege in such high esteem to imagine a world without it.

During my naturalization ceremony, when I got to lead the pledge of allegiance in my mother's very special "Old Glory" sparkly hat, it came to me that home is entirely where we make it; but if we choose a home which is not our native land, we have to fight for it just that bit harder. I could never give up the fact that I was born English and English I would somehow always be; a piece of me would always be over there with my parents and my peeps; but, in adulthood, it felt as if it was alright to adopt another land for my second homeland and to embrace it whole-heartedly. It means a lot to me that I am now half English and half American. Half English because I was born there and my family are English; (plus I really do love a cup of tea at 4pm; no getting away from that!) and half American because I love living over here, the divine land mass, the enormous opportunities, the excessive and amazing freedoms and the warm and open people; and I know that this will always be my home. My husband, my sons and my daughter are all American; I have many American friends. I live and work here; and when I am somewhere else, I think about being here in my home and look forward to doing that again. That is the essence of home and home land, I believe. Love, liberty and the pursuit of happiness; now isn't that what it's all about? Happy 4$^{th}$ of July, our nation's birthday! I shall be wearing my mother's "Old Glory" sparkly hat to mark the occasion. You won't be able to miss me in the crowd.

**Lucy is a proud Brit-American.**

# HUMANITY

# ACTS OF RANDOM KINDNESS

I was watching a lady in the store with some curiosity; as you do when you are in people watching mode and you're stuck in a long line, going nowhere fast. The store is one of the world's great places for observation. The lady in question was anxiously studying the prices ringing up on the cash register before her. She didn't have anything that would be called frivolous among her purchases, (don't be looking in my basket!) She had rice, beans, tortillas, milk, generic cereal, generic juice; and a few other staples. I observed the tension on her face; I sensed that she wasn't sure if she had enough money in her purse to pay for the things she needed; she had three young children with her, for sure she needed all of those things. "Twenty dollars and 85 cents," the cashier announced. "The lady pulled out a $20 bill and then proceeded to rummage through her scrappy old purse, eyes flitting back and forth in desperation. She knew she didn't have the 85 cents and I knew she didn't have the 85 cents. I produced a dollar bill and gave it to the clerk. "That'll cover the cents," I said quickly and quietly, wary of offending. The lady's eyes rose to mine and smiled. At that moment, we were both parents, nothing less. "Gracias", she said, her brown eyes glowing like rich pools of chocolate. What's a buck to me in any case? Pay attention in the grocery line; some one may be counting on you. A random act of kindness; what does it really cost to be there for some one you've never even met? Gave me the warmth of a cup of cocoa, I can tell you. And the lady in question? Maybe she'll return the favor, if she can one day, when some one else is a dollar short in the check-out.

A 'Drop-out Prevention Counselor' at a local school has, from my standpoint, the rather depressing job of trying to ascertain why certain children, some repeatedly, are not able to make it to school very much. Hers has to be one of the tougher assignments. Her task is to uphold the law – all children must go to school - and the law doesn't often make allowances for poverty, hunger, lack of clothing or childcare costs; but that is very often the reality that a drop out prevention counselor will have to face, when the names on a piece of paper become people. Face facts; if a child is not making it to school on a regular basis, the reason is probably not a pretty one. The counselor doesn't complain about the nature of her work; she'll win some, she'll probably lose a fair few, but she has a mission and she keeps on trying. She is a lady full of grace; it's written all over her face.

At this time of year she collects used clothing and invites many of the families she deals with into the school to have an anonymous 'free garage sale', as she describes it, to come in and see what might fit them and what they might need. Having been inside many of the needier homes in our community, she understands what a warm coat might mean to a mother who gives her all to her kids and it's still not enough; or a sweatshirt for a man who's grafting out in the fields in the early hours and his bones ache daily with the frost. She describes the pleasure she sees on their faces, as they're rummaging through the treasure trove, knowing that, for once in their daily grind, they're getting things they truly need, without having to worry about whether they can afford them or not. We should all know how it feels to have that kind of need; we would be better people for it. Get inside their closets for a moment in your mind, and then get into your own. My own pledge is that if I haven't needed it in 6 months, I don't need it at all. And that is coming from a person who is very possessive of her clothing! Sometimes you have to see the need to know it. Know it anyway. If it exists in our community, and trust me it does, and we, ourselves, have more than we need, which, guilty as charged your honor, many of us do; it is our humane obligation to make a difference where we can. Stop, look, listen; and then do something about it. You can't make it right, but you can make it better than it was.

Two young girls at the beginning of their bright promising lives take time out of their busy schedules to go and read stories to people on the back side of their lives in a rest home. Never mind that some of the residents kept asking if the story was nearly over, while the story-telling was going on and others commented that they either had to go and see their mother, (they must have been all of 90 themselves), or that they had to leave for work, (strapped in a wheelchair); that was not the point. The point was that some part of each one of them had probably appreciated the beauty of the children sitting before them and the purity of their voices and their intentions. That was the point. It is not what you get, but what you give. A simple lesson; a lesson in humility. One of the young girls is my daughter and she has discussed the experience several times since. Can you put a value on that? She gets to practice her public speaking skills under somewhat difficult circumstances, she gets to fulfill her reading obligations to herself and her school reading log, plus she gets to do something random and kind for people she doesn't know at all. This last thing has to help her to become a better person, who is better served to go out into the world and be kind to others; something so basic we never pause to consider its importance.

It is not what always what you do that is important, but what you do that comes directly from the heart. Commit an act of random kindness this week and start a trend. It may be that you start a tradition, create a meaning and make some one else's day. Start today even and tomorrow you'll feel a whole lot better inside yourself. You'll be a whole lot better and so will the community around you.

**Lucy tries to be kind where she can.**

# FALLING IN LOVE AGAIN

It has been a while since I fell this hard. I recall those tough and tortuous days of not so sweet 16, when the boy I adored was really some one's boy – then he was mine for a few short months – and then he was the same some one else's again. That was way too hard; the memory of the agony still doesn't sit well in the soul. This is better, but different. With maturity comes perspective. Were I 16 again, I would say "now is now and can now please be forever? I'll be your best friend!" From my current position in the universe, I say "now is now. If it's that good, watch out - it will probably change. Tomorrow is something so unpredictable; we're not even going there until she arrives!"

Now back to love and how deeply you can fall when you least expect it, regardless of your maturity. Maybe that was about love too.

"Look Mum, we found a baby by the gate!" my daughter came home on Sunday with a bundle in her arms. Not quite the Sunday paper I was expecting! She was carrying a brindle and white shivering bundle with large whiskers and mal-proportioned limbs to body size. In short; another dog. "Oh great," I said to just myself; and most definitely not her. "Now we have 12 paws in the house and those are just the dog ones! More darn kibble to buy!" grumble, grumble – as you do when you are a mature adult.

Judging by his general demeanor and the fact that he would evaporate at the very sound of my husband's voice, made me pretty sure that our newcomer's previous family had not been a very nice one, especially the males. Nevertheless, I made a sign by the gate where he was found to advertise the fact that he was lost, we had found him and we were taking care of him – a foster family if you will. I called the local vet's office and made sure it was well promoted throughout our little town that a rather sweet Jack Russell/terrier/who-knows-what-mix had been found and was being well minded until his rightful owner came back to claim him, (and give us in return a large bag of kibble for his keep – ha!) We waited. The call didn't come. We weren't much surprised. 'Smiley', as he quickly became known – though we were determined not to give him a name and then have to relinquish him to his rightful family - would smile in his own rather eccentric way when you spoke sweetly to him or gave him his kibble. It was almost a dance that accompanied this smile with all four paws going in different directions. So endearing I thought to myself, as I pondered who would deliberately abandon such a little ray of sunshine. Maybe he ran away from home and went out on a little adventure, then couldn't find his way back? There are all kinds of movies to that effect.

"Ha! There's a reason!" I noted to myself, as I arose and found little sprinkles in my garage where the floor was normally dry. Our visitor had found the tires to my car. My dogs did not tinkle in the garage. There were also rugs dragged around the yard and unusual holes to be found where holes had not been before. This little rascal had broken out of jail for sure and was on the run. He was one of those gangster types, running for his life and grabbing a bed here and there where he could. Fine, we knew his type. His peeps would catch up with him sooner or later.

Another few days passed and we realized that though he really was a rascal, the name "Roscoe" suited him for no good reason. My husband took it from the 'Dukes of Hazzard"; I took it from an artist. "Roscoe Smiley Jensen" – had a nice, unusual ring to it! I saw his mug shot on a wanted poster with his full name plastered across the top of the poster. "REWARD! Roscoe 'Smiley' Jensen. Last seen fully armed on Metz Road! Lock up your kibble!" His bereft family would come rushing to claim him, crying and grateful, with that huge bag of replacement kibble in their arms. I was dreaming again.

If you name, you claim, they say; but I wasn't ready to steal away some one's beloved pet that easily. If I lost one of mine, I would want the finder to make a huge effort to find me before they put a new name on the collar. I checked the Classifieds for frantic advertisements, desperately seeking an unfixed, smiling Jack Russell mix. None could be found, though I quietly checked every day. This was reminiscent of dog number 2 – Sophie "Halloween" Jensen, who we had actually witnessed being dumped out of a car on Vista De Soledad, one Halloween, as we were trick-a-treating down town. I saw her get thrown out, I knew she was dumped, but somehow I had to keep checking the classifieds anyway, in complete disbelief that a human could still do such a thing and mean it.

"You had better get his shots for 'parvo'," a wise friend noted. "If he's hanging with your dogs, the odds are he hasn't had his shots". Ok, what to do. Was he mine, or was he not? Was he going to be going home, or was he there already? I already knew in my heart of hearts that he had been abandoned at my gate by some one who thought he might find a home here and didn't have the courage or humanity to take him to the pound. I already knew – sadly - that some human being who had crossed his path had not been very kind to him. I also already knew that I could still manage a bit of extra kibble for paws numbered 9-12, and somehow scrape together quite a bit extra for the fixing and the shots that would come along with ownership of this little munchkin.

"Do you want to keep him?" I asked my daughter as we both perused our lawn, covered in the latest dragged-out pillows and blankets, courtesy of our newcomer. "I don't want to give him away to anyone else," she said. "He's been abandoned enough." So there you have it, love has a strange way of finding you when you least expect it. I imagine our newest bundle of ever moving paws will provide more color to our lives than we would ever have had without him, not to mention the sweetest smile you could ever see on a dog's face and a feeling that we did what we needed to, without really a choice in the matter. Take Smiley to the pound and carry those sad eyes in my heart forever, or know that I can provide as good a home as any out there and carve out another piece of my heart to another living thing? That's not really even a question, is it.

**Lucy is the proud mother of 'Roscoe Smiley Jensen', who has the sweetest nature of any living thing and who will live out his now happy days with our family.**

# HOPE FOR HUMANITY

It has been a terrible week, the one that just ended. I don't think that anyone will argue with that. Watching another senseless massacre on the campus of a city of learning, followed by copy cat attacks and irresponsible behavior of the media, in broadcasting the histrionics of a madman, made me not only wonder if the world itself had tipped over the edge, (and what we were all actually experiencing was the aftermath of the world's end), but also question whether I could ever put pen to paper again, as it were. I felt emotionally drained of thought, word and comment; which is rare for me. Those of you who know me will know that.

Young people should not have to deal with horror and sorrow on that level. Schools should be only places of fun and knowledge. We should be able to guarantee to our students and their parents that these locations for fun and knowledge are safe havens for our youth; worry only when they leave school and go out into the big bad world, that's what we should be able to tell them. But we can't. Mental illness is everywhere; and it can manifest itself even in the purest places on earth.

When I was at school, the biggest thing I had to fear was unpopularity or scorn from my peers. I never had to hide under my desk because our school was on lockdown, or witness any type of inconceivable horror story such as the world witnessed last week. Back in my day, if a student spoke back to a teacher, there would be a universal gasp of horror, the student would be dealt with and that "incident" would be the talk of the town for the day. The things some young people have had to deal with over the past few days are enough to guarantee them an instant fast-pass into adulthood. Their childhoods are over, for sure.

You want to protect your children. I have turned off any newscast this week when my daughter was in earshot; the news has all been so awful and so rotten. I do not want her to hear about anything that she doesn't need to handle before she is ready. Am I unrealistic, overprotective? Maybe. That is my right. I am her mother and my job is to protect and to nurture. Should she go to school fearing that an outcast will come in with a gun and start killing people? I would hate to wish that on her. Should you be prepared? Yes. Should you prepare them for the very, very worst that might happen on any given day? I have no response to that. Again, I am emotionally devoid of comment.

My colleague took on a foreclosure home this week – another source of bad, bad news in our world. It is never a good thing when some one loses their home. Did it happen overnight? No. Are the real estate professionals surprised by it? No again. Does it make it any easier? No. Lots of no's this week. Anyway, my colleague had to go through the process of changing the locks, expecting the worst of conditions on the home. When people are basically evicted from their abode, they do not go out with the best of will. Sometimes they show their feelings of sadness and dissatisfaction by trashing the place, sometimes they will lock the doors and throw away the key, because they can. What my colleague had to experience was not something I would imagine could happen in the civilized world. The family from the home was long gone, yet their dog had been left in a closed shed with no water and no food; the animal was nearly dead. My colleague told me that the cries she heard coming from that shelter were such as she does not care to remember. That incident brought the whole week to a resounding crashing end for me and that point I became almost comatose, emotionally void and crying inside for humanity and whether there was really any hope left for any of us.

Thankfully, with the dawning of a new day, I had another project I needed to attend to, which helped curve my attitude in the upwards direction. The "Steinbeck Young Authors' program at the National Steinbeck Center invited local writers to attend and coach young Middle School students on an assignment that they had been given only that morning, but on a book that they had studied in detail. We were coached as to our techniques as writing coaches – (teach 'esteem, esteem, esteem'!) – and then let loose on our students – one on one. My student – Julia – was a confident young lady. She loved to write; she had a lot of disciplines and a need to perform, a need to please. She was most anxious to receive honest criticism on her assignment and to amend her script with a maturity beyond her 13 years. I was surprised by her interest in receiving what I had to say; her resolve to modify and improve her piece. Julia - and the many other students who showed up and communicated with adults they had never met before - made me feel that, regardless of the horrible, terrible things which happened this week, whether on a school campus on the east coast of America, or a small shed in Soledad – humanity is basically good and that we have to keep on believing that, keep on hoping that the good will constantly outweigh the bad and prevail in this crazy old world we live in.

Thank you Julia and all the other Middle School students who gave us their all in their assignment at the National Steinbeck Center! You certainly gave me the lift I needed to stand up again with optimism to face the challenges of another week. Steinbeck himself would have been proud of you.

**Lucy, sometimes, has nothing to say.**

# KEEPING MEMORIES CLOSE

The Soledad Rotary was a more somber place to be than usual this past week with the news that our friend and fellow Rotarian, Red Skinner, had left us to go and share his Thursday BBQ lunch and smoke his cigar with some other people in St Elsewhere. Though I had not known Red very well, nor for long compared to my fellow Rotarians, I quickly learned that he had been a pillar in our community for many years; being a Veteran, a Police Chief and Fire Chief among other renowned positions. He was also a very cool guy with a quirky sense of humor to the last; that much I did know, and he will be missed. I'm sure other better qualified people will be writing suitable obituaries and honoring him the way he deserves. I look forward to reading the big picture about him and his life.

What really struck me though, as I dug through old newspapers looking for information about him and asking around his old friends, was how casually we all preserve our memories. I'm as guilty as the rest of you. Makes me want to rush home and start working on the last 5 years of photos, which are still sitting in their sleeves waiting to be neatly arranged in the albums I did buy 5 years ago. Makes me want to trace my family tree and write down all the names, which somehow escape me, of my great-grandparents and others who came before them and who are now less than just a vague memory away from non-existence. I need to do that now before I too am gone and they disappear entirely. Can't you see how sad that would be? I need to rediscover that sense of urgency I felt when I realized that I had forgotten which date my grandfather had died and how to go about finding it out.

When my child was born, I swore to take a roll of film a month of her and her antics. I fascinated my entire family and any of my friends, who would tolerate it, with pictures of her dribbling, crawling, falling over, crying, burping. You've got the picture. My mother announced that my child was the world's most photographed baby, (and also that I did not really need to send so many pictures all the time. She assured me that, as many pictures as I had sent them, they could never possibly forget how she looked!) But I'm glad now that I did, even though the habit has since slipped and I don't bore people quite so often with images of my darling. I'm also glad that I gained the dubious title of the family photographer back then; otherwise we would have had few family photos of anything really, and even less of my dear mother, who loathed being photographed and who required stalking in order to capture a frame.

My mother kept a record in her own way though, without realizing it. She was an artist and will forever have an archive of her considerable skills with me and mine on my walls and in my heart; though she would easily have thrown all her artwork away in a dramatic, artistic fit, had I not held out my arms and begged to be 'burdened' with it all. My daughter does understand somewhat what all of this means to me; especially now that Mother has also gone off to eat her BBQ with others in St Elsewhere and will never, that we know of, put pen to paper again. I impress on my daughter the importance of cherishing such things and she sees the happiness I get from admiring them and living with them every day, as treasures for my soul. I'm sure she will come to love and cherish them equally on her walls one day, when I leave them to her in years to come.

Our memories are our treasures. More than anything, they are part of our genetic make-up, our history and our being. We must take the time to preserve them and honor them for the generations to come. Record the holidays with your aging auntie; it may be her last. Frame that cute picture of your child doing something goofy; it may be the last time you see that particular expression. Repair that old hand-sewn, patchwork cushion your grandma made, which is becoming holey and thread bare. If you don't, it will fade away into nothing, (and your memory of it will follow.) We are all so incredibly busy fixing and doing and living; it often takes the end of an era, a passing on, for us all to stop, take stock and remember what is important. Shame on us; if we do not put the other things to one side and make our heritage a priority, before it's too late and we're all turned to dust! Many things can wait. This can't.

**Lucy is the official family photographer and keen memory preserver.**

# LAUGH YOUR WAY THROUGH LIFE

Whenever possible, we need to laugh more and frown less. Sitting in my daughter's classroom today, under the guise of marking papers, I watched the children doing jumping jacks and laughing at the same time. Not an easy task! The teacher's plan was to wake up all their little brains, which were obviously getting a big soggy before lunch; but for me, it sure made me laugh. The more they giggled, the less in sync their bodies became. They laughed, I laughed, the teacher laughed. We all needed that.

On the weekend, I dig through hefty newspapers oozing with death and destruction, trundling myself deeper and deeper into depression, desperately looking for my weekly dose of the columnist Dave Barry and his wacky humor. Why? Simple. It makes me laugh. I find myself seeking out the more humorous in my circle of acquaintances and want to sit a little closer to them. Why? There's an easy one. They make me laugh. There's a straightforward pattern here. Laughter is good, it's rich; it helps your head, your heart and soul. Never mind low carb- fat free-calorie-shy diets and an obsession towards general good health. Laughter must make you live longer; that's my philosophy. Ask any octogenarian you know. If they've made it that far, the odds are they have a good giggle every now and then, they don't take themselves or life too seriously and humor is an important part of their existence.

I used to call my Grandma in England every Sunday. Towards the end of her life, there were definitely days when she was not feeling so sprightly; but every time I'd say "this is your Sunday wake up call", (they are 8 hours ahead of us, so, naturally, she was at the end of her day when I was at the beginning of mine), she would giggle. Never mind any aches and pains I knew she was feeling, I really should have counted the amount of times we'd laugh during our Sunday chats. I wish I'd taped them, I wish I could remember all the things we laughed about, but I can tell you we did it a lot and it was good for her and good for me.

She's been gone a while now and every now and then, mostly on a Sunday, I will hear her voice again and her response to me when she'd picked up the phone and I told her it was her Sunday wake up call. She'd gasp, say 'Darling' and then laugh, without fail. She lived a good long life and enjoyed most of her vistas along the way. Why? Because she enjoyed being with people and people enjoyed being with her. Her grace and her humor made her a pleasure to be around right to the very last. There's a lesson there.

**Lucy was so fond of Myrtle, her step-granny – without any step to it, she used to say. We were very close and I miss her still, though find ways to still hear her inside my mind. She was an inspiration.**

# LEARNING HARD LESSONS

'LIBERTY, UNITY, BENEVOLENCE, CONCORD" – if you look upwards on Front Street – preferably not when you are driving - you can find this permanently inscribed on the front of the building above the Soledad Variety store as a statement of sorts, or possibly a wish from the author. Who knows what the inscriber intended. As many times as I have parked in front of that store, I had never noticed it before; but this time, I did; especially the unity, benevolent and concord parts that I was definitely lacking in the latter part of the week. I scowled at the slogan. Benevolence? I was all out of that, in addition to any goodwill to mankind I might have had previously and charity – she had left town too, leaving me behind in the gutter. Concord? No, we didn't have that anymore either; and the only reason for my current state of liberty was the good sense of the person who drove me to the local court house for our legal exchange and escorted me from the premises, fortunately before I had a chance to pop anyone on the nose.

And what would be the reason for the change in my usually pleasant demeanor? After twenty something years of living on American soil, I got my first taste of living in a litigious society, getting a few battle scars from my journey before the judge, and ultimately living to tell the story without even a contempt of court to my name.

I do remember years ago, when I was getting ready to move to America, that people warned me about this small factoid. "They'll sue for anything over there," they informed me. "People file lawsuits as easily as getting out of bed in the morning," I heard this, and yet I didn't really believe it for quite some time. It didn't seem right, it didn't seem possible that a so-called civilized society would tolerate too much of that type of behavior. But the more I read the papers over here, however, and the more I listened and learned over the years, not to mention, in my industry, the piles of real estate disclosures that we require people to sign in order not to be sued ourselves down the road, (and, in addition to that, we also carry a mandatory insurance policy for every house we touch just in case!) the more I came to realize that litigation is one successful way that many people travel from A to B in their lives, taking plenty of prisoners along the way.

My story was a mild, but an interesting one, in retrospect, involving a one-time one trip to the small claims court in King City. In my day to day job I meet all sorts. Some I'd rather never meet again, if the truth were known. This particular young woman was a single mother of four children who had been renting a home in town. Little did she know that her landlady had stopped making the payments on the home long before she stopped accepting rent money from the occupant and the state of California, (hello, theft?) When the tenant discovered that the home was now owned by the bank and she was soon going to be made homeless, the single mother was naturally disturbed. I took pity on her and tried to help her – or so I thought – to find another rental home, so that she and her many children would not be made homeless. However, it took her much longer than it was supposed to – according to the bank – to find replacement housing that was acceptable to her and, once she was finally ready to make her move, the bank stated there was no money left to pay her what they had previously agreed to pay in exchange for her keys. The contract had expired, as it were. Presumably the tenant had not made any rent payments for some time and she had saved up some money to be able to move on. Under these circumstances, most civilized people would just shrug their shoulders, thank the person anyway for trying to help, and move on with their lives. Watch out people. There are some who would not. Some know how to work this kindly system of ours in the western world. They recognize that public assistance can wear many hats. Not only can you get extra money for each child that you bear, but you can procure rental assistance, food assistance – oh and – I was to quickly find out – free legal advice through the public defender's office, should you find yourself in a situation where this might serve you well.

Once I was served with the court papers to appear, I began to prepare my own defense, as is necessary when you go to small claims court. The bank who owned the house had little interest in this trivial case, so I was on my own there. I still believed that the young lady would lose interest, find herself gainful employment, a reason to not join the long line of our society with their hands out, but I was wrong. She attended and she won. She also had a pending case to sue her landlady, in addition, in this same court room and I would be surprised, based on our outcome, if she lost that one. I learned something in that particular court of law. There are some who play the system and win; there are some that just work, pay taxes and afford the luxuries of a democratic society which defends all, even those who are playing the system for all she has.

I left the courthouse a little violated by the experience; certain that it wasn't one I ever wanted to repeat. The next young lady with a sob story will not get the kindness of my heart and the compassion you'd like to think you'd always be able to dole out as a humane member of the community. No ma'am; she'll get no help at all. We will go strictly by the book, she and I, according to whatever contract is on the table at that particular time. And if she steps outside the boundaries, she will be on her own - completely.

Liberty, kindness, benevolence? Hopefully they are not gone forever in the civil zone of my heart; but for this week I'm all out. Better check that my umbrella personal liability policy is all up to date and well stacked. The odds are I may need it again, if I continue to live in the land of love, liberty and litigation.

**Lucy was a little sore for a while, but she has since recovered.**

# LIVE LIKE YOU WERE DYING

"You're just going to have to try and live each day to the max," a wise man once said; and he was my husband and he was absolutely right, as he can be sometimes; most of the time when I'm not paying attention. "Try and enjoy yourself every day – live it as if it were your last." As some singer crooned recently – and, please, honchos of the music industry - do not bother me with your copyright infringement banter – 'live like you were dying'; it's a good line. Most of us seemingly well people do not do that. We take very little time to appreciate what it right there in front of us. We crash our way through our middle-aged existence, trying to not be late for work; endeavoring to make the bills, raise the children, feed the animals and not get divorced in the process from the children, animals, job or husband. To coin some 'Monopoly' jargon, if we "pass go and collect our $200" each tax time, we should give ourselves a big old hearty pat on the back, 'cos it's just not that easy these days.

I read about people who have a small slice of life left to live on this planet. "I only have 6 months to live; at best," they say, calmly; grace exuding from every pore. "In that time, I plan to climb Kilimanjaro, run the Big Sur marathon, donate all my worldly goods to worthy charities and try to find a cure for cancer. Then, when I die, I shall donate my organs to some one who needs them." If you have a deadline like that, it's amazing what you can achieve and how your stature as a human being can surmount most of the life that went before. What do the rest of us accomplish in 6 months?

When I talk to my 40-something friends, who barely have time for more than just a quick 'hey, how are u? I'm alive, let's do lunch,' type of email, received in abbreviated form with no punctuation, once a month; I realize that this is family life as we know it, for the non-wealthy 40–somethings in the 2000's, and we'd better just like it or wish our lives away. There's really no changing it. Long gone are the days and days of just self-indulgent time with one another, selfishly spending all our income on our own selves and not sparing a thought for the next person or the morrow. The here and now is the best we have with what we have to work with; and, if we don't start appreciating it, before we know it, we'll be on the downhill slope skidding towards eternity or, depending on your viewpoint, whizzing in the direction of absolutely nothing at a hundred miles an hour. Before long, we'll be reminiscing from our walkers and living precariously through our soap operas and our grandchildren. That is not a very optimistic vision, is it; but it's what seems to be ahead at the rate we're all going. Right now we can still walk, run a little – with a wobble or two - laugh, shop, clean, drive; all of those things we take so incredibly for granted, as we bemoan the loss of our individuality, our 'freedom', in short, our joie de vivre that is still a crystal-clear vision from not so long ago. We remember so clearly twenty years ago when our futures seemed such a buttercup of opportunity within the cluster of our youth. We exuded sex appeal and youthfulness; we raced around as if nothing could catch us. Looking back at those times, the years dissolved so quickly, like water we couldn't hold in our hands.

Two decades on and six months into the year, Christmas is just a hiccup away; again. The projects I had set for myself during the long grey wets of early January are still on my to-do list; just as well I do not establish an annual goal and punish myself for not crossing the finish line; I would despair of myself ever attaining a 25 percent ratio and give it up for life. And that's how it is most of the time when you are a working person with a house, husband, animals and more jobs than you perhaps want.

You arrive home on a daily basis to an upside down tip of a house without a clean sock in sight. Your refrigerator is a commercial waiting to happen for the 'Got Milk' ad, as the lonely milk carton sits alone on its shelf with just a droplet left in its nether regions, if some one was to choose to pick it up and tip it to see if a half a bowl of cereal might be possible. God help us all if it's already turned to cheese. Your windows are thick with the goo of several months of neglect and the cob webs weave their way across the ceiling of your life. All the phone lines are ringing at one time and the fax machine whirrs and jams, as the cartridge runs out of ink and the key document you were awaiting fades to oblivion.

So what can we do about it, except lose our minds? We can't hire a crew of helpers to make it all a little easier to survive. We can't hope that we will win the lottery and be able to sleep in on every future day of our natural lives. We have to try and live as if we are dying; find the glass half full and the rest of our lives, whatever that is, still to come, rich with opportunity. We have to grab a hold of the possibility of many gifts to come and so much to learn. Live as if you were dying; after all, we all are – some of us just quicker than others.

**Lucy tries to look at life with the glass half full.**

# OVER-EXTENDED

How far did we move away from civilization that we birth and then betray our young? What business do we have in procreation, when we strive to create and then only move to maim and destroy? Every day my thirteen year old has to deal with topics way beyond her youth. She is emotionally overextended for her thirteen young years and we should all have something to say about that.

I was at least 15 before I understood that sometimes people no longer wished to continue living and sometimes cut their own lives prematurely short. It was well into my teens before I appreciated that love and marriage did not always mean together forever, and sometimes people were raised with one parent only, (and the rest of the village that it took to actually build them up and make them whole.) I had no concept of domestic violence, or really violence of any kind until much, much later in life when I was emotionally so much better equipped to deal with such horrors, but could still be seen reeling from the shock of the cards that humanity can deal upon its own.

I witness what my daughter deals with daily at her own school in the countryside and wonder how far we have all traveled away from the civilized world, that children want to cut themselves to try and take away the pain, that they cry out for help – any kind welcome – in their desperate attempt to escape what they know as their stinking, rotten lives. I wonder, when my baby tells me that a certain friend is so afraid of being hit by her parent, that she no longer wants to go home anymore. I wonder also what my responsibility is here to step in, take charge, make things right. I know what is right – but what can I really do? I can tell her school, but well meaning though they certainly are, they are also inundated with such cases and are probably only able to deal with emergencies. I can call the police and send them to her home. Will that make things better? Probably not. A young girl brings a knife to class and cuts another girl. Where is she going from here? What does my child take away from all of this? So many questions and so few answers.

"Mum, you have to do something. Her mum is hitting her," she texts me, full of anxiety from the school playground. Our children are not playing games and laughing, as if their lives count on it in a happy play arena They are face to face, one on one, with some nasty realities of life in an adult playground that I resent them encountering at this fair young age. Middle school is full enough of angst without adult violence and abuse and a future certain of torment and torture infiltrating their developing minds.

How dare you parents do this to our kids? Stop and think before you cause further injury, please. Try not to raise your voice and don't ever raise your hand. Violence just breeds more of the same. Learn from your own mistakes, and please, if you feel out of control and you think you need some help, we have wonderful professionals all around us – in the schools and beyond – who will be proud of you stepping forward and stopping what you are recognizing as a dead end with dead feelings. This cycle of black makes me so angry. Poverty and lack of education are no excuse, sorry. Your humanity should guide you to a better place when you can feel you are doing your very best with what you have to work with. There are people and places that are qualified and ready to help you with all of your challenges. Ask anyone, they'll tell you how to get there.

I look around a small community and sometimes I am very afraid for the world at large. Our children do not need to learn fear while they are learning English. They do not ever need to flinch when a fist comes their way or an angry word flies through the air. They need to learn that respect is earned and love is not a birth right. Our youth have enough to deal with – all the modernities of our age, the challenges of technology and so much more than we, as the generation above, even conceived of.

Stop people, while you can, and save our children. You created them, it's your job to guide them into calm waters, to give them all the tools they need to go forward in peace and good faith. Don't go to church and say one thing, then go home and say or do completely another. Look in the mirror and promise yourself you'll be something better. I'd like to think that my daughter will not grow into her teenhood years already jaded by many of the adults around her and worried for the future of their offspring.

**Lucy likes to think we can save the children, one person at a time.**

# PEN TO PAPER; HEART TO HEART

I met Lizzie when we were about 4. The tale goes that my mother saved her from drowning in the local pond, so it was quite a momentous first meeting and one that had a good story to it to this day. She and I are 4 months apart. We were tight, tight friends, when we were young. We lived next door to one another on the East Coast of England; we lived inside each other's houses and pockets most of our childhood. Our parents and our siblings were friends; we were the best of friends. We evolved through the early years together and grew up as different people, but the same. It was an idyllic childhood and we were part of one another's through and through. We played tennis together, walked our dogs together, swam for hours together in the ocean. We bullied our younger siblings together and tormented her elder brother together. We lay down in the middle of the high street side by side on Saturday night and waited for cars to come that never came. That was the point. We pursued boys together around the streets of our village. We created characters together in our world together – she had one name and I had the other. We lived out these characters and when they became boring or obvious we created others. We wrote stories, drew pictures, made audio tapes. We had a very connected relationship as we grew up – it was an enormous world for us and all we needed.

Once we hit teen-dom and the dawn of awareness of the opposite sex, things changed once in a while – either she or I would have a beau on the scene and we would be jealous of the beau and missing the other half of ourselves – that's how it was. When the beau faded away, we'd pick right up again as if there had been no lapse. I calculated that we have now been friends for 40 years and that is a heck of a time.

Nowadays she doesn't even reside on the same continent as me. For a while she did, and for a while I really felt that she would get closer to me not further away in physical distance. We created other dream worlds that we lived in for a while – this time including our husbands and children in the mix, but those fantasies eventually became even further away than the ones we had when we were ten.

If you have a really old friend such as mine, you can be away from each other and still see each other and instantly know what the other is thinking. You can say one word and have the other in stitches. Your family history intertwines so deeply there is really no separation between yours and hers. There is no greater thing than an old friend. Even if we can only really catch up once every two years over a two hour lunch and two bottles of wine, that is enough, if that is all we have. There is never enough time these days. We had no idea, when we young, how precious those days and weeks and years were. We had no concept of how we would be forced to steal time together later on and always feel that our time was no longer our own to give.

Last Christmas I sent her a card and did not receive one back – funny how you always notice the cards that are missing on your mantel that time of year. Sometimes you think that maybe you have been away too long and they have decided that enough is enough, you had your time together and now it's over. Sometimes you wonder if something tragic befell their family. Mostly you know that they are just as busy as you are and a card was just not up there on their priority list. This year I received my Christmas card from her in early January. It was a rare hand-written missive. Years ago, we would write to one another in the character of whoever we were evolving at that particular time. Our envelopes would be decorated with our jokes of the moment, our creative spirit. Her hand written envelope hit me as a blast from the past, a time tunnel. She sent me pictures and news. She filled me in on the months gone by since our last communication and apologized for the silent times. She said she would try to write again the way we had before. I thought about that. No one writes to me any more. Even my father seldom puts his spidery scrawl to paper these days. It's an email or nothing. In my mail box sits only bills, sadly.

It took me about 4 days in all to get the ink on the paper, but I wrote back to her and agreed. "Let's try to do that again. We haven't made it a habit for probably about 25 years now, but let's try to pick it up again." Though I have carpal tunnel these days and my writing is a poor excuse for some one who had some fair penmanship years ago, there's no excuse. I can take a few days; I can pick up a pen and put it down again when my wrist hurts. But ultimately I can complete a nice few sheets of news, I can paint a picture for her of my life and my world, I can lick the envelope and send the bundle on its merry way. I can give her the pleasure she gives me when something arrives that is not adult and boring and tedious – something that takes us back to when life was simpler, with less people and complications in it.

Last night I received a letter from her in my mail box. I saved the scratchy missive until bed time when I could indulge in peace. It was very late when I pulled out my reading glasses and opened out the thick white pages. She took me back to when we were young, she took me forward to us as adults and she reminded me of how everyone has things in their lives that are challenging and demanding. Now we are all grown up, we are no longer characters in our own play acting; we are our own people, no fantasy land permitted. She reminded me, also, that though you can't go back, sometimes you can go back in your mind, and sometimes, that is all you need to do to take a little vacation outside of your world and into a special place back then, when things were simple and all the people, so important to the play, were still in place and performing.

**Lucy still has her oldest friends in her life. Every once in a while they will send each other a good old-fashioned letter.**

# THE BEST HOUR OF THE WEEK

One of the nicest things that the citizens of Soledad do every year is to nominate, from among their peers, the Citizen of the Year, the Business of the Year and the Friend of the Soledad Chamber. Though the event is traditionally a chamber event, it has grown to become a community platform that service groups, the school district, the city, fire and police and other businesses use as their own forum to commend the best in their midst. Through the good years or the bad – this is done every year in our small town and many other towns just like it.

But this year – just because we could – we added some additional categories and a little extra fun into the mix. The Awards Banquet committee of the Soledad Chamber added two junior volunteer of the year awards – students from Main Street Middle School and the High School – as well as a Coach of the Year award. We also decided that it would be nice to add an element of whimsy and surprise people, with their new found fame, in their place of business with a balloon bouquet; and so the plan was hatched.

This is not as easy as it sounds. First of all, you have to swear the people in the know to secrecy and that is not a simple thing to do – especially if you live with the person whose coach is being elected Coach of the Year – or you work closely with the Friend of the Chamber and you are just itching to give him a hint. No, this had to be sealed in the vault of secrecy and carried around in our heads and hearts until we were eventually allowed to spill it out.

Steve Pritt of Eden Valley Care Center and the Soledad Medical Center fame was to be our oh-so-deserving Citizen of the Year that year. Steve contributes so much to our community; not just his commendable work within the award-winning healthcare district and that rose in the valley also known as the "Eden Valley Care Center", but he contributes on so many levels in our town from the Soledad Rotary to the Soledad Chamber and beyond. We knew that Bud Sarmento – President of the Board of the Soledad Healthcare District – was good at keeping a secret, but did he have the strength and expertise to corral the colorful Steve; especially on a Friday morning - Friday the 13th no less - when Steve was getting ready for a nursing graduation and luncheon? That remained to be seen.

"We have to meet with very important people in the morning," Bud warned Steve in advance, after I had begged him to come up with a fool proof plan to round up our newest Citizen of the Year. That obviously was enough to get Steve's curiosity going. "What kind of very important people could you find in Soledad on a Friday morning?" Steve couldn't imagine the Governor was just popping in for a chat, and tried to get the info out of Jack, who was also in the know and not sharing. "Oh, just very important ones!" they tried to palm him off. As Steve strolled through the parking lot with Bud and caught us hovering – not important people at all – just us regular folk with some balloons and our local reporter, now he became really concerned. I could see the cogs in his brain whirring and wondering what that motley crew could possibly need to meet about on this Friday morning. We followed him into the meeting room, he invited us to take a seat and we told him we couldn't; we were just too excited. Then the beans were spilled and he truly was surprised! Mission accomplished. We had delivered our message out from under the blanket of secrecy where she had been hidden for about a week and it had had the desired effect. Congratulations to our Citizen of the Year and all who helped him get there. We look forward to saluting him at our banquet here in town with all his favorite people in attendance.

Next the crew moved on down town to the home of Soledad Auto Parts in search of our Friend of the Chamber, Fur Quintero. The lovely thing about the power of the nomination is that the most deserving folks are the ones who wouldn't in a million years think themselves eligible of any kind of recognition, let alone an award. Those are the best. Fur saw us wandering in with balloons and imagined simply that they were for his boss – that was pretty priceless. We told him that, much as we loved Sandy, we were actually there for him, and the tears started springing up. From his work on the local coaching fields to his endless support of whatever the Chamber might need in the way of help, Fur is just one of those local diamonds who help make up the fabric of a town where you'd like to live forever and raise your family. Whether he is cooking sausage for a youth team fundraiser, selling

Christmas trees for the Chamber or schlepping stuff that the Chamber needs schlepped, he has a wonderful can-do attitude and a demeanor that most of us should strive towards. We look forward to seeing some more of those tears at our awards ceremony, where we are sure he will speak from the heart and I can guarantee that the heart is good.

Ever mindful of a room full of teenagers having to sit down, be patient and wait quietly, we needed to make sure our third stop was a timely one. At Main Street Middle School, we hid in the Principal's office with our balloons, until the teachers had coordinated the necessary maneuvers with the kids in place and the Coach of the Year on site. Our Coach was definitely not happy about this "drill" that they were being forced to do. She had things to do, a class to teach; and the fierce scowl on her face made us all tremble just a little, as it should.

As necessity would have it, all the teachers were in the know – as would be a mandatory thing when you are trying to coordinate 600 children and all kinds of teachers and support staff to entirely change their schedule and be in one place at one time for the benefit of us making an award to one of their group. We really appreciated their efforts, and all the texting that Melissa and I had to do to make sure of the absolute right time paid off.

As we strolled out to where the youthful masses and their teachers were waiting for us, (and my daughter's face sunk down to her Nike's as she spied her mother strolling in), the Coach of the Year started to wonder just a little about this whole drill thing. When I got on the mike and admitted that we had lied just a little about the drill and we were actually there to honor some one who went above and beyond every day for our kids; some one who took our kids to games in Stanford, coached them during the vacations and was even taking them roller skating tonight and to Washington DC next month, the coach of the year - Glenda Woodrow – recognized herself and started to choke just a little as she wished the ground would swallow her up. The kids and teachers cheered and we all laughed along at her surprise – such a gift for us all in her presence, that such a deserving person, who would never in a million years expect to be honored for what she loves to do day in and day out, felt the love and gratitude of us all showering down on her for just a few minutes that morning.

In a world of tricky times and challenges, it is amazing once in while when you can stand back and say "that was the best hour I had all week." To Steve, Fur and Glenda – thank you all for your services to humanity and thank you for giving me, the Soledad Chamber President, the best hour I had all week and such sweet, sweet memories for coming days.

**Lucy was the Soledad Chamber Vice President for many years and Chamber President for two. It's a big job!**

# THE WEEK THAT WAS

Sometimes you can squeeze so many events into a week of so many different colors that you can be literally blown away by the emotion of it all and can end up requiring twelve hours deep sleep, and at least two bars of chocolate, plus, maybe, a bottle of wine, to get yourself back in your proper place. Never mind that the cats have no food, no one has vacuumed the floors and some one locked husband out of the house; they'll all get over it - this week was one for the memory banks in its rich color and hue.

It began with my daughter getting a home run at baseball practice. Not that I understood at the time that that was what it was. Where I'm from we don't play baseball, so I am clueless in that department, (and could not even figure out why she would wear a large glove on her left hand when she was right-handed, which made an American friend of mine laugh in hysterics). But I did manage to ride on the excitement wave of all around me at the practice session and realized that her speeding around all the bases without stopping was a pretty marvelous accomplishment. As I continue to say, she teaches me new things every day.

Move stage forward to a setting by the sea, a somber day of pomp and circumstance: the burial ceremony for our fallen Soledad firefighter Mario. Somehow, I've noticed, the toughest of days can have the brightest blues of sky and, somehow also, I always notice the sky at funerals. As the procession of over a hundred fire engines from all over the State neared the church, many were overcome by the shoulder of support leant to our small city of Soledad and its family of firefighters; a brotherhood to behold. Not only firefighters were strong in their masses, but also police officers, emergency workers, highway patrol officers – many were strangers to Mario, but all were brothers in service – incredibly enough, they had all felt moved to be there on that day to honor him and him alone. As the priest so eloquently stated, "there is no greater love than giving up your life in service of another." We can only hope that Mario was hovering around in that crystal clear sky, gazing in awe at those who had showed up – many strangers, many not - just to honor his life and his sacrifice that day.

Another change in dynamic: the celebration of 90 years of life, a life that had witnessed so many tremendous things in our history. Ruth Schrenk, mother to Bobbie and Carol, now resides in our local Eden Valley Care Center and has grace written all over her face. In celebrating this special milestone, she got to laugh at Grandpa Sparky the clown, and eat delicious cake with all her friends and family around her at her 90th birthday party. Doesn't get much better than that! Her eyes sparkled and gleamed with pleasure – a rare vision – one for the memory banks.

Another set change. No birthday cake this time, but a celebration all the same. The South County YMCA wrapped up their annual Capital Campaign, which raises money for scholarships. It's never easy to ask people for money; but it' s way easier when you really believe in the cause, and the people who show up for campaign meetings on a Thursday night, they're believers alright! Despite some tough calls and more than our share of 'no's', the campaign looks to come in very close to their goal and above the last year's total. A measure of some achievement! The campaigners were served a good dinner, given fun prizes and were made to feel pretty special for participating in a good cause. I would imagine many will be back next year for another dose of 'how to feel good when it's not about you'.

And then we're back to the ball park, which puts everything into perspective. Sitting in the fresh outdoors, watching little munchkins so cute in their uniform and so desperate to please and impress, makes your heart proud. You look back at the week that was and spare a thought or more for those who can't see how green the grass or how blue the sky today. May their healing begin and allow the hands of time to soothe their sorrow. You hope they will again someday, not too far away, be able to enjoy the gift of life and, that, in time, the sky will seem a little bluer once more. Grief is, after all, the price of love; and, without that, where would we all be. For the rest of us, let's aim to eat cake and smile at the clown on our 90th birthday, let's love one another as if there was no tomorrow and let's all try to live with a little more purpose every second of every given day. None of us know how long we've got.

**Lucy is still trying to learn the rules of baseball.**
**At my school, we played 'Rounders'.**

# TURNING ANOTHER PAGE

Another page turns, another day in the life, another birthday greets me. In the early dawn hours of my fortieth something year, I knew it was my birthday, but I couldn't for the life of me remember how old I was. I tried to count back to the year I was born and figure it from there, but my brain was still too coddled with slumber to come up with a good number. If it hadn't been so early in the morning, I would have woken up my child and asked her – for no good reason, she always knows.

A friend sent me a little cluster of age-related e-joke mails this week, knowing another birthday was on my plate of goodies to deal with for the week. "Age is a question of mind over matter," so the ditty went. "If you don't mind, it doesn't matter." I thought about that. I don't think about age, so I guess it doesn't matter. Not a darn thing I can do about it anyway, so why would I waste time minding? I mind so little, in fact, that I never even know how old I am. Other people I know mind so much that it becomes an obsession. (For what? So that they can eternally torment themselves?) You really do have to wonder about that.

"Wrinkles don't hurt." I read on. "Time may be a great healer, but it's a lousy beautician." Well, there could be a hair of truth there. I look in the mirror – something I seldom bother to do. I'm always giving the face a little lick of make up before I head on out the door. The light quality in shadow of my bathroom mirror is so poor anyway, that that face could be a fresh-faced twenty year old one for all I know. But if you take the time to look - to really look, which I only recommend with extreme caution – you do see the effect of the lack of sun-block during your youthful summers when you hadn't a care in the world. Sun sleeping, lathered with olive oil on beaches of the Greek isles have all played a part in the lines around the eyes, forehead and mouth areas not to mention the neck. You can see all your life scars smiling back at you if you take the time to look.

Friends I know go to the dermatologist now almost as often as they go to the store. It's a happening place to be. They get the surface of their skin scraped to all intents and purposes. Lasers are used, special creams, needles. Lots of money is spent. It's all beyond me. As terrified as I am of needles, it's not a place I would ever go anyway.

As I slap on some more cover up with a snatch of powder, I do wonder about the huge industry machine that has made all us women of a certain age – and we seem to get younger all the time – care so much as to expend lots of money on creams and treatments in our efforts to halt the ageing process. My magazine for the over 40's, which deals with lovely subjects such as menopause and age spots on a regular basis, makes bank on ads for all measures of highly expensive age fighting treatments. "Guaranteed to obliterate signs of ageing in 2 months, or your money back!" it spurted. (The differences on the before and after photos were impressive!) I checked out that same product at the drug store and noted that it was nearly 3 digits to purchase. It was so expensive it must work! I thought to just myself. I bought it, because my magazine guaranteed it - "miraculous results in 2 months or your money back!" - plus I wouldn't mind a 21 year old face coupled with the wisdom of something twice that age. Maybe this product would unleash the secret that millions of women the world over are furtively seeking? I brought it home ready to conduct my experiment. Once I had got through the fancy-smancy packaging, the little tube was remarkably unremarkable. My confidence was already waning. I conscientiously followed the instructions day in and day out until the little tube was squeezed to the end of its little life. I scanned the mirror. No change, not even a wee laugh line had displaced itself. OK, so the miraculous results take time to work, I figured; another month at least. I went out and bought another tube. Same thing. I went back to my 40 plus magazine. "The secrets to healthy ageing are plenty of sleep, water, nutrition, exercise and a lack of stress. Your skin can especially benefit from all the above!" it read. Hey, wait a minute! What about all the 'buy me' ads from the last edition! If you had just told me that last month I would have saved myself a bundle. Full of renewed energy to cash back in on my failed experiment, I searched for the receipts for the magic cream that had somehow lost its sparkle. I would show those turkeys! I would send back their wretched tiny tubes as an unsatisfied customer and get my buckets of dosh returned to me. Woe and behold, the receipts had gone the way of the newspaper recycling and I was left a little poorer and a little wiser. Hate it when that happens.

Wait! Here comes another ageing e-joke. "Wisdom comes with age, but sometimes age comes alone", I read and gave myself a giggle on the backside of the cream purchasing fiasco. "Today's mighty oak is just yesterday's nut that held its ground." There's another good one. Well, I am here to tell you folks that this old nut has had it with miracle ageing creams and even bothering to glance at the ads for overnight skin repair. They are all fudgsicles in my newly wise opinion and those clever companies aren't getting another dime out of yours truly. I shall continue to buy my large pot of Nivea moisturizer, try and get enough sleep and enough water on a daily basis and endeavor to put the lid on the stress fest once and for all.

Here's a last one for you. "Forget the health food. I need all the preservatives I can get." One thing's a for sure in this uncertain world we live in; laughter is a superb medicine for all afflictions and maybe I need to add that to my list of going for the gold in the race to conquer the ageing process. I'll keep the laughter lines if I can continue to find things to laugh at; such a deal.

**Lucy still reads the 40 plus magazine once in a while, but she hasn't purchased any expensive 'miracle' creams since.**

## 'VALENTIMES' – THE BEST AND THE WORST OF TIMES

When my daughter was young and still allowed me to read to her, we used to read the "Junie Bee" series together. One of our very favorite, laugh-out-loud novels was "Junie Bee and the Mucky-Blucky Valentime". Though seasonal, it was one that we could pick up and re-read any time, howling with laughter every time – such a pleasure it was. My daughter enjoyed her own season of Mucky Blucky "Valentimes", as she called them back then, (and we never corrected her because the vernacular was so cute.)

Back when "Valentimes" were big at elementary school, I would have to buy boxes of colored cards for every possible taste bud – Power Rangers, Super Man, Barbie and Minnie Mouse – later followed by the Crocodile Hunter, Bratz, race cars et al., and I would have to make sure that I shopped early for these "Valentimes", because selection was all and we would never really know which assortment was going to be in vogue at the vital moment of need. It was a fun time and so innocent. No matter what – friends or not friends, girls or boys – everyone got a Valentine's card. But times change as times do, and suddenly we moved on from the cards and I was required to make cup cakes with frosting for a whole class of 36 plus the teacher, like tomorrow, or provide enough chips and salsa for the "Valentimes" party that afternoon. This year: nothing.

"You don't want me to buy any candy, cards or anything?" I checked with my teenager, having seen rows and rows of buying opportunities as I passed through a local store rich with reds and pinks, which startled me into the realization that – oh heck – it was that time again and I had not done a darn thing about it. Valentine's Day is, after all, a huge retail day in America, close to Christmas I believe in dollars spent and tears wiped; and here I was, a hot-blooded woman and a mother – not in that order - participating not one bit.

"No, Mum. Nothing," she replied. "We are just having a school dance – that's it – and I'm not even going." Though I was tempted by the Snuggly Cuddlies and the cute little cards with hearts on them, I abided by the rules and bought nothing, de nada. I felt a little naked leaving the store with no love bites, no hearts, not a loving greeting to my name.

"I got only two cards and one was from a girl," she snorted after Valentines Day was over and we were all in the clear. "Honey, you didn't buy any cards either," I reminded her. That didn't help. Ack, it's such a tough time, this teenage lark. The rules can change the very next moment.

When I was her age, I was at a mixed boarding school in England. Valentine's Day was sheer torture and thrill at the same time all wrapped up into a tight ball. During the run up to Valentines, there were heart covered boxes strategically placed at the bottom of the boys and the girls' stairwells, positioned ready and able to consume all those heart-felt thoughts and feelings. We were pretty elaborate and very anonymous in those days. We would go to town and agonize over the most suitable card for our heart throb of the month for several days on end. I was pretty long and sincere with my feelings. One particular athlete had my heart for around 4 Valentine's Years in a row and probably only ever knew about 2 of them. At breakfast time on Valentine's Day, the Valentine Cards would be handed out. We'd be sitting on long wooden benches trying to act really casual about whether we got cards or not, while we chewed on our cornflakes. The pretty girls and the handsome boys stacked them up. Plain ones like me were lucky to get one or two and mostly from our bestest girl friends. It was delightful agony you just don't have to go through – thankfully- when you are as old as me and mostly just forget that that certain day is even here.

"What do you want for Valentines, dear?" I asked my husband.

"A day off," he responded quickly. Just what I was thinking! (And also – "well that was really good because I haven't got you anything!") In the end, I did write a short poem just for his lordship and he made me a beautiful copper coffee table fashioned from some piping from our deck and a neat top he found along the way, so we didn't give each other nothing; we gave each other tokens that said more than just the 'I love you' cards we could have found really quickly in the appropriate aisle of the store. We gave each other a little time. Our daughter received a "Hugs" teddy bear that seemed to even please and surprise her some what.

Some things are more important than retail – those things you realize so much later in life, when all the heart ache of the Valentine's cards has long since faded and you are on your way to some maturity of attitude. Valentimes? It can be the best and worst of a day; this year we saw it all.

**Lucy is so glad those agonizing school years are over. Angst and heart ache! Who needs it?**

# WEDDINGS AND FUNERALS

"'Twas a nice day for a white wedding," to coin a very good white wedding song; and so it was. After months of hefty preparation, attention to detail, fittings, re-ordering of several items, more fittings and details and re-orderings; everything came together nicely on the day; as it mostly does in the kingdom of weddings.

People traveled far and wide to my friend's recent wedding. They dressed up and bore gifts - some of them - (despite the missive not to do so). They even made it to the church on time to witness the love of two people be sealed for eternity.

As one of the wedding party, I had been along for the ride all the way and, during this journey, I learned many things about the customary joining of two people; which is deeply entrenched in tradition, and customized and personalized down to the last detail in the lives of mankind. Since it is June, one of the biggest months of the year for nuptials; I felt moved to share all that I had learned on my journey from bride – twice - to bridesmaid, an impressive three times:-

1. People love a good wedding; (much more than a funeral). They will literally travel across the ocean to be a witness to an age-old custom. There is little they will not do, in fact, to be able to watch friends in their best clothes, show up and be appropriate and link themselves for ever before the most complete gathering of loved-ones, matched only by ones funeral.
2. A wedding is your opportunity to stun and to surprise. Just because your usual attire is shorts and a Hawaiian shirt, does not mean that you cannot wear a white gown, a veil and a tiara to your own wedding. It's your day; have at it! Just check that the groom has had his heart checked beforehand.
3. It is not your responsibility as the bride and groom to invite only people to your special event who get along together. If they cannot behave themselves and either avoid or be civil for your special day; then they really

need to get over themselves. That day will be about you, not them.

4. You will be stunned, when you plan your wedding, how many people consider themselves to be your friends and how shocked they can be when they never receive the anticipated invitation, regardless of mega hinting over the period of several months. Makes you wonder whether eloping to Tahiti might not be an easier plan in the larger scheme of things. Cheaper too.
5. Don't ever plan to lose weight to fit into your special outfit; it never works. Trust me; if you go up a size, you can't go wrong. Stress makes you eat and drink quite a bit more than you do usually.
6. One rehearsal at the rehearsal is never enough.
7. No alcohol should be served prior to the rehearsal.
8. Alcohol should actually be banned at the rehearsal and the dinner afterwards.
9. A wedding planner is worth her weight in gold. Simply stated; the event will not happen without her. She may have to be really, really bossy during the rehearsal and quite the principal of proceedings on the day; but that is her job and you'd better respect it.
10. A wedding does cost the price of a small house.
11. Feeding 200 people is no small event.
12. Trying to cook steaks for 200 hungry people does require a mini-act of god.
13. If you have a best man, make sure that he really likes you and has nothing juicy on you. Remember, he will be making a speech at your wedding; and the subject matter is wide open.
14. There may be more tears at your wedding than your funeral.
15. Check the sound system at your rehearsal. (That's right after you have checked that no one has secreted any alcohol away during the rehearsal).
16. Do not allow a pre-wedding/post rehearsal dinner party. Some of your wedding party may be a little more rough for wear than you had planned on the day, especially if the temperature is above 100 degrees. You'll have to see the results of the night-before party in all the wedding photos

that you had planned on being perfect. The dark glasses are a dead giveaway.

17. You can't pick your relatives. Some will come, some won't; just like at the funeral. Don't let it hurt your feelings.
18. Have a sign-in book anyway –it will make for interesting reading later.
19. Take lots of photos – professional and amateur – ditto the above.
20. Don't even think about running off on a honeymoon right after the event. You will need to sleep for a week first.
21. Make sure to stop and breathe in the delight of so many people bothering to show up and put their other lives on hold to celebrate yours. Few days are ever that memorable as the one you are currently basking in. Sup it up and feast on the memory.

As bridesmaid, I tried to behave appropriately, to be on hand for whatever might be needed along the way and, on the day, to escort the wayward cowboy groomsman in suitably leadership manner, to fix the bridal make-up whenever needed and stay cool at all times, regardless of the heat. There should be an academy for such things! I also tried to bask in the moment a little myself and take a snap shot of all the gifts which were whizzing by on the agenda, as we laughed and we danced our way through the hours.

Like funerals, weddings are civilized traditions of the western world. They are some of the rare meetings of the masses, the occasions that clans come together, break bread and toast or eulogize. We should salute them in all their solemnity and delight and preserve them for the future. They are a day of love and salutation far, far away from normalcy to be cherished and adored. The bride in her white dress, a far cry from her usual Hawaiian attire, symbolizing not only the change in her marital status but a proclamation of life's truest thing; real love.

Congratulations; John and Sandy. And what a day or two it was for all of us.

**Lucy was happy to play bridesmaid.**

# GRIEF

# A LIFE CUT SHORT

The death of a local 10 year old on a freeway close to town really hit home in my house. It reminded me, once again, how brief life is. Not only do I have a young girl of my own, but she attended the same school at the time as the lost child. The parallels would make any parent quiver. When I became a mother, my greatest fear became that something would happen to my child and I'd be left behind on the planet without her. I still feel that way; most loving parents probably do. "If something should happen to my baby, that would be the end of me too," I said to husband as we discussed the tragic incident; and I meant it. Grief such as that is inconceivable, inconsolable, eternal.

Sadder even still is the knowledge that the little girl's death should never have occurred on a Soledad freeway, when it did. She should have been back to school, right afterwards, with only a few cuts and bruises from the accident. However, this little girl was not wearing a seat belt. There were others in the same vehicle, who were wearing their seat-belts and they survived. The crash was, therefore, very bad, but still survivable. I feel for the family; that they have to carry on the rest of their lives in this knowledge.

Clicking in a seatbelt is an easy thing to forget, yet such a vital component to living a safe life. We get caught up in our chaotica and our tight schedules; we rush from one obligation to another and we sometimes leave the details behind. Things happen. If we're running late, the view gets even worse. I see people tail-gating at 80 along the freeway, trying to apply mascara; I see others trying to check voicemail in the fast lane at 85, I see babies playing in the front seats of moving vehicles without a belt in sight. It all happens so quickly and alters the paths we walk on so completely.

I am a self-confessed seatbelt Nazi. Ask anyone in my family and they will tell you that I am a complete pain when it comes to buckling up. As a nine year old girl, I recall watching my mother on the phone, shaking with sobs, as she waited to find out the outcome of a very bad car accident involving her father, mother and child – my younger sister. I had never seen my mother cry like that and it's a picture which has stayed with me over the many decades since. I can still put myself back in the room, in the poise, in the outfit – it is a moment frozen by time - a little girl watching her mother fall apart; not a good memory. My grandfather died in the car crash. He was not wearing a seat belt. My grandmother and my sister were; they survived.

After that life-altering tragedy in my own family, my parents became belt Nazis. My mother would stress if we traveled in cars with anyone else; we were required to always check in where a car journey was involved and she hated us driving any distance whatsoever. (Just as well she never knew about the motorbike riding I did in France, or the many car rides she didn't have on her check list!) Fortunately, planes never bothered her in the same way; since I was always whizzing back and forth across the pond; though I knew that candles were always being lit throughout the trip, in her mind to keep us safe. Now I find myself behaving in a very similar manner. I'm not too keen on other people driving my child; and I always remind them and her that she has to use her seat belt. Never mind that my daughter does it automatically, I still have to remind her; it's ingrained into my being, it's my thing. Some wounds stay open and gaping; no matter how the passing of the years.

And what of the person who caused the terrible accident in Soledad? His life must look immensely different now from where it was before. He made a bad error of judgment, at the very least, and changed not only the lives of those he hurt and killed that night, but also his own family, his relatives. It's a ripple effect, which permeates the entire community beyond the families immediately affected. It should bother us; we should talk about it. We should tell our children what happened and why. If, as a society, we don't learn something positive from something so horrible, then what hope is there that our children will grow up and be able make better judgments themselves?

If they don't already have it on their radars, I would like to see the local schools call in the police or the highway patrol on a regular basis and have them use their scare tactics into sharing with the young and fertile minds what can happen if they don't buckle up, what will happen if they make bad choices, then drive, when they are older. It can never be too young to start learning some of life's lessons until life's lessons become second nature.

Tell the children that it is against the law not to wear a seatbelt; that they have to be accountable for their own belt, if mother or grandma gets busy and forgets. If you tell them enough, it will become part of their routine. Ask my child. She'll roll her eyes and say, "of course, I put on my seatbelt. I always do."

My hope is that, when I move on from the planet, my child will take over from me as the seat belt Nazi in our family. I'd like for her to annoy her own children equally, as I annoy her, with the lessons I learned from my childhood about bad choices and unsafe decisions and the overwhelming repercussions they can have on generations of a family. If she does that, perhaps we will go some way towards protecting the next generation. Have you belted up today? Better make sure you do; your life does depend on it.

**Lucy is a cautious driver and belt Nazi.**
**Seat belts do save lives.**

# A PROPER GOODBYE

During the recent good bye to another sweet soul from our community, I had the chance to reflect on how little we actually know about people until we stand face to face with their mortality in the column of a newspaper, or at their farewell service. It is sometimes only then that you read the story of their life and are able to admire them from afar. You knew you liked them; now you understand, at least partially, why.

Much as I suffer at funerals – as you rightfully should – and struggle with the fact, every time, that I really do not want to attend the service and run through the gamut of feelings that you experience, every time; I always go anyway and enjoy reading the program, as it were; learning more about the person sometimes than I had when they were alive. Having known the person in some capacity, but not as well as I would have liked, I relish the biography and imagine them listening to the last celebration of themselves and smiling at the group of people gathered together in their honor.

We do not wear our hearts on our sleeves, most of us. The best of us do everything for other people and say nothing of ourselves. Unless people specifically enquire, we do not broadcast who we are and how we got there. If we got to write our own obituary, most of us would say something like, 'she was a fair mother, a reasonable wife and a good friend; most of the time. She loved her family. She worked hard and didn't play enough.' We would downplay our entire existence on the planet and what made us special to those around us. It is therefore fortunate that most of us do not get to write this last tribute to ourselves!

Saying good bye to friends and loved ones should be a celebration of their life and their achievements. Their funeral is a chance to lift them up high and salute them as special people and significant cogs in our existence. It should not just be a time to share sorrow for their passing from our sphere, but an opportunity to build bridges through shared expression and repair old ones which needed some work. Crying should be viewed as an extension of laughing; emotion is good; we don't feel it enough on a daily basis, unless in attendance of a wedding or a funeral.

During a recent farewell, a sister from the church stood up and told the congregation a funny story. Laughter resonated through the church halls and made the candles flicker. I looked around and saw everyone laughing, even the most aggrieved. It was right and it was good. As the last song of the service was heard, 'The Wind Beneath my Wings,' birds came into sight way up high above us, flying across the tall windows of the church hall with a grandiose blue sky behind them and lush green tree backdrop. Lots of people saw this. It was right and it was good. It was a delicious and fitting finale to a touching event.

Attending some one's last service can put into perspective the rest of your own life. I tell myself that, if I live as long as that person did, then I may only have another 20 or so years to go. How would I like to spend it? Do I want to spend much of my time stressing over nit-picking details at work? Do I want to rag on my daughter daily to pick up her room and do her chores, only increasing my frown lines and crows' feet and her poor memory of me? Or do I want to look at the brand new day and tell myself that it's all mine for the making. Why don't I run the dogs over the hills and feel the cool air in my lungs? Take the children to the beach and let them eat the largest ice cream on the menu? Plan a fabulous dinner for the family and shock them when they see I can actually cook it and they like it? Plan the best birthday party in the world for my child and give myself a giggle remembering how my mother planned many just for me? Yes, all of that and much more. That is what I should endeavor to achieve; we all should. Make every sunrise a pleasure and every sunset a gift. For after all, we never know when the dawning of a new day and opportunity may be our last.

**Lucy will attend a funeral when she thinks she should and, when she does, is always glad that she did.**

# COMING TO TERMS WITH THE INEVITABLE

Though people dying is as inevitable as babies being born, it's still a heck of a lot harder to deal with; the process, though equally natural, doubly difficult. No matter how many times you walk down that road, every time is new and fresh in its pain and individuality. For mostly selfish reasons, we – the living and the well – wish we could keep the dying and the sick with us a little longer. It's pretty simple; we know we're going to miss them; we wish they could stay around a little longer. In short, we discount their suffering, their lack of quality of life, in our profoundest wish to make it all better again, for them and for us. We want them to see it as we do; yet the clock is ticking, the plates are shifting. It's all beyond our control; it's a maddeningly frustrating time.

My daughter's grandfather, my husband's father, is dying. He's been dying for about as long as we've known him – from one ailment or another – but he's really dying now. Since I was privileged enough to be able to go through the end of life journey with my own mother; I am somewhat familiar with the process. I recognize the signs. Having had the luxury of being able to travel with Mum to her last breath, I'm crazy for other people being able to do the same and getting to say everything they've ever wanted, while there's still time. Forgive me for saying it; there is nothing worse nor more lasting than regret.

This will be the last chance you'll have; that you know of, to open some doors and close others. For the person on their back – and someday it will be you or I – they/you/we all have to seize the power to make the last hours and moments precious ones. Somehow the departing have to be able to muster the courage to say "you and you out of the room; I never liked you anyway. You over there; you mean well, but you're annoying, go home. The people I really want to talk to are my wife, my kids and my grandchildren. I want to tell them what they have always meant to me; I want to remind them of things that will make them laugh down the road when I'm not there to play 'Go Fish', or create crazy cartoons which make them howl. I want to tell them that I'll miss them when I'm gone, but that I'll be just fine and so will they; as if I'm going on a trip and I won't be back for a while. Keep my picture on the wall anyway and laugh with me often. Talk to me still, as you always have, and maybe I'll talk back. I want to tell them who I'm looking forward to seeing when I get to where I'm going and what great views there will be on the way. Then I need everyone to just let me go on my trip, 'cos I'll be done for now. It's my right not to want to do this anymore. It's no longer any fun; so quit all the fussing, all of you, and let me be on my way. .." Sounds simple, doesn't it.

But there's a heck of a lot of work that needs to be done, in order to be able to slip off and away without leaving a big old mess behind you. Most of us do not live the tidy lives we should; in that, who cares how clean your house is, or how perfect your yard; but that your crucial records had better be in order, or your family, in the midst of all their own grief and suffering, will be dealing with life issues you could have saved them from. When some one dear is dying, you do not want to be racing against the clock preparing powers of attorney, looking for paperwork, tearing up the house wondering where the copy of the will went from 20 years ago. You want to be sitting at their bedside enjoying an occasional smile, a word. You need to be right there offering comfort and courage to the person who needs it most, savoring the last warmth in their skin and letting them feel yours. The experience is numbing enough; you do not need to be scrambling for detail that should have been dealt with light years away from the raw emotions of living grief.

Before I resolved to change things, it was a source of much angst to me that my own life was not in order; and it bothered me until I did something about it. To have ones life in order is one of the most selfless acts I can think of to bestow upon my family and friends and, in my humble opinion, we should all work towards that goal. Look in the papers, pay attention. All around you there are professionals willing and able to help you prepare a living trust. Start today, by digging out your papers and making copies of vital stuff. Get your life together today, so you can breathe easier tomorrow. Your children will thank you for it; and your last moments on this earth, whenever they may be, will taste so much sweeter for everyone.

That was my resolve anyhow, as I tried to entangle myself from the mesh of emotions which swept through our family in the midst of losing one of its members. It's a tough time; it's inevitable; we all go through it time and time again; best try and make it the best that it can be.

**Darrell Jensen passed away peacefully in July 2004.**
**This column is dedicated to him in fondest loving memory.**

# EMOTIONS TO SHOW

We have seen tears flow this week in our small community; as the flags stood at half mast, and our city paused in bewilderment and doubt. That is all as it should be, when a community is faced with inconceivable horror, such as we were last week, when we lost our young firefighter in a senseless hit and run accident. Grown men have allowed themselves to cry; others have wept and embraced openly in the unification of grief, as the huge shock of losing a local man and firefighter spread across the community and infiltrated our communal heart.

Small communities embrace their brothers and sisters at times like this – whether they really know them or not – and it is truly something to behold. You can literally stand back and be amazed at the outpouring of rich and overpowering feeling, when people touch upon deep emotions such as these in an effort to make themselves whole again. People want to do something; they'll, in fact, do anything to get away from that powerless feeling of actually being able to do nothing that will really make a difference at such a time. Restaurants donate food for the services, companies donate money, people from all over donate whatever they can to try and ease the pain of the unthinkable. We commend all of that; it is right to rush to our brothers' side in time of need and feel their pain alongside them.

What is worrisome in all this is the visible scene of people hoping to be *seen* to do what is right. A great man once said that the mark of a truly great man is to do what is right when no one is looking. I was reminded of that saying this week, when people from all over felt moved to do things for people they didn't even know; however, some of these people were doing these things when everyone was looking and that somehow, in a really sick way, was their purpose. I heard people bragging about their alleged relationship with the person who was lost, if that could even be humanly conceivable, and it just did not sit right. I heard others relating over and over the services they were providing to the grieving of the involved family and, listening to them, completely negated all that they had really done to try and make better of a truly sad and foul situation.

You only know yourselves what it is that you do. Are you unkind and spiteful for no good reason in your day to day lives? Are you quick to criticize and slow to commend? Do you find yourselves filled with envy or sharp of tongue? Are you humane and all-embracing in all you say and do? Are you magnanimous towards all people – those you mix with and those you don't? Unfortunately I have witnessed much interesting, some bad behavior recently, though none, you'll be glad to hear, in relation to our fallen firefighter. Those types of behavior are reserved for the living, the breathing, those who might equally do the same against us. And so it goes; the mean ol' cycle of life; which should not be.

A friend cried down the phone to me recently, because a person, she thought was a friend, had been spreading unkind rumors about her. Another person exclaimed to me that she couldn't believe this other person, in the same industry, would circulate such unforgivable lies about her within the profession in which they both work. Do these same people troop to churches on a Sunday and profess obedience to a higher power? Do they visit prayer circles to try and forget how really low they themselves have stooped? Stop the hypocrisy and listen to yourselves, one and all! We are none of us perfect; but, as adults, we need to be mindful of the things we say, responsible for the damage we do. We can stop the bleeding now; and we must. Our humanity depends on it.

I hear someone I know saying hateful things about people from other countries and I do not stop her. I wish she would not say these things – I myself am from another country and I subscribe to others' customs – but I do not have the strength to stand up for us, for all of us, and stop her saying the things she does. That makes me worse than any. I know it and I hang my head in shame and avoid listening to those words I know are coming. Same place, a different time; a crime. Challenge that person! Let them know their stance is unacceptable, unforgivable. Forego the relationship before you forego the loyalty to yourself. We all need to work on that. I listen to another bragging about a service to another. I do not stop the brag, I nod and half smile and move on; another crime! Challenge the false pride, force an illumination of the good deed, put the do-gooder in the spotlight to radiate their claim! It may not look as good in the harsh light of day.

For my part, I intend to be kinder to my neighbor; not just when they're hurting. I hope to be kind anyway. I intend to be generous of spirit, not just of goods. I aspire to seek not to be honored for goodness done, but just to be good anyway. You too; try to open up your heart and mind to a world without mean spirit and imagine how good that would be. However the chips may fall; aim to be good anyway. Work on being a good person through and through, when no one's looking.

**Lucy tries to treat people as she likes to be treated.**
**It's a good maxim to live by.**

# LOSING A CHILD

At 2.50pm, I could be seen standing at the window looking out over the empty street, watching and waiting for those two familiar little legs to come walking up the hill. She was late. 3pm came and went; now she was really, really late. The mind cushion hastens back to that time when she had explained to me that the bus driver had got lost and all the kids arrived home late; but, even then, I tell myself, it was never this late.

At times like this, all rationale goes out of the window. "She has been kidnapped", you tell yourself. "You're never going to see her again! Time is of the essence, alert Amber! Call the police!"

"Wait a moment; don't make a fool of yourself!" You hear another voice. "Call the school!" the voice of reason pervades through the fog. You call the school. It's 3.05pm; "school was let out early", you relay to the other voice. On a slow day, she would have arrived home at 2.40pm. You face the facts; your child is still not home.

"There must be a reasonable explanation", the reasonable voice asserts itself. You call the school. The office staff at the school takes like what feels like an eternity to ascertain that your child did, in fact, get on the school bus that day and yet, somehow, the bus is already back in the depot and your child is not at home where she should be.

At that point, what I can only describe as fuzzy, sick mayhem takes over the brain and you know this is not a good time for a crisis; you just can't help it. Everything you thought was important prior to that time goes to mush and, thankfully, you realize that something of this enormity is not to be handled alone. You call your friend and ask for immediate help, not knowing if this is the last day that you are ever going to be considered 'sane' for the rest of your life. The face of Polly Klaas flashes by, as do so many smiling young things, who are no longer with us on this planet.

It just takes a second for something really awful to happen, something so inconceivable that you would never be able to fully operate ever again. "My child is missing," I screamed hysterically to my friend. "I need your help". "Should I call the police?" I gasped. "Hang on a second," she said. "Let me come over to the house." My first thought was 'oh no, that is a real time-waster … if my child was in the house, I would have seen her.' In retrospect, it was a smart summation. You have to start at the core and work outwards; it gives you a base of operations.

Half-way to the base of operations, I get a call from my daughter's friend's mother. "Is my daughter with you?" I yelled at this poor woman, deafening her I'm sure. "Yes," she replied and then I collapsed with a tirade of abuse. What I actually said to my daughter that afternoon probably does not bear repeating. Let's just say that she knew I was very, very upset and the ear-bashing that she received that afternoon was not something she would want to repeat.

What had actually happened to send my world into such a tail-spin was that my daughter's class was kept a little late and she had missed the bus. Instead of thinking clearly and realizing that she needed to go to the school office and call her mother immediately, she imagined that she could quite easily go home with her friend and call her mother from there; not realizing that her friend's home phone was not working at the time. So there, her situation went from poor judgment to mayhem in just a few minutes. In short, she was "missing" for about 25 minutes while she had to wait to call me until her friend's mother came home with a cell phone. Though I'm sure we'll face further scary scenarios before we're done, I just don't think that particular situation will happen again.

For the rest of the day I was shell-shocked by the might have beens of that day; of how transitory life is and how we all live on the borderline of life, death and hell every day.

My daughter knew she had put me through something very stressful; she knew not how stressful. It goes back to the ultimate fear, when you have a child, of one day losing that child and realizing that your life from that second on is over.

My mother lost my baby sister once in "Harrods", the largest department store in the world. The memory of her hysteria stayed with our family and was told and re-told as a cautionary tale of 1) how not to behave in a very bad situation 2) why you must always hold Mummy's hand. That feeling really does something to you though and it's hard to ever recover from it. You raise your children so that they can go forth into the world and develop as rational human beings; you cannot escort them through life as their human shield, even if you'd really like to be able to do so.

For me, I have had to take two steps back for the one I had taken forward. I am nowhere near ready to let her go forth into the world and conquer, but I still have to force myself to allow her to ride the bus and hope that I have reinforced the obvious that she should call from the office if she misses it.

**Lucy has been accused of being an 'overprotective mother'; more than once.**

# MONSTER ON THE HORIZON

The monster is back in the home. He appeared while we were all out to lunch. Finding a crack under the door or an opportune key hole, he slipped into the room and made himself comfortable, amidst all our piles of seasonal cheer - just like the Grinch in that famous story.

It was the holidays and everyone was having a grand old time, as may of us do that time of year. Presents had been purchased and wrapped, festive meals prepared and the wine opened to breath. Even with all that preparation and adornment of tradition, it can take a mere second for a monster to breathe his poisonous fire and remind you of his presence, shatter all the laughter and joy of the season and of life itself even. He crept back in when no one was paying attention. Once we were forced to become aware of his presence, however, we realized that he had been there all along. We just hadn't wanted to notice.

My baby sister had breast cancer when she was 32 and goes in for her check ups twice a year. The further away the memory of the diagnosis, the easier it seemed to forget the horror and seal the belief that that whole nightmarish episode had just been a hiccup in our family's life, not to mention my sister's, which would then be allowed to continue on its way with the experience firmly behind us all.

This year was different. Ironically enough, I am always in the habit of asking my sister how her bi-annual tests go, but this year I had become so comfortable, so blasé perhaps about her consistently clean bill of health, that I never even mentioned it. I am ashamed to say that it didn't much spring to mind. The gloomy reality came quietly to light over the festive season that her cancer markers were up three-fold. If you are from a 'cancer home', you know what that means. Sis had not wanted to share any of this with us. She knows how we worry. Her plan had been to tell us when there was really something to tell; but the news of her bad check up slipped out right after the monster slipped back in.

Full of foreboding, our family speeds back immediately, as a unit, to the time mother's markers were found to be "up" and the evil beast had been located yet again somewhere back in her body.

Though this was several years ago, such a moment whizzes back to you as if it just happened – a demi-second frozen in time. Once that sentence was proclaimed back then, I recall the anxiety, the wait, the long, long wait, as the determination was made as to where 'It' is and what happens now. This time, we all become frozen in time once more. We are back in the waiting room, anxiously listening to the tick of the clock and hoping that some one is going to wake us up from the dark dream we are currently living and say that it has all been a terrible mistake and that we can carry on now. We had been carrying on. We had watched my sister recover from the dreadful purge of chemotherapy - her braveness and her fortitude as the chemicals chewed her up and spat her out, the good and the bad, her enormous lack of fury at her lot and her persistent great humor - ("Wow, look at these curls!" she famously exclaimed, as her formerly thin hair grew back luscious, dark, curly and thick after the chemotherapy treatments. "Good hair like this? It's almost worth going through chemo!")

She steered us all through a very dark time in our family's history, through and through and out the other side; or so we thought. And now we are back in the oily waters, where we were before. But before, we didn't know the wretchedness of the journey she was going to have to make; we only knew that she was going to have to take it alone. Now we know; it makes the wait even worse and the outlook of the journey even harder; the steps she has to take forward even more treacherous and more lonely for her, with us following several steps behind, where she likes us.

In the meantime, while we wait and we ponder with monsters pressing to move back into our lives on all sides, my sister is back in her home in Turkey, where she wants to be, with the people she wants to be with. She just enjoyed a splendid New Year's Eve celebration with her buddies over there and she optimistically looks forward to the year ahead. Her mind over matter is still a spectacle to behold and a lesson to us all, this time, just as it was the time before. Live each day as if it were your very last. My sister does, and that attitude will surely guide her into brighter waters, with the wind behind her and her sails full.

**My sister Rosie dealt with the bone cancer diagnosis as she handles all of her life – with a wonderful spirit and great humor.**

# MOTHER IS THERE IF YOU LISTEN

Mothers and daughters: the history of our relationships has been well documented over time and, is for many, a source of fascination.

I am no exception. My mother and I: a documentary of peaks and furrows. I scope out books on the subject and tear them up avariciously.

When I was carrying my own baby girl, mirroring my mother's age, dates and situation 30 years before, our relationship became even closer. The last few years I have had more conversations with her than I would think possible.

When I doubt myself as a parent, she will firstly agree with me, because she loves it when we spar! She will then reassure me that I'm doing a *reasonable* job; considering I spend so much time at my job, (in her mind most dissatisfactory; but then she was from a different generation and an artist to boot!)

When I'd play tennis with my daughter, she'd tell me to let her win, ("*children need to be raised with huge esteem*".) She'd also tell me to kiss and tickle her during the game, ("*You can never spoil a child with too much love. Look at how the Greeks raised their children*!" She'd say. "*Such civilized people!")*

She'd remind me to read my daughter at least two stories a night, to make sure she remains highly literate, and would chide me with a nudge when I didn't take her to enough movies or plays. Sunday, I'm reminded that church can be important, if you are that way inclined, but Christian behavior is better.

She still reminds me, almost hourly, of what a superb husband I married, how I should do a better job in the kitchen and to not let him "*do everything,*" just because he is so very capable. She laughs when I say I "*do the laundry*", as if I am out there with an old-fashioned scrubbing board, digging my arms into icy water. "*No Lucy, you do not do the laundry*!" she challenges me again. "*Your machines do the laundry!*"

She pokes at me when I have less than charitable thoughts toward teenagers, (never mind if they are deserved!) She nudges my conscience that all children need a mother and don't necessarily get the one that birthed them. My doors should remain open to all and supply copious amounts of food, as needed and whenever, just as a mother should.

The days when she is quiet, I know she is busy chatting with some one else who needs her more. I'm still there deep in her heart, but perhaps Jackie or Doreen need her that particular day. She's never too far away, though, and seldom stays quiet for long.

That day we were at the beach, the last time we were all together, she told me to stay away from the waves, or I would get '*dragged out*'. She walked along the tide line, beach-combing as ever, and keeping one beady eye on the diving cormorant bobbing on the wave. She helped us to find the treasured piece we lost on the beach, half a mile down from where we had originally left it. She laughed at me a little more kindly this time, when I cried, and she said my name in a soft sing-song voice that calmed me.

My mother, Una Bagnall Theodora Benedicta Mason, died on November 9, 2000, at 9am, after she called me into her room for the last time. I held her close to try and stop her from leaving, but she refused to stay, skipping away with "*Our Lady*", just as she had planned; having prepared for her departure, given her clothes away and purchased all her presents for Christmas before she left that day. I had been in England for only four days when she departed. She and I have been chatting like maniacs ever since.

There are so many theories about what happens when you die, but I like to think that my mother's soul went inside of me that day and the many people who loved her. Simplistic? Maybe; but who's to tell me I'm wrong? Look at it this way: all of us who want it get a little piece of her laughter, attitude, advice, and even orneriness. Some of us even retrieve gifts we thought we had lost. She lives on. The memory is rich and lasting. We see her full of joie de vivre and sunshine, feeling good again, kissing us the way she used to and telling us which movies we couldn't miss.

For those of you who hear your mother's voice the way I do, you might agree. There she goes again! "*Kiss your children like the Greeks do! You can never spoil a child with love.*" Go ahead, spoil them rotten; and, while you're at it, listen a little more carefully for the voice inside. She might be trying to tell you something.

**Lucy still chats to her Mum. She's just around the corner, somewhere in the other room.**

# OUR HEARTS ARE FULL

Absorbing the end of life testimonial at my father-in-law's funeral service, I was struck by a few significant things, as you are at such times; with so many thoughts and feelings swirling around in the mind. The first thing, quite obvious, but not something you think about every day is how fragile a species we are; how close we are to death every second of every day. A man breaks his leg and goes to hospital. 6 weeks later he is gone and a family's status quo is shattered, its dimensions forever altered. With that kind of cause and result, you find yourself looking back over the past 42 days and pondering the pointless, but inevitable "what if's" of tasks not done and questions not asked. You are raised to trust in the training of the medical profession; to follow their lead and heed their instruction. We did; it didn't work out. This first thought sent my sadness cascading downwards.

My second thought, close on the heels of dissecting something you can do absolutely nothing about, (and then deciding that this was a really bad idea), was that, since the life in question had obviously ended and we could hardly change that, could we; how lovely to have a humorous, but accurate tribute in the funeral service at the end of it all; how totally divine to be able to build a portrait of a life in just a few minutes' careful description. Though he had never met Dad, the minister had spent considerable time with the family prior to the service and was able to draw with tender detail a picture of the man we all loved. He depicted my daughter's grandfather as the kind, funny individual he truly was. In our grief he made us laugh. Through our tears he drew a smile. It made it right; it almost made it better. And that would be how we would all want our final story to be told, is it not.

Makes me think I should start compiling my own end of life testimonial right here and now; or begin working on the material at least. Firstly, I need to strive to make lighter of the things which are light, and stress less on the things I can't change. Teach us to care and not to care; teach us to sit still; so some one clever once said. Laugh more, play harder, be nicer – all those things I must strive to develop a little better; so that my obituary may be a tad more wholesome, or at least funnier, down the road.

"I want a really funny testimonial like that at my funeral," I commented to my daughter later in the day. "Draw a humorous picture of me like that for my final service and then sprinkle me on the ocean, so I can always be around you. When you miss me, you'll be able to find me. Don't forget to take a piece of me to the water, so I can be reunited with my ma." My daughter looked at me as if I had gone slightly kooky; but at least she knows now, and she'll probably never forget.

"Yeh, sprinkle me on my land," added husband helpfully. Having listened to us discussing the costs of plots and coffins over the past few days, she was probably already counting her blessings and her pennies at the thought of the cheap sprinkling of ashes on land and sea sometime in her future.

Some family members you only ever see at weddings and funerals. Though our family gets together quite a lot relatively-speaking, it is a challenge to get so many people in one place at one time; but watch somebody die, and see how easily it all comes together. The gathering of cars after the service was enough to get the tears going again. The back yard resembled the parking areas at Disney. People poured out of cars, hugging. Folks showed emotion like they never had before; shared photos and old stories, laughed at Dad's cartoons, raced across rooms to greet one another. Copious amounts of food and drink were consumed over the course of several hours' time; the last supper of sorts stretching out as if to stop it from ever ending. The children forget where they are and begin their games, chase around, laugh, giggle; as they should, and as he would have wanted. Made it right, made it almost better. The sun shines brightly, no coastal fog on this day; it was ordered special. Visitors from years ago pop in as old friends and share their memories. Old acquaintances are rekindled and made new. All these gifts can and do happen when some one passes on and it's a sight to behold, no matter how much clearing up of dirty dishes it requires. Our daughter got the gift of new cousins she had never met and was drawn to instantly. One of them had the exact same birthday; same day, same year, same hospital. We all wowed over the coincidence and exchanged phone numbers. Plans were made for fishing trips and travels, connections and communications. All these gifts were exchanged the day we buried Dad.

And now, though all cried out, our hearts are full. We are tired and a little sick; we need a day of no tears, no talk, just slumber and rest. We need to sit out on the lake in our boat, so to speak, and watch the sun come up and go down. We need to absorb all that has happened and find our peace where we can. We need to call all those people we promised we would and make the burial day more of a beginning than an ending; the first supper; not the last.

Another thought I had during the service was how rare and exceptional dad's last days were. Being able to die with dignity, surrounded by all measure of loved ones from both past and present has to be the best way to leave this planet; the ultimate, the Mecca of existence. It's a gift we should all aspire to hold in our hand at the end of a happy life; a treasure to touch, and then give away to those left behind.

"I've seen heaven and it's beautiful," said Dad as he popped his head back around the corner, shortly before he left us for good. "I've seen Mac and he's waiting for me." Who are we, mere mortals, to get in the way of such a precious exit from our world and a perfect entrance to another? I'll say it again; our hearts are full.

**Darrell Jensen died on July 31st, 2004.**
**His brother Mac died in the Vietnam War.**

# THE FROG POND & OTHER GIFTS

The night my husband's father died, we heard our first frog in the frog pond. "Hello Darrell," we said; as you do, in complete disassociation, when you are reeling with shock from something so terrible and are, simultaneously, tickled with something else so funny and so far out, it remains an eternal association in the mind. The moment stayed with me frozen in time, as something I shall always remember.

My husband had been building up his frog empire for some time before we heard the first magic croak that fateful night, some years ago, when his father finally gave up the fight on this planet and snuck off to the back shed of some place extraordinary, where he could finally have his smoke in peace and fry his potatoes at 4am without comment.

Husband had been building up a barrel fountain on one side of the house, as you do if you are the eternal craftsman, and he had been trying to coax frogs into coming over to live not only mildly in the barrels, as they had been doing, but also vibrantly in the new pond area on the other side of the house, which was where he really wanted them in the first place. If you have ever tried any kind of extraordinary experiment with nature, you will know that it does not work. The 'if you build it, they will come' concept does not always fall into place as it should. Nature has a way of marching to its own peculiar beat, and it doesn't give a hoot how the human race tries to manipulate it. Husband had constructed a water feature on one side of the house, so he built one on the other side to match, as it were; a frog experiment of sorts. Surely the frogs would know that if they simply hopped over to the other side of the house, an utter frog paradise would be waiting for them in the form of warm secure ponds, bugs galore and amazing marshy places to hide themselves in and croak themselves silly. Well, they obviously did know that; they just waited for the evening Darrell departed the earth to let the rest of us know it.

Along with the astonishing shooting stars we witnessed that night, the frog croaking became an ever-present reminder that those who reign in the memory are never too far away. Though sometimes we will close our bedroom window, which is located right on top of said frog pond, and proceed to lock out the noise in order to get a good night's sleep, most of the time the frogs are an ever constant reminder of home and all that is constant in the here and now; as well as the ever pervasive reminder of those who have gone before. Something we can count on, any season, any day; rain or shine, the frogs love it all.

Wherever Darrell went, we'll never truly know, but knowing his sense of humor as we do, we can only surmise that he did have quite a lot to do with the association between himself and the arrival of the frogs that night and for the hereafter. Darrell was a good cartoon artist – we have many of his pencil, line-drawings decking our walls of various family members in funny situations – some we could share with these members and some most definitely not. If only I could one day wake up to a sketch of my husband and I listening to Darrell croaking for the first time in his new life as a frog in the lily pond, I would then be a forever believer in something much larger than me.

If you talk to folks who tune into nature on a deeper level, as I think I do these days, you will see a pattern emerge. I have heard all kinds of wonderful and mystical nature stories from those who have witnessed the passing of loved ones and looked further into the ether for communications beyond the spoken word and the physical presence, and found things there. Humming birds have a strong connection with those residing in the after life or the world of the spirits, it seems to me. Many, many people think of their loved ones and have close humming bird connections almost simultaneously – just ask around! Being some what of a hummer lover, I have had several myself.

"Hi, Mum', I say, as a rather splendid green with a red-chested hummer buzzes my head and hovers knowingly above the orange blossom, eye to eye with me, her beak pausing just a millisecond away from the nectar. For a mere second we are one. I also greet her as the hawk swoops across the property, or the eagle glides high, way high in the sky and pauses just a second over my yard as if to glance down and say, "There's my girl! Good morning darling!" Mother is always and forever the cormorant swooping over the bay and the new bird that arrives in our yard trying to mingle with the old. Don't tell me I'm crazy; it is a wild and beautiful thing.

My mother was born in 1933. She died in 2000. I am always finding 1933 associations falling into my lap. My crème de la crème was my rare 1933 penny, which I now covet as a jewel in my grasp and mark it as the beginning of my rather strange penchant for collecting old coins with significant dates. It arrived in my life in a most opportune time; a time when my faith was fading and my spirit low. It perked me up and made me look around. '1933?" It said to me, emphatically. "Yes, I'm here, thanks for noticing." Every now and then when I least expect it, a 1933 'reminder' will ping me with a gift. I will get an order number with a 1933 at the end; my seat number will be 33, my new bank account – yes, you've guessed it – ends with 33. There are so many wonderful pieces of mind candy and comfort to be extracted from the mundanities of life, if you just open up your brain to feed. Nature, or the powers that move her, cover us with gifts every day – from the giant pumpkin that we never planned to the sunflowers we never planted. 12 heads of a sunflower that just showed up in our yard and smiled heavenly at us has to be something of a bit of magic. "Thanks, Mum', I say to that and wave to her knowingly, as she hovers systematically by the honeysuckle and gives me a show. Darrell's doves also swoop over our yard daily in a ceremonious hello. He used to religiously feed his doves in his yard and now it's their turn to feed us.

Hark, a chorus of frogs sparks up and it's time to say good evening to Darrell and the band. Though Darrell has technically been gone from us physically for several years now, we welcome him back into our memories and our humors every time the band strikes up and he passes through our memory stream once again.

For those of you who miss your loved ones, as we all eventually must in the way of the world; look around and glean the comforts that are available to you when you open your eyes wide to the universe and then move just a step further away. Pick up the penny and wonder why it arrived at your door step, look in your garden and find the gift. Stop, listen, breath, take a moment to soak in creation. Wait; was that a frog calling your name? I really think it was. Go outside into the darkness and see what the message is. The shooting star may be sending you a memo, the howl of the coyote may be singing you a song, or it could just be Darrell and the band serenading the love they feel for you every single day and the way they feel best served to deliver it under the circumstances.

**The 'frog pond' is now three ponds and home to lots of goldfish and, of course, plentiful frogs.**

# THE OTHERS COME BACK

A friend of mine just lost her mother. Regardless of the fact that ma had led a good long life – much longer than most, in fact - and therefore her departure could not come as a huge surprise to any of us, the searing pain is surprising; it always is. With her parting, comes back the loss of all those who have gone before. The pain throbs just the same as it did the last time, and the time before that. When it's your mother; the loss is eternal, the hole permeates for always. You wonder again, what it is all about. There is life before you lose your mother and life after; or, at least, that is my solitary conclusion. They are different places.

As you get older, you become more accustomed to losing people; almost better at it, if there is such a thing. You condition yourself and prepare your defenses for the inevitable which awaits you just around the corner. No matter what; how expected or anticipated, it still catches you, makes you gasp for air, rearranges your levels, moves your days into nights, suns into moons. With every loss of a beloved, the others lost before them all come back to remind you they are gone too and you are, once again, cut to the heart. With the return of memories, both sweet and bittersweet, you weep big, salty tears and wish it were otherwise.

I realized this week, however, that exercising my memory was a good thing; tears or not. With the loss of my friend's ma, I got to visit with my own, now dearly departed a few short years ago.

"How are you?" I asked her as the white angel hawk flittered overhead in the swirly blues, swooping the long patchwork valley up and down, down and up, playing games with my eyes as she stayed in my field of vision and then left it. From the soil to the heavens to the soil and back; and how suitable is that.

"Ah, yes, enjoying the sunshine as ever?" I chattered on to mother, who was a sun worshipper from birth, cursed to live in a country as wet and gloomy as England and always longing for the sunshine beyond her own physical world. "I knew you would like it here; isn't the countryside just gorgeous! Can you feel the sun on your skin? Sorry about the olive tree; we'll get another one in the ground, I promise you." She and I twittered back and forth, smiling to one another and feasting on each other's company, soaking in the serenity of our engagement.

"Well, of course you're here! It's your birthday this week. 73. Seventy three? That wouldn't have done at all!" I laugh out loud, or even just to myself. "Happy Birthday, anyway, Mum. I miss you," I say and she flutters off. Even though I had done most of the talking, the visit had been a good one. Later, I would pick some roses for her and light a candle, honoring our connection in the sphere of the unknown, or that place just around the corner that some of us really believe is there.

I thought of my lovely granny, after the news of ma's passing, and the fact that my lovely "Myrt" has been gone nearly a year. I watch her watching me every morning as I read my paper and prepare for my day. Her photographs sit beside me and exude the deepest of love and affection. Her eyes are warm and kind; her smile radiant to eternity. She helps me with the tough parts; her grace rides through my veins and makes me better, not just in the mornings, but throughout.

Ma's departure from our local area this week has given me a lot of gifts. Not discounting one bit the place setting she has left vacant at her table, nor the chasm she has left behind in her family, she has forced wide open personal memories that had been snoozing there for a while; and probably not just for me.

Ma gave me a chance to visit with friends in honor of her memory; to spend time in her church and feel the power of her spirituality all around. She gave me an opportunity to look back at her good, long life and imagine how it had been all the way back, when she was young in this once tiny community, which now sports more than a passing coffee shop and just about all we'll ever need for survival. As an immigrant, ma knew her fair share of going without and giving all you've got; she knew war and hunger and discrimination more than the most of us. Most of all, ma bestowed her wisdom and her love for those around her to spread and water; her crops were nurtured and distributed, as nature does in any valley, in her own way. In this valley, ma's legacy lingers beyond herself into the skies, the hearts and souls of those whose memory is rich with her. Thank you ma for all the memories you reminded me I need to nurture, gifts I need to share, spirits I need to engage.

To the angel hawk last seen swooping down towards Greenfield, close to ma's home, come back I say, come back. I have cake for your birthday and oh so many things to tell you about the week that was. Was that a tear I detected in my own eye? Isn't it a wonder; the imagination or the spirit – however you look at it – can still take you to places you thought you'd never go to again.

**Lucy still likes to visit with her mother in our valley she calls home and by the ocean her mother adored.**

# THE RIGHT PLACE AT THE RIGHT TIME

Location, as they say in real estate, is just about everything that matters. Once in a while, in life not just in real estate, you can find yourself in the perfect location; completely in the right place at the right time, without remotely realizing the power of your decision; except perhaps in the rear view mirror when you realize that you couldn't have planned it any better, if you'd tried.

For whatever reason, my sisters and I were gathering recently from all points of the globe at my father's house, during the rather evocative time of the anniversary of our mother's death. November; a time when leaves fall from trees and slide into mush, the sky can be slate grey and foreboding and the mood full of anxiety for the long winter months ahead. It can also be nail-bitingly cold and wet on occasion. That has always been my November experience in the past; it'll probably always be that way, even perhaps just in my mind. Several dear, dear people in my life have left me in November; hearts have been broken and hope lost for a while. I get bronchitis in November, depression can hit me hard, and I can stress about all the things I didn't accomplish that year and wonder how the heck I would get them done for next year either. It's not one of my favorite months.

But 6 years on from losing our mother, my sisters and I had gathered to toast her more this time than to mourn; to look at her perhaps a bit more realistically than we had in the first or second year of her passing. We could also easily imitate some of her funny ways and play-act her mannerisms; a private joke between us that no one else could possibly appreciate. On the actual day and time of her departure I was on my own, unusually, in the house where she had died, my dad's house, with me beside her. I closed my eyes and checked to see if she was there; she wasn't. That's right; she had come over to California with me. How would she still be there? It was pretty conclusive for me. Right time and place and all that.

It was also a rare time for the three sisters to be at home with dad and to drive him a little potty with the constant movement of the hot water in the bathroom, the copious amounts of food and drink to cater and provide at regular intervals in the house and the rush of people and conversation that perhaps you forget can exist when you no longer have it around you all the time. He managed pretty well and we all had some good memories to take away from it. In fact, I think he loved it and wished we could do it more often; despite the ravaged fridge and scavenged wine cupboard. My baby sister also let me go along with her to her annual doctor's appointment, where they had studied her scans and given her the green light for another year; at least where the cancer was concerned. I felt quite privileged that she allowed me to go along and listen to the surgeon. Again; one of those things about being in the right place at the right time.

At the end of it all, I kissed my sisters goodbye; as usual wondering how long it would be before I saw them again.

My dear, dear friend who I continue to miss so terribly all the decades down the road from when I left her alone without me in London town. She found me too at the right place at the right time; or I found her. However you look at it; we were together at a time when we needed to be so and that was all that mattered. She was at a horribly low ebb in her existence – the culmination of many years or layers of "stuff" in my unqualified analysis - and I, by chance, was flying in to be there. The days we spent together; the long, lost walks over rich green meadows and past ladies' swimming ponds and the lovely bridge, the 'Christmas Dinner' at the old pub, the cups of tea and long deep chats; those pictures will help cross the bridge of where we both currently live and the broad friendship we have which surpasses all time and place.

Location, location. Yes, sometimes we can get it right when we least expect to. I had no idea when I planned my impromptu trip to see my dad and my sisters how very important it was that I go. Something had rooted itself in my gut and given me the freedom and the mechanism to make those valuable days away possible. I shall always be grateful that whatever power it was – or merely my own need to go back to basics and recall where I came from – moved me on to manipulate myself into the right place at the right time and be a part of something much larger than just me.

**Lucy increasingly listens to the voice inside her head that tells her to do or not to do certain things.**

# LIVING IN THE MODERN WORLD

# 108 DEGREES AND WHERE DID WE GO WRONG?

Watching the sun dip down gracefully behind the Santa Lucia Mountains this evening, my bare feet warm on the stamped concrete of the aftermath of this day, I did have to challenge Mother Sun in all her serene, lovely gracefulness, even as she blushed pink and bowed her head down for another day, allowing the cooling process to begin. The calm after the storm, as it were. "So, what was that all about today?" I asked her, as she smiled back at me silently in her sweet knowing way. At one point, during this heat-taxing day, the thermometer hit 108 plus and I thought that maybe I would have to faint and force some one else to take care of this overheating body and put me somewhere cool to chill out.

I knew it was coming with the week our world has just endured. From complete wretchedness and devastation in China and Burma to aggressive tornadoes in our own Deep South and East Coast, the Charmed West Coast couldn't get off 'Scott free', as they say in the old country – there had to be some kind of earth-shattering quake or raging wild fire to get us off our couches of complacency and into the grief that much of the rest of the world is suffering. California cannot always be about free living and the best weather in the world. Global warming? It's global something, I can tell you. If I were a religious woman, I'd be working on my ark right about now.

Well, I'm here to tell you, bible-believers, that today *was* something to behold! The day started off early with that smarmy haze only witnessed at the beginning of very extraordinary and extreme climatic experiences. I knew it as soon as I opened my eyes. "Oh boy," I said to just myself. "You'd better get yourself psyched and ready for battle with the elements today!" No clouds to hide beneath, just a whimsical puff of white, as if to say, "Hey fool, you're on your own today!"

Years ago, I spent too much time living in Louisiana – another long story. There was a memorable time when I recall sitting in a traffic jam in high summer in my 1977 4-door Buick LeSabre sedan, which had no air-conditioning. Baton Rouge, LA, high summer – is not a place for the faint of heart and most definitely not for the British with no air conditioning to protect their tender selves. I could be seen literally skidding around on the red bench seats of my old jalopy, hanging on to my steering wheel for dear life and spitting with anguish and discomfort, before it came to me that in some situations in life you literally had to force your mind to take control over your body. I taught myself to think cool on that well-remembered day, and from then on, I can still muster that level of elevation if I need to.

As I entered the City of King, when she was about to have a record temp day and I was about to have to spend it in her sweaty arenas, I realized that it was another one of those days when I was going to have to muster memory of my Buick-with-red-seats-strength from a Louisiana summer a long time ago, and do my best not to whine and, definitely not to faint. It wasn't easy though. My friend and I were doing our stint as volunteers at the Salinas Valley Fair – yes, volunteers. We were not being paid for this torment. Such is the whim of weather, I clearly recall two years ago, during volunteer work of a similar kind, when it was cold and wet and the crowds stayed away because of the inclement clime. Today we think they stayed away for exactly the same reason but different. People walked slowly from shade spot to shade, ice cones were consumed and water bottles dripped on heads - it was a sight to behold, not to mention the poor children trying to keep their animals cool and free of anxiety attacks in the barns and the vendors sweating over their efforts to still tout their hot beef sandwiches and cups of cocoa.

Life is very much like a box of chocolates – you never do know what you're going to get on any given day. I knew, however, at the beginning of that hazy-heated day that it was going to be one for the memory banks, I just never knew how glad I would be when it was finally over with and I could watch that lovely last glimpse of sun smile her last for the day and sink down over the mountains. Only then could we all breathe a sigh of relief and enjoy the cool evening air on our skin and the embracing sheet of darkness wrap around us, as we contemplated another day of extreme heats, cotton candy and where we all possibly went wrong.

**Lucy adores our mostly mild climate. She'll take the wind any day over the other.**

# A DAY IN THE LIFE

Most days in adult life just blend, if you are really honest about it. You get up, get the child ready for school and rush off to work, stressing all the while about the challenges laying wait in the day ahead. You rush to the store for bodily nutrition, stand in line, stress again about all the things you didn't accomplish that day, eat supper and fall asleep in front of the news. When I was a wild teen, scooping up life with both hands wide open to the world, I do not recall imagining that this was how my adult life would mostly turn out to be. Probably just as well. (I do recall thinking that I would be definitely dead by 29, because after that, what was the point, but that is another story entirely.) Some days are naturally more uplifting than that, but, most of the time, the pattern of regular daily life is not the ingredients for a great tale.

Some days do stand out though and, when they do, I think it is important to give them some kind of marker, even just the casual stroke of the written word. Casting the mind for such a jewel, there was the recent tournament day that springs to mind, when the Volleyball League Champions – Soledad – met their arch rivals, King City, in the final of the 8$^{th}$ grade tournament. If blood, not just tears could have been shed that day, we would all have been bleeding ourselves to a certain death. The game was volleyball at its best – super close play and nail-biting tension – the material of wonderful sports the world over. It was unfortunate that some one had to win. That was a memorable day I won't forget really quickly. I also remember asking my husband to have me check my blood pressure that night – I didn't think it could stand pressure that intense for so long!

Then there was the wild-west day this past week when we lost our lovely sun we had been enjoying most of the past year, our growling, backwards wind picked up and our trees swayed – again backwards. Ominous, grey swirling clouds raced down the valley as if to say, "she's coming, she's coming! Watch out!" It was the same day my mother-in-law called me bawling her eyes out. Her brother had gone to sleep in the chair the night before and never woken up. It was the same day that thunder cracked through the heavens, causing our nervy dog to break his way out of the fence and go careering at top speed, miles across the vineyards. He was last seen racing like a greyhound around 3 miles away from the house, and heading flat-out for salvation in the hills. Luckily, he had the common sense to run right back home again when the thunder stopped; but that was, for sure, one memorable day of the week; when we were forced to contemplate life without Baxter, as well as life without uncle – and both on the same day.

Some things do make you stop in your tracks, pause, contemplate and even re-evaluate somewhat. And that is a good thing. That is one really good service of the winter months, I have always thought. In the summertime, you are so busy soaking up the rays, feeling the wonderful benefit of vitamin D seeping through your skin, entertaining outside, being outside, that you don't spare a thought for the inside thoughts that it is important to have once in a while. When I lived in England, the indoor lights that you gave yourself, not to mention the warmth that you had to have, were a vital part of getting through the harsh winter months, when the skies are mostly slate grey, the pavements mostly wet and the cold searing to the bone. Here we don't get much of that and we are very fortunate, trust me.

But on those wild and windy days that we do have, we should take the time to stop and think about the week that was. What was significant last week or even yesterday? Were you especially nice to some one or some one to you? Did you make any kind of difference in some one's life? It is not the life you lead but the life you change that counts in the larger scheme of things. A while ago – when I had more time or made more time – I used to write down 5 things to be grateful for every day. Some days it was nothing more than 'did not yell at child' or 'child did not yell at me'. Other days I was grateful for my good health or my loving husband. Some days I was simply grateful that I made it through my waking hours and did not kill anyone.

The way the weeks and the years whip by, I shall endeavor to take stock a little more of the significant things all around me that should count every day. Not just the days that Baxter runs away or a family member takes off to pastures elsewhere. I should not discount those ordinary days when I can look back a few hours and say to myself, 'wow! What a great day! Nothing really awful happened today. And aren't we lucky?'

**Lucy is a firm optimist, no matter how stormy the day.**

# A GROWING COMMUNITY

If you travel the highways and by-ways of our local community on any given weekend or holiday, you will see trains of cars, literally, headed northbound towards the shopping areas of Salinas and beyond, where they will bestow their hard-earned dollars on goods and services they elect to purchase in other places, while donating their tax dollars to those areas over there. Those areas get to use those tax dollars from over here for the betterment of their community over there – their police, fire, children, parks – you get the picture. Most people in rural areas have become accustomed to traveling on a regular basis to St Elsewhere for many of the things that they might need. It's not considered a crime to go to Costco in Salinas or Sand City and spend a few hundred, or even visit the malls, the outlets – all of those places are palatable in most people's book for polite conversation. But bring the topic of a box store into your own local community and you would have thought that they were directly spraying for the apple moth over the middle school, even after they had proven the spray was lethal.

Growth is inevitable, especially in an area where land is so plenty. Competition makes us better at what we do. Years ago when we were in the midst of a housing boom and they were throwing up houses as if there no tomorrow and definitely no lack of people to fill these houses, I recall a comment, that it was all very well to build all the houses, but what about all the stuff you need to go around the houses – the businesses, the shops, the jobs and so on. Those needed to come too!

When I first moved to Soledad over a decade ago, we had no shopping center. We had no large grocery or drug store. We certainly had no world-renowned coffee shop or popular drug store. Soledad was just a small community of small business back then. A lot of the old-timers liked it that way and worked hard to preserve it. People still went to Salinas where they had a choice, sometimes, or just for the heck of it. They would go there to do a big clothing shop, to go out to dinner, to visit the movies – or very often – to visit a big box store where everything would be in one place. People have always done that, and small business continues to survive – they may have to alter the way they do some things or provide an alternate service, but they can survive and they can thrive.

Small business will always provide something just that bit special, just that bit different. You will never walk into 'Bullitt' in a large town and have some one say to you, "How are you today, Lucy? Anything I can help you with? And how about real estate? Is the market picking up?" Oh no. In 'Bullitt', it's a very impersonal in and out experience. Those experiences are alright once in a while, but not for your everyday. Soledad is like a "Cheers" experience, where everyone knows your name. The clerk on the photo counter asks about your dad and when is he coming back to visit. The guy in the auto parts store not only knows your name but wants to actually install the window wipers you just bought because he knows you can't. The server in the restaurant knows how you like your meat cooked and she gets it ordered just right every time. The guy in the tire shop knows you're pathetic and can't check your own tire. He's happy to do it for you. A big box is not going to go there and we wouldn't want them to.

We should not be afraid of growth – it is inevitable. Most fear is bought out of what we don't know. When you face your fears, they no longer exist. Growth brings diversity, challenge and interest to our community. It will bring new visitors and tourists, even. Look at all the homes we have built over the past few years! Were we afraid of that? No. Did we comment when people said Soledad was a bedroom community for people who could afford to buy here, but still had to go and work and shop elsewhere? No, that didn't bother us a bit. So why would we be afraid of a little competition? Anyone who shops in our larger grocery store knows what I'm saying! You can quite easily stand in line with the masses for 45 minutes before you pay for your goods and get out of there. We have quite a community of shoppers, trust me. And we can accommodate more. If we have extra shopping, the neighboring communities will come here to shop too – and they won't just stay in one corner of town, they'll be all over the place. Just look at Paso Robles! It has some pretty extensive shopping, but it also has an interesting downtown with wine tasting, restaurants, antiques. They recognize in Paso that their downtown is still their heart of town and work hard to keep it that way.

There's a lot of rumor and innuendo going on anytime things they are a-changing. I honestly feel that there is room for more people and more business. With more business comes more jobs and that has to be a good thing. With more business comes more money, more tourists and that is how the world goes round – the hand that feeds the hand. There's plenty for all, I truly believe that. Yet again, the sign is not lying – it really is happening in Soledad and we are all hopeful witnesses to her evolution.

**Lucy loves the little town of Soledad, but would rather give more of her tax dollars to her little town than to Salinas?**

# A NEW WAY OF LIVING

"I can't believe you threw away the wheat bread. I just bought it!" I exclaimed. "And where is my All-Bran? Don't tell me you .." The brow was raised and the bristles up. Husband had done the weekly shop and made the mistake of cleaning out the old food and replacing it with the new. He thought he'd done such a good job.

"Don't waste food!" I ranted on. "Why would you act as if we were rich people?" The poor guy nearly got on his hands and knees and dug through the trash to rescue said discarded items; but it was too late. I was already exasperated.

This little exchange got me thinking. We are a society of waste and excess. We think nothing of throwing away perfectly good bread, because the new bread is better. We are so far away from the war generation of my parents who would still freeze perfectly good bread to stop it going rotten and eat up every last morsel of existing cereal, stale or not. This behavior, several decades later, has nothing to do with whether they could now afford to do so or not, but it had become an in-bred life style during the tough years, which bled into the less tough years, and that is no bad thing. I used to be poor myself, really poor. Even now, I will clip coupons from the weekend papers with good intent. Most of the time, I forget to use them, but intrinsically that habit has never really died. I can still be really thrifty when I put my mind to it.

"My husband has fewer hours at work these days," my friend told me. "We've really had to cut back." When I asked her what that meant, she explained that they only have fast food maybe once a week now. It used to be the norm for that quick dinner on the go of the modern American life. Maybe her husband's cut in hours will actually constitute an increase in the quality of life, I wondered to myself; it's a concept. Maybe they will all sit around the table for dinner and have a home cooked meal together most nights; maybe they will grow a garden and have fresh fruits and vegetables to eat year round. Maybe all the family will benefit from a more healthful lifestyle – lower cholesterol and higher ecological behavior. Your mind can broaden quite widely when you touch on this subject in our current economic climate. Generations before us had no pre-packed anythings; every thing was freshly grown and often home grown: fruits, veggies, chickens, rabbits and more. When did cancer really start to be so prevalent in our society? You do have to wonder about the connection there. Parents used to sit down with their children over meals and talk about their day on a daily basis, not just during the holidays – the family was an unbroken circle, in a sense, that came together around the table. It was a circle not to be broken. Were there problems with gangs, with children having no sense of belonging and seeking that most natural of things wherever they could get it? Did families inevitably fall apart the way they seem to now? Again food for thought. I'm no expert, I'm just picking around in the dirt, pondering the state of our union and where we all go from here.

With all the gloomy forecasts of our nation flailing in a condition of distress that is likely to last for a while, you can end up feeling a little helpless; and helplessness is no good to anyone. What I propose is that you do what you can do with what you have to work with – no more, no less. You can look at your own family's budget and see where some healthy changes can be made. Do you write down all the additional things you spend money on over the course of the week? How much goes to your morning Frappucino, or that quick burger on the go? Could you take your coffee in a flask or wrap up the leftovers for lunch? You'd be alarmed how much could be saved there. How much pre-packaged food do you buy? What if you were to buy fresh food for an entire week and document not only the monetary savings, but the way your body began to feel when it was not chugging along on preservatives and coloring? You might be surprised there. Do you have a small patch of dirt where you could plant a garden? There are many nice nurseries which would be happy to give you tips, or do some research for yourself on the internet. Perhaps it could be something you learn to build and grow with your child. Imagine the pride they would feel if they managed to grow a bunch of carrots or a green bean from a small packet of seeds. It's a small thing, but a large step in the right direction. If you'd rather buy your produce than try to grow it; be sure that you are shopping local. Read the labels at the grocery store. Why, in the salad bowl of the world, when broccoli is for sure one of the top crops that we grow, would our local store stock broccoli from Mexico? I'm no produce expert, but that small fact really bothered me. I need to make sure that as much of my money stays in my valley, while so many families are struggling to make a living and I will be more attentive in that arena in future.

How many vehicles can you drive at any one time? Do you really need the extra three? Maybe you could even walk to work, or ride a bike on occasion. Much as our public transit system is not perfect, it does exist in most communities and you could slash a huge sum of money on repairs, maintenance, insurance and so on, if you were to modify your life and recognize that you could easily live without our four-wheeled machine that has become such a well-oiled cog in the wheel of American living.

Bottled water? Whoever created that was a genius. If you had told me there would be one day such a business phenomenon, a universal movement out of something that we can more easily just open the tap to, I would have laughed and told you to package up the air that we breathe while you're at it. Now all the plastic bottles are filling up the land fills, as the well meaning humans desperately trying to switch from sugar filled soda pop to healthy water and glug their way through cases of the stuff. Please, buy a reusable bottle and just fill it up. Much cheaper and sweeter, ecologically speaking.

Now I shall get down off my green podium and make some lemonade from all those lemons I have been growing. I shall go out in to my neighborhood and share my lemons, have a conversation with my neighbors and ask them if they would kindly keep a watch on my young one when she gets home from school. We could act as if it were the olden days of home grown values and neighborly behavior. Maybe if we practiced it enough, we'd all start watching out for each other more, sharing our home grown veggies and making sure the kids were raised right. Before we knew it, maybe the world would not be quite so off kilter, the future so dim and the vegetables an icy ball that falls out of the freezer once in a while.

**Lucy loves the old-new concept of living.**

# ALL IN A DAY

Some days I collapse into bed at the end of the day, relieved to have nothing more asked of me, but the freedom to have a sleepy eye on my book and a hand around a cup of tea. Some days I care to remember little of what went on during the last few hours, but that I survived its helter-skelter and nobody got hurt. Over time though, I have learned to try and pick out a few jewels from the day and wrap my mind around them, as one might take time to bask in a luxurious tub or feast ones eyes on a splendid rainbow. You do have to try and drag the diamonds out of the dirt in order to seize the best out of life. Some days, it can be quite an exercise; but, regardless, it does help to remain up, to remain happy, grounded and all those other essentials necessary to keep on keeping on and to ultimately be successful in most of your endeavors.

Just the flitter of my morning green-breasted humming bird on the orange plant outside my window is such glorious eye candy when I first wake up, that it can kick start my day entirely in the right direction. I love how the hummers shoot and dart around and then remain completely still, but not, and focused on their one quest, the golden flower nectar. Quite the fairy tale! Their divine colors and elegant shapes make me want to plan a whole garden around just them. That is one pure thought I can have first thing, which helps me move onto the next thing. Another can come from the intensity of the hug from my teenager before she goes to school. Never mind that she seldom tells me she loves me; I can mostly tell exactly how she feels from her squeeze first thing. The hug intensity is much the best when she is first waking up and not quite her entire teenage self, still a bit of a baby if the truth were known. It can take me back to the early days of motherhood when I was so completely her entire world. That flashback can only last a second, but it's an important one and one that can sustain me through the entire day. Then there's the bear hug from husband, if he doesn't forget to actually say goodbye. It's a whole wrap-around embrace that most people should experience most days – it does a body and a soul the utmost of good.

Moving on from the early morning stuff comes the chit chat with my dogs, as I give them their breakfast and they love me so for it, their tails wagging as if they might actually spin off into the ether. Then comes my quiet time with my paper and a second cup of coffee. That can also be accompanied by a flitter of the odd hummer across the lawn and this can make me happy all over again.

Then comes the main bulk of the day and that can sometimes give me very little happiness, but take a lot of the zest and patience out of me. It can suck the flitter of the hummer away and the loving smile of the dog. It can wrench the super bear hug from my husband and steal away the tiny suckling babe I had again in my arms for just a moment. The constant drone of the phone, the list of tasks and late tasks, the endless re-working of the list and reorganization of the priorities. The incompetence of some and the idiocy of others. The bad machine that refuses to work and the blackout of the phone, followed by some more phone droning and a fax without toner. Papers falling off my desk, as I wallow, in danger of drowning – death by paper, a sad way to go. The bulk of the day can revisit like a bad dream which won't leave you alone and, at tea time, you can already find yourself longing for the sanctuary of your bed and the flitter of your hummer, reminding you that all is ultimately well. You are in a safe place where no one will hurt you. The phone is turned off, the papers crammed into the brief case and the fax without toner somewhere you can't think of it. The world did not end.

And that is our lives. We run on the treadmill every day and lie exhausted and spent, as darkness falls and we have little else to give up to the world. It is important then to recall the gifts of the day, write them down even and save the odd one for a real gloomer, when the cloud never lifts and the babe leaves without even looking at you, let alone loving you. There are gifts around us all the time – the gift of not being hungry, alone, sad, sick. So many gifts, so little time. We have so much we barely spare a thought for all we should stop and ponder. At least try to find yourself a picture-perfect hummer on an orange flower in the morning and see if that doesn't help you make it through.

**Lucy is always looking for her daily gifts.**

# CALLING FOR SERVICE

Though I am not exactly in agreement with a national day of mourning being turned into a day of service, the proposal I heard discussion of this week did give me food for thought. There wasn't a darn thing I could personally do about anything that happened on that treacherous day in 2001, when some of us really thought the world was coming to an end. But what could I do in my own small way to try and make the planet a better place from thereon; to move towards the concept that, though there are evil people the world over who wish us harm to the highest degree, most people of every shape, color and size just want to live in peace? If most people the world over made up their minds to do just that – to put lots of small ways together and make a large and lasting path towards a better world; why would that not create just that? Togetherness is a very powerful entity. Just like the recycling of plastic or the turning off of a light bulb, we have to start somewhere and make our small contributions along the path of humanity, in the hope that somehow, along the way, it will make more than just a small difference in the evolution of our world and what we are handing over to the next generation and beyond.

And so I contemplated my own call to service. What do I do to make a difference? Not just for my family – that is not so much a calling as much as a duty of love. I have a responsibility to provide and cooperate in that particular arena. I take my responsibilities seriously. I do my best. But it is not a call to service. A call to service denotes a certain lack of emotional attachment; an aspiration towards a higher calling and a higher goal perhaps – giving to people you will most likely never meet. Giving and never expecting an acknowledgment.

I thought back to the 'Back to school sports night' at the high school and the rows of chairs filled with parents eager to show up, be present, be an active part of their children's lives and assist the coaches and teachers who guide them. "If the school site council could have a room full of parents like this, we'd really be on our way!" the principal expressed, optimistically, to the crowd. The school site council meeting rolled around and present was a very small proportion of that same crowd who showed up and wrapped around a dry meeting table for the two hour meeting; not because the majority of the parents don't care, but because sports is fun and planning meetings tend not to be. I show up not for the fun; but to do my part, share in the burden; maybe, possibly, make a small difference where I can. You do what you can in your small, small way and hope for the best. It's not just about my kid; it's about all of our kids the planet over.

Creative minds can make a difference. I am convinced of that. Just look at the recent evolution of a Soledad Freshman Volleyball team. Motivated minds put their brain cells together and started a new movement whereby the local freshman girls had a team to play in and games to play. That didn't just happen because it needed to; it happened because caring people stepped aside from their daily track and did what it took to make things happen, change some lives. Call it small town stuff if you like; but it just might be something big in the lives of our local youth. Maybe one of those girls will have the course of her life changed by this; maybe she will go on to coach her own freshman league, or see her way ahead to escape a tough home life. Who knows? We only know, by giving up a small piece of ourselves, that we have an opportunity to enhance pieces of others; most we will never know about.

Pouring beer for the Soledad Chamber at the recent Soledad Fiesta Days event, it was a slow, cold Saturday in the late afternoon, with the sun quickly sliding behind the mountains, and the beer was not pouring quickly enough for any of us. In retrospect, the hot chocolate stand was probably doing a lot better than us! During my 3 hour shift, I had the chance to stop and think about the event and where it came from. It is entirely manned by local volunteers who donate many, many man hours to put the event together for the benefit of the town. The people come, listen to music, have fun at the carnival, eat and leave. They spend their money but they do not give a thought for the backbone of their pleasure and what it takes to put the whole thing together. When a child receives a college scholarship from the Soledad Fiesta Days it is from the "free" labor of those volunteers, meshed with the donated dollars of those visitors to the event; and bingo, you have a winning combination. They don't even know that they are working together, but they are. Small pieces can come together and create something large. Maybe the child who gets the scholarship will go onto do something fabulous in their higher education. Perhaps they become a doctor and then return one day to serve the community that, years ago, gave them the scholarship and their start in life. We don't always know how that works; but we can only be hopeful that our service to our community gives back in multitudes of ways we will rarely see. I'd hate to think that my cold toes from pouring beer at the Fiesta were for absolutely no reason at all!

Most of us are very, very busy in this modern world in which we live. We have full time jobs, children, bills, stresses piled up and ready to drown us on any given day. We have sports games to attend, we have commuting, we have groceries, we have debt, we have families. Just another task might possibly take us over the edge, we think. However, I have always found that stepping outside of your world and into another can mostly be refreshing and rejuvenating. It will make you less tired when you discuss budget cuts with the school site council or fundraising with your freshman volleyball team. When it is not about you but it is; the burden becomes a mission and the mission becomes a goal. Check out something that calls you for service and see how light you feel. If we all do that and take a bite out of the things that need doing in our communities one small nibble at a time; just think how much would get done and how the trickle down effect might spread down the valley and beyond to the world at large.

**Lucy has enjoyed being a community volunteer over the years. To give back is to receive ten-fold.**

# ESCAPE FROM LIFE

When you gotta go, you gotta go. Sometimes, no matter how very busy you are in your stress-filled life; how, in fact, you are really too busy to take any time off at all, you start to recognize the signs that it's time to escape life as you know it and be just you, away from them. Some of the signs to watch for: you stop noticing how pretty the sky is, (was it really sunny today?); you sit your child in front of the electronic babysitter instead of reading to her, because you're only half way through your to-do list and tomorrow is half-shot as well. You start to yell at your partner, ignore your kids, fall over the cat and lose the list which told you to buy milk. Hence, no milk in the house and the kid wants cereal. You forget where you left the phone, leave the expensive dry cleaning in the car in a nasty heap to become un-drycleaned, miss the appointment you'd long awaited and can't reschedule until next year – you get the picture. You fall asleep over a book with all the lights blaring and eat cereal for supper while you work, spilling milk on your precious keyboard. You're answering two phones at the same time and trying to retrieve a fax – oh and get the laundry out of the dryer. At this point, people, it's time to take a stance; learn how to 'say no' and stand back from your life. It is time to stop, before you explode and, people, kid you not, I have arrived.

How did I get there? You may ask, if you care, (or if this story has any parallel at all with your life!) Quite simply: of my own accord. I sign up for everything and then get mad when I can't get it all done. I want to help; I like to show up and take part; so I say yes. Sometimes, even when I say no, they take it as yes and then we're really in a pickle. "Mrs. Jensen", the phone message went. "You will be elected to yadda yadda board on such and such a day". "Whoa!" I yelp accusingly at my answering machine. "Who the heck signed me up for that?" I'm just reaching for the phone to get a hold of my partner, (around the neck), when I realize, "No, no, sweetheart, you did that all by yourself". And then I have to scrape back in my memory bank as to what the heck it was for and why, so I can try to get out of it. Maximum overload this disease is called, and it seems to be pretty hot and heavy these days in small towns, or even just the modern world of 'Superwomen' and all who sail in her.

At the moment, I have so many jobs; ironically, I don't have time to make any money. Yeh, that's really quite funny, isn't it and amazingly sick, if you think of it. I recall a preacher once, who was so busy helping all the needy people in the world, that his own kids were neglected and grew up to be 'weirdos', or at least problematic. Now that's a parable for you. "Ooops", I say to the world outside, "can't make that appointment, folks, I've got Rotary. No, tomorrow won't work either, it's Chamber. Friday? That could work if we do it after the YMCA capital campaign … oh no, drat, that's OSBA …. What, sorry? Forget the whole darn thing? Yes, that would probably be best …" So the dialogue might go and I wonder why I'm so busy I don't notice the overdraft charges on my bank statement, the fact that the cat has left home from lack of attention, and, oh, what is that pile in the back of my car? (Oh darn; that's the freshly laundered laundry, which is now not so fresh). Life gets mad if you let it.

It stops here people. We've gone as far as we're going to go on this particular adventure. That's it. I'm leaving my life for the weekend and I won't be checking in. No phones there, anyway; so don't call me! I'm traveling down South to the wilds of Big Sur and beyond, where the fairies play, the ocean is awesome and the fogs are cool. I'm going to the land of the condor and the hippy; to places where cell phones don't work and no one needs a computer. I'm going away from myself in a sense to find out again who I really am. We all need a special spot to do that kind of thing, and I'm not sharing mine with you! (It wouldn't be so special now would it; if I was to arrive in my own special haven only to find the population of South County all trying to find the same thing).

The spot my husband and I chose is a secret little delight we found many years ago when we were looking for a shelter in a storm; in more sense than one. When life starts to get on our nerves, we yearn for a taste of that magic, a smell of the sea and we go back there to remind ourselves what it's really all about. Since there's no television, phone system or computers in our hideaway, we also have a conversation or two while we're there, which makes a change and the change makes it good.

Look inside your own lives and be honest about them, the way I try to be, when I'm not running for bust on empty. Then, if you're suffering from the same affliction, or at least feel as if you could use an escape, find a secret spot all for you and go there. It may just be the bench at the bottom of your yard, or a sandy beach with otters feasting on abalone and horses cantering along the surf. It could just be inside a book or scratching down a piece of writing. Wherever you need to go, and how far you need to travel to make it right again is where you should go; and don't let anyone tell you otherwise. If you'd like to share your adventure with me, and you don't even have to tell me where you go, I live to hear from you. The sharing makes us all feel less lonely amidst the insanity.

**Lucy loves to escape from life once in a while.**
**Sometimes even just in a bubble bath with a book.**

# FLY OUR FLAG

'Patriot's Day'. It does have a nice ring to it. When I first arrived in this country, I was surprised by all the American flags flying in front of regular homes. You don't see that where I come from – just large flag poles over royal palaces or government buildings. I found the concept a bit alien. The longer I lived here, the more I came to appreciate that the United States is a congregation of, for the most part, people who truly adore their country and all she stands for. Once I became American myself, I really got it. If I knew all the rules of flying a flag, I'd fly one myself proudly outside my own home, as if to say, British born but America chosen. I hope I'd have that right. Maybe I'll learn the etiquette one day and surprise you all.

I especially came to understand the depth of pride behind the flag, on that infamous day, September 11th, when I truly wondered if the world might be coming to an end. It has not been a subject I have been able to write about in any depth. Years on, the memory does fade somewhat, but we don't really forget, do we; we just secrete the awfulness back in a padded cell of stacked pain that once in a while gives us a jab and reminds us that it has never really gone anywhere; it's still there.

I remember the horror my husband and I felt at what we initially perceived to be a 'plane crash' into one of the towers that morning, as we watched the early news. I remember how the horror accelerated to the point of near panic when we realized that an accident had not occurred; it had been a precisely planned and executed triangle of horror that the world witnessed that morning. That framed moment of realization stands still in the memory to this day. There is life before that moment and life after – it was a defining moment in our time.

Things came back to me this 'Patriot's Day', a day when things are supposed to come back and remind us that we must never go there again. I recalled my staff crying at the newspaper in sheer panic, once the realization came over all of us of what had really happened and I wondered, at the time, if I should send them home. And then I wondered again – but for what? There was a bomb scare at the courthouse across the street that added to the panic. This was new territory for me. My sister worked for the government in downtown DC and I worried for her safety especially – phone lines were jammed for a long time, I couldn't get through to her, and, again, there were moments in time I care not to remember. My young daughter drew a colored picture of airplanes crashing into and people jumping out of buildings that I had forgotten until this year, but kept somewhere tucked away, not for public display but private reflection. I do remember being almost grateful that my mother had died in 2000, not a year later in 2001. The horror of that day would have grieved her more than I can say. I was glad, at least, she was spared that, having been spared so little a year earlier. There were many, many things that came back to me this time on this remembrance of the year we were attacked, that had not come back to me before.

Memory is funny that way. Perhaps she protects you until you are best able to deal with it. Maybe your brain only allows to filter what you can properly process – the rest is forced to wait for another time – like grief, horror and other extremes of feeling. This year was, perhaps, my time to open the subject and look at all I had put away in storage, not knowing quite what to do with it.

'Patriot's Day' is here and we have come some way in awareness of our new world, the way we have to live with eyes in the back of our heads and a glance around at things we still need to learn. Whether it is traveling on an airplane, dealing with new levels of security on all levels of life, or simply flying your flag and getting all that that means, we are living in a different world this 'Patriot's Day' than we certainly were back in 2001. However, many are still proudly flying their cherished flags the same way they were doing back then on that day and cherishing all that goes along with it. May we never forget.

**Lucy is a proud dual National.**

# YOU CAN TELL A LOT ABOUT A PERSON BY THEIR LIPSTICK

I know I have said this before, but adults do not laugh enough. Ever. Once in a while, in the course of a regular work day, you can have a really good giggle; and oh boy, when you do, it does a body good. You can almost feel your facial muscles waking up after a long winter's hibernation.

A friend walks in the office. "Aren't you supposed to be at work?" We immediately laid into her for fun; as you do. It was a weekday morning. "I needed to take a half-day just for me," she said. "You know – Starbucks and make up, that kind of thing." I could not ever remember taking a half day off for coffee and lipstick, but I was intrigued; it was a concept. "You can tell a lot about a person by their lipstick," she went on, producing her rather sad and flattened version and her explanation of endeavoring to be all things to all people at all times, hence the flat lipstick. "Now you," she wagged her finger accusingly at our office manager, "would have the kind that comes to a perfect point, nothing flattened on the sides." We laughed, knowing that she had hit the nail entirely on the head there! And what kind of a lipstick person was I, I wondered; if this formula was to work for everyone. I set about thinking I would have to check my lipsticks in my spare time and figure it out for myself. I doubt my sides come to a perfect point, ever; that's all I could surmise at the time.

In the meantime, I have no time for lipstick analysis and I can't even blame real estate. Without even having the slightest intention of going there, I have become entangled by social networking and the pitfalls that such a web can weave. I'm a people pleaser, what can I say. And what kind of a lipstick does a people pleaser own? Probably one that other people would like to also use and you'd let them.

For the longest time, I have popped in and out of the 'My Space' web site to chat to one of my oldest friends who treats the web site as an equally old friend. I have so little interest in being there, if the truth were known, that I haven't even bothered to put up a picture of myself let alone any information. It is just our little private chat room where we visit and share secrets, she and I.

Then, all of a sudden, another friend invites me to join 'Face Book', another electronic social arena. "Everyone I know is on there," she twittered. "You can look up old friends, make new ones – it's such fun!" I was only mildly curious at the time and immediately got busy, as usual, and otherwise diverted. Then I received another invite for the same thing. I wonder - if I ignore it - will the person on the other end get a message that I ignored the invitation; or would they be so busy inviting other friends of friends to be friends that I would slip through the cracks and they'd never notice? Would my silence be tantamount to saying, "no thanks – I don't like you, never have, never will and, no, of course I don't want to be friends"? If I then saw that person out in the street or at a function, would they whisper to their colleagues that they have no idea why I have such a problem with them and that I was just a mean and despicable human being for being so openly cruel on 'Face book'? We wouldn't want to go there, would we, for the sake of a quick email response and confirmation that yes, of course, I'd love to be friends? Alright, so I accept the invitation to be their friend. Won't take a minute and then we will be done with it. They'll probably forget then that I ever existed and I will fade back into cyber oblivion, where I mostly belong.

Another email pops up. "Julie is friends with John who is friends with you. Julie invites you to be friends with Julie." What? Are we back in kindergarten again? What a dilemma! Every second email is an invitation to make more friends than I would ever have time for if I were to live three lifetimes.

"Hey!" a former colleague pops up from a darker part of my past. "Whatcha been doing for the last 10 years? Send pix." I mean really – how are you supposed to respond to that? If former colleagues had actually turned into real friends, then we would be emailing or talking on the phone like regular buddies as an ongoing thing, not pop up after a decade and say, "hey, how's it going?" Perhaps I don't have enough time on my hands for all of this idle banter. Maybe I am just too old and too ornery to really give a flying fish about any of it; but it is a social movement, I can tell you that, and, if you are not really careful, it could become a full time occupation that entirely consumes you.

"Babe! Put a picture up!" I get another email splurt in my mail box. "Babe?" I have never responded to that from any one and who, if I had any extra for the taking, is trying to get a hold of my friendship now?

"John Hernandez is asking you to be his friend," the message read. John who? I cast about in the dark recesses of my past and tried to come up with some one of that name who might ring a bell. This networking stuff will give you a brain work out, I can tell you that! There was a John Hendes who worked at the hotel where I worked in Louisiana way back when at the end of the 1980's. I remember him mostly because he had a huge lisp and couldn't say my name right, so he just called me 'ma'am' to save us all embarrassment. I don't think he would have reason to chat with me about anything. So who would this be? I elected to ignore Mr. Hernandez and see what kind of an impact this deliberation might have on my life.

Lipstick? I really must take a look at what I have and what kinds of slopes and flat areas I possess in the recesses of my make up purse. I do know that I never throw anything away until it is past time and the same probably goes for my lipsticks. As for friends; I don't throw any of those away either, unless they were never really friends to begin with. And, as for social networking, maybe I just need to come back with some thing really bizarre to scare away the folks who have too much time on their hands. How about asking them about their lipsticks; that might do it! John Hernandez would most likely immediately retract his invitation to be my friend and the old work colleague would instantly evaporate from my computer in-box.

**Lucy tries to keep up with all this social media banter. How on earth does a person keep it all in check?**

# MARRIAGE TAKES SOME WATERING

Watching a swan-couple glide sweetly and harmoniously along an English river this summer, as they metaphorically held hands until eternity, recently brought to mind a question: are we mere humans, like swans, really made for this 'til death us do part marriage lark? Swans, doves, road runners and other more tolerant breeds seem to be able to make it together for life. When their partner dies, they forever wander the area where their loss occurred in dreamy grief-filled state. Remember that they do not, however, have the ability to speak in the way that we do and therefore communicate in the way that we do or do not in some cases; which strikes me, in some ways, of considerable benefit. In fact, it could explain the longevity of their link.

Marriage between two people can be tough; no matter how you color it; a constant work in progress. I look at the wedding announcements in the paper full of white froo-froo and glossy sickly smiles. "Oh yeh," I say to myself, quite often. "Wait until the honeymoon's over!" Even if you *are* married to Superman, as I claim to be; even, good ol' Clark in his appealing tights can get on your wick on occasion. He can ignore you, when he's supposed to be talking to you, do one chore when you really need him to do another, not pay attention when he's supposed to and pay too much when you'd really rather he not. As mere mortals, we can miscommunicate daily on so many levels it's not even funny; and that's just the beginning. Digging back in your mind and recalling where the two of you came from; now that is downright dangerous. Do you dare to remember the adrenalin rush of dating and not being able to eat in front of one another; the high romanticism of the wedding and the rose-colored vision of your future together? In time, the bloom fades; it has to. You cannot live together day in, day out and not have the ardor pale a little, the fire turn to the warmth of a comfortable, less passionate, familiarity between you. Probably more the rule as opposed to the exception, if people were really honest, (which they are sometimes not in the matters of the heart!) Faced with dirty socks, piles of bills, another chore not completed in a timely fashion; all this and many more insignificant details can make the engine miss on a regular basis, as it were.

And, before you know it, you're wondering to yourself if the flame between you has forever been extinguished. You can barely speak to one another without tripping up on yourself; things get very awkward. You call said significant other at work and then wish you hadn't. In a very short period of time, you swiftly begin to doubt it all, the whole package. You see trouble on the horizon in the form of Barbie, and she's after your man, or Ken, your woman, depending on your perspective. Barbie's on her way to throw her skinny self into his lonesome arms and give him some of that ardor from way back when in the memory reserves; those sun-kissed days before the mortgage, the kids, the debts, the land mines in the yard; the life full of detail of miniscule importance in the larger scheme of things.

When the word "split" is uttered between you; sometimes that can put a stop to it right there and then, and you can quickly get a grip on the chasm that is being created here. Sometimes it depends on how far apart you've allowed yourselves to get and for how long. Sometimes, the concept can hit you on the head like a frying pan and make you wake up to your life and what really matters. Does it really matter that the shelf you want hung is still sitting on the floor waiting for its new life? Is it of huge consequence that the one thing that was the priority for you does not hold such enormous importance to some one else? What really matters are the basics of love, companionship, caring. Pry into your heart: do you still love this person? Ask yourself if you honestly do and what does that truly mean, in any case. Do you still like living with them? Another toughie! Are they good for you? Should have asked myself that one in the first marriage! Soul searching is an occupation that most of us make little time for. We race our way through our schedule-rich hours, not imagining life without that particular person, or consequences for letting things get completely out of hand in our personal life, because, after all, we have a meeting to go to. The word "split" can rouse so many of those key questions and move your mind to a vision of the future without said key person. Surprisingly enough, this is a very healthy exercise.

A wise woman once told me that men and women are completely and utterly different. "Well, duh," was my response.

She went on to clarify that each sex is only really capable of so much and that our expectations of one another are simply, consistently, too high. Pause. I think to myself. True? We cannot expect to have a husband, lover, friend, handyman, father and some- time individual in their own right all wrapped up in one perfect little package. That package does not exist and, if we force the issue, we may be sorry. Basic marriage 101: do not expect so much. Get what you think you're missing out on in other ways. And I'm not talking about infidelity. If your wife is a lousy communicator, talk more to your family or friends. If your husband is a lousy fix-it guy, hire a guy that is; and so on. It has to stop the nagging and the demeaning; it must reduce the stress and make the home a more all-round happy place to be. It may even save your union and stop your kids from becoming another statistic.

"Marriage is like a plant," my father once said. "Rip it up by the roots and see how quickly it dies". Yes, like a plant in the arid soils of California, a relationship does need watering; truthfully, every day. It needs pruning and tending to. It needs talking to and it totally needs your undivided attention. It needs to know it is loved. Say there yonder in busy-busy land! How's your garden growing?

**Lucy is a long-time married broad.**

# PIECES OF LIVES

When I first got into real estate in California, I had visions of cruising out on a sunny afternoon and showing a house or two to well-qualified buyers who were ready and able to sign on any dotted line I presented to them, there and then, cash in hand. I had dreams of helping innocent first time home buyers with the largest purchase of their natural lives and the gratitude they would feel towards me when I handed over the glistening keys to their slice of the American dream, (and they then asked me to be godmother to their first born). I had fantasies of being self-employed and gliding around in fancy cars, taking long lunches and kicking back in luxury and counting my many beans, while the workers I left behind in their Fortune 500 fortresses sweated over the 8-6 schedule at the office, fought the traffic home and went into a deep sweat Sunday night at the prospect of their motivational Monday morning meeting. Yes, a few of those thoughts actually did run through my over-active imagination and out the other side, when I left the corporate world a few years ago and went to work for myself. I look back sometimes and laugh at myself – which is very important for us to always do, especially if we are employed by ourselves.

What I had not envisioned was the constancy of work when you are self-employed. It is never over and you never leave it at the door. You carry it around with you in ever-increasing brief cases, bags, baggage and anything else which will handle a mound of paper. You transport it from your home to your car to your lunch break, back to your home and the spare bed where all the paper will proceed to get mushed onto the floor by the overactive cat who hasn't seen you all day and has no concept or caring of the life of the self-employed, where you return home to eat and change, only to swiftly move on to some more very important work of the day. You also take the work to bed with you and it can and does plague you in your dreams.

You buy all amounts of techno-equipment to make yourself more efficient from the Smart Phone to the lap top to the Wireless to the navigational. We are so systemized these days it's amazing that we can choose an outfit in the morning without consulting one of our systems. I recall my early days in newspaper when we would carry around a pocket full of change to call clients from the call boxes and fix up our appointments. Can you imagine doing that today? If my cell phone leaves my side for just a second, I am distraught – like a mother who has lost her child – and I cannot function until I find it again. I remember the arrival of the pager and how self-important business people back then would carry the black object in a special carrier on their belt, making sure to hitch up their sweater just a bit so everyone could see they wore a pager and were, therefore, very, very important and successful people. We thought we had really arrived in the newspaper industry when we were each "given" a pager that we did not have to pay for - unless we lost it - and we were told that we would be "regularly paged" throughout the day, as if it were a good thing. There was that particularly bad time when my office was paging me, as if the house was on fire, and I couldn't find a phone box that worked. In some ways, that was the beginning of the end. Pagers didn't work, phone boxes no longer were reliable – they had to come up with more techno for all of us to go ballistic over. That never ends either.

Another thing I had not anticipated when I received my California real estate license in the mail was the sort of work that I might have to encounter when the blissful days of putting a sign in the ground and receiving three over-full price offers cascaded over into the market of frightened buyers, alarmed sellers and record levels of people walking away from their house payments. Back then, I had absolutely no idea that that could ever happen. My work can now consist of assisting people with cash for key arrangements so that they will peacefully vacate their homes, dealing with the aftermath of people having to leave their homes and not feeling happy about it, as well as the ultimate toughie – the eviction with the sheriff's department and squad cars all over the streets. There are always pieces of people's lives that we are forced to pick through and cast aside for "trash out", (a bank owned term when the personal property is removed from the property.) One particular case keeps coming back to me, when the former owners had refused to leave, were forced to go by the sheriff's department and had effectively tried to burn down all the walls in their house before they left. For a few scary moments, I thought they had abandoned the only thing decent left in the house, which was their tabby cat. Fortunately they came back for it. We thought they had come back for fisticuffs, but they actually came back for the cat. Incidents like that don't leave you quickly and your work always comes home with you on days like that. That was not what I signed up for.

Real estate deals with real life and real life is not always easy. Being self-employed, I am working for myself all parts of all days, unless I manage to steal some sleep if I am lucky and stay away from the ghouls which visit me sometimes in the dark. Most of us have to work and many of us choose to work for ourselves. It requires a huge balance that some of us manage and some don't. At the end of the day, it's important to be able to step back, close the office door, wash off the office work and say to one self, "I did what I could with what I had to work with." Some days that's all you can say.

**Lucy has been a licensed California REALTOR since 2003.**

# PROUD OF OLD GLORY

I have been a citizen of this fair country for a few years now, a legal resident for two decades plus, and though there have been the odd time over the years when I have been less than proud to announce to the world where I chose to lay my hat, I do have to say that this week was one for the pride books.

Trying to learn how the political system works over here has been quite a challenge that I did not entirely take on, I have to admit, until I actually had the voting rights (which was around 18 years after I actually claimed her as my home of choice.) I am therefore quite ashamed to say that I lived in these fair lands as a non-voting legal resident, listening to all the blah around election time, (voting caucuses, super delegates, what exactly is that all about?) and really wondering how regular people put their heads around it.

Fortunately, they force you to do a mini marathon of the American political system before they allow you to take the pledge of allegiance; so I did glean some info along the way to prepare me for the histrionics of late. Since I became a voting citizen, I have taken my privilege very seriously. I study the issues – however tedious - I read the ballot, I force myself to peruse other opinions and ideas before quietly selecting my own. My journey to this point has been a long and rocky one, but I'm really working on my credentials as one of the voting public, I can promise you that.

It's been quite a ride, America. No matter what side of the political fence you sit, any reasonable person needs to take a look at the Democratic race a while back, where the white woman was pitched against the black man and say, gosh we have really come a long way, haven't we, America. As a woman and a believer in freedom and equality of rights for all – always have been – I really enjoyed watching that race.

Thinking about the contest and the outcome took me back to my years in Back of Brusly, State of Louisiana, when I had almost just arrived off the boat as it were - or central London, if you really must know - and stepping inside that odd mixed community felt as if I was living out the film “Deliverance’ and hoping, daring to hope even, that I would eventually, one day, get out of there alive. For those of you not in the know, Back of Brusly was not even Brusly, not remotely the city of Baton Rouge, but merely a tiny community of 8 trailers and a bar with a boat ramp nudged up against the bayou at the end of the line, end of the road, the end of humanity in some respects. Cajun people lived there. There was some mixed breeding that had gone on over time, with the children carrying the evidence as a life-long sentence for having been born. There was a railroad track dustily crossing the road. On one side of the track were the black people, the other side the whites. I was naturally living on the white side in the trailer park, though I felt no kinship with these people. I would drive past the black shacks on my way to work and wonder at how far back I had traveled in time and proximity to civilization. I could not believe that people still lived this way. We were poor, but the blacks in the shacks were way poorer. They didn’t even have electricity; some of them not even a front door. You’d see them on the porch of a summer’s evening, sweating and scratching with their shirts off and waiting for another lifetime when things might be better. They would watch you drive past, their heads turning slowly in unison as you touched their life for a second and then left it. People told me that the black people never went back to the Back of Brusly, they never crossed the railroad track. Was it the bartender’s rifle over the bar that kept them away or the wretchedness of their expectancies when they got there? I imagine a bit of both. I have to wonder how things are there now –if the invisible line at the railroad track has faded away. Not that I would ever want to revisit that experience, having got out of there alive, (the Cajun people found me even more foreign than the black people); but I am curious as to whether time could ever really stand still in any part of our magnificent land- even in the back of Brusly – and continue to ignore how dramatically some things have changed, pervasively, entirely, and, we can only hope, for the better.

It’s Election Year again and we have a few more months of positioning, posturing and rhetoric to go – there will be a lot of talk about change and we hope, some super game plans for how to enact the further changes that need to be made. There will be debates about issues, there will be characters dug up and dragged through the mud. For sure, there will be some politics as usual, which will have the cynics among us quickly skating away from the media and praying for it all to soon be over. There also has to be a lot of fresh curiosity arising during these months ahead from our youth and newer citizens like myself who have in recent times turned up the interest level in our national politics and tried to use our vote in a responsible and forward thinking way. From my own perspective, I am looking forward to the months ahead, the many tough issues which will be on the table and the end result I hope to be a part of. I look back to an old world in Back Brusly and hope it has been demolished. I do hope those old black people on the porch without the front door have turned their faces out to the world and realized that big things have happened to us all and it's absolutely past time to cross the tracks and stand up for all that is right.

**Lucy resided in Back of Brusly on the Cajun Bayou in 1988. She hopes things have changed since then.**

# RECESSION PROOF ATTITUDE

Many folks find our local and national news programs so depressing these days that they can watch only the weather. Factoids such as tainted peanut butter the world over, job losses, crashing stocks and money worth nothing; not to mention the housing market, will take you down into the deepest depression from which it's hard to climb. There's just not that much good news to be had, if you continue to pick up the papers and glean the local news programs.

When my friend came over to visit us recently from the UK, she channel-surfed on our television stations for a few minutes and then declared that the "Weather Channel" was the only thing she could stand to watch. "At least then you can look at the East Coast from your sunny position on the West and say, look at me, aren't I the lucky one!" she commented facetiously. "Everything in the world is so depressing at the moment!" These days most people have a hard time stating that they might be the lucky ones, lest they blink and everything changes in an instant. We've seen it happen. Caution is the cousin of insecurity, and there are a lot of their other relatives around at the moment, bobbing and weaving and shifting our plates for us. Most of us watched over and over in awe the tape of the captain landing the plane into the Hudson, in amazement that, finally, there was some truly good news to report. We got all teary at the visual of the passengers standing on the wings of the fallen plane and the neighboring boats and skiffs nestled nearby to rescue anyone who might slip off the wings and give that captain a less than perfect landing score. America needs more good news stories like that.

So what do you do when our world seems all petrified currently in resolutions of pale depressing grey and never ending rivers of pessimism are floating off towards an uncertain nebulous future? You go to the city, that's what you do! That can be so good for the soul. "A change is as good as a rest," as my Granny used to say. Having spent many of my formative years in London town, I concede that, every now and then you do need a city fix in your life.

Downtown San Francisco never ceases to amaze me and always seems so welcoming, when I visit, with her arms wide open to azure blue skies and sweet sunny climes. I never get any of that cool foggy stuff I hear about up there, so I always feel positioned for a good stay from the get go. Thus far, she has never disappointed me. San Fran has to be one of my very favorite cities. She has the regular problems of cities the world over – the large population of homeless people, the bad traffic and the general-overpopulated frenzy, when you are trying to move yourself from point A to point B; but she also has oodles of personality. She has the benefit of the ocean breeze and the odd city gull cawing overhead. She has a neat downtown, bustling and bright with cable cars clanging and street bands strumming. She has nice places to stay that won't kill your credit card and a good variety of shopping, galleries and restaurants that you can happily walk to. She has a lot going for her.

My friend and I always stay in a comfortable hotel off the square, when we visit; where the staff never changes and the tea is constantly a-flowing. It has an amenable atmosphere to it, topped only by its location close to the hustle and bustle, the corner musicians and the clang of the cable car. We feel as if we are really far away from all the bad news merchants when we are there. This visit, we went to the Wharf - it was busy. People were shopping, money was changing hands. We went to the movie house, Mel's and the Cheesecake Factory. The Factory was so busy, we couldn't get a table! We shopped downtown and crammed ourselves onto cable cars – there were lots of foreigners bustling around and buying. Hey people – California is open for business, I heard her say! French, Italians, Brits – they were all there and they were feeding our economy. Mission and Market were teaming with shopping bags and purses open. From early morn to late at night, San Fran was doing quite well, thank you very much and it was good to witness. In fact, if you only watched the "Weather Channel", as we did while we were there, you would have thought that America's economy was sailing pretty sweetly along.

From the buzz of the city, we came back home with a few extra pairs of bargain shoes in our cases and a feeling of refreshment in our bones. The world was not going to end tomorrow – we ascertained that much from our trip up north. We should all be dusting ourselves off and adopting the brace position for what would surely be difficult, but not impossible times, over the course of the next few months. But survive them we would and there would be better times ahead. That much we bought back with us.

From our few days up in the city, we traveled back via Carmel, where there was nearly not a parking spot to be had in the village. We popped into the shopping center in Monterey, where the scene resembled the weekend before Christmas and we later stood in line at our local grocery store, noting the large carts packed with groceries and the distinct lack of pessimism in the air. In the store, I noticed people sporting bags of chips, cans of beer, quarts of ice cream and more Unnecessities – all signs that folks had excess dollars to splurge on fancy extras. This is not to say that everyone has money to spare and our times are not still tough ones for many; but this was just a snap shot of my experience over a few short days that I think is important to share, when much of what we are currently absorbing with our daily bread is the negative topped with some really gloomy economic forecasts.

Perhaps it's time to tune away from the weather channel and back to the real world – maybe she's not as bad as some would have us believe and we will all recover to see another day and spend another dime towards our nation's economic recovery.

**Lucy noticed the recession start mid-2005 in her industry and imagines it's past time for our media to be full of good news.**

# REPORTING FOR DUTY

I opened my official envelope with cautious finger-tips. It was from the Monterey County court system and therefore required a little more respect than just my regular bills. It was an official jury summons and I had never in my life received one before. Having completed my US Citizenship a mere 21 months ago, this acknowledgement of my pledge of allegiance had taken its time in coming; but here it was in official seal. Here was one of the great privileges of citizenship; I was going to be allowed to rule on people's lives, have a hand in enacting the will of the Constitution – "Liberty and Justice for All" – this was going to be such a big day for me; or weeks possibly, if I got selected for a big trial.

I cleared my calendar accordingly around that particular day; my first appearance in court. In my diary, it looked like a big white empty pond amidst a sea of intense scribbling seaweed; but there it stood proud and available; ready for service. "You have to show up to court, man. No excuses," my husband told me empathically, as I grumbled about managing to fit my life around my jury duty. "Otherwise they arrest you." That was frightening. I did not want my first day of service to my country to end up in the slammer in blue denim. That would not be the way to go at all. I pondered my outfit for the day. You could show up, apparently, and they would still not choose you. I decided that I should not be too severe or professional looking, or equally too eccentric and wacky; or even too "British", as I have been accused of on occasion. I would go in sedate mode; Mrs. Normal American Person.

The important envelope sat proudly on my desk, and I kept checking and re-checking it to make sure that I hadn't misread the date, or somehow got my months mixed up. "You are advised to call on 5pm the night before your service is due to start," the message read rigidly and call promptly I did. "Lucy Yensen" – they mispronounced my last name, which wasn't a great start. "Juror number 0087634." (Would that also be my prison number if I failed to show?) "Thank you for your service. You are excused." What service? Excused! Excuse me? But I had so much to contribute to the legal system! Some one as opinionated and educated as myself could be of such great benefit to the scales of justice when analyzing the wiles of the human soul. They just didn't know it. "That's it for 2 years, man," my husband said helpfully when I informed him they couldn't use my services. I felt a little cheated of my rights to serve. They didn't know what they were missing.

All this build-up to my non-service – my brush with the law from the other side of the bench – moved me onto ponder the other forms of service that I have performed throughout my various chequered careers. I started waiting tables when I was about 13 and growing up in a small coastal town on the east coast of England. I will never forget the large bowl of Oxtail, (very brown), soup which I spilled over the carpet and the pink silk dress of a very large lady I was trying to serve. Just one of those things; never forgot it. There was also the memorable event when I was working in hotel marketing in Louisiana and we had booked in a huge tour group of French-Canadian tourists to arrive exactly a week after they thought they were supposed to arrive. I say 'we' as a matter of course. It was actually entirely my error in incorrectly booking the date that caused the entire fiasco. That was one of the scarier times. (Ever wanted the ground to truly open up and swallow you on the spot?) Then there was the time I was working at the security desk of the State Department and I failed to recognize a rather key diplomat, requiring that he produce his pass and not taking no for an answer, (yes, things were a little looser in those days). Ah service; I've really done quite a lot of it, paid and not so paid, and here I am, still really rather bemused as to why they discounted a perfectly service-oriented member of the American Citizenship Class of 2005, when she obviously had left such a strong trail behind her.

**Lucy has still never been selected to serve as a juror.**

# SPELL CHECKING

"Greivance" is a serious word – the attorney began her power point presentation on professional standards and grievance filings for the REALTOR training class with a howling spelling mistake that she went on to repeat three more times throughout the course of the class, without even noticing. And this was an attorney. "These are an unprecedented time in our industry," she went on to say, and I kept expecting Ashton Kutcher to leap around the corner and wake several of us up with the "You're Punked" line! With that level of education, you can only imagine the hurdles the attorney must have climbed over to reach the bar with this monumental spelling disability on her back. This lady was clever, but she could spell no better than a fifth grader.

I was unsettled. Oddly enough, this meeting coincided with the 'Spelling Bee' weekend where the 4$^{th}$ and 5$^{th}$ graders gather their finest at a local school to spell it out to the last. I remember so well coaching my daughter for her "Spelling Bee" performance two years in a row – to the finals no less - and realizing what a lesson it was for all of us; not least my husband who still can't spell his way out of a paper bag – (he is not a reader). Though I was always a pretty decent speller in my time – (I have always been a reader) - that helps – my grammar was consistently poor. It was an aspect of language arts that didn't grab me as it should have when my brain was young and formative. My English teacher back then had no interest for it either; he preferred to let children express themselves in flowing prose, however they so wanted. So it was not until I studied Latin that I was required to have an understanding of the structure of my given language. What a tough apple that was to bite back then! Even now, I draw a blank as to what is required mid sentence, as a pause – just ask my editor!

But back to my disturbing experience with the attorney! Look around you and see how many people bother to pick up a dictionary these days. Unless they are engaged in a to-the-death "Scrabble" tournament - as my family usually is when they get together - why would they? Spell check is available inside most computers – take it or leave it. Most people will probably not call you on it. Examine why people use email as an "ez-speak", a modern day vernacular, never bothering to capitalize the 'I' or add a full stop to complete a thought. Even my pedantic father – a professor of history no less and very old school – can send an email in entirely lower case letters, without a comma in sight. He does know better, but he likes the casual forum of the email. Heck, he's not writing a dissertation on an important historical figure, or spelling out instructions to his stock broker, he's sending a quip to his daughter, so why not relax, linguistically speaking? I know I do it myself, but I'm not sure that it is a good thing. Once in a while, I will pull up my socks and get real with the capitals and the semi-colons. I notice that is mostly when I am sending a serious conversation, more like a formal letter, or responding to a client who doesn't yet know me. Who am I trying to impress? Why don't I just do it all the time, as I used to be required to do throughout my schooling? I can just imagine my Latin teacher – Miss Stubbs – tolerating the type of language I scatter throughout my communiqués these days. I would not only have a lot of her red ink to contend with, but I can see a certain Saturday afternoon detention in my rear view mirror.

Texting is a whole other language. "When u cum" my sister sent me a text from Turkey to the USA – amazing that, the extraordinary technology of our day and how we have come to view it as being completely ordinary. My sister has a Bachelor of Arts degree, as do I. She is also, scarily, an English teacher. "9 June lunch' I replied and stopped to look again at the dialogue once it had 'pinged' the announcement of its departure from me back to her. We had had a whole conversation between America and Turkey, across the time zones, with no punctuation and not a whole sentence between us, in the space of about a minute. Though the language was convoluted and not really English at all, I'm convinced that we both had understood the dialogue and we'd have no problem communicating in that way again.

"Face Book" or 'My Space' – now there rules a whole other language. These social media forums are like a texting mecca of instant communication with the danger of feelings and photos in the mix, of being moved from some one's "tops", (top of their favored list), to their "bottoms", (bottom of their favored list,) in just the stroke of a key, of being 'friended' or 'unfriended' in the blink of an eye. I noted to my daughter that I was okay being consistently on her "bottoms", because then I could never be disappointed. I watch that whole social networking lark with the caution and fascination of some one who had grown up needing a quarter in order to call some one they wanted to talk to – who had never been surrounded by any of the constant and instantaneous electronic gratification and conversation as our youth of today. In my home growing up, we had one house phone on a long cord, eternally within hearing reach of my parents. We sent letters as our form of written communication. No portable phones, no instant message, no flippant emailing back and forth. Is all of this immediacy a good thing? Probably not. Can we do anything about it? Most likely not, unless you use its removal as a punishment! It's how our children function these days and, whether you know it or not, they are probably exercising this form of conversation with all of the people they consider their nearest and dearest most minutes of most days.

With all of that said, I do hope our modern educators are correcting our children when they spell 'grievance' as our attorney did, or forget to capitalize when a capital is required in the language that we should hold so dear. I'm sure they are, but I do worry about the anarchy of our language and whether ez-speak will eventually become the accepted vernacular of the modern world. The possibility of our attorney communicating with us, "when u cum class", and us accepting that as a regular way to enquire when we were coming to class is really quite frightening. If we are not careful with our language, she will creep away under a rock, the way that Latin did, and become a dead language of books and church with the rest of civilization functioning on a diet of ez-speak and texting lingo, splattered with not a comma or a consonant in sight. Thoughts, anyone? I know what the under 18's would tell me, but then maybe they are not really qualified to say, not truly knowing what we know in their young years.

**Lucy is a former Latin student.**

# TAKE A BATH

"I wish we could find a way to slow it all down," bemoaned husband over the holiday season. "Time goes by too fast." And it does, without a doubt. We helter-skelter our way through the hurricanes of time, rarely pausing to even take snap shots of our lives, let alone stop to take inventory of all we have to be very grateful for.

Looking back at my mother's era, it seems to me that she had more time for all of those things. She didn't work outside the home. She would take us to school, do a little gentle food shopping for fresh goods to eat that day, return home to her house which was cleaned by some one else to admire her garden which was cultivated by some one else; take time for herself, whether to paint a canvas, stitch a patchwork quilt or merely sit in a sunny window and read a book. She had, seemingly, captive hours of peace to give back to herself and make herself whole, before she picked us up from school and put herself back to "work" as Mum and wife.

It seems to me that my generation is expected to do all of that, pretty much, plus work full time outside of the home. It's no wonder that many of us need medication just to get through our mega days; never mind that the quilt never gets patched, or the canvas painted; those things we reserve for dreams of our retirement, when we will awaken late to sun-kissed bedrooms and wonder what we shall do with all the unfilled hours before us in our day. Realistically, by the time we are blessed with "retirement", you can bet that we will either be raising our grandkids, be forced to continue to work outside the home because we won't be able to make our bills otherwise, (social security being bankrupt by then), or be in such poor health that retirement means nothing; we are just waiting to die and, the quicker the better, since the price of coffins just seem to be going up too. That may be a rather pessimistic and extreme outlook for some one so usually half-full about most things; but it's one way of looking at the state of our universe and the train many of us seem to be riding on.

So what is to be done with what we have to work with? Take more baths, I say; that's a good start. There is something about lounging in a bath on a cold winter's evening that is so luxurious you can practically taste it. You set your own scene with a closed door, bubble bath and candles, a good book or magazine, a glass of wine or a cup of cocoa. You take time for you and you replenish yourself. Most people will not bother you while you are in the bath; or, at least, they should know better. After your bath and your slice of peace, you'll feel fortified, as if you had bought yourself the loveliest gift; and you have. It is called the gift of time; and the gift of time to yourself is also called 'giving back'. Play hooky from your daily grind; it'll improve your sense of humor if nothing else.

Make time to read good stuff. Turn off the box and limit yourself to programming that really does something for you; either it gives you vital information or it diverts you in some significant way, or makes you laugh; that's important too. Otherwise, turn it off. Life's short. After I graduated from college, I made a pact with myself that I would only ever read something that grabbed me. If it bores me after a few pages, I put it down. In college we had to keep going; no matter what. One of the benefits of being older, for sure; no tedious college texts!

A friend gave me a tremendous gift for Christmas; thank you, friend. It's a book called 'Simple Abundance', which has thoughts for every day of the year to help pick you up and move you forward towards living in a state of increased grace every day. Sound like a utopia? I enjoy picking up the book daily; generally as the sun is creeping up over the mountain and seeing what I can glean from the page, what I can extract from my life's ledger to take me on a better path as a nicer person that day, or at least a more content one. Find a gift for yourself, as I found through my friend, and pass it along to another; then it becomes a gift double given. Now that is shelf life!

Find a passion, a hobby, to help you get your mind away from the tedium of everyday obligations and lift you up to your natural born talent. Give yourself a little time to work on your passion, be self-indulgent, as it were; let your creativity flow like a stream and see where it ends up. It may be that what was your passion can become your source of financial settlement; that inadvertently your working to live can evolve into working for life; that should be what we are all striving for; but in the meantime, take a nice bath; why not.

**Lucy thinks that there is nothing nicer than a hot bath to put everything in its proper place.**

# TECHNOBABES

I distinctly remember being totally impressed, circa. 1975, by the inaugural visit of the electronic calculator to our classroom.

"This does not mean that you do not have to learn how to add and subtract," our teacher said primly, to some resounding "boos" from the raucous young audience, "On the contrary. But it does mean that you will be able to very quickly verify your work and check formulas. This is an important development for the future," she said with confidence.

Little did I know back then that that would be the beginning of a life-long techno journey for myself; mostly a struggle to accept all that I could never know, because my brain just doesn't seem to work that way. Though I resisted that scary machine back then, just as I later resisted the electric typewriter – with my father insisting that I take typing classes, because "you have to be able to type to do just about any job" – I have gradually, over the years, adapted to living with machinery, some easier to operate than others, and even, on occasion welcomed the odd machine into my home and co-existed with it in a semi-cheery way.

I love my personal computer – as long as it is behaving itself and not refusing to shut down or refusing to save. I like to use my email, save word documents and even download and mess with the odd photo. That is about the extent of my tech-expertise. Beyond that, and I panic. During a recent argument with my machine over its refusal to close out its anti-virus or shut down how it was supposed to, I realized, once again, what a techie-dumbo I still am; years away from my first encounter with the electronic calculator or even my first pc.

"You are trying to shut down with things still open," my semi-techie sister pointed out. "It has got stuck." She closed me out, as it were, one window at a time, and all was quickly well again in my tech-world, to my greatest relief.

"It needs de-fragging," said my brother-in-law, I assume discussing some serious computer surgery that the machine was now in desperate need of, as he tapped around in untouched pastures of hard and soft drives.

"Oh great," I sighed, as I tried to download some photos after all these many computer operations were dealt with by various different semi-tech folks who paraded through my office, which was also temporarily masquerading itself as a visitor's room. "It's broken again!" Somehow my camera was now refusing to have a conversation with the now unstuck, de-fragged machine. The techie clan gathered quickly to my side to point out, with a bit of a snorting scorn they probably couldn't help, that the camera cable was actually unplugged.

"Whoever wants to use my computer, please make sure to leave it as you find it," I squawked to anyone who was still in the vicinity. Deep down, I was a little mortified that I remain still so deeply tech-stupid that I cannot even recognize when there is an unplugged cable.

And there's probably little hope for me now. I will always choose simplicity in any type of machine, I want as few buttons on my camera as feasibly possible, I have never been able to program a VCR, ( and now they're obsolete), and I have decided that most Sony machines were made by men for engineers and should be strictly avoided; (the case in point being why I gave my very expensive Sony video/camera to my son after it had sat for two years in the closet and I still needed the instructions to turn it on).

Recently my daughter reached the pinnacle of her money-saving goals in life, and had saved up enough cash to purchase her very own lap top. Once she had secured all the various boxes and disks and cables that one needs when one buys one of those super-tech items - (don't believe the sales price on the circular; it adds up to way more than that) - we drove home and I stressed who the heck was going to put together these pieces of modern wonder without the whole chabang at least blowing up. I shouldn't have worried. By the time we got home, my daughter and her friend had pretty much got everything ready to go, except for the router – whatever that is - which she explained she would need to set up when we got home. As I watched her cruising around this fine machine, with all its bells and whistles, now successfully installed and running its various programs, I realized that the tech generation, i.e. people way younger than me, is completely at home with machinery of all kinds. They have been raised on it, from x-boxes to cell phones to computers. My generation had to learn all of it later on in life; and some of us will never really get there. We went to school with paper and pens. We used notebooks, we got carpal tunnel syndrome – some of us - from all the handwriting, and learned to count in our heads – some of us. We put records on the record players and we recorded music on tape cassettes. We used regular film in easy, back-opening cameras and processed our films at the drug store. This generation has spell-check, digital everything, "PSP" machines, photo phones, email phones and quick and instantaneous everything in their fast lives.

I try to keep up; really I do, while endeavoring to keep it all as simple as possible. Why should I learn how to put music on my IPOD when my daughter gets a kick out of me not knowing and, consequently, totally handles all of it for me? So take what you really need from this modern day life and leave the rest for the techno kids; that's what I pledge to do. If I really tried to get my head around the latest gadget, I'd get with the program, pass the test in my own mind at least and already be technologically obsolete by breakfast time.

**Lucy is okay with all that she will never know in the tech world.**

# THE AGE OF SERVICE

In today's economy, there are so many uncontrollables weaving towards us erratically on any given day, that we might easily lose sight of what we can still control in our desperate efforts to stay afloat, make the bills, cut the corners or keep the doors open. We might forget, for instance, that regardless of the world situation, people will always do business with people they like. It's not just about the money or the deal. We also might bypass the importance that it is not the product or the service that will make people keep coming back to you for your goods and services, but how you make them feel. If you walk in a store and they forget to thank you or give you no eye contact, you might forgive them once. The second time, you might notice and hold in memory. The third time – as in my particular case – you will simply shop elsewhere; whether you just need a gallon of milk or a full shop. There is a certain wine tasting room locally that I will never frequent, whether or not I might like their wines. I didn't like the way they made me feel when I walked in the door that one day. (And I won't even go there with how they made my friend feel.) I haven't been back since. There's a restaurant that takes an hour to bring you your food and has no apology or explanation for it at all. I just don't like the way they make me feel. If I sound like a record with a scratch, it's intentional. If I think there are many, many businesses that could give themselves such a shot in the arm if they just examined the above concept, I think many of them might just do a lot better in the future; recession or not.

Customer service, or lack of it; what a concept! Go back in your mind to the corner shop of yester-year; the five and dime, the local store that would lend your mother a few vital items until pay day to feed her family, the center of many people's universe during tough times. There was a mutual relationship of trust and reward back then that worked. We now live in such an instantaneously gratuitous society where everything is expected to be fast and immediate. You'd better have the cheeseburgers fresh and ready by the time I get from the order box at the drive in to the pick up window one minute later, or I'm going to be sighing deeply and wondering why I hadn't just got out of my car and walked into the restaurant. If I don't have the money to pay for said cheeseburgers, you're not going to trust that I will honestly bring you back your cash for the burger, when I get paid. Luckily that is no problem! If I don't have the money, I will simply give you a credit card. If I don't have any credit on said credit card, then the cheeseburger will be but a memory by the time you realize that. My charges for being over limit will also be about ten times the cost of my cheeseburger in addition, but we don't worry about that in our society! Can you see a pattern of destruction emerging here?

Serving the customer, such a concept! My office manager tells me that, instead of saying 'you're welcome or de nada," when a customer thanks us for our help, we should respond that "we are here to serve you." Old-fashioned though that may sound, maybe she is right and we don't thank our customers enough. For, after all, one happy customer will generally create two or three more and who really knows how many more besides. There is an arena of optimum business growth that occurs when some one you trust tells you to trust some one they themselves have learned to trust. It is a glorious and unsolicited thing.

In the olden days, when I used to work in newspaper advertising, one of my jobs was to go out and personally call on the customers. They expected it. We visited, we talked about their business, their lives, their kids – sometimes these relationships developed personal connections even. We would go way beyond what their upcoming ad campaign would be, but that was part of their personal service. If I called on them one week and they told me they weren't going to be doing advertising with me anymore, this was normally not an arbitrary decision; but something life changing. They were leaving the area, selling the business – disconnects of that sort. No one ever told me it was because they weren't getting any service from me.

With our remote controls worn out and our systems obsolete, my husband and I recently opted to change our satellite television provider. This was after an 8 year "relationship" with the previous provider. This "relationship" had solely consisted of them setting us up with the original equipment moons ago, and then collecting the fees from our credit card every month. That was the extent of our service. Once I saw what the new provider could give us for less money, I was angry. Why had our original provider not given us an ounce of customer service over the years? They had simply assumed our relationship was still good every month, when we hadn't cancelled the credit card, and hoped for the best. They didn't ever care that our equipment was obsolete and we should have received some kind of customer longevity appreciation discount long ago, not to mention the fact that our remote controls were worn out. Ironically, we have had more calls from them since we cancelled their service than ever before. Another interesting comment on customer service! Hello, take care of the customers you have first! Such a concept!

Think about it! How often do you get customer service satisfaction these days? Most of the time – especially on the telephone – you are inconvenienced with auto answer machines prompting you for the reason for your call and trying to avoid having you speak to anyone with a pulse. These machines are seldom set up for people with foreign accents anyway, so I find myself trying to trick the machine into thinking I am native; a task in itself, especially if I am laughing at the time. The one time I was nicely surprised was when I needed some help with my IMAC and called the Apple help line. "Apple, can I help you?" the voice answered quickly. I paused, thinking this robot sounded spookily like a human being. It was. This live person was present and available to help me with my challenge. In fact, she stayed on the line with me for over an hour while she sorted out my problem and I was back in business. We even chatted about who we were and where we lived. Customer service like that will keep you a customer forever, regardless of cost. She has the knowledge, I have the money. She needs me, I need her; it's a wonderful thing. I'd call her again anytime. She knows computers, I don't want to. Now that is customer service. Another refreshing call to Apple, about my blue tooth this time, came back with an unusual response. "Oh yes, that seems to have a design flaw they're working on. You might as well buy a different brand for now." I appreciated the honesty.

If you are wondering what to do with your small business and keep your people coming back, it is really very simple. Treat them as you like to be treated. If you are a restaurant, serve them decent food in a timely fashion. If you are a satellite TV provider, don't imagine that your customers are sheep and will keep paying even after their remote control has worn out. If you are a corner store, be friendly with your customers, thank them for coming, look them in the eye and ask after their daughter. It is the simple human communication that will make all the difference in the world. If you look back to the five and dime and the corner shop that extended credit to pay day, things have changed, but really not at all. It's all about the way you make the customer feel and probably always will be.

**Lucy loves to get a live person.**

# THE MODERN WORLD

In the modern day world, it seems to me we have way too much of it; way too much of everything, in fact. Our days are spent cascading from one late appointment to another. We drive too fast, speak too quickly, eat on the run, yell at our children for no good reason, we multi-task in desperation, trying to fit it all in and get it all done, all in the course of one day. We can eat, put on make-up, talk on the phone and drive simultaneously, sometimes also writing down a vitally important phone number at the same time. We can do all of that without wondering for a second what would happen if the system were to break down and all of that not be achieved at the designated time. What would happen if you crashed the car while applying your mascara, or if you knocked some one over while you were desperately trying to retrieve that vitally important phone number which had just fallen on the floor? Most of us fly through this modern world without a thought for any of the ‘what ifs’. If something happens to make us stop and think, we consider it an inconvenience, a barrier to us getting to where we need to get to in the allotted time frame. Most of us don’t look for the signs that everything is rapidly tumbling down hill on an ice slope and the mess at the bottom will be a culmination of many years in the making.

I recently needed to stop the car crash, which I looked back over my shoulder and realized had become my daily life. The red and blue lights started flashing behind me and my brain suddenly advised me that I was in overload mode and I needed to quickly make a change before something really, really bad happened.

After my mini-melt-down, when I had no choice but to cease and cease immediately, I was forced to stop and think and not multi-task the rollercoaster, as I cascaded down the slippery slope. I was clinging on for dear life and I came to realize that the body is a machine; for many of us a vitally well-oiled machine and it is capable of more than we will ever truly realize. It also has its limits, and many of us push those limits on a daily basis. Watch out! Your brain will tell you when it’s time for the body and brain to take a time out. I learned that recently.

I thought that my sleeplessness was just a sign that I had had enough sleep. Wrong. If you go to bed so exhausted you don't even remember closing your eyes and you wake up with the brain racing a thousand miles an hour at 2am, then that is not a normal thing. Take heed.

If you think that working until 7pm at the office without taking a lunch break is a normal and acceptable thing, or you go through the course of the day without checking outside to see if the sky is blue or grey, and then you return home to eat a quick bite standing up at the kitchen countertop, do a quick head count of the inhabitants of the house, and then go back to work – then there is something very wrong with the quality of your life. Stop and see what you can do to level out the playing field, give back some of your work, prioritize your life with some you-time indispersed into it in a more civilized manner.

If you don't have time to go to the grocery store and your child is forced to have her cereal without milk in the morning, and you are okay with that, then there is something very wrong with your current situation. What your child ingests is almost entirely up to you. If you only have 'Hot Cheetos' in the cupboard, they will be able to make an entire dinner out of the 'Hot Cheetos' and not have a problem with it. You should have a problem with it. Some one should be providing a well balanced meal for your child every evening – their health and well-being depends on it. The other option is not okay.

If you haven't picked up a book, taken your dogs for a walk, watched a movie or even had a conversation with a nearest and dearest in a while, sit up and pay attention, people. You may be headed for the same place I was just a few days ago. It's a place you can find yourself in very quickly, without really any advanced warning, except for the sleeplessness. (That hazy condition might be quite a clue for some one who normally sleeps so soundly.)

I am not Superwoman, not even close. I'm just a regular working woman with many things to balance in the course of most days. I am Mrs. Normal and there are so many of us around. We expect everything from ourselves and anything less is unacceptable. That is unless the power and strength of our brains force us to stop, sit down, take stock – and maybe rework the plan. That is what I have been working on the last few days, and I highly recommend it to those of you in the same boat. In the last few days, I've noticed how my daughter has grown, how the hills are now lush and green. The blossom is already white and glorious on the apricot tree and the wild flowers are poised and ready to bloom on the hillside. I've also given myself quite a talking to these last few days and promised to try and change how I run myself and my life. Once in a while you need to treat your body as a machine and oil its engine. You need to sit down, stop and think. Anything else is just inadequate. We only have a limited time here on the earth - that we know of. Be a little kinder to yourself with what you have left.

**Lucy is a former Superwoman.**

# THE TOUGHEST PURCHASE

I am not one of a car salesman's favorite people; I hate to buy vehicles, I have little interest in vehicles. I just want to jump in the thing and go as successfully and comfortably as possible to my chosen destination. The last car I "bought" was about 10 years ago, when I was given the keys to my current car – an older BMW – and told to drive it. I have learned these past few weeks, however, that there is quite an art to the purchasing of a car and I have also learned more about cars than I ever thought I would find interesting. It is never too late to learn new things; so they say.

There comes a time in the life of a REALTOR when it is really not cool to ask your buyers to follow you to see a home – only because you cannot accommodate them in your small car. There comes a time in a person's relationship with its trusted vehicle, when, like a pair of shoes with the hole in the sole and the toes curling up at the end, you have to admit you have taken the best out of your form of transportation and you had better start shopping around for its replacement.

"Just get me something at the car auction," I said to a friend of mine, imagining that they could see into my tiny car brain and imagine exactly what I needed. When what I needed was not exactly what they could find for me at the auction I stepped back from this whole vehicle purchasing lark and gave it some deep thought. You cannot just buy a car on "EBAY", as it were, and imagine that it will be something that'll make you happy for the next 10 years. No, this was going to have to be something which I studied and analyzed, whether I liked it or not; just like the buying of a home. I expect my customers to pick and choose the home they are going to live in for the next few years. No one buys a house unseen! Why would I think that you would do that for a car? And so the investigation began and I learned more about BMW's over the next few days than I thought possible. I visited all the web sites, examined the different models and years along with their options. I quickly became a savvy member of the general car-buying public; like it or not.

I was ready with my factoids and my victims in number of preference when my friend and I finally went out car shopping. "This is my number two choice," I said boldly as we strolled onto the lot. There she sat, the white beauty smiling at me and asking me to take her home. Now that would be easy! Stroll on the lot, take a little spin, pull out the check book and live happily ever after. Not so fast. "This one smells," I told my friend as we did our customary spins and stops in the "Toys R Us" parking lot close by. "Do all used cars smell?" Much like people's houses have their own odors, none of the research I had completed had explained to me how I was going to have severe problems with my nose leading me away from purchasing perfectly good cars. "That one too," I sighed, as we test-drove about our 8th vehicle. This was not as easy as I had thought.

"This one I like," I said, triumphant at last; but the price was wrong and the nice Persian car salesmen immovable on that particular subject. Having learned something along the rocky road about the techniques of car negotiations, I whispered to my co-pilot, ("at what point do we walk?" "Soon," she said. "And then they try and call us back in.") That seemed like a game we could usefully play; so we stepped away from the table and went to lunch. "Ah, gotta go; we have more cars to test-drive!" we said breezily, as we walked out of the office. "You have our number!"

We ate a good lunch and waited for the call back from the Persians. It never came. We test drove some more cars and then limped home as tired as if we had done a full day's work.

At 4am I awoke with non-buyer's remorse. "Dang it," I said to just myself and the black sky outside. "Should have bought that lovely car with the low miles; she and I would have got along so well!" I explained my condition to my co-pilot and she reconnected with the Persians. To cut a long story short, we set off again for the land of the automobile; this time resolved to buy. We had done our research, we had seen how awful some used cars could be; we had driven a lot of dogs and hailed a few beauties. We'd passed the test and learned so much along the way.

I shall never again underestimate the purchasing of a vehicle; it is a life decision that needs to be taken almost as seriously as buying a house or marrying a man. When I purchase the next four wheeled German monster in about a decade's time I shall be better prepared for my adventure, you'd better believe it. They should have college courses for this type of thing; or at least a survival kit. Car buying – like real estate – is not for the faint of heart.

**Lucy and her car 'Oprah' are still living happily together.**

# TREADING WATER

There is an old English term for doing a lot of moving in water; without drowning, but going nowhere. This technique is known as "treading water" and is a requirement of all young swimmers before they graduate to the deep end of the swimming pool. It came to my mind, since I have been doing a lot of swimming recently, that my life involves a lot of treading water; so much so that, at times, my mind can draw a complete blank and require me to go entirely back to basics. Superwomen of the world know what I'm talking about.

The need to tread water is naturally a result of overload; the dangerous land of over-promising and under-delivering to the majority of areas in your life. At this point the sane human mind will take over, thankfully, in all its power and its glory, and not explode, ( which is what you think it's going to do), but force you to "stop" whatever you are doing and be still. Being a busy career person with a family and a gazillion other things that you are involved in, you cannot simply hide under a rock for a few months. What you can do is to stop almost drowning with where you are in your life and start to tread water a little more carefully and selectively. I'm not ready for the deep end right now, I tell myself. I need to take baby steps only, or at least put a rubber ring around my middle. No, better still; I ought to sit on the steps of the pool and just watch. So that's just what I did.

When I did that, I realized that the world had been carrying on without me perfectly competently, as she does in her inimitable way. Somehow the hills beyond my house had completely lost their lush green of a few months ago and turned to burnt corn. When did that happen? Their parched agonies reminded me almost simultaneously that autumn and then winter would soon be here; and maybe even the odd drop of rain and ground frost. How did I miss the change of the seasons? That should never happen. The cannons are going off in the vineyard, heralding the ripe berries and the call of the harvest. Is it really that time of year, I pondered? Last year's harvest was so like yesterday. The children are back to school already and my child is now at the top of the elementary school system. And how did that happen? I recall her so clearly as a suckling babe needing me at every turn; not to mention her first day of pre-school with her little blue boots and nervous clenching of my entire arm. Now I'm not allowed to hold her hand if anyone's looking and kisses are definitely rationed. How did her need for me evaporate so quickly over the years; or maybe it just crept up when I wasn't paying attention and it's actually been there for a while. So what do you do when you feel like you're running a race against time and she's definitely winning?

You do what I have been making a concerted effort to these last few days; a lot more thinking, a lot more of nothing and a lot less drowning. I look at my calendar and I say to myself; "nope, completely booked up that day. Tomorrow is not looking so good either. How will next week work for you?" Then I go out and buy a book I'd been craving to treat myself to – hardcover or not - I sit out on the patio in the sun, watch the birds twittering and the sunlight caressing the hills; and I stop. I tread the waters of my life gracefully and with control for just those few minutes; then I read my lovely book and remind myself that I am a human being first and foremost and I had better take a little better care of me.

Treading water requires great concentration, I've noticed, but very little actual effort and absolutely zilcho on the stress scale. You can tread water and look at the hawk swooping down on the field mouse. You can tread water and play with your dog at the same time, think about your day, even touch on tomorrow. What you cannot do is to stress, be moody or sad in any way. I call it a drink of water for the soul and I plan on treading more and drowning less in the future. Maybe, that way, life will move along a little slower and a little more contained; I will taste more the treats and acknowledge more the change; more of a country drive along the highway of my life, as opposed to a rocket launch to the stars in my quest to get there first. Tread water; try it; you might find it will work for you too.

**Lucy is a fond swimmer.**

# VENTURING FORTH

It is still surprising to me that driving in the city can be a scary thing. I learned to drive in London's grimy streets, where you are perpetually squeezing a car down a slim line between two parked cars on both sides, while you career head on with a car speeding towards you on the same slim line. That can teach you a lot about aggressive driving, I can tell you. Then there's Paris. France, not Texas. If anyone has ever driven there, they know what I am talking about. I have a survival memory of riding a motorbike on wet, dark cobbles in Paris during the rush hour, or there was the time I made the mistake of trying to overtake a Porsche on a German autobahn in my teeny Renault 5, but those are whole other stories.

But now I am a mamy-pamby country dweller with our wide-laned highways and empty country lanes, I have become a vehicular coward and I kind of like it that way, except when I venture up to the city and am reminded how people can change over the course of time and how your driving skills can become part of your general ageing recession.

My friend and I were going up to San Francisco for a few days. Since we are in America, it never occurs to us to do anything but drive places, like everyone else. You do not stop and ponder, like the people who actually live up in the city, that it might possibly be better to take the train, or, god forbid, leave your car at the Bart station and enter the city that way. City drivers the world over are very unforgiving and very much in a rush. You are quickly reminded of this. They do not have time to wait for the preambling tourist who does not really know where they are going. You only have one opportunity to make that turn, or you will find yourself zooming over the Bay Bridge towards the toll booth, which is not where you want to go, and cursing the day you ever left home. As you enter the city, they should issue bumper stickers to us country-dwellers. "Be kind, we are visitors! Let us drive quietly in peace and make all kinds of mistakes! In exchange, we will leave lots of dollars behind in your fair city, (not to mention the 8.5% sales tax!)"

As you head towards San Jose and the blend thereafter, (which is commonly known as 'The Bay Area'), the lanes get wider, the line between life and death slimmer. You white-knuckle your way from thereon, thinking of the yummy time you're dreaming of when you pull up in front of your hotel and some one takes the keys from you, assuring you that you do not have to drive anymore until you leave and head home again. I practically kissed the ground once that happened and was able to look back with a wry smile at the lady who nearly sliced off my bumper as she cut me off and the "gentleman" who did not want to let me in his lane, (even though I had innocently made a mistake selecting the one I did), and I even waved sweetly to him as he raised his finger at me. Myself and my passenger, not to mention Oprah – my car – we survived it all with just a mere few missing paint chippings to show for it.

But it was all worth it. We had such a lovely few days up in the city, walking all the time – not a steering wheel in sight – or riding the marvelous cable cars. The sun beamed every day we were there, in uncharacteristic San Francisco way. The people at our hotel were friendly and helpful. We ate out and cruised around in dutiful tourist way. We spent many a dollar at mostly shoe shops and gulped at the dollars which bled through our fingers. We had a lovely time, we really, really did. Originating from London, we marveled at the clean streets and the clean buildings. It was almost a vacation, though I live here, kinda.

Leaving the city behind, I nearly high-fived myself as I safely moved away from the blend they call, unattractively, "Silicon Valley", and back into the rolling lush hills of home, where everything moves a little more slowly, you don't need to white-knuckle to get anywhere and nobody, well almost nobody, will use a nasty hand signal if you innocently choose the wrong lane.

**Lucy is a former city dweller. Miss it? Not a bit.**

# LEARNING FROM OUR CHILDREN

# A DAY OUT AT THE BEACH

"Mum, can we please?" "Mum"? 'Mum, when can we ..?" "Mum, you said we could!"

I had really put this off for a long time for absolutely no good reason except that I didn't have the time and didn't seem able to make the time to save my life. My probationary period had expired. "Mum, you said we could take the dogs to the beach in Carmel and we never, ever did. Can we, Mum, please? Please, Mum!"

And, as a parent, you really do have to ask yourself if that is totally too much to ask for? Around me, I heard whispering plans of what people were doing in honor of Spring Break. They were taking their kids to Disneyland, they were off to Cabo, they were taking a trip up to Oregon, or down to Texas. All around us, people were taking full days off and more to go and do something different, to travel, spend time with their children; and here, I couldn't even spare a day to take my child to the local beach with her dogs., something she had been craving for way too long? Not acceptable.

The beginning of spring break week quickly moved towards the end, and here we had one precious day left before she went back to school. "I'll take you on Monday," I ultimately promised her and swiftly put a line through the entire day in my planner. I had better make that happen, I told myself or I shall be a failure as a mother, forever memorialized as the mother that couldn't ever take a day away from work for her child. She would grow up disabled by her over-busy mother who had forever scarred her with her lack of care, attention and time – or at least time. Anyone knows that if you over-promise and under-deliver, you quickly become a flake whose word is dirt – less than dirt - nothing. Mothers of teenagers do not want to go into that category so quickly into teenage-dom, so there you have it. Sunday I could be seen studying my planner anxiously and wondering how I was going to fit everything else around the vacant Monday that I had now positioned into my life; but I was going to do it, gosh darn it, no matter what.

Monday blooms and our free day arrives. I skate off to work at the crack of dawn to try and attack the most critical of the day's mass before my little beach-loving darling even opens up her blue, blue eyes to the blue, blue sky of her perfect day out at the beach. I rush home to the picnic I had already prepared, the clean towels and whatever supplies had seemed vital at 6am. We pick up the chosen friend and take off – two children, three dogs and myself – for our day trip to the beach. It's hardly a "trip", since the beach is a mere 45 minutes away from our home, but it did feel like a trip to us, after all we had had to go through to get there.

"I've never been on this road!" my daughter's friend exclaims with delight. "This is a really pretty road! Look at the cows over there! Look, look, look, I see the water! I've never been to Carmel before – this is so nice!" And so the banter went on and I watched them in my rear view mirror, wondering why it had taken me so long to be able to load them up in the car with panting sweaty dogs in tow and get them away from their daily routine and down the road – 45 minutes worth of road to be exact – to a distant exotic place that at least one of them had never visited before and the other one had been craving for way too long.

It was one of those rare Peninsula days – not the heavy chilled fog kind with the deep scent of seaweed and the coolness that makes you wrap a scarf around your neck. This was one of the perfect jewels, reserved for the big eyes of small children and their memory banks, in reserve for those less than perfect days that invariably come after. Clear blue skies with just a creamy puff of cloud rolling by. Rich, warm sunshine, green seas and the most amazing array of dogs exercising their owners you'd ever seen. For those of you not in the know, if you have a dog Carmel Beach is the place to be. It is one of the few places where you can still let your dog run freely and not get a ticket – I think – don't quote me on that. At least, if you can get a ticket, nobody cares about that – they all run free anyway. Our mutt, Baxter, could hardly stand himself – this was a friendly dog's playing field. He raced around in everyone's business, sniffing and running and high on life the entire time. Little Sophie – our other mutt, two feet smaller - followed close behind – avoiding the large dogs which always terrify her, but keeping a watchful eye on her man and his marauding eye on the other ladies on the beach. Little Maxie, who rounded up the trio, trotted along in her own inimitable way – the smallest dog on the beach – and enjoyed the admiration she received. The two-legged girls walked up and down the beach and around the curve, in the rock pools, in the ocean (fully clothed I might add), and up and down the beach again. A kindly lady handed them a kite to fly and the sunshine kite flew suitably over my head, as I crowned myself queen of that particular day. I sat in the middle of the curve of the beach on a towel with my book and sunglasses in hand. Though it was a relaxing place to read and ponder, the scene was so fascinating, (yes, dog owners do always seem to resemble their dogs!) I spent much of my beach time doing some restful people watching. We ate our customary cheese, tomato and sand sandwiches and the hours passed by so pleasantly, I forgot all of the things that I had been stressing over in the morning.

Gradually, the sun began to move down towards the water, and I realized it was time to pack up our lovely day and pop her away in a basket for another time. The drive back was beckoning, plus some wet children's' clothing needed to be changed and lives prepped for the next day, that first day back to school after Spring Break.

I dragged the tired, sun-kissed children back into the car along with the exhausted dogs, and we trundled, reluctantly, the 45 minutes back home. The smell of damp dogs and kids escorted us the entire journey home. "I must try to make a habit of this in the summer," I thought to just myself, as I studied the happy faces of dogs and children in the back of my car. Not to mention the bliss that the girls enjoyed for several hours of this peaceful day, the dogs and myself all felt that the change was as good as a rest – as Granny would say - and why was it really so hard to make the time, to give the time, to make everyone so very happy and to give them a sweet memory to hold for the days to come. All I really had to do was make my mind up and put a line through the planner for that one special day.

**Lucy is a busy lady, but fond beach goer.**

# BIG READ FOR BIG MINDS

It's that time of year when books are brought back into the focal point of our existence. Anyone who picks up a paper or listens to the news at this time knows that 'The Big Read' is back in town and it's an important time for all of us, or, at least, it should be.

There are not enough book shops in any given town. That is my opinion. Count on fingers and toes the number of clothes shops and eateries in any community and you will be hard pressed to find a book shop, second hand or not, that can stay alive. If you go to cultural communities such as Berkeley or Santa Cruz, you can find places where people will still go to look at, buy and enjoy books. Sadly, over the years, I have witnessed the book shops in our local communities dwindle and die – such is the state of our techno-obsessed world.

I was raised with books, so forgive my nostalgia. From my earliest memory, I can hear my mother's voice reading a nursery rhyme to me – now horribly obsolete – or a Beatrix Potter story, complete with amazing illustrations. Whether or not I could understand the words from such an early age did not matter a bit. I found her lilting tone and the presence and feel of the written word concealing worlds behind worlds something I learned to crave. She read to me for many, many years. Every night before I went to sleep she would read me a story, or continue something we'd been enjoying together the night before. It was our time together, our down time and such a comfort. I had no idea how I would look back in time, and in wonder and nostalgia, and crave and long for those long gone days and marvel at how precious those times were. At the very end of her life, I read to her and it was the perfect circle.

I fight to continue reading with my child now. Some nights it gets too late, or she's too tired, but still I persist. I crave that snuggle time with her when we read a little something together. We lie down and we relax. We laugh and talk about what we read. It's our time. It's the mirror image of my mother's time with me thirty odd years ago. Maybe she'll read to me at the end of my life too.

Last year I helped out at the local Steinbeck Center and the studies of the County's middle school students. They were reading

'The Red Pony' and I was among a group of local writers volunteering to coach them on their writing about the book. As usually happens when you intermingle with young people, thinking that you are going to teach them something, it ends up being completely the opposite.

I find myself swimming along against the tide most days in the modern world and craving the company only of a book, when my days' work is done – or even when it is not. Give me a page turner and I can be the most peaceful companion you'd ever know. You can find me standing up at the counter eating my supper, or knees up in the sun chair, or propped up in bed, and you will definitely find me armed with a spine full of a world outside myself. During recent days when I needed a little escapism from my own life, I found myself fleeing to the world of the written word and craving the embrace of her arms more and more.

I delved into Jodie Picoult, my pick for the week, and took myself into the difficult world that she depicted with such clarity and accuracy, that I couldn't take myself away from the pictures she created. Though they were tough pictures, she created these huge images of a troubled world way beyond my own that made me care about what happened and crave to turn again the page and hope for better times for the characters.

Take your child to the local library, if you can't afford to buy a book – it is such a wonderful resource that we take so completely for granted. Your child can get arms full of books to take home with him or her for absolutely no money at all. English or Spanish, it doesn't matter – they are both there and in all levels of skill and fluency. We are blessed with free reading in our free world. I'm afraid that it is a dying right that we have to fight to conserve.

That is why I enjoy all the publicity of the 'Big Read' and will do what I can to further their cause, whether I coach the middle-schoolers in their writing skills or simply rev up my own child's reading habits and insist that we continue to read together until, further down the road, it's time for her to read only to me. It's too important to let this monument to learning pass us by as just another week. Reading is a gift we should all take great pleasure and pride in. Don't ignore it.

**Lucy is a life long reader and believer in the wonders of books.**

# BRINGING OUT THE BEST

At a recent chamber general meeting, we were stood up by the speaker which we were expecting that day; a bit embarrassing I'd have to say the least, for the Chamber Board of Directors. However, our stand-in speaker more than made up for the embarrassment we suffered with his heart-felt presentation which touched the crowd that day. Our speaker had been given about 20 minutes notice to prepare something for our captive audience; but I came to realize that you don't need any preparation at all if, in fact, you are speaking from the heart.

It doesn't take any great intellect to absorb the simple issue that busy children have more chance of staying out of trouble. Experts the world over get paid big bucks to do intense studies of child psychology and analysis to come to the same conclusion that the rest of us can also come to, which is that if we do not give our children a healthy structure and family in their lives; then they will find one that is not quite so healthy. Just look at the gang problem so prevalent in so many of our communities and you have a clear picture of what can become of our children if we can't or don't pay enough attention to them.

Lots of people pay lip service to this topic. They complain about the graffiti and the crime in town; they avoid the clusters of gathering youth in shopping centers or on street corners. They try and turn a blind eye to what is an overwhelmingly obvious problem with a solution; we need to give our children constructive things to do, reasons to strive for better in their lives; hand out a little hope to them for the future.

Sports have always been a winner in this realm; no matter where you go in the world. Put a child in a sports team and not only are they moving around in a healthy environment, burning energy, working together within the team concept, under the controlled guidance of some one whom they respect and who helps them pay attention to the rules; but they are given consequences for their behavior and rewards for their achievements. These are winning combinations. It's interesting to me that sports has become a bit of a sideline in our schools, a part of the curriculum which comes way behind math and English in some school districts; but should be treated just as much of a priority because of what it brings to the esteem of the child and other key issues such as fighting gang recruitment and obesity.

Our chamber speaker explained to the group that the Soledad youth football team had basically moved to Salinas – a long story - and with the move of some of the players and coaches, the team itself, as it had been known and grown in Soledad, became extinct. Though the speaker's son was now too old to play for the team since he was moving up into the high school team; the speaker still felt moved to push for a re-birth of the team that he had worked so hard to build, and to fill the gap for all the youth of Soledad who needed a team, a place, somewhere to go and feel good about themselves. In short, it was so much more than a place for his son to play; it had become a mission from his coaching heart.

As he worked to put the team back together, he was reminded of what a great place South County is when you need something. Farmers, ranchers, educators, teachers, wood crafters, real estate professionals, pizza parlor owners, auto parts people; heck, they are all there for you when you talk about youth and trying to put a team together. As our speaker recalled all the people who helped him to get the team back on its feet with uniforms, a place to play, a clubhouse and so much more, he became emotional. As he proudly displayed the pictures of his teams from before and the plaques of gratitude he received as their coach, you could see that all that he gave to the kids and the teams was given right back to him and more. There are lessons there for all of us.

**Lucy is a proud supporter of youth sports.**

# DENTAL PHOBIA

"I hate going to the dentist," I proclaimed boldly to the poor dental receptionist sitting down in the chair before me. "I'd rather be in labor." "Oh dear," she responded meekly. "Don't worry. You'll be okay."

Forgive me father; it has been 2 years since my last dental visit; that memorable day etched into the recesses of my mind, when the hydraulic teeth cleaning torture lady dug down so deeply into my roots and hence my nerves, I thought I was going to have to howl in pain and run screaming from her clutches, splashing mouth wash and sweeping dental instruments out of my way.

"Not putting myself through that again," I said, leaving her office way back when, as I mentally gritted my teeth and committed myself to a life free of the white coats and weapons of torture. "My teeth are good; I drink lots of milk. I come from a long line of people with good teeth. I could go the rest of my life and never need to go to the dentist. I floss; I brush religiously, I rinse. I do it all." I had managed to deceive myself for a good while with my stubborn insistence, to just myself.

However, if you are a parent and you try to lead by example, you want your children to have good, healthy teeth and you must therefore show them, as you lead them to the dental chair, that you are not mortally terrified of going to the dentist yourself; even if you are.

"You're 40 plus and you've been through a lot in your life," I tell myself, as I am awakened the day of our tooth visit, with a big black cloud hanging over my head. "Why would this be such a problem?" I asked myself quietly, heart pounding in chest. "Dare I say; you seem to have a phobia?" (Some of the very best conversations I have with me on my lonesome.)

"I hate going to the dentist," said my daughter stoically, as I brightly announced that I would be picking her up early for this momentous occasion. "Nobody likes going to the dentist," I responded cheerfully, "but it's just something we have to do. We'll give ourselves a nice treat when we're done."

Daughter was in and out without incident, no cavities required. A nice fresh clean mouth and a new toothbrush; in short, a slam dunk. X-rays had to be performed on me; since it had been so long since my last check-up. ("What a waste of money!" I'm thinking, "charging me for something that is really so unnecessary. Just hurry on up and dig those sharp metal things around in my mouth, flush in a little fluoride; then let me run off and get my treat for being a brave girl!") Some of my most rational conversations go on quite successfully inside my own mind.

"You have four cavities," pronounced the calm young dentist.

"You must be kidding me!" I retorted, not impressed. Me? The queen of the best teeth in the west, who wouldn't need any more dental visits for the rest of her natural life? He showed me the gaping holes on the x-rays. No, he wasn't joking. "Why wouldn't I have felt any discomfort?" I challenged, trying to comprehend the magnitude of my condition.

"Some people don't," he replied, "until it's really bad and they need a root canal." Oh well that did it. I fired myself instantly, as a self-diagnosing medical expert and began some deep breathing exercises, which I've heard is very good for both conditions of labor and intense trauma, such as the one I was currently experiencing.

"If you can pay today, we can do it today," the nice money lady said with her calculator in hand. I couldn't foresee stepping out and away from said dental instruments and then being able to persuade myself to voluntarily return, knowing what was ahead of me and how much of a big coward I really am.

"I'd rather get it over with," I said solemnly. "Please can you let my cavity-free daughter in the waiting room know that Mummy will be some time under the knife, as it were; she has four cavities." I felt like calling my husband and having a good cry; ringing my friend for a last rights conversation of consolation and reassurance; but I thought that the dental crew might decide that I was going to be a bit too much work for one day and make me come back the next. That would be too much to take.

I braced myself, pinching nails deeply down into skin; the theory being that if I make that one thing, i.e. my hand, hurt very badly, the other thing will be a breeze. It didn't work for childbirth, by the way; why would it work for this?

The bright light shone intrusively into my eyes and I thought about how wonderful it is that sedation dentistry is becoming quite a norm in our society and how, maybe, I'd be an excellent candidate for it. I thought of happier things elsewhere in the world, as they poked and prodded around. I remembered my Mum and all her trials and tribulations with gum treatments, (she'd be wagging her finger at me right now!) I thought of pretty flowers and frolicking lambs; that didn't help. I imagined all the nice things I could do when I eventually got out of that chair and on with my life ….

"Ouch!" They put a sword into my gum. Not nice. Another sword and then, maybe, a cheese –slicer went into the flesh; or at least that's how it felt. Luckily, the numbing effect of the shot gushed over pretty sharp-ish and I quickly realized they were cleaning my teeth. Never like the part where they scrape around the nerves of the bottom teeth and remind you that you're still alive. Then they stopped and the nice assistant asked me if I'd like to rinse. "Ish I can," I dribbled, unable to speak through oral paralysis. "Have you finished?" I ventured.

"Yes, with the cleaning," she responded. Eek, the drilling was yet to come! How could cleaning take such a long time? Yes, sedation dentistry would be perfect for me, I'm thinking, beginning to hyperventilate and sweat like an athlete. Good, here comes the nice calm dentist again! No chance of an escape, (which I did once, when I was much younger, at another dental visit in another life.)

"It'll be alright," he says, eyeing my perspiration, (what a tough profession! Always having to reassure people that you are not going to maim or kill them on purpose!)

And it *was* alright in the end. It was not a walk in the park, it was not lambs and pretty flowers, but it was over pretty quickly. I was a little poorer, a little paralyzed, and, as you do every day, I had learned a few valuable lessons:-

1. You must go to the dentist every 6 months; it is one of life's necessities; like it or not. It will make things less painful in the long run.
2. Do not self-diagnose. There are reasons why you are **not** paid to do this. Self-diagnosis will only end in tears.

3. It is okay to let the professionals know that you are afraid. They deal with cowards like you 7 out of every 8 hours of every day and they know how to be calm and nice and say, "Don't worry; it'll be alright." You do not have to believe them, but it is better for you if you at least try.

And the moral of this story is lead by example, at all times; even when you'd really rather not. Confront your fears; it might make them go away, at least a little. If all else fails, ask for drugs. Every dentist will have a little sedation dentistry technique at their finger-tips, which they may be able to use on you.

**Lucy is a big wimp who hates going to the dentist.**
**Always has, always will, most likely.**

# EVERYTHING I KNOW I LEARNED FROM A CHILD

Somewhere in my 40 something years of education and development, I had forgotten that cows have 4 stomachs and chew their cud most of the sun-kissed day. Maybe, in my English upbringing, I never knew how grapes are picked in the first place; what the different names for chickens are– male and female; also that a packet of broccoli seed could cost over $300 and how many stages it takes to get an actual bunch of the stuff to put on the table. I was reminded of these facts, plus many more, when I attended 'South County Farm Day' recently with multitudes of third graders, many of whom seemed to have more of these facts under their belts than I did.

Sitting on the school bus, squished between young ones, on the way to King City, I had some radical flashbacks from my own school trips back in the days of yore. Realizing that it had probably been 30 years, since I had last sat on a sweaty-seated school bus, made me truly aware and afraid of the rapid passing of time! Sometimes you can be swiftly reminded of just how valuable it is to use every minute as if it were your last. You can never recapture a third grade trip; you can never know how important it is to your child that you show up and pay attention; you can never fully appreciate how much you really learn from them and you can never know how wonderful it makes them feel when they know you're doing it all for them. Never mind, they don't know that it's also for you.

It would have been so easy to have made my meeting a priority, (can always do it next week, if I really put my mind to it); or to feign extra busy, because, of course, I am. But no, somewhere in the deep dark recesses of my mind, I am sensing that there will come a time, very shortly here, when the child will no longer really want the support systems of her family around her, especially me. She will want to go on trips with friends, not snuggle at night with a book and me, or cuddle close in the early morning when we awake; she being cold and me warm. Sooner than I dare conceive, she will want money for clothes, money for this, money for that, freedom to be out in the evening, liberties to date boys – god forbid; in short, she will want her life away from me in the scarily foreseeable future and she will, probably, beg me at that time to please not go on school trips with her. She will continue to teach me at that time; but most likely from a distance. I'm sensing that all will change here very soon; so I'd better grab a hold, while I can, and savor the now.

"Do you want me to come and help out in your classroom, dear?" I ventured cautiously. "Yes, every day", she responded assertively. Now, every day might be a bit detrimental to actually earning a living in my case; never mind the feelings of the teacher who might anticipate that an invasion was about to befall her. No, once a week, I reckoned would be enough to show that I care; that I am committed; that I want to know what's going on over there and how I can help. Once a week would be enough to learn more from the third graders than I'd dare admit! So once a week it is; and lord help any organization that might get in the way of me getting there.

My first week for helping out, I got to observe all the little munchkins and how well-behaved they are, (things have changed since my day; we used to make paper airplanes and throw them at each other in class. I also recall a poor music teacher once being locked in a cupboard by an unruly student with a strange sense of humor, when she, poor teacher, was desperately trying to find some sheet music!) Yes, these days they run a pretty tight ship and it's good to see.

"For once, don't get in line, bunch up, class!" hollered the teacher above the ruckus, when we were trying to get an up and personal look at some draught horses on 'Farm Day'. The kids looked at each other in confusion. 'Not get in line? Well, how would you do that?' they said to each other. I watched that subtle little expression of the disciplines they subscribe to and I smiled to myself.

That evening, our minds were further enriched, beyond the sights of calves feeding and seedlings sprouting; if our brains could take any more, we had yet another educational experience to fill us up. It was the School District's 'Science Fair' event. "Mom, we have to go!" stressed Daughter. "I have two meetings to go to. If you're so desperate to go to Science Fair, then you'll have to make the meetings too," I responded helpfully. "I have to go see if we've won," she demanded and so it was settled; two meetings equals one science fair, and maybe a McDonalds.

After quietly sitting through the two meetings, we arrived at the fair and eventually found our booth. I say eventually, because there were so many awesome demonstrations to behold and distract me from the mission in hand! "Second place," she grouched, when we found the booth. "That is not good."

"It's not the winning, it's the ..."

"Don't go there, mother," she cut me off threateningly and it was then that I realized her life experience was fast approaching the level of my own and, in a very short period of time, I probably would not be able to 'go there' without a retort. Face facts; soon I would not be allowed to ride on the bus and I, most definitely, would not be helping in class. Better learn everything I can from her now, while I still can; that is before she knows everything and we have to go round and around.

The moral to this story, people is, don't ever look back where your children are concerned and say I "shoulda, woulda, coulda"...... It will be too late then and regret is the worst. Consider yourselves warned; do it now, while you still know everything.

**Lucy was allowed to help out in class until about 4$^{th}$ grade, when the teacher – if not the kid herself – put a stop to it.**

# GIVE THEM A HEAD START

If I had my way, team sports would be a sport for everybody, no exclusions allowed. There would be team A, B, C and all the way down to team Z, if necessary, so that all the children could be involved, could feel part of a constructive team, could know how it feels to do well and be cheered, could have a chance in life to step up to the next team, without somebody shooting them down. They could wear the uniform of their peers and feel proud that they belonged to something strong and something enviable, way above the day to day struggles many are forced to deal with. Maybe that is why so many children are drawn to gangs, destructive team though that so obviously is. They get to wear a uniform and feel proud to belong to something. We should all think long and hard about that. I know that not all the kids can be a part of the sports team, but that shouldn't stop us from hoping that they would want to be. It'd be a start.

It tears my heart out, as a parent and a human being, when I read about another young life being uselessly trashed for absolutely no good reason on the streets of our cities. It warms my heart when I read good stories like the one about the store keeper in Salinas recently who made it his mission to get a couple of unrelated kids to start going to school. All the children did was go into his store once in a while, and he not only helped them with the applications and the red tape to get them accepted at local schools, he bought them the clothes and supplies that they would need when they got there. Though the children were not even remotely his family, he made them so. We should all think long and hard about that too. Family should be more than just blood. If there is a young soul in trouble, we should all be people enough to reach out to another. Making a difference in one life is to, equally, make your own worthwhile. That should be a religion we all subscribe to.

Recently it was my family's privilege to be involved in the middle school volleyball tournament once again, thanks to the belief of our schools' coaches that it is good for our kids and regardless of the fact that it was their day off. Schools from all over the Monterey County area showed up at 8.30 in the morning, bright and smiling in their team colors and ready to play for their own families, coaches and fellow team members. For any of you who have never witnessed such a thing, it is quite a sight to behold, not to mention the noise and the enthusiasm which exudes through the walls and which you will still experience hours later.

I always learn something when I watch youth sports. In the game of volleyball, I really like it that the girls touch hands when one of their team members makes a mistake. We all make mistakes all the time, but in this sport, the one making the error is made to feel a little better and move on. The hand of the error-maker gets stroked by her team mates, as if to say, "it's alright, we're in this together." When the team makes a good play or wins a point, the team all clap; I like that too. I also like the fact the team members who don't play as much as some others are just as much a part of the team. They clap and cheer in their shiny uniforms just as heartily as the rest of them, and are always ready to take their place on the court in just a second's notice. I really enjoy the end of the game when both sides of the tournament touch each other's hands and say "good game", whether it was or not. It's an important gesture and one that reminds me of the old skills of sportsmanship, not to mention humanity. Treat people as you would be treated; it's a pretty simple maxim we should all work harder towards. Maybe the kids can teach us the rules.

I think again of the store keeper and his kind watch on the youth who frequent his store. He must sleep well at night knowing he's basically saved a life or two at the very least. I look at the coaches of our local schools and I feel the same way. They save the lives of our kids every day with their commitment to helping them to the next level, their love and support in striving to make these young ones be everything they can be; not to mention the eternal gift of hope they give to our youth that being part of a group can be a wonderful and positive thing, it just has to be the right group. I see all of that and more when I watch youth sports.

There was so much that showed up this week for the volleyball tournament. Of course there were the team players and the coaches, parents too. There were team colors, enthusiasm, Gatorade and a lot of bouncing balls. There was also hope, love, courage, kindness and family – they all showed up this weekend at the volleyball tournament to rally around our youth and hold them up high above all the challenges that they face every day. Thanks to all of you who make such a difference in their lives.

**Lucy loved it when her daughter played team sports.**

# GO FORTH INTO THE WORLD

"Go forth into the world in peace. Be of good spirit." I still recall those words from our High School Principal at his closing address to us, his graduates, at Friends School, Saffron Walden, U.K.; Class of 1979. We were leaving High School; we were going forth into the world. If the truth were known, we didn't really care less what our principal had to say, because we were shortly headed for the biggest party of our lives that night. I'm surprised that I even remember that particular line from his long and mostly humorless speech. Maybe I remember it because, at the time, it seemed pretty random. Now I'm a little more mature, it seems most pertinent. If you can hope for nothing else from a high school graduate, you should be able to hope that he or she goes forward into the world in peace; that he has made some of his mistakes and learned from them, that he has covered his curriculum and learned from it, that he is a better human being coming out than he was going in.

I recently had the privilege to go to our own Soledad High School and present a scholarship at their awards night, which I make a point to do every year when I can. I do find this a humbling experience. I stand before the educators, counselors and administrators who have raised these students to the peek of their potential and now stand ready to move them forward to the next level of their achievements in life – to college and careers to be proud of. I always feel so small next to them. To have nurtured and encouraged so many lives to such fulfillment has to be the pinnacle of achievement. I take my hats off to them every year. And our young people! There they sat quietly in their rows receiving their certificates and awards! How proud they were and how excited for the future! You want to take a snap shot of that moment and send it down to the classes below, the struggling and the unfulfilled. It might help them aspire to other places than where they find themselves in their own particular non-graduating class.

"What do you mean there are kids who aren't graduating?" I questioned my daughter, when she informed me that there were a few students at the middle school not walking with their class.

They don't get to wear their cap and gown and feel proud of their achievement; they don't get to enjoy the fruits of the graduation ticket – the trips, the picnics, the BBQ's. They don't get to feel that they belong to a movement larger than themselves; they get to feel like the underclass and that is good for no one. It makes you feel that there is nowhere for these individuals to go but even further down in esteem and productivity.

Knowing the school as I do, I do know that the non graduates are members only of the class of last resort. The teachers have continually done everything in their power to try and help those children to be able to walk with their class, feel proud of what they do at their school and visualize their way out of whatever slows them up in their day to day and get through it ultimately with achievement. I have to know also – deep down – that it is not our teachers who have failed our kids in these instances, but the parents of the kids and the kids themselves. Years ago, when my child started at preschool, her teacher told me that, regardless of how good the teachers are, the parents are always the primary educators and they alone have the power to make the difference between success and failure for their children. I bought that at the time and I buy it now. Who is at fault if my child doesn't do her home work? I am. Whose fault is it if my child goes to school tired or hungry? Mine. Where does the responsibility lie if my child is disturbed or stressed by her home life or its circumstances; so much so that she takes it to school with her? Mine alone. I may not be able to accurately teach her the timelines of the Vietnam War or the intricacies of geometry, but I can certainly make sure that her mind is clear and ready to absorb information and that her psyche is free of the burdens and stress that should await you only in the arena of the adult world when you are mature enough to be able to deal with them.

I look around at some of the parents I have come across these past few years and I see again the challenge for the teachers. I see the selfishness, the chaos, the lack of concern for the lives that these parents themselves created and then quasi-abandoned. I see abuse and neglect, I see suffering, I see quiet, young voices crying out for help and there's nobody home to listen. Amidst all of this, we expect them to graduate with their class? It makes you weep for our youth and all the things that they shouldn't have to deal with at this young, young age.

I can only hope that our young people who, for whatever reason, were not able to walk with their class this time or the next, will find the inner strength to stand up against the odds and resolve that it will be different for them the next time around. Next time, they will be walking and they will be walking with glory. They will be sitting on the benches with the scholarship awardees and they will be the class of the awarded not the discarded. To all of you, please stand up and demand to be counted. Do not give in to the adults who failed you and your own acceptance of this failure. Be angry, be there, be counted.

To all the graduates in our valley and beyond, well done - all of you. Many of you have climbed multiple obstacles to achieve what you mastered this summer and some of you did it only with your teacher at your back and your faith in your pocket. To our local educators, administrators and coaches; some of us do recognize what you do every day for our kids and we thank you deeply for it. Many of us - myself included – could not do what you do every day for the betterment of humanity and we salute you for making it happen.

"Go forth into the world in peace; be of good spirit." Please do – all of you. Have a wonderful and safe summer.

**Lucy knows enough to know that she could never be a teacher. She holds them in the highest esteem.**

# I'D LIKE TO STAY 12

The bridge between child and teen is apparently as difficult for them as it is for us. I was surprised when my 12 year old proclaimed that she wanted to stay 12; she didn't want to turn 13. She also announced that she didn't want to go to middle school either; a place where, apparently, the kids would be even more scary than at elementary school! The frightening concept of heading off to a place where the pressure to be popular and pretty would only get "huge-er" – her word not mine - was already growing large in her mind; with half a year still to go before she'd officially be at junior high. I had no idea.

It is our job as parents to protect our young; even when they feel that they no longer wish to be protected; when they stumble on that bridge between childhood and adulthood, and they don't let us catch them very much. It's our job to stand aside as much as we can and allow them to walk a little more solo through these really difficult years, when everything changes and the world becomes wonderful and terrible all at the same time. I feel my protective mother skills still as sharp as a tigress, yet, increasingly, with no place to go.

"They called you what?" I exclaimed. Not sure that I had really heard what my daughter had just told me.

"They called me 'Wonderbread'," she replied, which made me immediately burst out laughing – I had never heard such a thing and I have heard a lot in my long life- before I realized that this had been hurtful to her, not funny, and I retracted my initial reaction. This simple word – a brand name for white bread, for those of you not in the know - was referring to her ethnicity, and was not supposed to be received in a nice way; according to my tween.

"Do you want me to do anything about it?" I asked; daggers ready, mother-tools packed into the mother tool belt; mother claws sharpened. In the past, she had allowed me to intervene; to contact the school, stop whatever it was that was making her day less than pleasant; in short, deal with the bullies, no matter what.

"No Mum," she said with resignation. "I've got it." And so, she has got it, I suppose; and all by herself. She went off to school the following day walking tall, with an attitude as big as her back pack, and we haven't talked about white-sliced since. In that particular sphere, we have crossed the bridge between mother protector and mother redundant and I'm left at the gate with fury in my heart, waiting each time for her to come home, hopefully unscathed, from her treatment by the world at large and some of its cruel inhabitants.

"She has to learn to handle these things herself," my husband tells me, ever the voice of reason. "The days are over when you can go running off to her Principal and fixing things for her." I accept that reluctantly; just as I accept that she no longer wants me in the classroom watching over her and stressing anxiously as she runs around the playground, waiting for her to fall so that I can pick her up. In my heart she's still my tiny baby, relying on me for nurturing and protection; still needing me for absolutely everything in her young life. But I get the need to survive thing; the necessity to be able to stand on your own two feet and face the world as the world faces you. That part I get; I totally get it.

That is until she is sick and I feel the regression. Then she wants me to nurture; she wants me to cuddle and baby. And there's the mother in me again; ready, willing and able to perform the job that I thought had gone the way of the diaper and the pacifier. I'm almost doing a dance as, in her feverish state, she allows me to cuddle and to kiss her; to make her chicken soup, as it were, and tuck her into her bed. For a minute there I'm transported back to a time when I was number one in her life; I was everything; I totally rocked.

It doesn't last. She's feeling better the next day and brushes me off as she struts towards the bus with that powerful back pack swaggering behind her. I try to sneak a kiss and am foiled, forgetting the no kissing in public rule. I understand her breaking away from me; I understand the rationale, I understand the evolution of the species. I get it, I totally get it. So why do I long for another sick day, just one more day of holding her tight?

**Lucy is always amazed at the swift passing of the years.**

# LEARN BY WATCHING

There are many things that you can learn just by watching, but to learn properly, you have to watch properly. Over my twenty years in this country, I am ashamed to admit that I have accumulated only a very mild knowledge of your sports of baseball and football, (by watching the handsome young men dashing around in their very fetching, tight-fitting uniforms!) Unfortunately my knowledge has never really grown very much beyond the attire, because my attention span is slight and my leisure time minimal, in that order; so I move on always before the 2$^{nd}$ half or the first down, or who knows what. I have to confess at this point that, two plus decades into my life on this continent, I still do not really understand the rules of either game. I know; I should have my citizenship revoked. My feeble defense is that where I come from we had neither sport infusing us as young ones, neither on the playing field nor through the television set, so I had no head start there.

However when your child is an eager participant in team sports at her middle school, you had better darn well sit up and pay attention. Just as I eventually got with the wonderful game of volleyball – no, we didn't play that either when I was growing up – the season was over and we had to quickly switch gears and go in another direction. I felt rather sad about having to let go of a sport that I was just becoming rather affectionately attached to. Just as I was learning the vernacular of spike and kill and so forth, we had to move on to another enigma in my book, another arena of non-knowledge for me: basketball.

Now, that is a blood and guts sport, I have learned, and only for the strongest of the pack. We didn't have that either at my school. We played netball which is of a similar concept – balls and nets - but with no bodily touching, whatsoever. Basketball seems to me a full-on, take no prisoners, the more bruises the better and especially if the bruises are on the opposing side type of battle field. It is a little more like the sport of rugby, which they do play in the British Isles, and which is especially favored by large, hairy men who have no problem rolling around in the considerably muddy fields and often injuring themselves. I have to confess to my health insurance provider that I am mortally afraid for my baby every time she straps up her high tops and goes to war out there, sporting only a light uniform and lots of attitude. And these are 13-14 year old girls we're talking about – not bully bruiser macho men, but something does happen to these sweet girls out there on the court, when a competitive monster takes a hold of them.

At the recent game against King City, I was not only impressed, (or rather intimidated), by the aggression of our young girls, but I was also alarmed by the adult supporters around me. It was so very important to them that their team won, that their language declined rapidly as the game progressed and their vernacular got more vulgar as the game played on and the tension heated up. I should have moved away and sat with my own team's supporters, but I was strangely fascinated by how far these grown adults would go. It gave me an insight into how terrible emotional scenes can even occur in innocent youth sports games.

With this said, I do hope by the end of the season, to be able to get a bit of a handle on the rules and understand who is fouling and why. It sure is a fast and super game and terrific exercise for our young ones, but why, oh why, all the pushing and shoving, the wrapping of body around the ball and the strange calls on what is obviously a foul? I think back to my own favored sport - the civilized game of tennis – and the sweat and emotion of those tournaments where the ball was obviously in or out and there didn't seem to be much of a grey line anywhere. The only thing that got bruised there was my ego. Basketball seems to walk a much greyer line, in my ill-educated opinion; but maybe, by the end of the season, I'll be a bit of a pro at this whole basketball-watching occupation, I'll be up on the rules and the fouls and spitting my own harshness at the other side. Or maybe I'll still be as clueless as I am now; I'll be, at least, sitting with my own side at the game and praying that that particular fall does not constitute a larger bruise on my baby than the last one.

**Lucy used to love watching the team sports at school.**

# LEARNING NEW THINGS

I learned something new this week and it's always a marvel when you teach an old dog new things, isn't it!

Like most American sports, I do not understand basketball, never did. Back in the day, we played netball at my school in England and I had imagined that basketball was a little similar to netball. Ha, was I ever wrong! Netball was a rather sedate game for girls only, which involved passing the ball, (no running with the ball and certainly no dribbling), and then shooting into a hoop. Though it could get a little fast and furious sometimes, it has not even a passing semblance to the great American sport of basketball. I learned that this week.

My daughter is a sporty girl. Like most parents of teenagers, we strive to find healthy occupations for the minds and bodies of our swiftly evolving offspring. I have told my husband that, whatever sport she wants to do, we will let her try out for the team. If I had been involved in more sports in my youth, I think that I might not have tried some of the things I did and strayed down some of the paths I wished I hadn't. The way I see it, we can only strive to correct errors we made ourselves in the lives of our children.

My daughter adored volleyball and made the team. I ended up loving it too, once I learned the rules. I was sad when the quick season ended. She is now on the Main Street Middle School basketball team and she loves that too, bruises and all. I realized this week, as I looked forward to her third game of the week and reorganized my work schedule so that I could make all the games, that I had fallen quickly in love with it too. It is a wild rush even with $7^{th}$ grade players who are only just starting out and learning the game themselves. The look of drive and anticipation on the players' faces, when they get the ball and sprint along the court with it, is a pleasure to behold.

Saturday morning, when a lot of people have a choice to still be in bed, there were the many basketball fans – old and young alike - and all in the Gonzales High gym waiting expectantly for the games to begin. I looked around at the families and the pride they felt as their youth sported a uniform and tried their best for their team. The flush of vigor after they sat down on the bench after a good effort and the roar of victory when a team member made a basket made me ponder. This is exactly what our youth needs – boys and girls alike. They need to play more sports in teams when there is a consequence if they foul another player. They need to be accountable for their actions, ("there are 5 players on the team not just you!" our coach yelled at one of the players as the player tried once again to do it all herself.) They need to know the euphoria of winning and the sour taste of defeat – these are life building experiences which make our players more solid as people. I looked at these coaches too – dedicated teachers who spend much of their so-called "free" time practicing with their teams and working towards their next performance. They give so much to our children, a mere thank you is not enough.

Soledad beat Gonzales in Saturday's game. It was a good game all round and nobody got hurt, (though some of the scrimmages are quite alarming as a parent to witness!) The teams will be revisiting each other on the Soledad turf this week and the result may be an entirely different one. Whatever the result, that is not the point. The point is that the teams show up sporting their colors and their pride, they play for their school and they do their best, whatever that is on any given day. When the players' parents show up, that adds an important element to the game. The players may act as if they don't care, but, for sure, the presence of loved ones makes them feel wanted and admired, the familiar face sitting in the stands and occasionally clapping and smiling, so much better than the absentee. When we show up for our kids, it gives them an unspoken confidence and stature in their lives, that we are most definitely setting them up to most likely be more successful in other arenas. It may not always be possible to stand on the sidelines of your kid's game and herald their victory or commiserate on their defeat, but try and be there for them most of the time. It's more important than any of us can know until much later, and you'll probably end up having a really good time there yourself. You'll also learn something.

**Over the years, Lucy was always one of the proud parents in the stands.**

# LOCAL CARE FOR OUR KIDS

We are totally blessed to live where we do. If you have a child, you know what I'm talking about. Maybe you just haven't stepped back from the gift we take advantage of every week day and really looked at it in a while. So, we need to work on our test scores – look at your own, how do you fare? So, there's room for improvement – isn't there always? Could you improve on anything in your world? Stop sniping and be thankful for our schools and their support systems. My daughter's teacher explained to me that there is little time for art or play in their classroom these days; they've really got to just work on raising their test scores. Now, that's dedication. Our children are well-taken care of by professionals who have a passion for what they do; that counts for a heck of a lot in my book. We all need all kinds of things we may never get, but if you look at the big picture; South County, we're a very fortunate lot and, if you keep reading, you're going to be reminded why.

My child transferred to the local school system from her private school in Salinas at the elementary level, (which, by the way, involved a commute and a fair chunk of change, plus dealing with over 35 kids to one teacher in her class every day.) On my fact-finding mission before the transfer, I meekly approached San Vicente School on Metz Road, our local school geographically, wondering what on earth I was going to find. Since my baby had been at the same school in Salinas since Kindergarten, I was not really equipped with slews of knowledge about our local education system here; and I have to admit that I was a little reluctant about the prospect of stepping out of our comfort zone and throwing her to the Soledad wolves, so to speak.

"Oh, yes, our Principal is here, if you'd like to talk to him", informed the cheery Receptionist in the school office. (This was an impromptu visit; I didn't have an appointment.) "Certainly", I responded, very surprised that talking to a live body without an appointment was still possible. The Principal duly appeared and was most helpful about my concerns and needs. He treated my child as a real person, even though we had never met. "Aha, the mark of a good educator", I say to myself. Some one who cares about the students and the parents; such a concept! I was able to do various tours of the classrooms and made to feel really comfortable about my decision.

My little blessing was easily transferred, with minimal paperwork and effort. She was placed into a class with only 17 children, and I was amazed to find that I did not even have to supply one pencil for the pleasure, (move stage back to private school, where you are required to supply 25 boxes of Kleenex and all kinds of other essentials to finance your child's way through the school year; and that is in addition to the registration fees and regular monthly dues.) I sent her along on her first day with a box full of pencils, just in case. Some habits just die hard. Her hot lunch only cost about 80 cents a day, (you try and do a boxed lunch for that, as I did for years!) Our yellow school bus would pick her up every day on the dot and deliver her safely to her place of study. People, we are so very lucky to have such a wonderful support system within our school structure!

After school the Soledad YMCA will walk down to her school, (or drive, if it's raining), and pick her up from school, then deliver her safely to their big pink building, where she gets a snack and is able to do her homework and play a little, until her doting parents can pick her up. Look at the image of secure child in arms of safe community, and all for very little money at all. Oh boy, South County, we are lucky. Did I say how lucky we are?

During the vacations, the YMCA hosts holiday camps for our little blessings. For little money again and a lot of peace of mind, your child will have fun, get much needed exercise, plus make all kinds of new friends and other people not such good friends to prepare them for the real world, which is guaranteed to hit them in the head down the road. Networking is part of a larger life experience and I wouldn't have had her miss it for the world. School and after school programs; so important to the systems of a well-oiled working family! In South County, we have it all.

**Lucy was always so grateful for the care her family received when they first moved into the Soledad School District.**

# SEND THEM OUT TO THE BALL PARK

As the sun falls behind the hills and the chill quickly hits the ground where I am currently crouching, I am swiftly reminded of how it is to sit on the side-lines of ball practice in the early season; absolutely totally freezing and not really a comfortable situation for those of us who actually feel the cold to the bone and beyond. Can't believe that I had already forgotten about last year and how it was exactly just so! I am sure it is always just so; but, as the season progresses, the memory does tend to fade with the increased warmth, and you find yourself looking for shade under the nearest bush.

Eccentric though I am anyway, much of the time; during this season, I take the biscuit for fashion faux-pas. If you were so inclined to try and track me down this time of year, I can be found on the softball practice ground somewhere in town with a Mexican blanket over my head and tucked around as much of my body as it will stretch to, a hat covering as much of my head as I can make it and various other loaned or stolen articles of clothing draped around my body. Being out on that damp grass and watching a squad of young 'uns continually reach and miss the ball in the late afternoon in very early spring is a labor of love, I tell you; either that or a demonstration of the purest insanity there is. As I watch my little angel pumping her heels around the diamond in the near dusk and listening to the bark of her coach, I feel the love in every step, with my teeth chattering to the swipe of every ball. I also find myself wondering where on earth I left the hip flask.

"Hustle! Hustle!" the coach shrieks, willing the little people on to a performance level fit for their first game, which, thankfully, is still a few weeks away. "And why do we do this to ourselves after a long hard day of grind in the American money machine of life?" I can't help enquiring of my chilled bones and any remnants of brain matter that haven't been frozen to smithereens.

With the obesity epidemic so rife in every level of our American society these days, that is why we do it, among other things. It is an investment in the good health and well-being of our children, which we, as responsible parents, must make. Looking around, it's a crying shame that there aren't more kids and more parents showing up at the ball park and making a stand against the scourge which is just about eating up more people than cancer.

Considering how many chunky kids we are breeding who will, with more than a shadow of inevitability, turn into even chunkier adults, we need to get our entire family up and moving much more than we do, people. This is America, the land of much more than we'll ever need. On a daily basis, we have way too much choice in the way of yummy stuff to put in our mouths, encouraging the gorge to park itself on our over-loaded frames. We have no real concept of the power of fruits and veggies and how they're supposed to be the major part of the portion to fill up the plate. We no longer send our kids out to play, but in to sit on the 'Play Station'. In short, we have become a world of sedentary observers who actually need only a lettuce leaf in kilojoules or calories in energy to sustain us, but who consume enough for a small army. That's the reality, America; and, unless you want your child to waddle around for the rest of their lives and struggle with their esteem for absolutely ever and ever, you'd better get their little tuskies out of the chair and up onto the ball park.

Forgive me for making this sound so easy. It's not easy at all. The coordination it takes to facilitate the little blessing coming out of school, going to the YMCA, taking care of the homework, changing for the practice, delivering the child -or manipulating some other unsuspecting person to deliver the child- to practice, being there on time … it's all a feat of some considerable weight. And that's if you already know, ahead of time, where and when the practice is being held; which has been quite a challenge for us the past few days, I can tell you!

But it's an important thing and you have to make it happen. It's for you, for them, for their children and for the universe at large, come to think of it. If you instill in your offspring a sense of esteem and worth in the way they carry themselves on the ball field; give the energy they use to exert their little bodies some significance, as well as their efforts to do very best against their peer group; you're giving them a gift for life. They will have more energy to play more sports and aim to be healthier throughout their entire lives. They will have higher self-esteem; they'll most likely strive to excel in many different arenas, not just sports. They will then mix with others who have the same goals and possibly stay away from others that don't have such a positive creed; at least, that's what you hope.

In time, they will reinforce their own success stories with their children when they come along. They'll be out there on the ball park at the very beginning of the season with the blanket wrapped around their head, wondering why the heck they're there; but deep down remembering their parents and the parents before them who cheered and waved and suffered the elements, full of love and promise; and all for their little blessings to have a better chance at making it to the finish line with everything they might need to make a really good go of it. Or, at least, that's the plan.

**Lucy was always there, cheering on the side lines.**

# HELTER SKELTER OF LIFE

My lovely babysitter, who watched my darling for me from about the age of 2 months old and would do so even now, used to tell me that all children are born angels. "They walk through my door full of goodness", she'd say. "Then you meet the parents and you sigh for the child, knowing how they'll turn out". With over 25 year's experience of watching angels turn into devils at her daycare, her sharp judgment is not to be snorted at, in my opinion.

Recently, my child was socked in the belly by a child at school. She did not apparently antagonize him in any way; but he somehow felt it necessary to knock the wind out of her. Having never been hit before in her life, the shock, more than anything else, made her cry. What can have induced this kind of behavior? We need to look in the mirror, look around us and try to figure it out, one little person at a time. If that young man doesn't learn now that that is totally unacceptable behavior, there's little hope for him down the road. He will be the one to later join a gang, beat his wife, terrorize his children, and commit unspeakable crimes, perhaps. Am I being extreme? Maybe. To their enormous credit, the school dealt with him very severely, and showed him that there are harsh consequences for offensive actions; but what happens to him after school? Does he watch violent television; does he play aggressive video games and flaunt weapons around the place as toys? Parents arise and awake, we need to take a look at what our children are learning every second of every day. As little sponges, they soak up everything around them. We are their teachers too, don't forget; their primary teachers. We cannot rely solely on the trained professionals to steer them through the quagmire of life. When we, the parents, say bad words, they imagine that is okay and repeat them. When we exhibit unattractive traits, they emulate them. When we don't punish unacceptable conduct in a serious way, there is little to prevent them from re-offending. Parenthood is a very serious undertaking and they can't teach us how to do it successfully at school. All of us just have to learn as we go along, and sometimes that leaves large margins for error.

When asked how the little boy was now treating my daughter at school, she responded that he was very sorry and that he wouldn't do that again. "I feel sorry for him, Mommy" she said. "He's really in a lot of trouble. He spends every day with the Principal". Well I don't feel sorry for him at all, but her compassion for her aggressor was touching. We can only hope he can move on from this experience and adopt greater communication skills for the future. Though I don't know him at all, I'll be watching him with interest from afar.

Children are always on a precipice trying to fall over the edge. Sometimes we can save them; sometimes we just have to let them fall. My oldest son left home and moved to Tahoe. Fed up with the same old thing of the steady job, nice shared home with friends and comfortable home town he grew up in, he thought he'd go and make his mark on the world; go snowboarding, feel the speed, live a little. I encouraged this; since he was still such a young twenty one year old with no responsibilities except to himself. I've always felt that traveling is such an important part of education. However, he did not take the good advice we gave him, did not plan the move so well, did not wait until a certain traffic ticket was paid, did not have quite enough money to pay for expenses up there 'til he found his well-paying job, did not think out the life beyond snowboarding and girls. He also did not think about the repercussions of getting behind the wheel when drunk. Unfortunately, he is now in trouble with the law and limping home, just as his father predicted he would. Terrible though it is to have to stand back and watch him fail at a life excursion he felt so passionate about, we are letting him do this walk alone. At some stage, in the parental proceedings, you have to stand back and let the apron strings fall where they will, you have to exercise the technique of tough love. If we were to bail him out again this time, it would be a life sentence for us of paying and bailing; a lesson not really learned for him. Hard though it is for me, (the nurturer comes out every time); his father is absolutely right. If he's old enough to make these very adult decisions, he's old enough to stand on his own as an adult. Like the little boy in the playground, perhaps he will learn from this tough experience and, from now on, work harder to make his life better. One can only hope.

On my end, I plan to open my eyes a little wider and be a bit more cautious about the exposure my younger child gets to the world outside. Not that I want to coddle her to the point that she doesn't learn and grow, as she should; but I still need to protect her, while I can, from violent influence. I can stop her from watching nasty things on television; I can step in if she is being forced to deal with mean children; I can help out in her classroom and pay attention to the people she spends her day with. I can do all of those things; with very little effort. After all, it might just make the difference necessary to keep her compassionate nature intact for the future, while still developing an innate sense of right and wrong; and, when the boundaries get blurry, still being able to forge her own pathway towards a civilized adulthood. Maybe, with all the warnings we as parents receive on a daily basis, you'll try to do the same with your children?

**Lucy did the best with what she had to work with.**

# SPELLING ABOUNDS

Denying all copyright infringement, our family has been literally "*spellbound*" these past few weeks. Through our wonderful local school, our daughter became involved in the County 'Spelling Bee' frenzy; meaning that all of us in the family, from husband down to our fish, Chubbs, became enmeshed in the essence of word soup: spelling mania, eating, drinking and spewing a large, difficult mish-mash of vocabulary from noon until night, just about. The mania infiltrated our house, to the point where we were actually walking to the school bus stop in the mornings with our spelling list in hand and testing any poor unsuspecting students who were waiting for said bus, when we got there. It's a contagious disease without a cure, (except for the finals – that cured us pretty much and then there's always next year to get back into the insanity...) Thanks to the enthusiasm and the participation of our local school – yeh, thanks, guys - we were bitten by the bug and there's probably no turning back from hereon, until our sweet baby becomes a teenager and then, your guess is as good as mine. By then she'll probably be spelling 'get out of my life' and not a whole lot more.

It's been quite a different scene at home recently. My husband, not honestly much of a speller, bless him, has been seen putting his tongue around such tantalizing sensations as "inappropriate" or "miscellaneous", in his endeavors to assist in the humongous project of preparing our daughter for the next level of spelling bee-itus. He fell sadly by the wayside at "bureaucracy", which left our daughter tittering with joy and sharing his lame effort of "all Dad could come up with was B-something" with the unsuspecting group at the bus stop.

Yet, in all its madness, it really does feel that we, as a household, have been striving for something more significant during the "Spellbound" madness than even spelling victory; something more than even a larger vocabulary, though I'm certain we got at least that. No, it was more of an unusual unity which came about in our family's determination to help our daughter cross over the finish line at each Spelling Bee crossroads we faced; and then, miraculously, move her along to the next level, when we realized that she had somehow managed to cream the contest and graduate to the next round.

"How comes you're in the finals?" a super nice kid enquired of our daughter. "You're not even the smartest kid in class!" There's no good answer for that; except that sometimes the little blessings can be really something, can't they! But it serves to say that, smartest kid in the class or not, our little 10 year old really got her teeth into this challenge and was on a mission to do her best, whatever that may be. You do not have to be the best to be the most successful at something; we all know that. With that "yes I can" attitude she may go all the way in this particular spelling bee of life; but, in any case, her courage and her tenacity will give her all the perfect grades in my book that she'll need for future use. Disciplines such as study technique, determination and courage come to mind; as well as an overriding ability to quell any performance nerves which will most definitely arise.

Watching the movie of the same name "Spellbound" made for some interesting observations about the striving that we pass along to our children; some positive, some otherwise. I am not a believer that, if you force your child to read the dictionary they will instantly become enamored of the written word; far from it. I also do not subscribe to the doctrine that if you want them to excel at something and you want it hard enough, it will become so; again, far from it. I do, however, believe that children are sponges and that if you soak them up with enough good stuff they will retain at least some of it. The Spelling Bee is more than just proof that the child can learn and retain vocabulary beyond their given years. That young person has to perform, sustain their posture, overcome their nerves; all types of human behavior come into play when they are on stage at the spelling bee and there's silence in the house. You try it and see how easy it is.

In our house, the written word is an important thing. We read a lot of books, we talk about books, we talk about current affairs; we listen to the international and local news and we read the newspapers. We are informed and our children see us hungry to stay informed. This, in its turn, makes them want to be informed. It's a gift that a generation can pass down to another generation without there being any obvious demonstration of intent. Studying for the spelling bee is not going to take away from the knowledge you get from books or the satisfaction you get from completing a story, but it does pad the edges and make you into a life player. If you can perform at a spelling bee and not lose your marbles, in my mind you're ready for it all; go out and grab it.

In retrospect, the Spelling Bee was a great race. We didn't win exactly, but we learned a lot and we came out from under it a little wiser. As the educated adults in the audience struggled with such beauties as "isosceles" and "alchemy", let alone "pneumonia" or "prejudicial", you come to realize that, educated or not, our general knowledge is pretty feeble in the larger scheme of things and we will spend the rest of our lives trying to absorb the many, many things we don't know.

Put your average adult on a stage in front of a floppy microphone with a tag around the neck and make them spell something really significant in front of the Principal and their peers; most would fall apart! Just showing up and giving it a go, means that you are a player and you won.

**Lucy looks back at that time with such fondness.**
**Her daughter is still an excellent speller.**

# THE ANIMALS TEACH US EVERYTHING

# DOG PEOPLE & CAT PEOPLE

Growing up there was a clear dividing line. You were either dog people or you were cat people; there was no mixing the two. Maybe it was the fact that we grew up with the cartoon series 'Tom & Jerry', where the bad, bad cat always got the rough end of the stick and nearly died in almost every episode; but my family was just not very fond of cats.

If the truth were known, I was actually quite afraid of them. At about the age of about two, I do somehow recall the terror of reaching out to touch a very large black and white number and it reciprocated with a searing weal down my arm. The horror and the terror, not to mention the pain, ensured that I never went close to cats again. That was until I met up with my husband-to-be and he had four of the pesky creatures, plus a dog, in addition to the two charming teenage boys and it made for quite a household; but that is a whole other story entirely.

Back to cats! At the time, I was literally forced to at least acknowledge that these sly, four-legged whiskery things had a place in the universe. We had the black and white 'Thumbs' with, yes, an extra digit that looked exactly like a thumb; Fester, who was the slyest female I have just about ever met, woman or feline, and two others who left home shortly after I moved in, either feeling the competition of the other woman or sensing my non-feline vibe. With Fester, she was determined that we were going to be friends and so we became, over time, in the strangest way imaginable. Fester would pop up on the counter while the dishes were waiting to be washed and see what we ate for dinner. That would drive me ballistic, and I'd end up chasing her screaming up the stairs, (the idea of animals up on the counter tops were beyond my level of comprehension!) When we moved to the country, Fester would wait for me patiently at the bottom of the hill (how did she know when I was coming home from work?); and then slowly stroll up the hill in front of my car, while I furiously tried not to stall the darn thing, or mince her little biosky, which is what she totally deserved.

When Fester went off to cat heaven or maybe met her fate at the snarly paws of a hungry coyote; we searched for her for some time. We kept expecting her minxy little body to come sleeking up over the valley and demand her wet food, then lie next to her fire and toast her silky black coat. I have to admit to a very sad feeling when I realized that she was never coming home again; and even now I can get sad when I see a photo of the old witch. I have come a very long way from being a cat-loather, I can tell you.

A few cats later, and then along came Joey. Joey was a rescue kitten and bad to the bone from the beginning. When he was just a mere fur ball, he was bouncing as if electrocuted through the house and attacking just the twitch of a toe. We should have known back then what we were in for. If there was something ludicrous to be done, then Joey would find a way to do it. From parking himself on top of the roof and watching the world while he wondered how he would get down, (he has a broken tail and no sense of balance), to lying in full airing position on the carpet and clawing anyone's arm who dared to think he wanted a belly rub. Joe has become a legend in his own time in just a few short years. Though now 'mature', he still has his eccentric ways; his overwhelming yearning for wet food, his adoration for becoming a thick scarf for any unsuspecting visitor to the spare room, his squalling when my daughter is not at home to sleep with, his odd twitches when something gets moved or changed in the home, (such as the annual positioning of the Christmas tree). Yes, Joe is quite something and we still don't know how he selected our home to rest his thick tabby coat in, except that, perhaps, we are quite eccentric too.

Yet, when my father came to stay – another seeming non-cat person – I came to realize that animals can have quite magical powers in addition to all their other surprises. "Come here, Tiddles!" I heard through the half-cracked windows; and there were father and Joseph having a little morning chat, which they proceeded to do every morning of his visit. Both sitting there, in their way quite resembling one another, and both liking things how they liked them with little room in between for flexibility. There were even some physical similarities, but we won't go there.

Dog person or cat person? I guess that I can honestly say it is possible to be both. I have several of both now, including Joey who doesn't believe he's a cat. They provide a richness and a warmth to life that I highly recommend. Anyone in need of chasing something on a daily basis from the counter top or entertaining the visitors; or even just a companion who'll wait for you at the bottom of the driveway and cause you to stall all the way up the hill; cats are a part of life's amazing layers and, on the whole, a pleasure to behold.

**Lucy was born a dog person, but is now a reformed admirer of the feline in addition.**

# DURING THE WINTER, WE DREAM OF THE SUMMER

"And during the dry times, people forgot about the wet times," (I'm paraphrasing some one famous to keep myself out of trouble); "and during the wet times they forgot about the dry times. It was always that way" …

During a sweaty spell in the summer when I just couldn't cool myself down; I'd get up in the middle of the night to take a cold shower, drink ice water until I felt I'd turn into a popsicle, crank my air conditioning to max and complain that it still wasn't cold enough, and generally be pretty grouchy with the general lack of comfort in my surroundings every waking minute. I also recall strangely wishing it were already winter. I recollect longing for my black clothes in the closet, my lovely leather boots and turtle necks, the cashmere scarf and snuggly gloves. I positively yearned for the blazing log on the hearth and the lure of steaming tea, hot soup and spicy mulled wine. I do actually remember thinking to myself during one toss-and-turn sticky night, as I lay awake to the annoying hum of the fan; "I wish it were winter already."

When I was in the UK, the grey chill rain began to fall from the grey chill sky. I watched the rain slide side-wards at me as I endeavored to tuck myself up in my anorak and basically ignore the wet drip-drip down the back of the neck, (hate umbrellas; always have. I'd rather get wet.) I didn't really want to go out in the muck, so I tried not to. I had already totally forgotten about that sweaty night in August, when I dreamed of winter and all her layers. When I finally arrived in winter, I was not enjoying what I found there at all. I was wearing my black cashmere sweater and white cashmere scarf and it still didn't make it any better.

Now we're deep in the throes of a Californian winter, (a contradiction in terms itself), and I still feel the seeds of discontent growing and welling with the frost in the air.

"It's cold in this house," I snap, as I force myself reluctantly out of my lovely warm cocoon of duvet in the morning and see my breath like puffy clouds before me. "This house is 58 degrees!" I continue, barking to the cat who's obviously listening attentively whilst looking intently at his empty food dish. "How can any one get up and out of bed when it's 58 degrees?" I bunker up in my husband's down jacket, my woolly hat and my clutzy gloves and I have completely forgotten my wishful thinking from August, when I longed to layer up and feel snuggly. The only way I feel now is like a deeply wrapped donut with a mobility problem. Even the cat doesn't recognize me and looks for some one else more familiar to feed him.

Deep in the winter time, people get the blues and need the counsel of at least one therapist. The bills are worrisome, as we crank every utility known to man, and stack up as many dollars as we can onto the greedily awaiting credit card gods, who know that the happy days have arrived and they are about to get real fat and sassy. The silly season can bring on all kinds of strangeness. Husbands and wives fight over silly things like the dogs' dirty paws on the carpet, when they are really letting off steam about all the other anxieties which come out to play this time of year. It's an unsettling time of frost and mud and 58 degree homes.

It's also a wonderful time of change. Long gone are those sticky, sweaty August nights; the wine flies buzzing around your head; the need to constantly be outside and enjoy the sunshine, because, well, the sun is shining and it's too nice to be inside. No, a Californian winter – or any kind of winter really – is time to do all the other lovely things you've been depriving yourself of. Light a log fire, put a vat of mulled wine on the stove, light a candle, read the book you've been hanging on to for too long, without guilt and without reserve; and do all of this in the middle of the day, because you can.

We're never happy are we, humans? Take a look at your dogs and learn something from them. Unless they are ill, they are always happy, regardless. This morning it was well below 58 degrees in the garage where the dogs were sleeping. I opened the door in my donut outfit and there they were, the little blessings; jumping up and down as happy as can be, delighted to see me and thrilled to greet this lovely new day with optimism and verve; no matter that they could see their breath and it smelled like last night's dinner, plus they had icicles hanging from their eye lashes without even a skimpy sweater on their shaggy frames.

And, in the meantime, while you are learning things from your animals, enjoy the winter while it lasts. Before we know it a heat wave will hit us, probably in February, and we'll be sweating to the fan and wondering when next we can dig out our black cashmere and donut outfit. Come the summer time, guaranteed we'll have forgotten about the winter; it'll probably always be that way.

**Lucy is a former sufferer of the British winter and is happy now to winter in California.**

# FRIENDSHIP ON THREE LEGS

When I first met Jake, it was via reputation only; and that particular quality had heartily preceded him.

"He was just strolling along Metz road like he owned the place." My British neighbor related. "In fact, he was hitchhiking, if that's even possible. I stopped the car and gave him a ride – as you would – and took him home where he belonged." Our neighbor, already charmed by the indomitable young man, didn't mention the fact that she ruined her lovely white mohair sweater in the process of escorting said gentleman to his abode of record.

Quite the wanderer, sometimes young Jake could be seen skirting in and out of private properties, always charming to the last and constantly on a very important mission. On occasion, he'd bring the odd female companion back with him from his travels, but they never seemed to stay long and were perhaps not the prettiest women he could have chosen to share his life with in any case. His taste in women was strange; proven by the fact that when he first met my young son, he fell deeply in love and couldn't understand that the affection was not reciprocated in that way.

The relationship between Jake and his family was an interesting one. There was a great deal of unspoken love there; as well as a good amount of mutual respect. They knew his capabilities and watched him closely. He had a small house; just the perfect size for his small size; but preferred the much larger house belonging to his very large brother; and, despite the size difference and obvious strength disadvantage, Jake had no problem staking his claim there. The same went for the soft toys, which also belonged to his brother. Jake wanted them; they became his; it was just how it was.

Despite locked gates, he had a knack of disappearing and not showing up again until dinnertime. Though he never wore a watch, he had an uncanny skill for reappearing just in time for meals, and always with a smile on his face.

As time went by, he'd encourage his younger and more gullible siblings to behave similarly and ensured that locked gates became fortresses at their home for all of their good. He had an in-built skill for totally leading his siblings astray. Never mind closed doors and locked gates; within their fenced yard, Jake found loose fence boards which, at the right angle, became his challenge and his opportunity, and enabled an easy escape out into the world, as he deftly bounced himself up several feet high into the air and through the boards like an acrobat, to everyone's complete amazement. One time, I had the complete pleasure of taking care of his welfare while his parents were away. I could not understand how I managed to secure the wily guy behind locked doors and yet, as I went out to my car to drive away, there he was standing by my car and smiling like a fox. We did this about 5 times that particular afternoon; the university grad versus the complete munchkin. It was quite a standoff.

Visitors to his home were similarly treated to his charming ways. The regular body shaking, three-legged trick and strange limping tendency were not indicative of any type of known ailment; they were just personality at work, ensuring an extra slice of sympathy cheese, or an additional loving stroke; not to mention numerous sweet words cast at his chocolate brown eyes which would glow back with whole-hearted adoration like deep pools of love; (ensuring another slice of cheese).

When our youngest boy spent some time in Jake's company, in the form of a sleepover, it was interesting to note how our boy returned home after the weekend, shaking and hobbling as if injured; sometimes also hopping on three legs. Such was the power of Jake's character.

When Jake got ill, it became suddenly clear once more, as it can in life, that often it is the brightest lights which burn out the fastest. He had loved, enjoyed and entertained his way through his short life as one of the world's great performers; a legend in his own valley; living life to the fullest and with more style and charisma than many humans I know.

Jake was a four – sometimes three-legged rat terrier with the black and white markings of a happy California cow. He was nine-ish when he died, but with the wily wisdom of way more than his 63 in human equivalent years.

I felt deeply sad at his passing; another dear soul in our universe lost to cancer; another friend moving on, missed but not forgotten. But I was happy, too, that Jake was suffering no more from that nasty disease - it totally slowed him up and cramped his style. I also knew, for sure, that in St. Elsewhere Jakey would be brightening up the other human and canine spirits at his next locale, wherever that might be.

Whatever he's doing now, he's having fun; you can be sure of that. He's hitchhiking along the galaxy of his existence, manipulating humanity with his ruse and his guile and making everyone love him to pieces. For sure he's also shaking his little black and white body throughout the spirit world and dancing on three legs to the march of his own band.

Rest in happiness, Shakey-Jakey, and if you can't rest, as you never could; enjoy every second of what you're doing, which is what you always did. There are many of us, mere mortals, who could only stand back, marvel and laugh a heck of a lot at your enormous being and the lessons you taught us along the way. Have a string cheese on me, old friend.

Dedicated to the large memory of my good friend Jake; rat terrier extraordinaire and chief Metz Road hitchhiker.

**Lucy adores naughty dogs.**

# IF YOU BUILD IT, THEY WILL COME

Ever since I was a child and found the story of "The Secret Garden" a magical one, I have always wanted my own secret garden. Ideally, this place would be a leafy, woody sanctuary hidden behind a large old crumbly wall, with a small wooden door secreted by climbers. It would have lots of ripened fruit trees inside it, rambling roses and a lovely serene pond. I always loved ponds and streams. Years ago, when we lived in the English countryside, we had a beautiful ornamental pond next to our huge old oak tree. When my little sisters began to move around and consequently become a liability, the pond was filled in. I never liked that.

Now I am a big girl and have a house of my own, my husband enjoys building little "areas" we can enjoy on our property during different times of the day and season. He builds them and I get to enjoy them; it's a wonderful relationship. The front of the house is lovely and calm in the early light of morning. The side of the house is great on a windy day; the deck area is divine just about any time, and so forth.

Another plan came along to the inspired. My husband thought he would build an area with a pond for a few gold fish. Our goldfish had overgrown his bowl and needed a larger one. We liked fish; it seemed to make sense. This area became a sunken garden, which I watched with interest evolving over time. With a few pollywogs – or tadpoles, in my language – soon we had frogs, and the sound of the frogs at night became a noise I got used to sleeping with. Soon the pond grew to three ponds. All of a sudden, we were enjoying the birds bathing at different times of the day on the muddy edges of the watering holes and new species were even flying in for a dip. This peeked my interest. Isn't nature an amazing thing! A beautiful lawn was put in one day into my secret garden, also rocks so that you could walk between the ponds. My husband and I would sit in our lawn chairs in our secret garden, sipping our tea in the afternoon and marveling at our little oasis. He planted special pond plants, lily pads and the like. He situated bird baths so that we could bird watch as we sipped and began plans for a gate to be able to close the dogs out of our paradise when they were getting too rambunctious. This was such a special gift; I began to look forward to my quiet time in my secret garden every day.

One day, as I drove home, a large black and white King snake was slithering across my drive way. I was forced to stop the car or run it over. For those of you who know me, you also know that I consider snakes appropriate only for shoes and handbags, so the running over option seemed quite attractive at the time. Callous though that may sound, I cannot stand snakes and I find the summer snake presence in these parts almost the only drawback to living where we do. Just the sight of a snake – poisonous or not – will have me locking my car doors and screaming at my husband to quickly remove said thing from my line of vision, my property and, if he refuses to exterminate the wriggling mass, at least move it onto the neighbors' lot where it belongs.

A couple of days later, the same thing happened, at the same turning point on my driveway, though I think it was a different beast. A worrying thought came to mind that, knowing my anti-serpent stance, these things were messing with me. My husband and I were sitting down for our nightly tea by the ponds. "Don't get excited," he cautioned and I immediately whipped around, as a brown and white King snake slithered across one pond towards another and I quickly evacuated the area, spilling my tea as I ran.

A day or so later and I found him giggling to himself; always a suspicious thing. "I figured something out," he chuckled. "I was lying awake thinking about how noisy the frogs were the other night, what we could do about population control and how they have no real predators; then I remembered all our surplus of snake visitors. Guess what, our snake visitors love frogs!" Oh my gosh, and that just made such perfect sense! How had I ever allowed him to build all those ponds and put all those frogs in said ponds? The chief snake-hater in the universe had just invited generations of snakes to come and visit, even move in for the duration! How preposterous is that? Am I out of my mind? Short of telling him to just fill in the blessed ponds, as my father had to do years ago - for children, not snakes - I knew not what to do. It was going to be a long summer; I knew that, with my eyes peeled for the comings and goings of the slitherers and my nerves on edge.

“I think he looks like a Leroy,” my husband noted, as said unwelcome visitor curled his way, in relaxed fashion, around the front lawn. It was the same intruder as our recent pond visitor. This was not good; I was starting to recognize the pest. “You are naming him!” I yelled at husband accusingly through the locked window. “Don’t even go there! Just get him out of here!” Husband just chuckled again and carefully escorted Leroy over to the shade of the olive tree where he could stretch out in peace and prep his appetite for a few more frogs from our ponds.

Since then, Leroy has pretty much moved in, as if he has some rights over the place, a passport to move around freely at will – at my place, eating my frogs. He has been spotted near the roses, around the lilies, round and round the front lawn many times and most definitely at close proximity to our frog ponds. “King snakes are good snakes,” everyone tells me, as I try to rouse the sympathy vote and do something extreme to remove these intruders from my neighborhood. “They’ll keep the rattlers away.” OK, so those are worse - and I have seen a couple of them in my time out in the wilderness, also called my home. With the arrival of Leroy came a resident water snake, which has, thankfully, yet to be named. He resembles a long sprightly worm and I don’t like him either.

And there it is. You may not always like the neighbors you are stuck with and some of them are just visitors and will only hang out in the summertime; but just think of it this way, some of your more permanent neighbors are worse! In place of your frog-loving peaceful dude – Leroy, the King Snake – you could have Hiss and Bite, the rattler, who also lives close by. I guess, reluctantly and quietly, I’ll try to take a live and let live attitude with Leroy this summer and not scream to the high heavens every time he’s around. I’d hate for him to get an inferiority complex and move on out, leaving Hiss and Bite to rule the kingdom of snake at my house. Most of life is about compromise anyway. If you live in paradise, there has to be a sting in there somewhere.

**Lucy is a snake phobic living in California snake country.**

# IF YOU NURTURE, IT WILL GROW

When we first brought Sarah home, she'd keep her ears back and spit in a most unattractive way; not lady-like at all. In those early days, there was no way to get close to her. "Oh no," said husband who had picked her out especially and brought her home for our daughter's birthday present. "Trust me to get the feral one." (He was already in trouble for having gone along with the 'buy one, get one free' offer from the rescue shelter and bought home eight legs instead of the four we had originally agreed upon!) This was an "uh-oh" of mammoth proportions for the chief animal carer in the house, i.e. me.

Sarah also had a real problem using the cat box we had strategically placed for her inside the house; the carpet seemed so much easier, I guess. We all know that kittens need to stay inside in the early weeks of their life; but sometimes the stress makes it just not possible, we discovered. Joseph, the resident territorial tabby, was simply not in the sharing mode, and wouldn't allow the two kittens to eat, drink or do their business in the right place. In short, Sarah - and her buy-one-get-one-free amiga – caught my wrath one too many times and went out to live in the shed. Though still supplied with shelter, food and water, we imagined that Sarah, especially, would further develop into every bit the wild huntress of the neighborhood she had seemed destined to become in the first few months of life. We envisaged we'd see glimpses of her white coat and calico coloring every now and then; but she would be, on the whole, an absentee pet. Or, that was what we thought.

Over a short period of time, Sarah became a quite tame and quite loving member of our family. She likes to curl around your legs and will purr with delight if you stroke her while she chomps on her nuggets. You can pick her up and nuzzle her any time you so choose; the true meaning of a love bug. The turn-around from wild to madly domestic in the life of this abandoned cat still surprises the husband and me to this day. She even likes our completely hyper dog, for heaven's sakes! None of our other animals like our dog!

If you pay attention, good things can come; that much is proven. Sporadic gestures of kindness can go a long, long way in the crazy life that most of us lead. So why do so many of us pay so little attention? Because, on the whole, we can; that's why.

That is until some one close to you says "things have not been right between us for the last 2 years." Last two years? What happened two years ago?" You drag back in your memory for a key to that particular door. The world, as you know it, stops right there. Life, as you thought you knew it, shifts its levels and becomes dark and unfamiliar all of a sudden; everything around you goes very quiet and very, very frightening. "Well," you respond, cautiously. "In that case, we had better sit down and have a conversation."

From there, you imagine life shifting forever in that direction. You see your new life stretched out before you, without that person in it. They will not leave you in the morning with a peck and return at night; they will not be there to do so. They will not fix your gates, repair your windows, or bring you flowers. The blooms inside your house you will deliver yourself, the car will drive itself into the dust - no chance of a reprieve in the repair shop, or even its bi-annual detail. You won't have that person to laugh with and plan and share your dreams. Lots of things will go to pot, but you'll hire some one to pull the weeds, because they wait for no one; we all know that.

The child will lament herself from a broken home and forever have that excuse that she failed at it all because her parents were no longer together. All of those things you can visit in a very short period of time in your mind, when you realize that you have not been paying attention and that other person, so special in your life, has realized it also and moved some way towards accepting it as being so.

"We have two choices," he declares, with an authority that makes you go unusually silent. "We can fix it, or we can fix it with counseling." Inside, the relief swells like a huge air balloon. "He's not leaving, he's not leaving!" (No mention of the 'D' word; that would kill our daughter. You can kill me, but don't kill my daughter; that's been the overriding goal in my life since conception".) The internal conversation rambles on excitedly. Inside just myself I'm giving myself an "atta girl"! If we were in the hugging mode; at that point, he would have got a hug.

And so, the conversation begins and, all of a sudden, this is not Mount Etna we're climbing or an impossible marathon race we're trying to win; it's two people who lost their way in the chaos they call their existence, trying to find each other again and realizing that they had actually lost nothing at all; they had just forgotten they needed to pay attention. What a relief: a reprieve, a second chance to do a little better. Sometimes you have to be reminded of how it would be to be without it, in order to wake up and revisit a rare gift.

The gift these folks had rediscovered came back to them like treasure they had never, ever had. They cooed over it and held it close, as if some one was going to take it away again, which of course they might, if they weren't paying attention.

Like a wild cat, you must nurture what you think you might lose; work on taming what you think is untamable. Fill your cup to overfull and hope that some of the drops will stay and water the soil to keep the life beneath it growing and blooming in the way that it should.

In time, perhaps, we will have mastered this mystery called relationships; in all probability, just in time to crumble and fall into the arms of eternity.

**Lucy is a busy person who sometimes doesn't pay enough attention to the things in her life that really matter. She's working on that.**

# IT'S A DAWGS' LIFE

Being a dog person myself, there are very few dog people that I cannot get along with. To me, real dog people epitomize all that is civilized in human beings. Dogs enhance you, they make you better. No matter how ugly or rotten you might really be, the dog can find the best in you and bring it out. I'm not talking about those fighting dog people – those would be equally at home with fighting rats or roosters. No, I'm talking about your honest-to-goodness, dawg lovin' types, who will maintain the maxim that most children will leave home eventually, but a dog is forever.

My black Labrador retriever shapes my memory of child hood. Her name was Julie and she lived until kidney failure took her from us at the ripe old age of 16. My mother swore she couldn't go through grief like that again and she didn't. Julie was the only dog we ever had growing up and Julie was a huge part of our family life. She nurtured the children, exercised the adults and made sure that none of us could ever be that mamby-pamby house-proud or the queens of car finickity that we couldn't tolerate the presence of a majestic four legged security system in the home or around our garden, or even dripping slobber down our necks as we drove in the car. Julie was the bomb – she was good for all of us. She kept us level. When my baby sister was sick, she walked circles around her in the garden to guard her and keep her safe where she lay. She was all we needed.

Several years later and Rosie was my next dog – a black Lab mix and wily as a mamba, just like her namesake – my baby sister. She was Louisiana born and bred and liked nothing better than to go out into the muddy bayou and sniff out a good Neutra-rat or two, regardless of the consequences. Her one goal in life was to get out of wherever she was confined, and in the modern day world, that meant that things got a little tricky with Rosie around. There was a memorable time in Texas, when we were driving cross country in the height of summer with Rosie and all that mattered at the time inside the confines of a Mercury Cougar. It was time to vacate the motel and get driving across the hot, boring, flat mass of land, also known as the state of Texas-in-Summer, when Rosie escaped our grasps and went off for a little illicit wander. My traveling companion at the time was so ready to leave Rosie to the wiles of destiny – but I could do no such thing, even if it meant another paid night in sleepy, sleazy motel 0 in the middle of absolutely nowhere. There was a bit of a fight about that I do recall. Rosie and I, we understood each other. Rosie had stopped that mean, drunken man entering my trailer at dead of night, when I was home alone way back when. Rosie was to be waited for, so I waited and, sure enough, she came back.

And now we have Baxter – a mixed mutt of indeterminate breed medley but with the sweetest chocolate brown eyes you could imagine and a kind, sensitive nature. Baxter, so the story goes, was abandoned on the freeway at Gonzales and picked up by animal control, where he was shipped to that nice shelter on Hitchcock where we found him, fell in love and adopted him. He was supposed to be a small dog, but that actually didn't work out. He is a fair size. Baxter lives in ag country, but has developed a highly neurotic disposition towards the vine cannons and guns, which, at this time of year, exchange their booms at fairly regular intervals to keep those pesky birds off the ripening berries. His neighbor is a vineyard and he has a hard time getting used to that. Every time a cannon is fired, especially the whizzy firework kind, Baxter needs to get away, preferably into some one's lap, or at least under the bed. If he is in the backyard and no one is around to rescue him, then he will do his darndest to dig out under the fence and away. It really is quite a sad state of affairs and one that may require a trip to the doggie therapist and a prescription for some doggie downers if it gets any worse. Laugh not.

As a dog owner, I am required to read the story about "Marley", the world's "worst dog", who is really just a large, rambunctious Labrador retriever with oodles of personality. I have learned a lot from my literary journey with Marley's owner and have realized that there are many, many neurotic dogs out there, who are freaked out due to absolutely no fault of their owners. They just have their own peculiarities which need certain, specific attentions – just like people. Marley, for instance, couldn't tolerate thunderstorms - a little like Baxter's aversion to gun shots and vineyard cannons. Marley would eat dry wall and become a "cutter" at the first boom of nature's wrath. Despite being on drugs, Marley never could get used to this particular aversion, so his family accommodated him and moved to Pennsylvania. Well, it wasn't quite all about him, but you get my drift.

If Baxter thinks he is going to be the one to make sure that we leave this paradise we call home just because he cannot tolerate a vineyard as a neighbor, then he has another think coming. But I do try and accommodate his neurosis as best I can. I let him snuggle up to me when he is suffering. I let him come in and away from the demons, when the demons are really giving him a hard time and I am in a position to rescue him from his wildest nightmares, which are, of course, just loud bangs in the vineyard next door.

And so it is. Dog people do just about everything for their dogs, just as kid people do for their kids and we all know that dogs would do anything for their people – the kids, we can't really say. It is a deep love that some cat people and definitely no-pet people completely fail to understand. A dog brings so much to everyday life that I really cannot imagine a significant existence without one, or preferably two, bringing their large personalities and sometimes neuroses to the family table and adding an added dimension of color and love that has no price.

**Lucy is a proud owner of two rescue mutts –Baxter, who is afraid of bangs, and Sophie – a quarter his size – who is definitely not. (At press time, she was up to 5 dogs.)**

# LEARNING FROM THE DOG

With all the many fears we mere mortals have to contend with on any given day – from the threats of global warning to pervasive terrorism in our daily world – it is no wonder that we tend to regress somewhat; resort to indulging in the simpler pleasures in life, the ones which do not involve analyzing whether the world is going to melt or explode in the near future, or at least today. It is no wonder, therefore, that we become a little obsessive about our animals; and in our case cats and dogs.

I have noticed an increase in this obsession over the last few years. Just travel over to Carmel and the doggie boutiques, or stop by the grooming parlors and witness the latest styles; it really is a sight to behold. Visit Carmel beach with your dog and see how many friends you can make in 20 minutes. There is nothing like a four-legged bundle covered in sand and salt water with a whipping tail, helping you join the club.

Dogs harbor eternal love and I have to think that many things I have learned in later life have been since I became a serious dog owner. I say 'serious' because I have always had dogs around me; just that mother used to be the primary doggie care giver, which is a quite different thing entirely. No, you have to be the chief caregiver, the dog supreme, the queen of Dogdom, as I feel I am now, which makes me entirely qualified to you unbelievers to advise that the doctrine according to St. Dog is quite simple:-

- True love is forever. No matter how many times or how frequently you leave and come back again; may it be a minute or a month, dogs will show you just how much love they have for you in licks and whirls and general crazy behavior. They have no sense of time and nor do they care. Humans only behave like that in the first week of dating.
- The main goal in life is to get inside the house. No matter that there are lovely cozy doggy beds situated on various parts of the property; both shade and sun accordingly, and human chairs that can be equally stolen for good naps; the bestest thing in the whole wide world is to sit with the humans in their human arena. That is when you will truly see a dog

smile. They will jump on the sofas, wriggle until all the cushions fall on the floor and doggie-chuckle with delight. Ah; simple pleasures.

- Dog food is okay, but what you're eating is so much better. No matter what the experts say; those discarded pork or beef rib bones with just a snickle of meat left on them are manna from heaven and need to appear more than as just a rare treat.
- Just as the main thing in life is to get inside the house where the humans are; the second most wonderful thing is when you appear with a leash and they know that life is grand from where they're currently standing and wagging. There is little in the world quite as delightful as watching your dog on the hot trail of a rabbit and tearing flat out through the vineyard in hot pursuit. They share your opinion there.
- You understand that they have to use those darn doggy necklaces, also known as collars and leashes, but once in a while, take them to the vineyard and let them run loose. Heaven is rushing through the vines after a chubby hopping bunny with the wind flapping your ears. Even though you can hear the humans yelling your name and they're getting more and more hysterical as they lumber behind you, the chase is the thing you crave; and for sure, they'll forgive you when you limp back, tail between the legs with deeply sorry hooded eyes, and sink your haunches before them. Men could learn a lot from dogs.
- Punishment is understood, equally, when the humans acknowledge that you are not actually deaf; you just chose to chase the rabbit instead of coming to heel. You get the loud words and the wagging finger; they just need to hurry up and get it over with and not bear a grudge. By the way, giving the other dog a snackie and not you is not the way to play fair; rabbit or not.
- Children rock in Dogdom. They are to be indulged and encouraged in all aspects of canine raising. Children know how to play; you don't even have to teach them! Let a few kids out with the dogs and see how much fun can be had. As for the adults; they can mostly use a little help. Chasing after the same ball time after time just doesn't cut it.
- Don't even try to enter Dogdom unless you're really committed. It's just like raising children, though without the

same sort of diaper training. Dogs need to be nurtured and cuddled and loved; not to mention walked and watered and fed; constantly. They are not a fish; don't treat them like one.

- As for cats, they can be fun too for the citizens of Dogdom; as long as the canines know who the bosses are. Cats can be great trainers of dogs; and it's so amusing to watch their education. One little scratch on the snout will have them eternally towing the line. Cats will not lick you or love you to death; but they can have their own place in your animal kingdom which also falls in line with some eternal – if aloof devotion; and definite leanings towards daily habits of ritual and preferences of personage.

In this time of doubt and stress; get yourself an animal to teach you all you need to know about living out the rest of your life in a more satisfactory fashion. They will make you love them; they will force you to think of things other than global warming and world peace. They will make you feed them and nurture them and forget all about yourself; no bad thing. They will also, on occasion, lick you to death with overwhelming love and devotion; and make you feel like you are the most desirable thing on the planet. We all need that once in a while. Men could learn a lot from dogs.

**Lucy is a dog-holic.**

# LEARNING TO LOVE LIZARD STYLE

Scooter has been a member of the $5^{th}$ grade class for almost a year now. Not your conventional class pet, the odds were firmly against Scooter ever surviving the first week of school, let alone the first year. But what most of us underestimated from the get-go was the over-riding power of love against the odds; the strength of caring to hold Scooter up above daily danger and inevitability and keep him thriving all those many days of commuting back and forth between multiple homes and little hands and the sanctuary of the classroom.

Scooter started out life as one of many, in all likelihood; though his parents were unknown at the time that our paths crossed. He probably was born and raised under a rock in the late summer of 2005. Though, in his early life, he was surrounded by fierce predators, such as the ferocious tabby cat always looking for an easy snack, Scooter was resourceful, for sure, from a young age. He acquired early survival skills, by managing to slip his slim self in and out of the rocks and wood piles for a quick bite, before ever being caught. The same could probably not be said for his siblings, since, by all accounts, he remained a lone ranger. We never saw any others remotely like him in our garden.

Scooter was captured prior to the return to school after the summer vacation of 2005. His first home in captivity was a clear plastic box with air holes and grass. It was okay – at least his new mother brought regular food and water to him. It was even better when she remembered to leave him on the shelf in the sunshine for the day in the warmth; then she really rocked.

One day Scooter thought the end had found him prematurely. He was bumped and bounced until he thought he had no more feeling in his little body. All of a sudden the bumping stopped and he was surrounded by lots of little faces and big eyes. He was at school, though he didn't know it yet.

"This is Scooter, boys and girls," said the lady in charge. "You are all going to have the opportunity to look after him and take him home with you." And so it went. The schedule was arranged for Scooter's sleep-overs each night; the permission slips were signed by any willing parent daring enough to take him on, and 5th grade took over the responsibility of lizard husbandry. Each day a new student would have permission to take Scooter to their home with the charge that they bring him safely back to class the following day. Almost every day the task was accomplished.

By the end of the school year, the students had learned a lot about caring for a tiny little thing, no bigger than their pinky. They had learned to nurture and feed; to be responsible for something other than themselves; to love even.

Scooter will be returning home for the summer vacation with his second mother and will then be released back to the wild. He will be free to return to basking on the peaceful rocks and snacking on bugs before falling asleep in the safety of the wood pile. We imagine that Scooter will live for a good long time; he's proven himself an unlikely survivor in a rough and tumble world.

"Look how pretty he is, Mum," said Francoise, his second mother. "He's shedding his skin." Sure enough, Scooter was stripping off for summer and preparing for retirement.

"I can't believe he's survived this entire school year," said Mrs. Morris, the 5th grade teacher, the lady in charge; (and surely not much can continue to surprise her, as a teacher of 10-11 year olds!) None of us can believe it; least of all Scooter, I'm sure.

They tell you to never underestimate children; if you do, they will surprise you every time. I myself deeply underestimated the caring nature of the 5th grade class and the overriding power of love. The whole experience was a pleasure to behold.

**Lucy will never forget Scooter and the 5th grade class.**

# PIGS, RABBITS & CORN DOGS

Have you ever really studied the buttocks on a pig, caressed the silk-soft ears of a rabbit or tasted a real fresh fair-made corn-dog with too much mustard sauce? I hadn't; up until this week that is.

I'm ashamed to say that I have lived in America for a good many years now and never really understood or enjoyed a good old-fashioned American fair. If the truth were known, I have really avoided them wherever possible. In England, where I'm from, a fair is a few scary carnival rides with names like "The Skid", or "Crashing Bumpers"; plus some nasty gooey pink cotton candy, or candy floss, as we call it, which gets stuck in your hair when the wind blows in the wrong direction, which is invariably what happens, to create a nasty, gooey memorable fair experience. You can also spend a lot of currency trying to win that soft cuddly dog on the top shelf of the English fair and end up going home with the pink plastic dinosaur on the bottom. You will, without doubt, spend a lot of currency; period. That was a fair for me back then; an experience that you could get over when you were 13.5 years old and never go back to. This could perhaps explain why 2006 was my first proper fair experience on U.S. soil and now, I believe, that I've seen how different a real American fair can be, I think I might be a little hooked.

The King City or Salinas Valley Fair is a very wholesome adventure in Americana and I mean that most sincerely. Everywhere you go within the fair grounds, you will see people you know waving at you with ice cream cones in their hands and a smile on their face; so very Norman Rockwell. Wonderful food everywhere; candy floss becomes a distant memory! I was bowled over by the workmanship in the arts and crafts booths; the flowers, photos, paintings, Missions, bird houses, quilts; you name it – not to mention the fruits and vegetable displays. What you have at your fair is a veritable modern day museum of contemporary arts and agriculture. So many man hours and constant attention to detail have been bestowed on each and every project. Made me want to get out my scrap-booking and whip out a new photo or two. Our young people really get their teeth into these projects and are proud to show off their work; we need more of that.

We strolled, slowly, through the animal pens in those enormous dark red barns and admired the young people in starched whites, nervously spritzing down their pigs or sweeping an animal pen. My friend knew everyone in these barns, so we kept having to stop, pause, talk, stop again; and I was then able to stand alone quite a lot and admire the scene. I was amazed that this is really such a family affair; deck chairs were arranged around the animals' pens, picnics laid out. Everyone was taking the day off from their busy lives to support their child in this significant venture in their lives. This strikes me as such a key factor for children; we have to pay attention to them, we have to praise them where praise is due. We have to teach them to nurture. Animal husbandry helps us all do this. The fact that the children have to be so solely solicitous of their charge for a period of time teaches them life skills they couldn't get in the classroom. I learned a lot myself just watching all that they had learned.

For those of you for whom the fair is an annual event; a part of your forever eyes; just put yourself in my shoes and see what I saw for a minute. I saw a whole community behind your children; watching and supporting and admiring the fruits of their labors. I was also informed that this same community would also bid highly for the fruits of these same labors on another day. I have a hard time imagining how my own child would be able to give up an animal she had bestowed such tender care on for such a solid period of time, but I hear that it happens and it happens a lot. It teaches them great business sense, they say; some clue of the world ahead of them.

And so my launch into the world of the County Fair was a quiet, timid one; very few people would ever have known that such a novice was in their midst. That is they wouldn't have unless they caught me examining the interesting shape of a pig's buttocks, the different qualities of corn dogs throughout the fair grounds, or even the smile on the young face of the competitor who had entered the race, worked hard and done very well, thank you very much, even though it was her first year.

**Lucy went from being a fair novice to the mother of the Reserve Grand Champion Hog and FFA Champion in just a few short years!**

# RATS AND CARS AND ALL THINGS NICE

If you had told me even last week that I would be living in my own home with a pet rat, I would have laughed and said "there is no way in hell", plus that I would have to completely lose my mind before that ever happened; but then, even I can forget that children can be so persuasive as to be termed manipulators.

My daughter is an animal obsessive. If you were to check medical journals, there is probably a condition associated with her affliction. If she had her way, we would have every type and shape of critter living in our home and around its periphery; horses, goats, cats, dogs, snails, hamsters, snakes, spiders, lizards, fish, cows; you name it; even rats. They would have a place in our family and we would never be permitted to crush, dump or flush them; ever. If they happen to pass away, as was the case of the tiny baby field mouse after its sad altercation with our big mean tabby cat, the proper thing to do is to make a plot in the garden, have a serious burial ceremony outside, shed proper tears, say a few words to help the tiny baby be escorted up to heaven, make an appropriate marker for the grave and then yell at said mean cat; (only to forgive mean cat later on in the day, when mean cat becomes soft and purry and wants to wrap around your neck). Such is the nature of love and forgiveness. Enough of the cat; now back to the rat!

My daughter did a deal with her father 6 months ago that if she did all her regular animal husbandry chores, such as the daily feeding and cleaning of all the other many critters she has persuaded us to buy or adopt over the years, she could get another small animal. Armed with 6 months worth of completed chores and a reluctant but growing attitude that maybe a hamster wouldn't be so bad, if in fact daughter would clean out the cage herself; husband traipsed off to the pet store, hand in hand with the biggest animal lover in the world.

"You have a rat," he stated simply to me on their return. Knowing how I scream at the sight of a mouse even, especially as seen recently in the bottom of my washing machine, this was a brave move on his part. "They bite less than hamsters," he added to his relatively slim information pile. My daughter went on to elaborate on all the virtues of our new pet; their affectionate nature, their comforting sleep patterns, their general intelligence; and all the while I couldn't take my eyes off its long winding tail and razor- sharp front teeth.

Meanwhile, back in the BMW, my son was trying to install himself back onto the family payroll at the ripe old age of 21 approaching 22. "I'll pay you back," he whines. "You're the only people I can turn to for help. I know I'm going to get this job and I will pay you back immediately." Then there comes the poetic pause and the line that he uses when he really wants to go for the jugular. "You are my real mother, you know," (I'm not).

Years ago, he had purchased an expensive and irresponsible car that he has carried on his back ever since; the weight of it practically dragging his chin down to the floor. We had not ever endorsed this purchase, quite the contrary; yet here we are presented with yet another payment for the monster that he's pleading for us to assist with. To date, he has never paid us back a dime of the so-called "borrowed" money; no matter what hollow promises were delivered; even in writing.

What is it with children when you say, assertively, "no", they know that you mean, assertively, "maybe"; and that you will forever be a sucker for a sob story and dig however deep they need you to if they just keep on pushing a while? The car payment is made. "This is the last time!" you say, frustrated to the core. "Don't ask me again, ever! And, and ....you had better start paying us back what you owe!"

"I will," he assures, like the cat that just ate the cream up on the countertop. "I will; as soon as I get the job." And so he skips out of your lives until he needs something else in the not-so-distant future, when he will fly back in with a sweet tale of sorrow and a bet on his life that you'll fall for it. He doesn't get the job and calls for the 2$^{nd}$ car payment request in two months. I relayed his calls for help to his father and, this time, the car payment did not get made.

Back to the rat; way easier than children. Rats are actually quite sweet; I can hardly believe we're having this conversation. They smile almost, they twitch and, I swear, they snuggle, given half the chance. A week after "Temple" moved into my house, I can almost say that I'm a little fond of her, (don't tell my daughter).

"Mum; the book says that rats do so much better when they have a companion," my daughter starts working on me 3 days after Temple moves in. "They live longer and are much more affectionate if they are not lonely." I could swear that her big blue eyes were almost swelling up with a tear. "Oh Mum, please, can I get another one; I promise I'll take good care of it. I always do."

"Maybe," I say, (kid's language for yes), and she smiles, knowingly.

On our way out of the pet shop, armed with "Ruby", rat number two, two harnesses and a stylish carrying case for critters, I had to really stand back and take a good, hard look at myself and the events of the past two weeks. Not only had I made another car payment I swore I would never do for the son who never seems to learn, I had two rats living in my house; and I couldn't for the life of me figure out how it all came about.

I came to the conclusion, ultimately, it's called blind love; that's what it is; and you're mostly going to do it no matter how much you jump up and down and say you're not. It's not a quantifiable madness; it's called parenting and it can and will surprise you every day.

And, while you're on the way to make your own child's car payment, stop into the pet store, why don't you? They have all kinds of rats available; and they're much more affordable than hamsters or even birds. Around every corner comes a surprise package. What is a parent to do?

**Lucy still owns the critter cage specifically for any additional rats needing a home.**

# SNAKES ON THE PATH

Valentine's Day and we are stripping off. It's around 70 degrees and the February air has a July feel to it. The skies are azure blue, the sun a resounding flaming ball, and, if you bought chocolates for honey on this day of love, they are by now melting in the car. Some days, you really do think the world has gone mad. The world's climate change theories, which they pound into our brains daily, have made us buy into the fact that summer can start in our hemisphere in February and we will just go along with that, for want of better research at this current time. So there you have it. Never mind the summer solstice – summer begins now on Valentine's Day.

Another nasty school shooting – (please, Mr. Media, stop broadcasting these horror stories, they only make more crazy people come out of the wood work and crave attention of this nature) - and the folks on the scene even give it a title to give it more credibility - "The Valentine's Day Massacre". (We got it the first time in all its Technicolor glory; it really doesn't need a name to memorialize it into eternity). This horror story on the day of love could not have contrasted more fully with the glorious winter day we were soaking up in Monterey County. I watched the families wrapped up in winter wear climbing up snow banks in Illinois on this terrible day for them; then caught a sweat myself, as I walked my dogs over the land and admired our rain-kissed, velvet mountains, our flowing river and that divine summery bask – all in February.

Then I stopped in my tracks. There was a very large skin on the path and it wasn't of a dead rabbit. It was of my least favorite animal in the whole wide world – the snake. Heck, it's only February and the snakes already think it's time to come out of retirement! The world has truly gone mad. I peeked again at it and the large hole beside it. It, no doubt, belonged to a very large reptile. "Come on dogs," I said, all of a sudden in a bit of a hurry. "Let's run up the hill and get dinner!" Snakes in February? What happened to their winter hibernation? The period when us walking people can calmly stroll through the grass without a care in the world, least all that we will wake up one of those scaly things snoozing in the soils.

The plates have indeed shifted on our planet. Maybe it was that mega-tsunami that messed with us all way back when. Maybe we really shouldn't be continuing to drive SUV's because of the toxins they toss into the atmosphere, creating Feb in July and vice versa. Maybe it's all a load of bunk and weather is as weather is. It comes and goes and there really is no rhyme or reason to it. I am no scientist – can you tell – but I do know that we should not be wearing t-shirts on Valentine's Day – there is something very wrong with that. One of the coldest days of my life – aside from the Siberian cold we experienced climbing the Great Wall of China – was at my sister's wedding, a Valentine's affair on the East Coast of America. Outside, the cold was such that your eye lashes felt as if they were freezing together, the cold made your eyeballs ache, your lungs cried with the insult and felt as if they were going to bleed. I had not known it was possible to feel that way and live, but it is. I recall that day as a day that I felt I had encountered a meteorological extremity of epic proportions and lived to tell the story. Those poor people in Illinois could probably tell me a thing or two about frozen eye lashes.

"When you look at that muck, you can't imagine living anywhere else," my husband commented as we sat in our February t-shirts watching the 'Valentine's Massacre' re-screening on the East Coast. Those poor souls looked like large bears in their thick coats, scarves and gloves. The pure white of the earth made the suffering even more desperate, the blood on the ground more soul-destroying in contrast, if that were even possible.

Valentine's Day and parts of the world certainly went mad. A campus in Illinois for sure – please don't give out the shooter's name. And a small area of Monterey County, where the snakes were out for a walk in February and the people stripping off for summer, wondering when winter was really going to arrive.

**Lucy feels qualified to say that Monterey County has the best weather in the whole wide world.**

# TERRITORIAL RIGHTS

I have had the most peculiar relationship with coyotes ever since I moved to South County; no, even before that. Before I moved here, I had a romantic vision of the coyote as a beautiful wolf-like animal, which would hungrily roam its sleek frame over the remote mountainous areas to hunt and seek food for their young. I never dreamed back then, that their chosen remote area for roaming would actually be more likely my back yard, or the garden path next to my bedroom.

Our first few nights in the neighborhood were spent listening to the coyote howls, closely followed by the screeches of the coyote traveling gang, as they hunted and were successful with their mission in our hood. We liked the eerie sound in the night air, until our beloved feline, Fester, went missing overnight; presumed dead; just like that. He went out one night, as cats do, and never came home again, as the song goes. That changed a lot of things in our house. After that, we no longer had any romantic visions of the beasts; they were vermin, murderers; they had slaughtered our poor helpless kitty and made us all cry for several days after the deed. They were foul and to be exterminated.

However, as time goes by, you realize more and more, that you are actually living in their hood, not the other way around. Just because there are houses and trash cans and noise going on in and around the luscious piece of ground you call home, does not mean that the original inhabitants, the coyotes, are necessarily going to move out. Gradually I have come to terms with the fact that we have to build a wary co-existence, the coyote and I – he's not moving out and neither am I, all being well. Just like neighbors; you don't need to like each other, but you do need to learn somewhat to live alongside one another and know each other's limits. On occasion we've even had a conversation; the coyotes and I.

Strolling down my path to the land, in broad daylight, I see a young pair hopping across the grass. "Get out of here!" I yell, as if I owned the place, which of course, in my world, I do. They stopped, sneered, looked at me, laughed to one another – it seemed to me- looked at me again, sneered again, sniffed the air and stood their ground, as if to say, "no, au contraire, Madame; you get out of here!" That's as probably as close as you'll ever get to a conversation with a coyote, but it was enough to really tick me off. "Can you believe that?" I retorted. "They're not even afraid of us!"

"They should be shot," said hunter husband aggressively, observing this exchange and taking the invasion of his territory as personally as any male would and does. "Except that I couldn't do it", he added. We both stood for a while and watched the pair coolly make their way along the banks to the caves over yonder where they probably dwell. As they glided, their bodies merged with the color of the sandy corn-colored grasses and became almost one. They were made to hunt those banks, blend into the color of the landscape, live anonymously to grow and thrive. If we had been made to roam these hills, we would have sandy colored coats too, which we obviously don't.

Everyone has an opinion about coyotes in these parts; mostly whether they should live or die. Sort of like politics, the coyote can arise as a dinner conversation and make for a most arresting topic. My dear neighbor and fellow Brit Mo has to be the most avid animal lover, I know, along with my daughter. She would not crush a nasty spider, even if it needed to go bye-bye before it nipped her first. She is the rescue shelter for waifs and strays; animals flock to her knowing that she will spoil them rotten. Mo – chief animal lover in Monterey County - has a definite opinion about the coyote. "They were here first," she says adamantly. "We're living in their territory." She might not feel quite the same if she had lost one of her beloved cats to them, but then she is as protective over her cats and as cautious with their movements as any cat-lover should be in this district. She knows her boundaries and her life discipline, living where she does. You get home before dark to get the cats in, you keep a vigilant eye out during the rest of the day and you make sure that the cats have always got a way to get on the roof away from predators. She hasn't lost one yet. My other neighbor had a totally different opinion. "The coyote will drag a calf out of the mother and eat it," she noted, after dinner was over, luckily. "They need to be shot." And so it goes, the coyote discussion, like politics, is one of such strong personal opinion, that, just like politics, it would probably be best if we all kept our opinions to ourselves, or, as our dinner table banter showed, agree to disagree, change the subject and have another glass of wine. If people maybe felt as passionate about politics, now you mention it, as they do coyotes, perhaps we wouldn't all be in the pickle that we are. It's a concept.

While we would have as hard a time rounding up the coyotes in these parts as they do the "trouble-makers" in other parts, the opinions are easy to come by. Perhaps the philosophy should be that we can't maybe rid a neighborhood of vermin, but we can learn to live warily alongside one another, not liking each other exactly but sharing a hood and keeping our distance, 'cos neither one seems to be moving out.

To the sneery young pair on the hill, I've got your number and your address, pretty much, guys, so I need a little more respect when you cross my land. To the older wily coyote, which got the shock of his life by being chased by anything, probably, let alone my little ginger-colored, foolhardy mutt, there's more where that came from buddy. Baxter is still strutting, as we speak.

In the meantime, I shall still stand back and be amazed at how they continue to blend so seamlessly into the landscape, no matter the season.

**Lucy is a cautious co-occupant of coyote country.**

# THE ONLY THING YOU HAVE LEFT IN THE WORLD

I read a quote from the notorious actor Mickey Rourke this week, as he contemplated his rise from the dungeons of stardom to the possibility of reincarnation as a well-paid movie actor: the prospect of an Oscar win. He has come a ways in sobriety and humility; you have to think, since his bar brawls of yesteryear. "Sometimes all that a man has in the world is his dog," he said and, from where he has come from, we knew he really meant it. His best friend, a Chihuahua aged 17, died this week, and I can only imagine his grief.

If you are a dog person, you know what he's talking about. I recall, very early on in life, after a particularly nasty row with my mother, putting my salty-teared face into the neck of my black Labrador and telling her that she was the only one who understood me in the whole wide world. She'd lick me and her breath smelt of fish, but it was okay, because she loved away my tears one pink-tongued swipe at a time. Even now, if I am in the foulest mood, I can go out on the deck and visit quietly with my four legged friends; knowing that I can whine and moan, heck outright yell, to my heart's content if I want to, and they will just smile, wag and pant and love me just for being there with them. You can't really say that for people. Anytime I whine and moan, I can empty a room really quickly. Give me my dogs and they will get as close as possible to the whining and the moaning. They'd all be on my lap at the same time if my lap would allow it.

So there you have it – the difference in loyalty between mankind and the kingdom of the dog – chasms apart in loyalty and affection. Humans in the business world will say what they think you want to hear to your face and then do something quite other. They will act as your friend on the one side of their face, and trip you over in the dark, given the chance, on the other. They will pledge their heart and their loyalty to you in the house of the lord and then cheat on you behind your back. And that is just a casual observation on the differences between humans and canines.

So who in the world are your real friends – in addition to your dogs, that is? You hope your partner is and your immediate family. You hope the people you spend time with on a regular basis - you truly hope they are and that you will not just become a statistic in their lives of the people they have used and discarded along the way. In my decades on the planet, I have learned that true, solid, lasting friends have to run the test of time and you seldom have very many of them who stay the course. They have to witness you at your worst with raging PMS, as you lose the deal of the century, all wrapped up in one, with an IRS audit sprinkled on the top. They have to deal with all of that and then still be brave enough to call you the next day to see how you're doing. Real friends will send you a plane ticket to come and stay with them when they know that you are right on the edge of your sanity and ready to fall into the abyss of being completely out of control. They will do that, pick you up from the airport, take care of your baby, take you out for your divorce party and let you get completely ravaged. Then they will buy you another plane ticket a month later, knowing you still don't have any money, and make sure that you are getting your life back on track and are not going to be quitting the race any time soon. Your real friend will send you miniature packages of all your favorite things over the course of time, when they know you need cheering up, and call you when they know you're sad. Sometimes they'll just sense it even. They have your history, they have your number – some things extend beyond geographical location and time zone. I remind myself often of the real friends I am gifted with, and they assist with how I deal with the shortcomings of the other friends who are not that real.

"BFF". I see my daughter share tokens of esteem with friends of hers. Best friends forever? Gosh, those positions become very quickly obsolete after high school and wildly unimportant once you go out into the world of work and have a family. I can count my 'BFFS' on one hand just about, if you don't include my dogs. They will always go into their own special category of "constantly adoring, ever patient, never annoyed, until-death-do-us-part" kind of *best-friends-forever* that money could just never buy. Sometimes all a woman does have in the world is her dogs – her daughter has locked herself away in her room, her husband is in hiding, and her friends are off doing other things; but her dogs are there and ready to give away some more sincere loving. She just has to show up and they'll show her what she means to them.

**Lucy adores all animals just about – except snakes.**
**A house without at least one or two dogs is not a home.**

# THE WONDER OF IT ALL

That's the wonder of life; isn't it? Just when you think you've got it all figured out, along comes a freight train with a different agenda; and you find yourself sitting on the tracks wondering what happened. You imagine that you've got your day all mapped out. It's in your planner, checked off in the palm pilot, or reassigned for tomorrow. It's all situated, as it were; until along comes a big surprise in a box all wrapped up with a huge bow. The note attached to the box tells you that "I know you thought you had it all figured out; however .."

In the land of the "tween" you don't do things quite the way you used to either, and most especially not at Halloween. Long gone are the days when you hold the little blessing tight by the hand and escort her and her cute little pretty-witchy costume through the scary cobwebs and spooky doorways to collect truckloads of candy. I never knew that such a little person could cling on so tightly as I recall in Halloweens past.

There comes a time – right at the doorway of now, in fact - when you are trailing said "tween" and her best buddy of the moment in stalking-like fashion, (following closely behind, but not too close in a VW Van), as the adolescents branch out on their own and maraud the neighborhood, acting all grown up in front of the peers who they inevitably bump into during the course of the night. "Yeh", I think to just myself as we master the art of trailing/stalking children without being too severely caught at each corner, "I have this Halloween totally in the bag. It's all figured out." That is until you see something so totally bizarre that you have to wonder if you saw it at all.

A Honda Civic appears in your view shed, as you pause momentarily on a side street, the "tweens" dipping into doorways close by. It's dark, but not so dark that you can't see the model of the car and the 2 individuals inside. They u-turn in the quiet, dim street, turn, u-turn again, pause and quickly drive off. On the sidewalk there remains a little quivering bundle, looking out into the big, scary night. I instinctively jump out of the van and coax the shaggy bundle to my hand. I pick her up. She is warm and trembling. Matted yellow hair on a skinny, shaggy frame with dreadlock twists does not conceal the sweet little face and trusting brown eyes.

"I can't believe that!" I snort as I jump back into the van, bundle in arms.

"You don't know .." says husband, ever cautious.

"I know," say I. We knew. How can some people live with themselves? Disgusting, despicable, but destiny all the same, enforcing her right as the queen of it all. What are the odds of complete animal lovers being at the exact spot on Vista De Soledad on the exact night when Mr. and Mrs. Honda Civic decide to dump the mother of their puppies? (Probably could sell the pups for a good rate; probably could not sell the mama, riddled with fleas and neglect and needing to be spayed and fed among other things.)

My daughter, the chief animal lover in the house, thought that she was having a religious experience when she saw the bundle we had acquired. My husband – ever wanting to believe in the basic decency of mankind - still held steadfast to the notion that we had got it all wrong and some sweet little girl was anxiously hunting the streets, looking for her pup which had got out of the security of her home and couldn't find its way back home.

"I don't know that I would return her even if I did know the owner was looking for her," I spurted out with usual candor. "She has been so horribly abused." To that, husband was quiet. He knew. We knew.

So, Sophie Halloween Jensen – a Chihuahua-Pomeranian mix with the loveliest honey coat, when clean, you've ever seen, was reborn that night and came to live with the Jensens in Soledad. Her older brother Baxter – also a rescue mutt found on the freeway near Gonzales – has a few lessons about delicacy and gentlemanly behavior he still needs to acquire; but I look at Sophie and I know she's happy now. She's safe, she's well fed and she'll never have to deal with any of that ever again. She wags and dances and yips at the delight and mercy of destiny and how you never know when you wake up in the morning what on earth's going to happen that day. That's the wonder of it all. And what will the morrow bring, we wonder?

**Lucy's eyes are always open to small mercies which can cross your path when you least expect them.**

# THE TEEN YEARS

# CHANGING MOODS

If you thought you were borderline unstable before you had kids, when they turn the corner and become teenagers, you will assume the fetal position of knowing absolutely nothing anymore and having no brain to comfort anything you knew you did know before. The rules, they change all the time, and you just never know when the curve ball is coming to smack you over the head and remind you that, yet again, you got it all wrong.

My daughter is going on 14. She's my own flesh and blood, my own sweet baby, yet I never quite know what I am going to wake up to.

"Good morning Darling, "I say cautiously to the mound also known as my kid, and then proceed to creep on down the corridor, lest I give her a bad start to her day. No matter what happens between that time and the time she leaves the house with her hair straightened, a back pack on the arm and a snarl on the face, I will steal a hug at the door and tell her to have a good day and that I love her. That is my job, my role, my goal – every morning as her mother. It just wouldn't be right otherwise. I steal a hug, as if my life depended on it, from that rigid, unrelenting frame that I produced. If I'm lucky, I may get a small pat in return or an "OK, Mum, that's enough", or a little wave as she leaves me to start her day and catches me watching her leave. You'll take anything at this stage; the precarious tightrope between childhood and adulthood. Just the mildest acknowledgment that you are alive and occasionally allowed to share the same airspace is something to be appreciated – such are the crumbs that you cling onto when you are mostly made to feel that you are invisible. The birds, they fall out of the nest quick these days, it seems; and they want to learn how to fly almost immediately.

"I'm a good driver!" she insists. "Dad lets me drive!" I nearly keel over. OK, attentive ears of Law Enforcement, so this "driving" you're hearing about is on private property and all; but still, I am as alarmed as you are at the thought. So much so, that I have nightmares about it and wake up in a cold sweat! My tiny baby behind the wheel of a death machine? My husband reminds me – she'll be able to get her permit in just over a year – and that she's going to be a good, cautious driver. What happened to the bottle, the binky, the 24 hour a day need for me to take care of everything? I see the snarl again on the face of my babe and the perfect eyeliner – on her - belonging to me - and I know that that my ability to nurture her, the way I still want to, is a thing of the past, at least until she has her own children.

Flashbacks – they come too, fast and furious sometimes, when you have teenagers and you've had them before. When we had two teen boys in the house we'd lock our bedroom door; not for the privacy issue, but simply because they'd need our shampoo, shaving cream, sweat shirts, socks or any of life's other essentials when we were out of sight and they'd see fit to simply pop into our personal space and take whatever they needed at the time. We got sorely sick of that after a while and would lock our door, much to their chagrin.

Looking for my eye liner the other day it all came back to me. I do have a key for my door! I can plan against a teen invasion if I really want to! And there it was, the innocent pencil, tucked away in my daughter's bathroom, because she needed it and I had what she needed at the time. "Grrr," I said, or words to that effect, to just myself. I then began to pick up stuff from the floor, as you do when company is coming to the house, and, lo and behold, there was an entire week of my daughter's clean laundry – that she had pledged she had already put away in her closet the third time I asked her to – there it was in all its scruffy undercover way – stuffed under her bed and away from my eagle eye. Still clean. I snorted, in anticipation of the big fight we would have tonight, when I would look her in the eye and inform her that she was severely busted, how long should she really be grounded and what did she have to say about her lies? We'd have such a show down and I would totally come out the winner – maybe with her even being forced to do all of her own laundry for the rest of her life, and perhaps even mine. I was almost gloating at my victory march, as I looked around for more things to convict her of.

And then comes the ice breaker, the one thing that was going to mess with the eye liner bust and the concealment of laundry – a small, sweet text from my teenager. "Happy Anniversary", it read, and yes, it was indeed our anniversary. "I love you guys." There, my heart melted. I don't hear that kind of thing very often and she has no idea how opportune a time that was for her, with the eye liner bust and the life long sentence of doing her own laundry and mine right before her. What is a mother to do? I'm down on my knees. I implore you – help me. I have several more years of this and I'm not sure a mental facility exists that can really help me.

**Lucy is still working through the teen years and assuring herself that, one day, there will be light at the end of the tunnel.**

# DO AS I SAY

"I came home and my son and his friends were baking pot brownies," my sister tells me.

"He is grounded for life." She sounded really sure of herself.

"Did you ever make pot brownies when you were 17?" I asked her. She didn't know what to say. We both know she did a lot worse than that; she just never got caught.

A friend tells me that her daughter is not allowed to date. She is 16. "How old were you when you were allowed to date?" I ask her, knowing the answer well in advance. She told me that was not the point.

This parenting gig is about the hardest job any of us will ever do. It beats out real estate and journalism every time; probably medicine and the law too, if the truth was ever to be readily conceded. Even really smart people flunk at it all the way along. Statistics show that some of the smartest, most together people have the worst teens.

"Be consistent; you have to," I find myself telling stressed parents of teenage boys, who I randomly encounter along the path of life. Since I am now a graduate of that particular class, having raised two myself and they are both still alive and not living with me anymore, I consider myself quite an authority on the subject. The boys are no longer teenagers gladly, and are living their lives mostly unattended with the odd sub from yours truly along the way. I, on the other hand, cover my grey hairs with bleach. Once in place, the scars of parenthood never really go anywhere else. And now we have a teenage girl and it seems, from this vantage point, as if they are so much worse. I am becoming quite an authority on that too, interestingly, since we are so very early into the game.

'Be consistent', people tell you. They are mostly the ones that have no kids or who have really forgotten what it is like to go through the teen years.

"You have to be consistent," my father tells me, then ponders. "Well," he says, "to be honest, your mother did all the child raising, so I don't suppose I really know. All I remember hearing was, "be quiet, or your father will hear you!" Yes, that was one consistent thing I do remember hearing."

Consistency. Really? I'm afraid, that is near impossible; but it is something I do dream of aspiring to. Our girl is such a super-manipulator and I am so cuddle deprived where she is concerned, that all she really needs to do is to snuggle up to me or even really just acknowledge my presence in her presence and I am putty in her hands; an adoring mother- mush of paste to be worked as she will. And that is not even the saddest thing. The shame is that I truly do know better. I know that if I let down my guard, back down on my word – which I mean to follow through on so sincerely at the beginning of the charade, that I can almost put it in writing to myself and believe it – I know I am truly lost to myself and all the super, successful goals I had set out with.

"I thought she had to be home all weekend," husband adds to the mix. It had been a homecoming week full of pure teenage excitement and exhilaration. I had told her, in no uncertain terms, that her grandfather was over from England and she needed to spend time with him over the weekend since he was leaving the following Thursday. Friday night she was out enjoying the homecoming, Saturday she spent time with friends and was then due to come home for the remainder of the weekend.

She arrives home Saturday afternoon and immediately gives me the most delicious teen girl hug. My heart melts all over again; I had missed her so. She snuggles up next to me. "There's a dance tonight," she tells me, her big blue eyes sweetly on mine. "No, no you're done for the weekend," I tell her firmly. She stands her ground, visits with the relatives, goes and tidies her room and puts her clothes away. She sidles up to me again; this time coming in for the kill. "Is there really no way I can go to the dance tonight? I've done all my chores and hung out with the relatives…all my friends are going ..", she persists. I start to falter. So why couldn't she go, really? Was she in trouble? No. Did my mother ever say no to me and really mean it? No. I start to wane. "Ask your father," I say, always a good sidebar to buy myself some time. Maybe he could dig up the goal for consistency which was already slipping through my grasp like water in the palm. I was falling, I was sinking; if she comes back around, all is lost and I will be driving her to the dance.

Driving to the dance, I did know that I should have held my ground and not let her go. I should have kept her at home and witnessed the closed door to her bedroom and her heart for the evening. I justified my failure as a parent by telling myself that we wouldn't have seen her anyway, as foul as her mood would have been; but deep down I knew that the next time would be harder still. I knew that because of my abject failure as a parent this time, I would have to severely dig out my backbone for the next round and the one after that, sure to last all of the long four years at high school. If I had a chance of surviving this with even a vestige of self respect left behind, I had to find that bone and find it quick.

Looking back with honesty, we weren't really that consistent with the boys either. Real life has a way of taking you and beating you to a pulp, as you endeavor to make a living, pay the bills and line up your priorities, flunking miserably along the way on many counts.

Needing to ground one of the boys at a certain time, we knew our patience was on the brink and we, selfishly, opted to ground him away from the house. Grounding him at home would only torture us further. This was so confusing for him at the time, but necessary for us. We needed the time out away from him; we had a lovely weekend without him. All the guilt we should have felt went out of the window in favor of our own peace and serenity. All these years later and he still remembers it.

In this battlefield also known as parenthood, it is important to remember your sense of self and self worth from the time the attitude launches to the day the front door hits them in the butt and the moving van takes them away. Never mind that it is completely unimportant and irrelevant to the teen against which you are battling, you must stand tall and say 'I am me and I have a right to be happy too." Arm yourself with the years worth of survival rations you're going to need – a sense of humor, a good strong partner and a handful of friends who have gone through the same thing – and keep trying to find that illusive 'consistency' that we all strive for and few find for any period of time.

**Lucy is still parent to a teen. The last one.**

# LEARNING THE RULES AS THEY CHANGE

*"CHILDREN! Tired of being harassed by your stupid parents? ACT NOW! Move out, get a job and pay your own bills ... while you still know everything!"*

---

We had this piece of yellowed paper touting the above words taped to our fridge for many, years when we had two male teenagers under the roof who both knew everything at the time; while we, the "ancient" parental unit, knew absolutely nothing. Who were we? All we did was raise three children, go to work every day, try and make our bills and feed and clothe our family, not to mention fulfill all of the teen boys' worldly whims within reason and attend all their sports games – without going insane. We knew nothing at all.

Our teenage boys would both scowl at the piece of paper on the fridge, as they passed us by on their way to something much more important – like the interior of said fridge, the shower or the phone. They would chuckle to themselves, snort and make the derogatory "stupid" comment, while they moved on to their very important lives of being a teenager; when all is circulated around you and, fortunately maybe, you little realize at the time how trite and limited that all is.

I recently found the hallowed piece of yellowed paper, which had survived several years in the bottom of a moving box, and smiled to myself all over again. Things change, don't they; but not really. Now we have a teenage girl in the house, it was time. I posted the sign on the refrigerator again, just like in the olden days, and my daughter in her turn remarked "stupid"; just as her brothers had done years ago. It was almost nostalgic and I got to have a laugh over it all over again.

When I was a teenager, I knew everything too and my parents were stupid and annoying. I remember that very clearly and it really just doesn't seem that long ago. I see myself sometimes in the reflection of my teenage daughter's eyes and I can see that she feels the same way. Luckily for me, I was the oldest child in my family and therefore my folks had no idea how to tread the tricky path, or battle ground if you like, whereby they made the rules and I followed them. They really were clueless, poor things. My parents were not yet versed at all in the concept of the teen manipulation techniques, whereby the teenager learns to maneuver things to their satisfaction and the parents adopt the maxim of 'anything for a quiet life' and duly let the teen do whatever the teen wants to do, within the realms of them not actually killing themselves – though it did come close on occasion. My folks got clued into the power of the teen manipulation technique right around the birth of their third child, who proved to be a really tricky little number and in need of the guidelines they continued to try and set.

Years down the road, it came to me why my folks were not really gutted when I informed them that, break their heart though it may, I was moving out and getting my own place. At the time, I do recall being really confused by the fact that they were obviously not upset at all by the announcement that, this time, I was really and truly leaving home. (That confusion was resolved for me a bit later in life when I had my own teenagers and they announced that they themselves were moving out. I would say that the feeling was a bit different from "gutted" and more like "euphorific", or at least heartily relieved.)

Moving down the road a few decades, when our oldest boy was a teenager, my husband and I got to the point where his grounding involved being effectively grounded from the home, not in it, as might be the norm in other family situations.

"You are grounded! You may not use the phone or the computer the entire weekend!" We advised him. This was serious stuff.

"Can I go out?" There was an air of caged desperation in his 15 year old demeanor.

"Why yes you can!" we responded. (In fact, the sooner you go; the better! Can we give you some cash to actually be gone the entire weekend?) Call it horrendous parenting, if you wish, but we called it survival at the time and it was sometimes the only way we made our way through. We had our share of stress, ("Marc is not going to graduate. He hardly ever even comes to school anymore," The Teacher said.) We had our share of fury at 3am, ("This is Watsonville Police. We have Marc.") We had our share of truly trying times. "(No, you may not take my car! Just because you have put the truck in a ditch and your own car into impound does not automatically give you the right to assume that you will ever be going anywhere near my vehicle, which is the only one we have left that is working and in one piece!") Yes, we survived that too, along with him systematically destroying every piece of working machinery in his path and being banned from driving at least twice that we knew of.

And now our oldest son is in his third decade of life and, since he is finally old enough to acknowledge that he really doesn't know anything about anything, we actually have a very good relationship! It was quite rewarding when he shared with us, not so long ago, that he had no idea what we went through with him when he was a teenager, until he knew everything, moved out and had to start paying his own bills. (You can't help but sneak a glance over at that faded piece of paper!)

"I remember you telling me to turn off the lights when I left the room," he noted. "I never really knew what that was about until I had to pay my own utility bill." Ah, the light bulb, people, the light bulb – it can sometimes illuminate of its own accord! It may take a while in some cases, but it can happen and it is somehow rewarding when it does.

In the meantime, my "baby" is 14 and she knows everything too, while I am the dumbest blonde on the planet – especially me, not so much her dad. I dress badly, listen to horrible music, wear my hair like a dork, say stupid things and am generally a waste of any space she might be breathing at the time. I am annoying when I try to hug her and irritating when I ask too many questions. I have vague uses in the early mornings when she is running late for the school bus and I am able to remind her of key items like homework assignments or gym clothes that she really needs that day. I am also okay when I manage to rustle up a last minute birthday present for a friend, or swing a quick five dollar bill out of my wallet for the sign up that is due that morning. I have my uses, but basically I am still dumb no matter what, and I am reminded of that regularly. It is lucky for me and my self esteem that I do remember so clearly feeling that way, and now my own mother is gone from this planet I wish – oh how I wish – we could go back just a bit, so I could tell her that I didn't mean any of it, I was just being a teenager. If only she knew how I really felt about her – and maybe she did all along.

I'll go with that for my own teenager and know that once she knows everything in life, she will move out and move on with her life, and then she will look back and realize just how little any of us truly do know and how humanizing that is in the end. I'm sure she'll also look back with fondness at her stupid mother and how deeply she loved her – really, truly deeply. Even though she'll surely remember that she knew everything at the time, she'll inevitably look back and one day be able to say she didn't have a clue. It is possible. We've seen it happen. Most of us have been there.

**Lucy remembers 14 as being a particularly tough age.**

# NOT MY CHILD

My child is confident and secure; she wouldn't do that.
My child is responsible and mature; she wouldn't do that.
We have raised our child well, so far, we think. We gave her trust and earned freedoms, as time passed, and she seemed able to deal with each extra inch of liberty afforded to her.
She wouldn't do that.
Other teenagers would do that; but not her. I know her; she knows better. She wouldn't do that.

It was early evening. We had arranged to pick up our daughter, aged 14, from a friend's house at 8pm on a Saturday night; a respectable time. The last text to this effect from us to her was received and acknowledged at about 7pm. Texting is a good method of communicating with your teen, without intruding into the sanctuary of their guarded personal space. We get less attitude that way and a quicker response time, we have learned.

The rice is put into the rice cooker. We are going to eat at around 8.30pm. The evening already has a nice organized ring to it. My husband goes to pick her up. "She's not here. She and the friend went out somewhere, the sister said." He calls me from the friend's house. How annoying is that! The nice organized ring to the evening quickly breaks. You immediately lose your good mood and begin to mutter about irresponsibility, selfishness and other qualities easily attached to the modern teen, when they are not where they are supposed to be at the given time. Husband returns home; not knowing where to go to look for her and give her grief. Almost immediately he arrives home and we receive the call from a friend's older brother. "I just picked up your daughter and her friend on the streets of Soledad. They are blind drunk." My ears hurt. I didn't just hear that; it must be some one else's child he picked up. But he knows my child and he had no reason to play a mean trick like that on an unsuspecting parent. Driving down to the friend's house where he has dropped them off, I have multiple images raging through my mind from disbelief to horror to fear to fury. How could this happen? Our two way communication was only a very short time ago and very concise and to the point. I was a responsible parent, wasn't I? Where had I gone so horribly wrong? What planet had she visited in the last hour where she had lost all her common sense and trustworthy ways? Any parent that says they can get their head around that crushing reality is lying.

I can hardly wait for the car to stop. I have an urgency to get to her that defies reason. I see her and don't recognize what I am seeing. She is so intoxicated she can barely stand up; her limbs flimsy like a rag doll. Her eyes are rolling in the back of her head, as if drugged. "What has she taken?" I grab her more sober friend by the shoulders. "What on earth has she taken?" I cannot believe this is my daughter. This is some one else's, not mine. This is more than alcohol; something has infected my child and it has to be removed. I am terrified at what I am witnessing; my sweet baby girl possessed by demons and talking in what seems to be tongues. She has been turned inside out by something and my baby is no longer present; she has left the room. In her place is a monster I don't recognize.

As we race along the freeway to the emergency room, all I know is that I have to keep her conscious to keep her alive. If she has taken something, I cannot let her close her eyes. If I do, I might never see them open again. I urge her to stay with me; I yell when her eyes roll back into her head and all I can see is the whites of her blue wonders. I breathe in the icy night airs of the open windows and wish I could now wake up from this nightmare. I want to go back to my warm kitchen where the rice would certainly be ready in my rice cooker and my sweet child open armed for a hug. I feel the car go faster and faster as I scream more and more at this unrecognizable rag doll beside me. I remember looking at the lit undercarriage of the 18 wheeler beside us as we overtake it at high speed, and wondering what would hurt more – going under it or going through this.

We arrive at the emergency room in what feels like hours, but is more like a few minutes. Our child falls out of the car onto the harsh concrete of the parking lot. The cocoon of the ER embraces us like the parent we all need in times of stress and swiftly gets our child prepped for treatment. A saline drip, a blood pressure monitor and more are swiftly hooked up to our child, once she is stripped and ready for inspection. This is not my child. Mine is the one at the dinner table ready for her meat and rice; joking with us about the antics of the cat or the barking dogs. This child is hooked up like an addict, laughing raucously as the nurses tried to hook her up and do their job. She is poked and prodded in regions she would barely pronounce in her normal sober life. She is scared. We hold her down for the tests for drugs, date rape and other horrendous 'D's'. I reel at the prospect of engaging the smell of semen on my child and all the chaos that would follow thereafter. I call the kids she was with that evening, pleading with them to tell me what she might have taken in addition to the considerable amount of vodka she had drunk for the first time with no idea of its power and its strength. I text the kids, call them, beg them. This isn't us; this isn't me. We are the cautious family, home on a Saturday night, having enjoyed our meat and rice and safe in the knowledge that our daughter is tucked up securely in her room. This here is some one else's family; some one that doesn't pay attention to their child or what they are doing. Some one who doesn't know their child's friends and where they are at any given time. This nightmare belongs to other people, never us.

They take her for a brain scan; she is scared, we are scared. She says her head hurts and she had certainly fallen on it more than once in that short period of time she was over the edge and out of the boundaries of her usual behavior, or so they tell us. I feel sick. You read about times like this, the surreal light of the emergency room, the other calls coming in, and the arrival of police with unknown voices behind the curtain. "We got a call about an overdose." I hear the voice of law enforcement with no person attached to it behind the privacy curtain. Are you talking about my child? My child's overdose? A sickness quickly overcomes you like a terminal disease you didn't know you had. The drug tests are shown to you – no heroin, no cocaine, no methamphetamine. You sigh with relief at the lack of check marks. The helpful nurse points out that not everything shows up. "The tests don't always detect the new stuff," she notes. We are unconvinced by the negative tests, as the child that used to be mine tosses and turns and fights with her blood pressure monitor on her gurney. She must have had something. What could she have had? The powerlessness seeps through your being like you are on the drip yourself. Again, your psyche begs to be woken up and brought back to something you can understand and put your head around, something you can control or change.

My husband goes to fetch coffee as we wait for the results of the brain scan. We need the caffeine; it is now turning from midnight Saturday into another day. I told him to put sugar in mine; I never take sugar. Tonight is one for nevers. But I think he also needs to go out of the crazy confines of the ER and into the sanctuary of solo dark time and the relative freedom of the fresh air to pinch himself and remind himself that this is indeed our child and our family and ask himself the inimitable question: now where do we go from here?

She begins to calm, the drip is working. The hallucinations begin to ease. They have pumped nearly the entire saline bag into her system. “You can take her home, the scan is clear,” the doctor says. The kind nurse comes over and lectures our daughter on the 14 year olds who don’t get lucky enough to leave the emergency room. “You’re a lucky one,” she tells her. “Learn from your mistake. Don’t do it again.”

We take her home. She was and is our child. She has made a huge mistake and we hope she won’t make one equally large anytime soon. My nerves are shattered. She soon becomes sober and sorry. So many people had worried about her; her parents had crawled close to the edge of hell and were now hanging off the cliff and looking down to where they nearly went in horror and disbelief. It would take a long time for them to be able to crawl back to safe ground and to a place where they could start over and make sense of any of this.

In the cruel light of day there are so many reasons to be grateful, yet so many steps had been taken back, the days ahead seem like an insurmountable project full of unforeseen holes and hazards. We creep on, one tiny baby step at a time on this vicarious tight rope known as the adolescent years and the slim ravine that many families find themselves hovering on between life and death full of bad choices and horrible mistakes. Yes, this was our child, this is our child and it happened to our family and continues to happen. Know that this could be your child and your family too - for no good reason and at no particular time or place. I write this difficult piece in the hope that you do not have to suffer any of this with your child. But know one thing; you may be the best parent in the world, the most guarded and the most caring –

and it could still happen to you. I used to think that I was that person in that place.

For the record, the children did not buy the vodka that was drunk that Saturday, but they obtained it from one of the grand parents' liquor cabinets while the grandparents were not home. Whether any drugs were put into the drink that day is still a mystery. This is a true story. It happened to our family.

**Lucy will never forget that night.**

# SINCERELY, MUM

We have come a long way from the long corded rotary dial phone, that windy plastic cord that I liked to play with while I chatted to my mates when I was a teen at high school and somehow, amazingly had a phone in my room, which my father used to threaten to take out - like all the time – but never did until years after I moved out. See! Sometimes you can even sound like a teen again, when you haven't actually been one for decades. I guess some things never leave us.

The most annoying thing in the world, I do recall, was when some one else wanted to use the one line inside the home and that person would pick up another phone while I was in full dramatic conversational swing and enquire how long I was going to be. The nerve of it! That was my own personal line, my connection to the vital outside world of which I was a huge important part! It was my line to parties and concerts, connections for hook ups over the weekend and trips away. We didn't have cell phones, the internet or even pagers in those days, so the home phone was an intrinsic cord that tied us to the world we lived to participate in. Those were the days that labeled you 'dead' or at least 'unpopular' - both almost equal back then - if you did not 'go out' on a Friday and Saturday night. We were 16 and we knew everything.

During a power cut, I will still dig out my trusty old thing with its twisted up cord that hides in the depths of the cupboard most if its life; and I am always very happy every time I still have the ability to speak out through the storm, unlike some of my non-corded neighbors with their fancy cordless numbers. I wish I still had the super classic black rotary number with its satisfyingly smooth dial and delicious clicks that I had in my room throughout my formative years; it would be quite the antique now and a period piece I would dust with joy. The cordless things we all have nowadays are horribly devoid of character and irritatingly disposable. However, it goes without saying that, if you have a teenager in the house, you can never find the cordless variety in your home anyway, regardless of the multiple numbers of receptacles you might possess. The odds are that they are somewhere in the bed clothes of said teen and likely to remain so for a very long time - with a completely flat battery for when you find said implement and wish to use it.

Years ago, when we had teenage boys at home and the cordless variety also; their punishment would be that the cordless ones would go on time out and, if they wanted to use the phone, they had to stand in the kitchen on the one corded variety and let the rest of the family listen in to their conversations – (a far cry from taking a shower with their buddy on speaker while they made their social plans for the evening to the sounds of rap music, a boy on speaker and the eternal drain of the hot water!) One especially memorable time had our oldest boy actually trying to climb into the wine cupboard with the corded receiver to his ear, in order to get some privacy while the cordless phone was on time out.

Nowadays I get the best conversation ever if I just chat to my teen daughter through texting. It is such a bizarre thing; I urge you to experiment with your young ones of a certain age. I can call her on the phone and listen to the heavy sigh when she picks up, followed by the 'What, Mum?" (I'm bothering her), followed by another heavy sigh, tinged with a slight tone of attitude; you get the picture. By the end of the exchange, we are both so disillusioned with our chat that we can barely stand ourselves, let alone each other. Texting however has a concise and efficient basis for practical, modern dialogue:-

"What time u finish practice?" (Do not spell out words or use punctuation; I have learned in the realm of texting. That is annoying and unnecessary practice.)

"IDK. Maybe 6."

"U want pick up?"

"Yeh."

And so it is. You never get into the 'why didn't you pick up your room this morning after I expressly asked you to?' or the 'why did you leave your cereal bowl on the side when you left for school instead of in the sink?" And so on. That regular annoying banter is much too long and tedious to try and text a conversation about I've decided, so you don't ever actually go there. That seems to breed a much more civilized environment for us parents with teens who have some communication challenges, even at the best of times.

Recently, our improved system has spread to email. In keyboarding class, the students are allowed to send emails once they are done with their tasks. One morning I saw a familiar yahoo email address pop up.

"Hey Mom! Wassup." It said. And that was that. Interestingly, this was followed by the sign off -

"Sincerely,

Frou"

OK; we can do this. "Hey Frou. Working.

Sincerely,

Mum"

"Watcha working on?

Sincerely,

Frou"

Really, she's interested in what I'm working on? Well, no, I'm not as foolish or delusional to think that, but it was a fun dialogue anyway and a change from the daily battle field on which we mostly find ourselves.

In the effort to keep the dialogue going with our teens, we parents will try just about anything. My folks were probably just trying to chitchat with me years ago when they picked up the other line on the rotary dial and asked when the line would be free. Perhaps they were hoping we could try a chat with each other over dinner, a civilized exchange of questions and ideas. Who knows? I do know, however, that I will keep texting and replying to the 'Sincerely Frou' emails which come my way, knowing that that may be as good as it gets sometimes during these tricky years. And, if I sneak in an 'X' after my 'Sincerely Mum' sign off, maybe one day she'll sneak one in after hers.

**Lucy tried to do her best with what she had to work with.**

# SOUP AND SCRAB

My family has always excelled at "Scrabble" What, I hear you say? Yes, really; that spelling board game which has seen little in the way of alteration or improvement over the past few decades - for that is how long I have been playing it. I secrete very, very old memories of my parents practically fighting to the death over a dubious Scottish derivation with a triple word score, which would score 45 points for one party and ensure a sound lead over the other. They were extremely competitive with one another around the Scrabble board. Put them in front of a board with letters on it and the battle of the intellectual versus the lucky would begin. I started playing quite young myself – a rite of passage in our house - and still love the way it can twist your brain and make you really feel like you are getting a cerebral work out.

Over the past few years, it has become an item for vacations only in my world. With the average game taking around 90 minutes, it is a luxury brain food you just can't squeeze in on any normal day. When my family and I traveled to France on vacation recently, a ratty old Scrabble board came along. It was played most afternoons in the heats of the Provence, while others around us snoozed. Sweat and Scrabble in the shade. A prelude to the early evening white burgundy perhaps; and both quite addictive habits.

My father is over 80 now and still a voracious player. 80 years of vocabulary and, not surprisingly, he has the edge on most people. One by one, we would line up to play a round with him and mostly he beat us. Not to brag, but I did manage to clinch a hand against him and quietly chuckled to myself as my Oxford grad of a sister failed to do so. I noticed that my daughter wasn't going there with any of us. She would just sit and quietly in the shade, watching the maneuvers, the techniques, the sweet words that would save you and, periodically, the bail out, when the smart thing was to throw in the hand.

There had been a time in elementary school, when our whole family had been in training with her for the "Spelling Bee" – two years in a row in fact – and she had placed extremely well there.

Surely she had to be a player in training for the blessed board? I pondered if it was just my bossy family that kept her away from jumping in and showing us the way, her way.

Back to America and I told my husband about the daily Scrabble playing we did overseas. As owners of two very large, very old dictionaries and one newer 'Scrabble' dictionary, we both agreed that we should play at home more than just when father comes over. Not being much of a wordy, let alone a reader, unless he suspects one of my columns is about him, I was surprised when husband mentioned that he would like to play. "If I'm going to beat your Dad when he comes over in October," he joked, "I'm going to need some practice."

I received a text on my phone that afternoon. "7.30pm - Soup & Scrab." I took it sort of like a date that you seldom get when you've been married for over a decade, and started to rather look forward to it. Even more surprising was that our teenager ultimately wanted to play too. There we were with our soup, playing our "Scrab". We played and fought and laughed more than we all had in a while. We tortured our 1971 dictionary and made a pledge to try and find a dictionary that at least sports the word 'computer', if not 'IPOD' and 'blog'. (Dictionaries are very expensive by the way if you investigate!)The next night we played again. Somehow, in our crazy lives, we positioned this piece of "entertainment" into our evening, like a piece of the puzzle that was missing and we'd never noticed until now.

Our daughter's friend came over and both girls wanted to play. This was crazy! Normally the door is shut with the teenagers in and us out and we don't see either of them until much later the following day. This time, the conversation was civil, the chocolate was shared and my daughter beat all of us around the board.

Not to say that this isn't just a novelty and '7.30pm - Soup and Scrab' will go the way of the work out equipment in the back yard or the treadmill in the living room, but it certainly has made a refreshing change from other places we have been recently, I can tell you.

If you are needing to have some valuable family time and don't know how to get there – or even just a civilized conversation with your child - buy yourself an old Scrabble board, (never mind the age of it – they haven't changed a bit!) Turn off the television, make a big old pot of soup and soak it all in. You will be surprised how entertaining this can be – for all ages – and how your brain will at least enjoy the work out, if not also your teenagers.

**Lucy is a long-time 'Scrabble' player.**

# THE BITTER SWEETS OF MOTHERHOOD

It was one of those rare days. The sun was shining, skies cobalt blue, with the wind not too vigorous. We had no plans; I did not have to work. (Who would go to an open house on Mother's Day, even if I opened one up?) No one had to come or go until much later. Days like that are rarities in the modern household. It was Mother's Day, my day; a day I truly make the best of every year; because I can.

The day started out impeccably. Husband made a pot of coffee, though he still insisted that mine is always better. I read the papers in bed and looked out on my world. Though my child was not home at that particular time – a sleep-over the night before having been a more attractive option – she was soon to return with whispers and secrets. A hand made card was produced promising a foot massage and pedicure, a gift produced – something I loved immediately. Everything was going along swimmingly.

Both sons managed to find time out of their busy days to contact me. One by phone, one by email; but I'll take it. When you are in your early twenties, life is still very much all about you; and I recognize that. I appreciated the thought, even by electronic mail box. My husband's mother appreciated her call. Check. A few chores were accomplished. Check, check. The rest of the day was mine. I read my book out in the sun, drank a Corona and dutifully counted my blessings, as we should do more than we do and with much more sincerity.

Within my blue, blue sky of my azure sparkling day, I captured a moment and popped it in a box for later. Life has taught me that I might need it. At one point my husband and my daughter were working on my feet at the same time. When I say 'working', they were sitting side by side on the patio chatting away. One was doing the massage, the other the pedicure on my feet; and I was lying in the middle doing absolutely nothing, book in hand. Times like this are rare, I reminded myself again; in fact it had never happened before. (Better put that one away for a rainy day!)

The entire day was lovely, lovely. No rain clouds scarred my horizon; not even a puff of a lost cloud. In fact, I wished that the day could go on and on for maybe a week, so that I could really relax and feel some more like I was feeling that day. But Monday always comes, doesn't she, in a manner of speaking and I needed to pop back into the box quicker than I had thought to touch my magic moments now swiftly vanished.

My sweet, lovely girl had quickly turned back from the adorable mama's girl on Mother's Day to a tween growl over night.

"What's the matter, darling," I ask, Monday morning, still swooning from the day before. I stroke her hair; she hates that.

"Nothing."

"You're not feeling well?" I venture, (she does feel a little warm).

"I'M FINE!! LEAVE ME ALONE ...GA'AAAAD!" (I run away quickly; she's scaring me.)

"Did you feed your animals?"

"Don't I always?"

"Mostly not until you're reminded," (the tones are rising).

"YOU ARE SO ANNOYING!!! GA'AAAAD!" (I run away again. Her teeth are grinding. She looks like an animal that might bite and kill me.)

"Did you pick up your room?"

Long, frustrated sigh. "I will."

"You need to put away your clothes. They've been sitting there for days."

Deep groan and double-grind. "I TOLD YOU I WILL. GA'AAAD LEAVE ME ALONE!!!"

And so the mother-daughter communiqué evolves into a game of cat and mouse with poor old dad, in the middle, counting the years until he can stop being an umpire in the hormonal ring between the two females in his life and have some peace restored to his homestead.

My baby is on the bridge between childhood and teen-dom; I am on the long bridge to middle age, old age and certain death. Both expeditions collide in the middle and create quite a spark. I refuse to let her treat me that way; she refuses to let me treat her that way. It's going to be a long walk towards finding any civilized communication and any lasting kind of truce, with the two of us battling it out along the way. Around 10 years I'd say; if I am recalling my relationship with my own mother correctly.

Just when I think I've got my role in the melodrama figured out, she will surprise me and want me to baby her once more. I then sink happily back into the role of nurturing mom, milk almost seeping with relief, and am, almost immediately, heartily rejected at the next corner; when I wake up to her snarl and realize that the rules have changed again.

As we walk to the bus stop in the morning, as we do every morning, the subject of a rattle snake comes up; the tiny little vicious baby with its one rattle that decided to slink its way across my patio last week, (where it ended its youthful days under the head of my husband's shovel.)

"Why did he have to kill the snake?" she asked; again. (We'd already been through this several times.)

"I know you're an animal lover, but rattle snakes are a different beast," I tried to reassure her; again. "They'd have no problem biting you or your dogs."

Gasp, sigh. "You already told me that," she snapped, (or, in translation: "are you really so stupid that you can't even remember what you already told me, like yesterday???")

I refuse to let her talk to me that way, or even just spit that tone in my direction.

"I don't think I want to walk with you anymore," I announced quietly. "It just starts my day out wrong."

She grabbed her stuff and jumped on the bus without a glance. She did not say goodbye, she did not look over and mildly wave as the bus left; which is her normal routine. I felt horrible, slapped, bruised inside. I traipsed back to the house and tearily revisited our exchange. Was I wrong to say that to her? Do I just take it and take it until I collapse in convulsions of tears in the privacy of my own company? I revisited my own relationship with my mother and how the ladder of years had some really tricky steps along the way. It's normal; it will pass, I tell myself. I call my husband for reassurance.

The mother-daughter thing will ebb and flow more than most relationships, but it will survive and it will flourish, ultimately, we hope. Much as I miss my own mother now; I know that to be true. For the time being, I just have to hold tight to my lovely memory in my special box of the handmade card and the wonderful massage and pedicure, and remember that such gifts are possible even in the kingdom of teen-dom, where life can be more than tricky on a daily basis and the simplest communication can absolutely result in tears; mostly mine.

**Lucy thinks that motherhood is the toughest job.**

# THE CHALLENGES OF SUMMER

As the huge wicked scorpion crabbed its ugly way across the floor, I was reminded that, with the lovely warm weather and the long buttery days, come some other gifts too. In summer we don't go walking over the property – too many snakes. We don't go out in the garage with no shoes on – scorpion alert. We close up the house and watch the thermometer on those pounding days when it never seems to get cool; those 48 hour days of daylight, when we think of winter and long for some respite – that long, hot summer. "Summer time; and the living ain't easy"; that should be how the song goes, but of course it isn't. The "other" song reminds me of the 1980's when I was young and single and on vacation and in quite a different planet and place. Summers did seem easy back then.

Here on planet work and planet parent, the children have now been out of school for well over a month now and the natives are restless. And that would be us and that would be them, in addition. If you don't have pots of cash to send the little sweeties "away to camp", or off to some kindly relative who'd simply adore to keep them busy the entire longitude of the summer; it can get a little tricky right about now. Our children have got over the novelty of sleeping in and going to bed when they feel like it. They're sick and tired of watching the shows they normally love on television and snacking on the junk food, when you leave for work, that's normally a treat. They roll their eyes at you when you mention reading a book, picking up the living room or doing some art. They're barely dressed at noon and can still be easily unwashed at tea-time. It's the dregs of the vacation here, folks, and we parents are knee deep in the overflow.

As for us adults, we'll still trying to keep on keeping on. We are not on vacation, let alone for 10 consecutive weeks. Smart people will take some time "off" when their babies are out of school and venture forth on a nice family road trip or a week away somewhere gorgeous and tropical; but if you are self-employed, that might simply not be viable; and so you have it; the summer vacation impasse between the working poor and the bored children. It's a war zone out there, for sure, and, trust me, I'm right in the middle of it.

Not so long ago, I used to be able to bribe my young sweet darling to read umpteen numbers of books over the summer and entice her with some lovely fuzzy toy or other, as her reward. One summer she even clocked over a hundred books, if I am recalling it correctly. We'd go to the library and return with arms-full of super literature which she would literally consume over the course of time; and I'd be proud, so very proud of her and me for my splendid idea. Those days are over.

"Go and read a book, honey," I coax sweetly. "No," she replies, without moving her eyes from the TV; and that is really that. I will then find her glued to some inappropriate date show on MTV, or building some really curious lives on the interactive "SIMS" computer game and I'll know, in a sense, I have really lost her forever.

I organize a lovely week at swim camp for her, thinking that she'll look forward to making new friends and having some structure for a week during her long summer hiatus away from real life.

"Oh God! Tell me; why am I really going?" she frets, when I remind her that she'll have to be up and ready in good time next week for swim camp. "This is definitely my last year of that!" she reminds me empathically. And I'm sure it is. Maybe next year I will be able to abscond for a few days and take her to Europe. That covers a good period of the long summer holiday. Maybe next year she'll expand on her pet sitting job of this year and take on a few more clients to keep her schedule busy and her brain tired.

We do worry, us parents, through these long summer weeks when our children are away from the classroom and we are in our regular lives, but out of our regular minds. It's not just the scorpions crawling across the garage floor, the rattlesnakes in the driveway and the constant fire dangers all around us. It's our little blessings and their enormous lack of schedule which frets us as we try to work and keep to our very important agendas, while all the time wondering what on earth they're watching on television now and why on earth they can't pick up a book and read it, just like you'd like to be doing right about now, and just as they did willingly years ago.

It's a tight-rope we walk, so many of us, as I'm sure, our parents did with us. Some how you get through it and look back and say, 'it wasn't so bad, really'. "A long hot summer just passed me by;' another summer song from my youth which fades; same as the sharpness of memory.

**Lucy remembers her 6 week summer vacation time back in England. That was quite long enough!**

# THE FRESHMAN

By the time you read this, my tiny baby will be a freshman at high school. Not that she is a tiny baby any longer – she towers over me in height and fortitude with a sizeable attitude to match – but, as a parent, you are always able to go back to the beginning of the first butterfly in your stomach, the first breath, the first step, the first word, the first day of preschool, kindergarden and so many other beginnings. So many firsts that your baby can't possibly remember and you can't ever forget!

Now we have another first; the first day of high school – and the rest of her life in fact, since after high school, real life begins in earnest for most people. Whether you go onto college or university and manage a huge course load, as well as a part time job and student loans, or you go out into the world and knock 'em dead in other ways, high school is the bridge between immense freedom and huge responsibility of sorts. Some how, after high school, people expect you to have grown up and be ready for the adult world in front of you. Fortunately most kids don't know that, when they enter those well-walked arches as freshmen.

When our oldest son was in high school he was the self-proclaimed bomb. He was a jock on the football team, he was popular, his life revolved around his friends and his fun. We, as his parents, were pretty much irrelevant through those years, unless he needed some cash or a signature here and there. I do remember getting a little teary at the mother-son ceremony on the football field, when he gave me flowers and a hug, with my name being read over the PA system, but that was a very long time ago. Now he is a few years out of school, he is mature enough to be able to look back and say, "I thought high school was everything at the time and it was. What I didn't know was that when I left it, I was nothing." It can be a crashing time. Our son crashed pretty badly after high school.

I sat in the courtyard of the new freshmen orientation this week at Soledad High and watched all the former middle-schoolers greet each other after the long summer apart. One would walk in the gate, the gathered group would stop, pause and then a loud set of squeals could be heard, followed by running steps towards a firm embrace of the new arrival. This was the same group that was so wholly sick of each other at the beginning of June, I wryly noted to just myself, that they could barely even speak anymore.

"I don't know who I am going to walk with to school," the freshman in our house commented with some intensity. "None of my friends like my other friends." Quite a problem to have indeed! I do remember my own group of three not working out too well at various stages between the ages of 14-18; and the inevitable fall out with some one always getting left out. It is not a surmountable problem at that age. At around 25, things seem to work themselves out. Right now our freshmen are entering the part of their lives when they are very likely going to make one or two friends who will stay with them throughout their lives. The rest will fade away, inevitably. They just don't know that yet.

I thought I was the bomb at high school too. I was into sports, good at academics, solid in the 'popular' group. I do remember wondering where all my "friends" went when we left school and had our own life adventures in the thereafter, meeting up only occasionally for a class reunion or a wedding. Now I don't see any of them. I only have two good friends left from around that era and we have now been friends for over 30 years, which is a scary period of time in anyone's lifetime. We've been through births, divorces, deaths; all measure of life's milestones together. We can communicate across the ether without regular means of communication, we can tell each other tough tales, we can always pick up and go on where we left off. The layers of history there are so deeply bled and engrained together that we will, for sure, be there for each other into our old age and infirmity – 'til death do us part, should the truth be known. I love old friendship movies – I see us there. I love sending over a three word text I know will have them giggling. I love finding the perfect top in a shop and knowing they will love it on their next birthday or the photo to email them that will capture their hearts. Friendship like that has to be earned and it is a rare and wonderful gift. Longevity has earned you the medal of being a good friend. You cannot get those medals at the freshman level. They just don't know that yet.

Hoping our freshmen all find the halls of their new adventure not only wildly exciting and stimulating, but also a solid basis for the rest of their lives. May they rise to the challenge, surmount their adversities, exceed all of their own expectations; and, for sure, be as lucky as I was to meet forever friends in those well-walked halls and be able to cultivate and nurture those relationships throughout their lives and no matter what comes their way.

**Carey, Kate and Lucy – class of 1981, forever bound. Our resident 'freshman' is now approaching her final year at high school.**

# THE GAME

"You're not really going, are you?" she said hopefully. "You're going to hate it!"
"You probably will," he agreed. "But if you do, it's okay, we can leave early."

That night: "Do you really want to go? We don't have to. You're going to hate it, you know …"
"Yes, I really want to go," I responded. In the way of the world, the more they urged me not to, the more I wanted to go.

And so went the presentation of my welcoming committee to one of the first American football games of my entire life. Watching my son years ago at Watsonville High does not count; since, in those days, I was chasing a young baby around the bleachers with never an eye on the game. I do remember how the boy adored the sport though and never questioned the amount of practices he had to attend or the grueling work outs they were forced to endure. The glory came at game time with the blazing lights over head and the thrill of the crowd. That much I do remember.

Never mind that they do not play that particular sport where I come from originally; and, in the twenty something years I have lived over here, the rules of American football have always somehow eluded me. Maybe I never really tried to learn them in the first place. In any case, it could be considered well past time that I made the effort to get out and watch another game, support our local team and see what all the excitement was about. I have always enjoyed the uniforms and the general "Rugby" feel to the game in any case; maybe I could move beyond those two things and into some general game understanding, if I really paid attention. It might even make the experience more pleasant for me!

"You're going to be freezing," he said. I took a jacket. "Take an extra jacket," she said. I took along my fur boots as well. I was well prepared for all eventualities, bundled up as if for an Alaskan cruise with my Aztecs sweatshirt and hat; layer upon layer. The only thing I left behind was the umbrella and the cash that I should have remembered for the snack bar, ( and cursed myself for leaving behind, as the family in front of me indulged on pizza and baked potatoes while my stomach simply growled for hours!)

There is something really moving about being in a crowd of happy people cheering and enthusing at a sporting event. I had forgotten that. You get stirred by the emotions also, ("oh no," they gasp, or words to that effect. "He fumbled!" "Go, go, go!" they shriek, as a young Aztec races down the side line before being tripped up by the opposition.) It really was very exciting, I had no idea, and wonderfully escapist. I couldn't answer my phone and pay attention to any work calls while I was there, even if I wanted to! The music, cheering and general noise were far too extreme. Should have changed my voicemail to say that I was in a meeting or some such near truth!

Never mind that sometimes there are several small trips and movements before there is a large one, momentum inevitably builds as the game progresses and you start to feel oddly at one with your home supporters and your home team. You have never seen them play before, but you want them to win. You really, really do. The principal and vice principal, along with the athletic director and coaches parade the side lines urging them on. Their friends are in the stands and many parents too. A lot of people there know each other. It must be a huge boost to the young players' spirits and an adrenalin rush that makes them want to play again and again. We talk about seeking positive influence for our kids; now there's something. Encourage your child to participate in a team sport and then show up to watch them; such a concept. Some of the young cheerleaders that night were searching the crowd for their family members and not finding them. What could be more important than showing up for them and seeing the smile of relieved recognition on their cute little faces?

My team did not win. We should have won, but we did not. It was a good game; in my unqualified opinion, exciting and hard fought. It was also a really thrilling way to spend a Friday night and an experience I plan to repeat.

"You're not going to go again, are you?" she said, the question heavily loaded. "Did I interfere with your time while I was there?" I responded to my teen, treading cautiously. "Well, just not every game," she went on, playing dodge ball as she went. "No, not every game," I could at least assure her of that.

As soon as the autumn nip evolves into the winter chills, I shall probably just have to read and hear all about it, feeling the cold as I do. I doubt I shall make it to the bleachers very often to cheer my team on in person; but don't tell her that, I just might. There's probably some full body armor made just for the die hard fan during winter football season – I see a large, billowy suit in purples and yellows that I could wrap myself into and roll into the stadium for my game. She'd die of embarrassment, but at least I'd be warm and out there, showing up and cheering on the team as you do.

**Lucy has since become quite the fan.**

# THE TEEN YEARS

Something happened at the $8^{th}$ grade graduation ceremony. First of all, she happily wore a dress and coordinating accessories; something that hadn't happened since she was about 4 and we were allowed to dress her in cute dresses and bows and shoes with buckles on them. (I've hardly seen her wear a dress since; mostly black rock t-shirts and jeans.) Then, at the graduation itself, she liked the attention the dress got her and, from there, she started primping a lot more in the mirror; working on the hair and outfit in a much more concerted way, significantly more than once a day, I might add. Then, we go away on vacation, and she asks me if we can "go shopping". Shopping? That had never happened before! Clothes shopping for her had previously been such a chore, I'd have to bribe her to go and power shop in the minimum time possible, then secure the bribe with a good Chinese lunch when the torture was all over with. In France, she wandered about the boutiques, checking out the colors and designs. I do recall chuckling to myself - in about 100 degree heats – as I thought of all the mother-daughter bonding we would be able to do, now we liked some of the same things. In London, she wanted to spend most of her time at the outdoor street markets, looking at all the wild stuff, and even buying some of it. We would get back to wherever we were staying at the time and examine her spoils every evening. We'd laugh together a lot and fall asleep close by. This was a transformation and a swift one. In place of the black and the grey, we had a lot of bright pink and yellow. In place of the closed bedroom door, we were in the same room and liking it. Sometimes we'd even giggle ourselves to sleep. With this temporary utopian existence, I had no idea what was around the corner.

Back to reality, to home in America, and the bedroom door is closed again. The music is on high, the shower runs forever and you wonder what it is that is living behind those mostly locked doors. There is a scent that comes from under the door that is a distinctly teenage one, so you assume that that is what lies behind the barricade.

You knock softly, careful not to annoy. "What?" A loud and obviously annoyed voice answers. Aha; she is alive. That is a good thing. "Darling, do you want dinner?" "No," the voice responds. "Can I come in?" you ask. You do wonder what she is doing in there after all, so you pursue. You are used to hanging with her all day and night, and, if the truth were laid bare on the table, right here right now, you miss her already. You hear an exasperated sigh and a sardonic, "Okay mother," (with an upwards lilt to it that suggests a high level of irritation.) The door unlocks reluctantly. She is on the computer, chatting on 'My Space' with her "Friends". The angst is intense in that arena, most of our teenage youth wearing their hearts on their sleeves and deleting their so-called "Friends", as they themselves are deleted. It is not a forum for the faint of heart, but a hugely important social network for this age group, where you see and are seen, like parties and pubs used to be for us. The phone rings, again. You watch her chuckle and gurgle like some one you used to know, as she greets her 'Friend' and chats fluently while you stand awkwardly by waiting for your turn. "Hang on," she says to the receiver. "Let me get rid of my mother." I had never thought of it like that before. She wants to get rid of me. I leave quietly, my tail between my legs like a dog. The door clicks to the locked position again.

Hours can pass with that door in the same position, the electronic media pumping out messages and more communication than any of us ever need. The phones deliver text messages compulsively and ring often. As I witnessed this renewed frenzy of friendships in cyber space and wireless, I realized that our time together abroad was just a resting place from the melee, a pause in the proceedings, so that she could gather up her thoughts again, line up her 'Friends' and throw herself back into the mix with renewed energies as soon as she returned home. It is what teenagers love to do in the modern world. If you say they can't, they will want to do it all the more and most likely find a way to do so; not a great alternative.

To try and blend quietly and have some sort of an understanding of what happens in the "My Space" venue, I got myself an account and tried to behave like a wall flower in mute mode. I did not want to call attention to myself in any way. This was all very well, until my little blessing got particularly irritated with me one day recently and deleted me from her 'Friends'. I had not estimated how gutting that can be, even though I am hardly a player on the 'My Space' playing field. If some one deletes you, you are truly redundant and you are made to feel that way. "So and so has deleted you." The message comes across loud and clear. If I were 14 and not 40, I am really not sure how I would be able to handle that type of rejection.

The door opens and the contents of that room is not in a good mood. You cannot speak to it and you certainly can't go anywhere near it for a hug or anything mothering of that nature. You stay away and you certainly don't knock or say goodnight or anything foolish like that. You hear the murmur of the voice until late at night and wonder why they are able to tell those 'Friends' of all the pain and suffering, but not those who gave them life and who will secretly nurture them forever.

You see the same person in the morning; the same, but different. The door is wide open to the soul, as the serenity of the sleeping babe shines through, the teddy bear thrust comfortingly under the head and the cat wrapped around the neck. You are relieved. You recognize them as some one you know. They are still there; they are still alive to see another day. They wouldn't let you comfort them, but the bear and the cat are in the realm and in the know, and that is something. You stroll away, telling your wounded sensibilities that this is normal behavior for the teen years; this is how the young start to want to break away from the old and mould their own existences. This is how we learn to want to let them.

"Hi Mum!" she gets up smiling, big blue eyes around the door frame. You pause. This is the same body that had the swiveling head and gurgling green foam the evening before? "Hi, babe," you reply, cautiously, because you are the adult and you have to be the mature one. She hugs you and she has no idea how much that means to you. "Do you still want to go out to Monterey today?" she asks and the gratitude that you feel fills you up so intensely you feel like you will over flow. You know you can't show any feeling though on this precious and volatile tight rope. "Sure, we can do that," you reply calmly and feel some of her sleeping serenity from the night before seep into your soul at just that particular moment like an intangible glimpse of hope.

It's just a moment but you'll take it. You never know what is around the corner; what is coming next to surprise or terrify. You never know when the rules will change, the mood will twist with the wind and you will be locked out, you will be ignored; or worse still, you will be deleted.

**Lucy is still the cautious-treading mother of a teenage girl. This too will pass, as her mother used to say.**

# THE TRAIN OF TIME

Whoa! It happened like a flash. As a comet speeding through the night sky in a time capsule, I was back there in the early months of motherhood. I was back in the day when I was everything to her and everything for me was about her; as it still is. As she suckled on her bottle and I held her, back then – one-armed – I remember thinking to myself, "the look she gives me; now that is love." I was her world, her universe, her everything. I moved; her eyes moved with me. Her eyes gleamed with adoration. We were one; still almost connected by the umbilical chord.

At the end of the tail-spin of the comet, the place where the collision happens and we wake up is the part of the movie when you're in a time warp and you discover that, somehow, 13 years have passed by, and a lot has changed. Life is not the same place now as it was then; it never is. I warmly touch the photos of her as a babe with a sentimental tilt to my head and I glance over to the couch and see this near adult slouching with long legs and big attitude and I say to myself, where did it all evaporate to? Where the hay have I been these past 13 years? I know I've been working a lot, but this is ridiculous!

My journey back through time hit me with galactic force this past week when my tiny suckling babe trucked off to middle school. My little girl now attends junior high. She will be in high school in 2 years and with every passing second, I'm losing her just a little bit more. It is truly frightening to be a parent, as the train of time hurls down the track of life; and we are left standing at the station going, "Wait a minute! I'd still like to be important! I'd still like to be your everything!" But it's over. The train leaves without us and we are left standing with our suitcase full of memories and our photos of other times when we were something.

I had been warned of this a while ago. My dear friend Barbara who left us prematurely for pastures elsewhere a mere 12 years ago is back in my aura this time of year. There she is reminding me of what she told me moons ago, and she was right; she was always right. "The time goes too quickly," she warned me as she held my newborn in the very early days. "Enjoy it while you can!"

"Yeh, yeh," I responded at the time, watching this tiny helpless thing lying all flopsy-bunny in my arms and looking forward to the time my babe could crawl, could talk, could walk, could accomplish all those monumental things which are now just kinda blended into one category of babyhood which was oh such a long time ago.

Now I find myself looking backwards with longing and looking forward with anxiety. The mother-daughter war of words has already started – on occasion. The battle for the female territory is brewing. I see her spark, I look in the mirror and remember the challenges my mother had with me, I remember the laws of payback, I look at the calendar again, and I take a deep breath. In about a decade's time, we should be friends again; I say to just myself. My mother and I, we sparred brutally at times until I was about 23; rather a lot of years to go still, if we mirror so many of the things that we have already mirrored; she and I and my mother and I; decades, almost lifetimes, apart.

But I shouldn't look at it that way; should I. I should brave each day as a fresh start, with its laughs and its challenges and give her a new opportunity every day to surprise me, to embrace me with her discoveries, and, maybe on occasion ask me for the benefit of any counsel she thinks I might have gained during my 4 plus decades on the planet. Every now and then, when she's really not paying attention, I can still try and play mothers and babies. I can still try to hold her like she's a tiny suckling thing that needs me more than anything else in the world; I can still look at her when she sleeps and remember how I loved to watch her as a sleeping babe and see her lips move as she dreamed and her mouth suckle as if she was drinking milk in her sleep. I can still play the game and she need never know.

In real time, I must enjoy her new adventure, almost as much as she does, and embrace her excitement and her absorption of that brave new world out there. It's the law of the species and the earthly given right. I have to step aside and let her go where I went before and thousands before me. I have to let her go without me. I have my memories and my experience; she has her youth, her drive and her future that only she can pave. It's all in the circle, and who am I to stop the train leaving the station; even if, sometimes, I want to so much it hurts?

**Lucy has always been a bit nostalgic.**

# SOUL AND BODY

# AWARENESS IS GOOD

I have always been a little suspicious of 'Hallmark' holidays. You know - 'Happy Halloween', 'Columbus Day Greetings', 'Happy 4th of July' and the like. I see the retailers' gleam of satisfaction as each celebratory event comes around and they get to make a buck on the merchandise, the cards, napkins, decorations and more associated with that one special day. Around the 'biggies' – Christmas, Valentines' Day and Mothers' Day – there seem to be plenty more celebratory days nipping at their heels.

Then I heard that October was 'Breast Cancer Awareness Month' and that stopped me in my tracks a bit. Having just recently had cancer cut out of my breast made me a little unsure how I felt about all that hoop-la with the pink and the retail support of the pink ribbons everywhere you look. Was this just a reason for stores to sell more pink items with the breast cancer logo on them? (See "Happy Breast Cancer Month"?) How much would truly be going to research and how much would be propping up the administration and marketing of this multi-million dollar industry? Do they really want to find a cure, or is this another commercial angle to sell product? I see the 'Happy Birthday' ads on television for the American Cancer Society and they make my mountain to climb seem just that little bit taller. Only 1 month out of chemotherapy and I don't know that I need to be reminded how long it will be until I celebrate a 'birthday' of any importance where cancer is concerned. Case in point, my sister received her 5 year 'all clear' anniversary, only to be re-diagnosed with bone cancer during her 6th year.

Then I stopped in my judgment tracks again, as you do quite frequently when life has put you up against a huge challenge and is still waiting on the sidelines to see how you handle it. Sometimes you simply practice your breathing exercises, which they taught you to do after surgery; as if you just learned how to breathe for the first time and still haven't, fortunately, learned how to speak. Sometimes, that it is all it takes to be able to pull yourself together again and move forward in your mind and your cognizance to the bigger picture; i.e. less about me, and more about 'it'.

It was at the volleyball game, that I got a hold of this awareness gig and held it tight. Some how our Aztecs team had acquired pink 'Volleyball For The Cure' t-shirts with matching socks – thank you coaches and Athletics Director - and our little blessings were jigging around and flying the flag prior to their game, when the team shirts needed to be worn. Sure, some of our girls would just appreciate the free shirt and clean socks; but some, like my daughter would be able to know, first hand, what breast cancer can do to a person and a family and be able to perhaps hold up, as she wore her pink shirt, a modicum of hope, that we were all in this together and that with hope – not to mention tireless research – we would, one day, be able to stop this modern day curse from afflicting the next generation and the one to follow that. As one courtside male after another put on the shirt, I felt touched by the reality that this was not just a female disease, this was a plague that touched our world at large and we were, truly, all in it together.

All of a sudden I am seeing products with pink ribbons everywhere, companies making donations towards research or awareness. I've been on my own awareness platform since about April when I was diagnosed and all of this attention does make me feel less alone. 'Early detection' is key to long term survival, they say, and of course that is true. I would also add to that, that 'early and ***thorough*** detection' is even more important. A lot has been said about the mammogram and its importance in the detection of breast cancer. Less has been said about the amount of cases – like my own – where the mammogram failed to show up any tumors - actually three times in a row - and a deeper examination in the form of an ultrasound or MRI might also be necessary. Had I relied on the results of a mammogram alone, I would still be walking around with my own breasts and an aggressive, triple negative tumor growing malignantly in the deep tissue of my body. Contrary to how you might think, breast cancer is very silent. I'm sure I would also still be feeling just as healthy as I felt the day of my diagnosis.

One thing that makes me very happy is that our generation is a talkative one. We share our stories, on the whole, and perhaps ensure a more informed generation to follow. In my Mother's day, no one talked about cancer. When she was diagnosed with breast cancer, she quickly booked herself in to the hospital without a word to anyone. Even my father just thought she was having a cyst removed. There was a definite stigma attached to this illness back then, which must have made the cancer victims feel extremely lonely in their plight. I am happy to say that I have not felt that. I have felt anger, I have felt sadness, I have experienced grief, fear and fury; but I have not felt lonely. Whether I am out in public with my scarf and chemo brows, or I am receiving an encouraging email from a reader of one of my stories, I have felt bathed in kindness and support from friends, strangers, family and community. I have felt love such as I have almost never experienced. I will always attribute a great part of my healing to that support and be ready, in my place, to pay it forward where it might be needed.

No one knows why so many have cancer in their lives. Can we inherit the likelihood of getting it? Yes. Could it be our diet, our modern day living stresses, our pesticides, our chemicals? For sure. Can we prevent it? Maybe. We can lead a good and clean life, eat well, sleep well, exercise, be straight forward and honest in the way we lead our lives. We can do all of that. Can we still get cancer; yes we can. But the awareness is out there now in the world as never before, and, nowadays, people do not avoid you or not hug you if have cancer. In fact, most people will embrace you more and hold you up so high that you can see the amazing view on the other side of the challenge. They will encourage you to work your very hardest, with their help, to cross over the cure line across the mountain you are climbing, your eye firmly set on the prize of a long and healthy life with faith, optimism and love at your helm.

**Lucy will, reluctantly, call herself a 'survivor' and more likely a 'warrior'.**

# THE BITTER SWEETS OF LIVING

It has often seemed to me that with the passing of one soul comes along the unexpected arrival of a new one; and that is the way of the earth as we know it. I recently had the opportunity to breathe in the sweetness of a new born and watch his fresh, new eyes watching me, as if we'd met before. I also had the honor to be present at the celebration of the completion of a long full life and the heralding of a passing soul, cherished by many. Both the arrival of the new soul and the departure of the older one were surprises to us all. The new born was a surprise, since he needed a home and my friend had been waiting to give him one; she just didn't know when he'd be arriving. The older soul had certainly not known he was ready to be called home, as quickly as he was; but he left us full of the life and humor he had always had and that life-full picture of him will be immortalized with his loved ones for always.

In light of my own latest 'surprises', I have been trying to extract the sweet from the bitter recently, in order to be able to live with myself and my 'new reality' over the coming months; not to mention attempting to lift a little of the inevitable burden from my friends and family. So, in light of all of that, here is my bitter-sweet pledge in black and white, with good intentions from the heart:-

1. I must try to pass along some of the kindness I have recently received to others who might need some of that for themselves. Whether it be in the form of a nice card, a friendly phone call, or just a flower from the garden to lift their day. I must step outside of myself and remember I am not the only one with life challenges. That is part of life.

   Recently, some one who had just lost their life partner and is currently immersed in helping their daughter battle the same disease as me, stopped by to give me a basket of flowers, a card and a hug. They did just that. They stepped outside their own realm of suffering and into mine for just a few minutes. I think we both felt a little better for that. I know it lifted me up and made me resolve to try and be a better person and find compassion in my heart for others who are also suffering. Another friend took time out of her day to talk to me about her own struggle with the illness and cheer me into believing I can and will get over it, the way she did. She also assured me that life, just around the corner, will again taste sweet. I needed that. Another friend made sure we had delicious dinners cooked for us every night; the fortitude of the body being just as important as the conviction of the mind. And that helped enormously too. Another friend sensed my anxieties and would some how call me when she felt I was at my lowest ebb and sitting alone with my diagnosis. She would talk me through it and out the other side. She would wait patiently, the international minutes ticking away, as I blabbed and sniffed my way through my own selfish agonies. I must remember all of these compassionate gestures when I am up again and on the top of my game. I must remember to pass them along, packaged in the same way that so many gave them to me.

2. When I come out the other side, I must also remember to thank everyone who helped get me there. From my friends at the newspapers to my family and friends from all over, to neighbors, colleagues – and not least my husband and daughter and animals – it will be a group effort to get me up and going again and back into the driving seat of my bossy self. I am not one that sits well and can tolerate any kind of physical challenge before me which will stop me getting up as usual and going to work. It will take a village to convince me that I will need to stop and heal and take the time out that my body will most likely require. I am thanking everyone in advance, because I know you'll be there to help me help myself. Contrary to how I currently feel; I'm sure the world will not stop operating, because I am not in it for a few days.
3. I must remember to document my experiences. What is an experience if not something that can assist some one else who will, for sure, be in the same situation somewhere down the line? It is a lesson to be absorbed. Even when I

am low and down and ugly with myself, I must put it down in the raw language of some one who is tasting the tougher side of life; and I must share it as a donation to humanity. If those who have gone before me were not sharing now the most intimate details of their disease, I would not feel the comfort that I do that I, too, can come through the other side and back to a wholesome life they promise me will still exist when I return.

4. I must stay true to my hero – my baby sister Rosie Emma Alexandra Mason - who has been battling with this same life challenge for about 7 years now. She is a professional to the core and has let me lean on her heavily through these tortuous early days of my diagnosis, even though she is still going through chemo herself and currently getting herself geared up for 6 weeks of radiation back-to-back. She has taught me a lot about how to be, though I am supposed to be the older sister. She has managed to cheer me up when she is herself not feeling so good and made me laugh, 'til I could cry, about the damndest things. If she wasn't busy being a teacher, I've decided she could certainly be a comedian. Her grace and humor, throughout this life ordeal she has been dealt, have made her rise to the top of people I enjoy being around. I need to be more like her and less like the vision I've seen in the mirror recently of this rather sad and wrinkly individual, who is feeling a bit sorry for herself and the deck of cards she's been dealt. I need to quickly shed that skin and become more like Rosie.

   With all that said, I will work very hard on all of the above while I am away. They say that if you write it down, you make it so; and herein you have my pledge. I will be cheerful, I will be kind, I will not be self-indulgent – please, call me on all of these things when I falter - and then, I will be back.

Enormous thanks to so many of you in this wonderful community I plan to call home forever, for lifting me up during what would have otherwise been very grim and dark days. Thanks too for helping me see that the spring flowers are, indeed, still gorgeous, the hills are still green, there are humming birds waving to me outside my window, my dogs kisses are endless and divine; and you – all of you – are what can make up a very, very sweet life I plan on returning to soon, very soon.

**During her illness and the period of time that she could not hold herself up very much, Lucy was held up by her friends, family and her community. She is forever grateful for that.**

# DRESSED OUT AND ON THE COUCH

"I need the 38's", husband said, an air of desperation in his voice. "I've put on about 30 pounds and the 36's don't feel so good anymore."

"Lose the weight then; I'm not buying them," I said helpfully, watching him consume a large handful of chocolate covered pretzels as he lounged in his chair, sighing his misunderstood male moan.

"Don't we have some 38's from before?" he pursued plaintively. "You know, when I was like a little bigger?"

"Threw them out," I noted, ever the helpful partner in the marriage. Sometimes we women have to save our men from themselves.

All women know that if a man sets his mind to it, he can drop from a waist size 38 to 36 in about a week with little sweat or agony involved. Mostly, this involves the male actually thinking before he puts something in his mouth. He does not have to pursue the cabbage diet or fast for even a minute. No, he can just cut out soda or junk food for a few days and you can notice a marked change. For us females to do that would take several visits and weigh-ins to Weight Watchers over a long period of time; most likely along with the services of a highly paid weight loss counselor, and countless visits at 5am to the gym, along with a severe nutritional program that we would suffer day in and day out before we could persuade the globby stuff to go anywhere at all. We all know men and women are different in every way; this is just one of the larger gulfs that separates us from one another. The weight loss divide; a cavern between the sexes.

To get a good start on our new regime, husband and I moved the treadmill from the sitting room, where it had become a towel rack over time, to our bedroom, where it presided over a lovely view of the birds and the ponds and where we would always be reminded of its presence as we passed through our sleeping space and out the other side.

The next day, husband appears in his work out gear, which constitutes a t-shirt he has cut off at the arms to resemble a muscle shirt and the oldest pair of sweat pants known to man, forever held up around the waist with a large rubber band. "I'm dressed out," he proclaims proudly to the world, as if he were back in middle school and likely to be sent to detention for not wearing the correct attire to PE class. "And what exactly are you going to do, 'dressed out' like that?" I enquired sardonically, (another thing that men miss almost entirely). "Oh, I'm going to sit in my chair," he replies. "I've already lost 5 pounds just thinking about dressing out." And sit down he did. The next day brought the same scenario. The man would "dress out" and then go and relax in his chair. He did not move, except for hand to mouth and hand to remote control, but I could swear the pounds were just melting off him.

Exasperated I spat, "And when exactly are you going to actually use your work out gear to – you know – like work out? Such a concept! Just putting the clothes on does not constitute an effort in exercise!" (Little did he know!)

Meanwhile back in girl camp, I am proud to say I have lost 15 pounds over the course of this entire year, which is a not very impressive success story of just a kiss over a pound a month, but it seems like a lot when you look at it as over 7 bags of sugar off this little body. My 'success' is the result of a few simple life changes I like to call my 'Mostly' plan. I have mostly learned how to eat in a little more controlled fashion, I have tried to mostly keep up on my exercise plan and I have also tried to avoid the more obvious temptations of junk food everywhere you go, most of the time. 15 pounds may not sound like a lot, but it's a lot for me and it's a lot considering the life we lead. If I could have replaced the word 'mostly' by the word 'always', I probably would have doubled the number of fat pounds lost, if the truth were known.

Alright, so lead by example; that's what they tell you in the parenting guides. If husband was dressing out and then sitting in the chair, I would show him that dressing out and then getting on the treadmill every day and drawing a little sweat had to be a much better thing for all than just sitting in the chair. I would encourage him to take the next step by showing him I'm not afraid to step forward and lead by example. "I did a mile this morning!" I bragged, totally impressed with my small self. "Another mile!" I gloated the following day. "Think I'll be onto 1.5 tomorrow!"

"Good for you honey," he smiled mildly and continued to sit in the chair in his work out gear smoothing his increasingly slimming lines. He still had no interest in actually getting it together and shaking that body on that moving platform. He just wanted to sit there in the relevant clothing, stroke his shrinking stomach and contemplate it. It was obviously working for him, so why fight it.

Whether husband will ever make it back onto the treadmill or not is probably beside the point. You cannot make other people do anything they don't want to do; especially when they are over 18. In the meantime, I shall continue to work on my mile and my mile and a half, in fact all my milestones. I shall continue towards my goal of raising my heart beat every day, if only for a few minutes over looking my ponds, and I shall persist on my journey to encourage my errant partner to raise his too, if only in the search for his work out gear and the solace of his couch.

One thing I will not do is to give in to his whinings to buy just even one pair of 38's for his closet, nor will I purchase that pot of macadamia nut clusters that he has been coveting to add to the resident tire around the waist he is currently stroking. I won't, I won't, I won't. In the meantime, just the thought of a smaller jean size is probably helping him smooth out yet another line in his goal towards continued weight loss success and we women are just left gazing in awe.

**'Coach' Lucy always seems to be about 20lbs shy of her goal, no matter what.**

# IT'S A SPORTING LIFE!

They say you can't teach an old dog new tricks! Oh yeh? I'm here to tell you that us old dogs can and do learn new things every day.

I thought that I was in the twilight of my sporting career; not that it was ever much of a career, more of an ungainly dabble; but I did always fancy myself as a pretty fair tennis player. I was once awarded the "Ladies Number 2" crown way back when in my home town, which is not too shabby, (and the memory lives on). I had thought that I might assume some late-in-life tennis doubles matches at some stage; (when we get our Soledad Country Club perhaps; if I'm not on my walker at that stage!) I had not anticipated that I would be actually learning some new sporting moves so late in life and, in fact, quite liking them.

The sport that found me is a different animal entirely. My daughter discovered volleyball recently; assisted by some lovely new grass in our back yard and a rather attractive net that my husband set up. (Also, perhaps coached by the fact that she will be entering middle school very soon and moving into the realms of the volleyball elite). Despite the new net, I had avoided playing with her for a while; citing the weak wrists, the carpal tunnel syndrome and the general lethargy I feel after a day on the grind; all very valid reasons.

"Please Mum; play with me. Here, I'll teach you," she encouraged. "I'll even chase the ball when you hit it out of bounds!" That was challenge enough. Off I went to be instructed by a bossy 12 year old on a sport which had thus far eluded me in the long line of sports I have played over the years from badminton to tennis to hockey to netball to racquetball to squash to soccer to table tennis; you get the picture. I am pretty sporting!

The first slap of the ball on the finger tips told me that I had better listen to my coach and get with the program. "No, Mum," she said. "You need to use your fingers like this. That way you won't hurt yourself." She's quite a patient coach, my daughter, I discovered, as I wacked the ball yet again out of bounds, hit it again like a frying pan into the net and had a good giggle at my own feeble attempt at serving.

The next night she got me again. “Mum, let’s play volleyball!” she said, practically begging this time. I could still feel the strange terse muscle aches in my fore arms from the night before, but couldn’t say no to that sweet imploring little face and the fact that she wanted to play with me at all. She didn’t want to sit on the phone with her friends, or close the door and play her IPOD or her video games. She wanted to frolic out in the fresh air with her Mum; no matter how lousy a Volleyballer her Mum might be and no matter that she would have to still chase all the loose balls up and down the hills.

As the darkness fell and we switched on the outdoor lights, I realized I had found my way to the crock of gold; the mysterious key to successful communication between teenagers and adults; indeed, the answer perhaps to obesity and depression. It’s really complicated; so try and get your brain around it: fresh air and laughter. Yes, really. If you run around with your teen, whether you’re trying to master volleyball and launching her into hysterical laughter, or you’re out on the tennis court trying to show her a few moves without making her mad. As long as you’re playing together and you’re inhaling the airs; it’s all good. It’s the road to the solution that most of us somehow miss along the way; myself included.

Somehow, somewhere I had lost what I knew; which was that if you find something that they like to do, they will still like to do it with you; no matter that they will be snarling at you again later – in most likelihood. You will have found a way to get them out of the house, away from the video games and bouncing up and down on their little legs; which is naturally what we all need more of.

I love volleyball, I have decided; and I didn’t even know that my entire life until now. How have I lived so long without it? It makes me happy. If only that she and I are laughing and playing together until darkness falls. She’s teaching me, I’m absorbing, we’re giggling a lot; and we’re both bouncing up and down on our little legs.

**Lucy learned to really appreciate volleyball.**

# JUMPING JACKS AND JILLS

Some smart person informed my daughter's class that, if they could not run a mile without stopping, they wouldn't be able to graduate 5th grade. What a great idea! Motivate our little blessings to get up off the couch and onto the running track; why didn't I think of that myself? And so we have it. With only just over 2 months to go before 5th grade "graduates", my daughter wants us to get in training for her mini-marathon. I say "us", because running alone is not an option for her and she does not want to get held back because her sprinting is not up to scratch.

Our first day of galloping over the land, I think I was a little fitter than she, since she was pulling me back by the hood and not allowing me to win. Since then, she's accelerated considerably, probably due to the 30 year age gap between us; but I give it a good go anyway. We don't puff as much either, neither one of us.

"They didn't have video games when you were young?" she asked me, panting, after a run. "No, we used to play outside," I replied, thinking to myself that, back then, you didn't see many overweight children around either. We would play outside until our parents would force us in to either eat or sleep; that was the only time we stopped racing around. We also didn't eat junk food or drink sodas either; another contributing factor, as we all know.

And so my quiet, private goal is to get my daughter to "play outside" more. We have started running together and we will continue this, much to the joy of our dog and chagrin of our cat. When the rain clears, we will play more tennis and go swimming more often. We have already purchased our new bathing suits ready for the summer ahead and, oh boy, by the time summer arrives, we will both be looking a little better in both of them.

At a recent meeting for "Girls Inc", which has so many valuable programs, many of them already in our local schools, I read for the first time, the Girls' Bill of Rights. One of the rights is that girls have a right to accept and enjoy the bodies they were born with and not to feel pressured to compromise their health in order to satisfy the dictates of an "ideal" physical image.

I have to look at my own hand in compromising my daughter's "ideal" physical image by the swift and easy meals I let her eat sometimes; the junk food that is presented as a treat, the candy ditto. I have decided I need to try and turn that around somewhat, so that her ideal physical image is not bogged down in early adolescence by the feeling that she is overweight or uncomfortable in her skin in any way. Young people do not understand that what goes out has to over-supplement what goes into the body in order not to carry the burden of extra weight. They do not comprehend at all the huge overall benefits of good nutrition early on; the enormous values of fruits and vegetables; nor do they care very much. We have to teach them and continue to do so. "Girls have a right to be free of vulnerability and self-doubt and to develop as mentally and emotionally sound individuals", so sayeth another clever bill of rights from the Girls' Inc. roster. If I allow my child to wander into pre-teenhood not understanding how she is solely responsible for the good maintenance of her body and the solid link between the physical and mental in all of our existence, I am doing her a complete disservice. As the child of a life-long anorexic, I am anxious not to push that nasty word "diet" and to lean a little more heavily toward the slant of "lifestyle". I can help it if she eats 2 cookies in place of a yoghurt; who does the grocery shopping anyway? I can help it if she goes the entire weekend without going out to play or going for a run. I can help it if her self-image suffers by the way she feels about herself. Just because children evolve from needing you the way they once did does not mean that your role of being needed does not evolve too. This all just came to me very recently and I hope it will be a wake-up call for others as well, which is why I am confessing my parental sins to y'all in this place at this time.

As Jack and Jill jumped their little hearts out on the playground recently to benefit the American Heart Association's 'Jump For Heart' fundraiser, so the national statistic hit me in the face that every one of two females will suffer some kind of heart attack or stroke; that is the cruel reality in our nation today. We have to protect our silent organ in a better way than we have been doing; I know that is the case in our household.

Grab your running shoes, dust off your stop watch and take your child out to play; why don't you. It'll be better for both of you, mentally and physically. You may even give yourselves a good giggle in the process, as is the case most days with my daughter and myself.

To quote the Girls' Inc. yet again, because I was so very impressed by their organization, their mission is to inspire all girls to be strong, smart and bold, to respect themselves and the world around them. I'm going to start by getting my girl and my self to respect our bodies just a little more, and then we can begin to work on everything else.

**Girls Incorporated is a national nonprofit youth organization dedicated to inspiring all girls to be strong, smart and bold. www.girlsinc.org**

# KICK IT FOR SUMMER

"Summertime; and the living is easy", as the old song goes in its sweet timeless way. It reminds me of lounging by the river on a warm afternoon and listening to the hum of the bees. As adults, we get little time to kick it, as it were; summer time or not, and we almost never have time to listen to bees humming. The living is seldom easy for the parents when the school summer vacation stretches out like a long arm of freedom around your kids' lives. You know you should be happy for them, not stressed for yourself, but it seldom works out that way.

At the beginning of the school holidays, I eyed the calendar warily; hugely aware of the enormous gaps between one summer camp/reassuring child care option and another. Long gone are the sunny days when the local YMCA summer day camp was considered an acceptable vacation location for my "tween", (sounds like pre-teen, shortened to "tween"). Horse riding and swimming are still okay in her book, but their schedules this summer didn't blend as well together as I had hoped; and it's all about me naturally.

And there you have it; a lot of sun-filled days full of nothing for my little blessing. Between "Urbz" on the X-box and unsuitable "tween" programming on the regular box, you hope that she will pick up her lovely copy of "David Copperfield" in between times; or even start working ahead on some fractions for $6^{th}$ grade; but I'm obviously not quite as tuned into the "tween" lifestyle as I need to be. So what is wrong with days of nothing, you might ask? Absolutely nothing, I've come to the conclusion; absolutely nothing.

Thinking back to the long summer holidays, as we called them, of my youth, in England, I had lots of delicious nothing back then. I had 6 weeks worth to be exact. Our family – except for poor old dad who had to stay and make the money - would go to our cottage by the sea and we'd stay there for the duration. I'd play with my friends, swim in the ocean, eat a picnic on the beach prepared by Mum, play with my friends some more, swim again, eat … I look back now and admire, from the huge distance between then and now, the delightful childhood my parents afforded us, with never a mention of fractions or Dickens; though we didn't play computer games either and seldom watched the box.

As I look at my own child and the current sleepover of the day, both still asleep at 11.45am with the remnants of last night's popcorn and cocoa scattered around their room, I'm getting better, I realize, as the summer progresses, in letting go, relaxing the rules, smoothing over my own boundaries. During school time, the regime is tight. Up at a certain time; bus at a certain time, (mostly running in order not to miss it!); school starts, school ends, homework, chores, reading, bed. Everything has its own compartment and it has to be that way. During the long holiday break, it doesn't have to be that way. It's okay to break your own rules a little and allow the littles in your house to do the same. The boundaries will still be there come August, when the parents are rain-dancing the day for back to school. At that time, I guarantee you'll find all your rules just where you left them.

For right now, let your children be children; allow them to indulge in their free state and help make some good memories for their future years, when they themselves are watching their babies sleeping in at 11.45am on a hot morning in July and remembering how things were for them years ago. Give them treats and let them stay up late and eat no breakfast, except for maybe ice cream. Let them play too much x-box and squeal with laughter as loud as they like, along with the latest sleepover who loves coming to your house because you're so easy. The other side of life will come back to them soon enough and the good thing is that they will probably be very ready for it when it does.

**Lucy has relaxed quite a bit over the years, as 'tween' evolved into 'teen'.**

# THE LONELINESS OF THE LONG DISTANCE RUNNER

"I've learned that you can tell a lot about a person by the way he/she handles these three things; a rainy day, lost luggage and tangled Christmas tree lights."

- Maya Angelo

How about the ageing process? I'm sure Maya has many really profound things to say about that! She hits things on the nail so perfectly. I'm okay with ageing; no really I am. I like myself much better now than I did as a teenager, a twenty or even thirty something. I'm smarter, nicer, more careful, more considerate, less selfish; all really good things, (and yes, I was quite a horror when I was young!) Plus I seem to make way better choices and that is an age-art in itself. Who cares if the price you pay is a few more laughter lines around the eyes, a few dents in the upper lip and a cleavage and neck that should really no longer be exposed to the cruel light of day? Doesn't bother me a bit! I happen to like cover up and turtle-necks. Most of the time I forget how old I am; I have to ask my daughter. Menopause messes with the memory; or so they say.

I am always interested in studying the people that ageing does bother though and seeing how much energy they expend fighting the inevitable. My mother worked hard to keep her body as trim as it could possibly be; to the point that she starved her bones, which ultimately turned to lace. She loved to wear jeans, dye her hair and mix with young people; all wonderful things. She stressed, however, too much, about the passing of time and tormented herself with her deepest wish that she might be young again. That is a tough burden to bear. We look at the calendar these days and say, "Mum would have been 74 this month," and then look at each other and say, "That wouldn't have done at all." And it wouldn't. She could not stand to be debilitated by age, or limited by aches and pains, or sickness, even when she really wasn't. The mildest common cold would send her, insulted, to her bed. She only lived to be 67, but 70 plus would have had her reeling; no doubt about it.

My sister insists that she is ageing well; she is. She spends much of her day racing up and down hills on bikes or running on her legs, or swimming in a pool. She is a tri-athlete and marvelously fit. She has found the cure for carrying extra weight and the partial source of her own sense of well-being. She is pretty concerned about ageing, but has no children or child-bearing scars to weigh her down. I hope she can continue to run marathons and race on mountain bikes for another couple of decades; and maybe she can. But I worry about the alternative. If her knees start to play up, like my husband's, or her hip is a little dodgy like our other sister. That will put all that vigorous exercise on the sideline and where would that leave her anxiety about keeping away the approaching shadows of ageing and the odd descent of gravity or an expanding love handle?

I sometimes read 'More', a magazine for the over 40's. It helps you not to feel so alone; there are lots of us out there, suffering with pre-menopause, or teenagers or a wonderful combination of the two! I look at all the anti-ageing creams you can purchase for serious money, the "Botox" and the anti-wrinkle serums. We - me and a whole bunch of other vulnerable 40 somethings - are their target market and, judging by the amount of intense advertising, there must be a heck of an audience out there ready and willing to scoop it all up with their credit cards, while they watch the miracles happen. I am heavily skeptical about all of that stuff and think that lots of water, a little exercise and good sleep go a long way towards helping us look and feel better, which is what it's all about; right? Oh and fresh air, good nutrition and lots of laughter; they're all way high on my priority list, now I've hit 40 plus and things don't quite sit as well as they did 20 years ago - from the top down.

Be happy with who you are and where you are currently on your journey. When I was a teenager, I did not think that I could live beyond 28. Don't ask me why; that was just the magic number at the time. It seemed to me that life would become so incredibly boring at two decades and eight that I would just have to evaporate away from all the tedium and cease to be. There you have it. I have outlived my own life expectancy and I'm happy for it. 28 was so over-rated, after all.

As the great Maya also said; "I've learned that even when I have pains, I don't have to be one." Don't worry, be happy; there are such great views along the way, forty, fifty or who really cares.

**Lucy loves it when you are old enough to really just be yourself.**

# MEET YOU IN MY DREAMS

I had a meeting with a salesman this week, as you do quite frequently when you manage an office. On his binder, there was a large photo of his young daughter. "Ah, so cute!" I said, looking at the 8.5X11 blown up photo; and I meant it. She was a bit fuzzy, but adorable all the same.

"I travel a lot," he explained. "It's hard for us to be away from each other." The salesman went on to explain that the one source of comfort, when they are away from one another, is that they plan every night to visit with each other in their dreams. They plan the place they are going to meet and what they are going to do when they get there. "This week," he explained, "we arranged to meet in a bird's nest, so we could pretend to be like little birds trying to keep warm in the grasses of the nest, while we took care of our babies." Other times, they meet at more "regular" places like Disneyland or Great America and they do extraordinarily fun things together, like going on lots of free rides with no waiting time, as well as eating a lot of ice cream.

I liked this concept; not just because little kids are so magic and they have such killer imaginations that you could just feast on them, but also because, as old as some of us are, we all need things to look forward to; whether they're just in your dreams or not. Right now I'm as burned out as one human being can be - in my mind – as well as in my dreams, when I can find myself constantly racing against the clock or being late for my plane; or even, on occasion, falling down stairs I don't even have in my "real" life.

I'm looking forward, in a really childish way, to escaping my day to day and heading "home" for some rest, some fun, and some totally different experiences from my usual reality; a trip which I shall be making in just a few short days. Not discounting the fact that I love my "real" home, my family, even my job most of the time, you just get that feeling sometimes that you want to meet yourself in your own dreams and find that person to be a more joyous, light-hearted human being than the one you're looking at in the mirror at right now.

When I meet myself in my dreams, I will not have so many frown lines, grey hairs or wrinkles; I will have lost the 20lbs I failed to lose. I will not only be lighter on my feet, but lighter of heart. I will dance at my own party, laugh so hard I can't breathe, and feast my eyes on all I have to be so very grateful for. I'll remind myself what I am leaving behind on my small journey to my "real" home and I'll completely enjoy the trip down memory lane, even just for a short while. I'll see my people, hug my dad, laugh with my friends and wrap up every pleasurable experience I can squeeze into that short time into a small package for viewing later; not truly knowing, as you don't, how many more visits I'll have like that with certain people for sure.

Maybe when I meet myself in my dreams, I will get to meet others too. Perhaps mother and I can be once again in Greece; we can drink our *Retsina,* eat our Greek salads and enjoy our *moussakka* outdoors on one of the harbor front restaurants in Chania, on the island of Crete; as the flaring sun falls down over the horizon of the now blackening sea and the air begins at last to cool. We will listen to the wonderfully spiritual Greek music. Mum will practice her Greek and I will practice the art of eating Greek food and drinking Greek wine and chatting with Greek waiters. I recall I did all of that very well. We'll adore the scene; the smells, the people, the journey from where we were before to where we are now. Again, it will become a part of our souls.

Perhaps I'll get to see my father-in-law in another dream; he's another bright light you'd like to bump into once in a while, if only in your dreams. I'll get to hear him laugh from his belly once again, as the kids climb over him giggling, and maybe there'll be a cartoon drawing created from that special day for us to hang in the bathroom and laugh over all over again.

There'll be lots of people I'd be able to catch up with in my dreams; if only I knew how to make it happen. Once in a while in your dreams, you get a visit from some one long gone and that makes you a believer for life. Maybe, just like a little girl, if you want something bad enough, you can make it so. I'll just have to work on that during my short trip away to somewhere else, where I hope to meet a more vivacious person than who I'm currently looking at; my own reflection in the mirror of life.

**Lucy has always been blessed with very vivid dreams.**

# MOODS AND THE MOON

Women I know of a certain age regard the moon with a great deal of respect. The larger she gets, the closer many of us know we are getting to that certain time of the month when our men friends need to hide, our children need to bow with respect no matter what and our work colleagues need to acknowledge that it's not a time to say something really stupid. Many women are tuned into the cycles of the moon; it's as simple as that. And that means – men, look around you and be warned – that many women in close vicinity to you are on the same cycle.

Not understanding tides or universal rotations, let alone my own, I stood back recently and tried to intellectualize deeply the impacts of the tsunami in American Samoa, the huge earthquake in Indonesia and our own tsunami watch here on the local coast line, not to mention the several small shakers that bounced around the area. It does make you wonder. I look up at the moon and wonder some more. Ah, the power of the moon, I say to her and her alone. Even the scientists don't always get you!

My friend hails me from the U.K. "Don't try and call," she warns from afar. "I'm in my tunnel and likely to remain there for quite some time." I know that kind of warning. It happens just about every month. I don't try to call and speak to her directly. She will not take my calls. I text her mildly from a distance and counsel her to drink cups of tea, take warm baths and be kind to her. She's on the same moon pattern as me, but time zones apart, so we are both crawling into our tunnels at about the same time. My daughter too. Like it, or not; she's on pretty much the same moon plan as me. Certain times of the month, my poor husband can be seen running for the hills with our neutered dogs fast in tow. What else is a man to do? There is no reasoning with power such as that! My daughter and I just snarl at each other like two hierarchal female wolves claiming their rights to the homestead. I am the adult; I know when to back down. She's fairly new to this; she does not. These are powers swirling around us over which we have no control. During these bizarre days, you become somehow numb to your real self as you crawl towards your tunnel, your tail permanently between your legs, as it were. Gradually, as you edge your way out towards the sunshine and the life and humor you once knew, you find yourself again. And this happens every month around a certain phase of the moon.

Certain times of the month strange things start to hurt. Not the usual things you would think. I will get a tooth ache – very often – and sometimes an ear ache. I definitely will get a spiteful headache around the temples. My memory will start to blur in and out of focus. I will walk into a room – very often – and forget why I am there. Odd things happen at night, most nights. Usually I am a deep, deep sleeper – my mother used to say I slept like the dead – (which is, on the whole, highly fortunate because I live with a deep, deep snorer!) However, during my phase of the moon, I suffer what mother also used to call "white nights". I flit in and out of slumber; the slightest noise, moon beam or snore can and does wake me up and then I am, what I can only describe as, in a moon mood. My brain will get up, get alert and drive me crazy with all the things I need to accomplish and stress over for the rest of my life. She will tell me I am hot, she will tell me I am cold. She will tell me to get up and get busy, because I have so very much to do and it's really not very long until the end of my life.

Sometimes I will wake to the moon laughing her bright beams through my window as if to say 'it's daytime, come out and play." I will look out across the valley and be able to see every thing crystal clear like a stage set, as if it were really day time and we should be out working, if not playing. I'll look at the clock – it is 3am and the moon is messing with me again. Any civilized person does not get up and go to work at 3am. The moon knows that, but she loves to joke. She is a witchy girl. There should be a moon mood 3am club just for the likes of us – when we females are woken up by the moon. We could text each other, just to know we are not completely alone. We could visit with one another electronically, without actually speaking, and share our feelings. We could compare our night heats and communally rag on those other heart beats in our houses which are happily snoozing, snoring and preparing themselves for the dawn of the morrow with fresh faces and good attitudes. Even the cat and the dogs are still slumbering intently and the male snorer heartily going for gold on his side of the bed.

In the morning, as the alarm bell cruelly clangs me out of wake-dream sequence, it is almost as if I have been to an all night party during my white night and closed my eyes not at all. How will I be able to get myself through this day? How long until I am able to lie down once more and do my moon dance again with the planets? There is something about daytime after a white night that makes you want to take the day off, call in sick – whatever it takes - and allow yourself the luxury of sleeping through the daylight, until you are completely satiated of resting, since the darkness had eluded your hours of peace so spitefully.

Back across the pond, my friend is limping out of her tunnel. "Sorry," she texts me. "I've been wanting to kill everyone for a while now, but gladly I did not. Came out and looked at the daylight today and it did not look so bad." Aha. Progress is being made over yonder. Maybe it's time for me to crawl out too.

From my own tunnel, I peak out with hooded lid and realize it's not so bad here either. Never mind that I haven't slept well in nights, I am now at least dreaming of complete strangers and not even work anymore. My body feels like a swollen vessel that is shedding its shell, my psyche is moving through her moon phase, she is calming herself and she is seeing that there may be life once more beyond the shift of the planets; at least until next month.

Meanwhile, the teenager daughter's horns have grown to a point that they will actually stab you and she growls rather than speaks. She flinches when touched and avoids any actual close contact of any kind. The bedroom door remains firmly closed, except to be briefly opened by means of escape and then slammed once more.

'Tis an interesting time, this bridge to menopause that many of us are crossing; especially when combined with cohabitation of a teenage werewolf and a snoring male who is consistently running for the hills. Somehow we will all get through it. Not without a few arguments, many night sweats and ever a swear word at the wiles of the moon. Close your curtains, I urge you, if you are trying to hide from her beam; her powers are convincing and pervasive at certain times of the month. Ask anyone in the 3am club; they'll tell you.

**Lucy used to be such a good sleeper. Just ask her Mum.**

# RAINDROPS & ROSES

Raindrops on roses & whiskers on kittens; green grass & horses and fresh air for skipping! These are a few of my favorite things", or so the song goes, kind of like that; except I never can remember the proper words and it doesn't really matter anyway; it's about the emotion. It was always a soaring song which helped me look for the diamond in the rough. Whenever I heard it, I would stop whatever I was doing – still do – and listen to the passion of the music, savor the words I could never remember; still can't.

"When life gives you lemons, make lemonade," my granny used to say and I never really got that either; still don't; except that I think it means something like play the hand you're dealt; always see the glass half full; something like that.

Too many of my friends and family have been dealing with nasty health scares and dire realities of prognosis of late. I awaken sometimes at dawn with a lump the size of the hunchback's from Notre Dame on my back; I feel anxious and doom-ridden much of the time, as if the very cancer was eating me up inside, as well as them.

"What really awful thing is going to happen?" I wonder. "What really bad news am I going to receive today?" I stress, with my eyes tightly closed, not wanting to get up and face another rough day in reality. Then, in this state of heightened anxiety, you naturally turn to yourself internally and ask yourself how you are really feeling. Why are you so constantly tired? You ask yourself. What is that lump? Is it bad enough that you should go to the doctor? And so the gnaw of self-doubt starts to seep in through the cracks and, before long, you are shrouded in gloom and not admiring the raindrops on the roses at all, let alone the whiskers on the newborn kittens, nor the chirping of the fresh-faced bird looking out at the world from its nest for the first time.

Sometimes it will take a simple slap to the heart to wake you up and get you out of yourself and your cloak of misery. A depressed person is of absolutely no use to those who have real reason to feel depressed; it's just hard, when you let yourself slip down into the mires of gloom and despondency, to pick yourself up again and smell the roses once more.

"We never do anything together anymore; you're always busy." She said. (First stab to the heart.)

"When we go out together, you're not even paying attention to me; you're always talking on the phone." (Blood.)

"You used to always tickle me before I went to sleep. You never do that anymore; you're always too tired." (Aching wound.)

"Even when you came to pick me up from the bus-stop with the dog, which you know I like, you were on the phone all the time, which you know I don't like." (Scar.)

"Do you want to skip with me?" she asked. I paused. (Never let an opportunity go by to right a wrong.)

"Sure I would, honey," (that's the last thing in the world I feel like doing, if you really want to know. All I need right now is a nap, not a skip.)

"Really?"

"Really. Let's have a skipping competition," I said. The smile that came back to me stretched from ear to ear, as the first of many daily skipping competitions began in our driveway; a tiny piece of time and attention away from the drab and the blah and the horrible diagnoses. We started to skip, my daughter and I.

When you haven't practiced something in about 30 years, trust me, you are about as rusty as if you had never ever done it before; plus the instruments of use have significantly altered, or, at least, this was my excuse. In my day, positively moons ago, a skipping rope was a lovely, long, thick soft rope with large wooden handles on the end, which made for a skipper's delight. These days the "ropes" are a harsh plastic and not at all kind on the legs when they whiplash you, which they invariably do, as you trip in your endeavors to skip forwards, skip backwards, (now that's a laugh), and keep your little honey giggling away. There is no greater sound, I have decided, than a little girl's giggle.

And so she beats me every time in our competition; she has to, it's one of the rules. She longs for me to trip and fail at my record of yesterday; and, daily, she strives to cream her own record, which is about 4 times higher than what I could ever aspire to. I'm making amends; I'm making lemonade out of my lemons, smelling the rain on the roses and, hopefully, strengthening the power of my spirit to help lift up the spirits of those most in need and hold them up high, way high, with their glasses half full and my optimistic skipping rope at their heels.

**Lucy has always loved the show tunes.**

# RAW ARENAS OF THE HUMAN CONDITION

When I was young and rich with the bloom of heavenly childhood and I would wake up with a cloud of doom over my head, it was probably because I was going to the dentist that day - my very least favorite thing to do in the whole wide world. You would have thought I was going in for organ extraction at the very least. I'd clench my eyes tight shut, grip my sweaty palms and console myself with the reality check that this time tomorrow it would all be over with.

"You will not have to wake up tomorrow and feel this way," I'd tell myself as if it would really help me at this point. "This time tomorrow it will all be over with for another 6 months."

I'd still go into Dr Fox, the dentist's office, feeling completely sick and nauseated. I'd still want to lock myself in the bathroom and try to evaporate, as I did one very famous time in our family when I actually locked myself in and my mother, horrified by my irrational behavior, threatened to break the door down. I'll never forget the humiliated fury on her face when I finally opened up the door to the rest room and allowed her to unleash her rage on me face to face, while the cool faced receptionist watched with curiosity.

No, this cloud of doom is completely different; it's not remotely about me, but it is of course, because it involves some one in my sphere and someone very dear.

I hate the cloud that she is waking up to at the moment, the nagging reminder that something is not quite right and yet none of us really know why, and therefore there is absolutely nothing to be done about it. It's a vacuous, horrid place to be; a large, empty hall where the clock ticks more slowly than normal, towards at least a time and place of knowledge and preparation.

It's the day of her big tests. I awake with a heavy, grey cloud over my head. There is tension in my heart, a nagging probe in the brain and an all over twitch to the body. There is nothing to be done to change it. This feeling intensifies as the day progresses and I know that my friend is undergoing some really terrible things that we have no control over; the undergoing or the end result. Suffering is a wretched thing and the human condition requires that we deal with it way too much.

I recall my mother's fury at the medications she was prescribed to "treat" an untreatable condition. "Are these keeping me alive?" she raged; "because if they are, I don't want them." We'd had many days of awaiting results back then also; it's almost an ongoing thing and I'm still no good at it.

My friend told me, at the end of her mega testing day, that they accessed her jugular vein to biopsy the organ they were studying; a surgery of sorts to investigate the realms of the unknown. In the meantime, I think of her husband and family wading through mud, as it were, in their long walk towards discovery of where their family would be forced to go with all of this and what it would mean for them ultimately. For me myself and I; at times like this, there is always less of me, myself and I and more of all of the other; never a bad thing. I am taken to the more raw arenas of the human soul; where we can feel a loved one's pain and empathize beyond our own small troubles and irrelevant daily trivia. The unknowing for all is the very worst indeed, I've decided.

For my self, I write it down and expel some of the tension within. I light a candle, as we have always done in our family – during times of need or even just a plane that will be landing with one of us in it - and I hope, with all the good intentions I have inside, that what seems so bad is, in the end, so inflated it's not even funny.

In the meantime, we are all sitting in the waiting rooms of our lives and hoping to turn a corner to a brighter day without the tension and the nausea of the great unknown where we are currently residing. To my dear friend who says so little about her own condition and behaves so graciously; you deserve a great result, truly you do. To the rest of us who stress and wonder and wait; we learn as we suffer for the next time, when we will no doubt suffer some more and hopefully learn a bit more also. My friend's unselfish dignity teaches us all another life lesson.

**Lucy has been down that road too many times.**

# SALVAGING THE SACRED

Religious or not; everyone needs a little bit of sacred in their lives. 'Find yourself a small space and cultivate it as your own', my monthly magazine told me. The space needs to have things you like to touch and admire in it. It does not have to be a large area, but a private one with a photo of a loved one close by, a candle perhaps, a pebble from your favorite beach; a treasured ornament. It needs to be something that you deliberately culture entirely for yourself; you nurture it and it nurtures you. Even if you think you don't have any space to spare, either physically or otherwise, you have to find it and make it your own. A window ledge even, a shelf, a comfortable chair with a view; when you start stretching your mind to achieving something so simple that will give you endless pleasure, it's amazing how creative you can be. Everyone needs a happy place that they can retreat to, stretch out in, as it were, like the cat beside the fire; and feel that when they are in that place, the world is okay.

I had such a place last week; a cozy reading room, resplendent with rich warm colors on the walls, wooden bookcases lined with books, art I enjoyed on the walls and photos all around. There are twinkle-twinkle fairy lights embracing the lovely drapes in sparkling whites and blues – husband put them up 3 years ago and I refused to let him take them down, ever. Photos of my grandma and my mother smile at me, as do the older stills of the living all around. There is only music, no television, in this sacred space; a room with a view which can capture the lovely early morning light just as well as it illumines the cast of the moon as she rises up and over the Gabilan mountains; such a treat. I could light candles in my special place, if I so chose, and sprinkle some pot pourri in a bowl if I was in the mood for that. The lighting is good, if eccentric and eclectic. You could sit quietly there in your space and watch the birds without them knowing about it; from the busy sparrows to the resplendent humming birds; you could almost watch the roses bud and the olives grow. In short, over time, I had achieved my special domain, my sacred haven.

When I say that I had such a place, I still have it as it were; but it has lost its title as my sacred place. It now has the markings of a male locker room, as well as a small gymnasium; and I have only myself to blame.

The treadmill is such a cumbersome beast. Why people can't just get outside and use their legs as if they were on the treadmill is beyond me; but some can't and that's just how it is. Treadmills should be banished to the garage where they can sit their large horrible black selves anywhere they darn well choose and not be such a blight on the landscape; next to the recycling bin or the cat food would be good places.

I had never liked the black beast living in our family room, but that was where it lived until one day, when we were studying our assorted pieces of furniture, as husbands and wives are wont to do once a year or so. Husband remarked that the treadmill didn't really work very well where it had always resided.

'Hallelujah!" methinks. "The light bulb has finally gone on!" At this point, I imagined that husband would be creating a large space in the garage for the beast to live in for the rest of its natural years, and I was naturally horrified when he suggested plonking it in my bedroom. That wouldn't do at all; so I diplomatically broached the idea of the beast sharing my lovely reading room; without thinking the thing through; at all. My motivation was to help the poor man get back on his exercise regime, which had sadly and completely fallen by the wayside to the tune of 15 extra pounds on his torso. It's what wives do; help their husbands when they are so clearly unable to help themselves.

Inspired by my spirit of foolish generosity, husband hurriedly got the dolly, before I changed my mind, and whisked the beast up the corridor and into its new home. Now the whole thing has become a sad and repentant affair. My pictures have to be re-hung, the esthetics of my haven have definitely altered for the worse, and, insultingly enough, when I'm sitting in my sparkly wonderland of cozy armchair and snuggly pillows, I am facing a large black beast, a set of dangling head phones and a large pair of cheesy gym shoes; not the most celestial way to begin or end a day.

So that is what they call compromise; or that is what they call marriage; I haven't quite figured out the difference. Now muscle man is wondering where the "Bowflex" might squeeze into the general equation of things and whether, in fact, I might need to move all my sacred stuff into the sanctuary of my bedroom, so that he can have a proper gym in there. He's lucky I'm a peaceful person; that's all I have to say about that.

In future I shall be very careful before I make helpful suggestions. Any one have a sacred place they'd like to share? I need an area in my life that is just mine; and I refuse to go out into the garage.

**Lucy has since moved the beast back to the bedroom.**

# SEEING THE WHITE LIGHT AT THE END OF THE TUNNEL

For most of us, the religious experience does not come when we are sitting in the dental chair. As I dug my fingernails into my flesh and squeezed my eyes shut for fear that, any minute, I was actually going to have to bite my dentist and run out of the chair screaming, I looked up into the bright light above me and appreciated what people might see as they were moving on into the next world; walking towards the bright light as it were. We've all pretty much met people who've had experiences such as this.

Not to say I was dying in said dental chair. Even my serious condition of 'dental phobia' could not be described in that way; although the guts that it requires for me to even make a dental appointment is a little sad. I would just about rather have an extended dinner with my worst enemy, plus an overnight stay, or be in the final stages of a long labor than step into that lovely friendly office with the great music and kind gentle dentist. He knows I hate it there; I tell him every time. Poor dentists; they must have to go through some serious psychological counseling to be able to handle that beat, especially dealing with big, whiny babies such as myself.

I am the kind of parent that has no problem scheduling a dental appointment for my daughter and not myself. I tell myself that we can't afford it right now – we have no dental insurance, she is the priority – the truth is really that I haven't geared myself up for the ordeal just yet.

I took my daughter in for her cleaning on time; no problem. I did not, however, schedule myself. November came and went – my due date for the dental chair – I then told myself that I needed to make sure and go in for my check-up before the holidays. Thanksgiving, Christmas and New Year - all those holidays - came and went. January arrives. I tell myself that I need to get it over and done with before my trip in March. Finally I tell myself "you're having such a tough week anyway; why not just add to the pile and get it over with?" With teeth literally gritted, I dialed the dental office.

"Would you like the 10.30am or the 3pm?" the nice lady asked. "Neither," I responded and I really meant it. I took the 10.30 in order to be rid of the whole thing before my day began in earnest.

As if I really had a monster growing on my back, I awoke that day doom-ridden with torture. Today was the day; there was no escape. "Be rational," the voice of mature rationalization harps in the background, "it's the dentist not the torture chamber"; but still the heart pounds in the chest, the palms are sweaty. Perhaps this is how people act when they are having an anxiety attack; though my "attack" is for a very silly reason. Laughable, really; if it was only about somebody else and not me!

"I'm going to be out of action for a while," I tell anyone who'll listen to me that morning, with dramatic pause. "I'm going to the dentist." I expect them to gasp or at least sigh with empathy. Most people just breeze right over it; others snort and say, "Oh I hope your visit goes better than mine normally does!" People, this is a phobia we're discussing here; no snorting warranted! I need you to escort me to the 'breathing lesson class for dental visits', or at least the nearest bar, before I am forced to face such an ordeal.

It was as bad as I expected. As I left the light of day and entered the dental office, I reassured myself, "The next time I see daylight and feel the sunshine on my face this horror will be over with for another 6 months." And it was. Armed with an extra piece of face armor in the form of a white filling and some raw gums, I strode bravely out of the dental office a little poorer, but extremely proud in the face of the defeat of my enemy another time. If you looked closely, I was also dribbling. Those that were really paying attention would have notice a little skip and kick box movement, as I headed towards my car on my victory march towards another 6 plus months of being dental free.

**Lucy has suffered this inexplicable, irrational fear of dentists ever since she was a young 'un in the dental chair of a certain Mr. Fox.**

# SHE'S BACK

Most families have subjects about which they skirt around, avoid, conceal, darn right tell lies; ours is cancer. Considering our quite long-standing relationship with the big 'C', this is quite a feat and a task.

My grandfather died of cancer back in the 1960's, my mother succumbed to the wretch just a few short years ago, with her cousin following suit shortly after that; to name just a few of our clan lost to the quiet wiles of that deadly disease. There may have been others among us who, I suspect, just didn't get diagnosed correctly, but left along the same path. Many of us in our family have had cancer scares, including lumps and strange cells; there seems to be a scary, growing pattern there.

My baby sister had breast cancer in her early thirties; chemotherapy, radiation; the works. Every six months she has her "check ups" and this is when, in its overriding anxiety, our family reaches its peak for non-communication skills. When 'C' comes to visit, as it were; we are strangely and uncharacteristically moved to silence.

"Has she been in for her check up?" the question is broached.

"She's going next week." Silence. The tension rises in the air, cutting the atmosphere with its veil of fear and foreboding.

"How's she doing?"

"Fine; she looks great, just great." (Wish it were already over with.)

"Oh that's great." (Boy, these check ups come around quickly. I hate it!)

A week later….

"Did she have her check up?" Silence.

A follow up question is required: "How did it go?"

Most of the time, the answer to this is "fine". This particular time it was not.

"Well, I wasn't going to say anything; but since you asked; there seems to be something there."

"Something there? What do you mean "something"? Do you mean It's back?"

"I didn't say that. I said there's something there."

"So what are they going to do?"

"They're going to wait and see."

"Wait and see? So it can grow some more?"

"I didn't say that. I said they need to wait and see if anything changes after 3 months. Then they will decide what needs to be done." And this is how anything turns into something, a shadow turns into a cancer and everyone is back where they were at the beginning, when all of this started.

And so it is. It's back living in our family again, as if it had never left; the uninvited visitor has returned without an invitation. This time we won't forget its pervasive existence so quickly.

After the trauma of a family member and consequently the whole family suffering the intrusion, the sickness, the debilitation of cancer; and, ultimately, they are given a clean bill of health; hope takes you up on her wings and makes you feel that, after such suffering as that, up is where you will all be staying for the foreseeable future. She does not give you any kind of inkling that "it" will come back for a return visit and rearrange the playing fields where you hoped you would eternally stay. When it comes back – small, unformed, scientifically unidentifiable at this point; it comes back in all its strength and overwhelming power. As a family you return to the stress, the unimaginable concept of possible loss, the suffering of a member and all of your members. The plates move in your midst, the dynamics of your clan shudder. In an instant, everything returns as it was just a short, short time ago, and everything else in your sphere becomes almost irrelevant.

So it has been for my family these past few days. We are now on the short list. We are in the waiting room. We have a few short months to go until we know what needs to be done; the waiting is the worst. We taste metallic, we feel nauseous, we lose our hair almost at the prospect of all we do not know and yet we dread with a flavor that tells us we have been there before. We are still with fear.

To all families who are traveling the same road as us; know that there are many, many of us moving in the same direction; moving, yet hardly moving at all. We are capsules in time, floating above our own existence and all we know, without destiny remotely in our sights. To my sister, Rosie who maintains a remarkable equilibrium and humor while we are all stumbling and fluctuating around her and saying everything while saying nothing at all; it becomes clear that it is truly in the face of adversity that we find our true selves.

Rosie is a warrior and her colors continue to shine above us all.

**Lucy's baby sister Rosie continues to inspire and entertain those around her.**

# SO, WHO IS GOING TO TAKE OUT THE TRASH?

It has been a confusing few days. I guess some weeks are just like that; geared and ready to shift your planets and make you look a little more closely at life and her gifts.

I have not taken out the trash since I was 9.5 months pregnant; there you have it, I have confessed. Simply stated - it is not one of my jobs; it is not what I do. I can't, I won't. If I hear the garbage truck zooming up the hill towards our home, my husband had better be wheeling our carts up our driveway, or, better still, to allay any lingering anxieties, they had best be already there. I also do not appreciate said cans staying at the top of the driveway for the rest of the day like two sitting ducks waiting to be re-emptied, or worse- two signals to any cruising local thieves that, "hey! These dumb folks are not home! They've left their trash cans at the top of the driveway!"

This week the plates shifted. My more able and domesticated half was felled by a nasty disease. The first day I was moderately tolerant. "Oh honey, that is too bad. Make sure you drink lots and rest. I'm off to work. I won't bother you with calling - I'll just text you to see if you need anything." That night was spent with him marauding around the house trying to find a place to get comfortable. I got up in the morning and saw his trails at every turn. Is he in the office? No. How about on the deck? Negative. What about the front room? And so it went on. There were unseemly trails of slimy pillows and blankets everywhere through the house, like some one who had had an all-night party and never actually slept.

The second day he didn't go to work either. He groaned a lot; sweated excessively and smelled like something metallic that had gone really, really wrong in its evolution. I had, reluctantly, taken the trash and the recycling to the top of the driveway in the morning. That evening, I moved the trash cans back down the driveway where they really belonged, gave myself a little talking to and broached the medical question with the patient inside. "How about going to the doctor?" (Also known as, 'How about we put a stop to this right now, fix you up and get back to the concept of you being as really helpful and useful to me as you usually are?') It didn't happen then either.

He wasn't eating; his skin was ashen and damp. He wasn't sleeping. He walked 'the corridors' at night like a nocturnal creature looking for something larger than himself, and spent the rest of his time lying horizontal and trying to find the cruel sleep that evaded him. This was not normal behavior. He had no appetite. Was he dying? Had something from the recent fires done something radically and permanently damaging to some of his vital organs? I could not explain his sudden decline in any rational way, other than I needed a serious medical diagnosis and I needed it quickly, while there was still time.

"He has the flu," my friend said helpfully, in her most matter-of-fact way. "No, you don't get it," I urged. I explained some of his dark and disturbing behaviors to her. "Yep, the flu" she said knowingly. "Take him in." And there it was. This male was not going to get well on his own-some – it was going to take a medical intervention.

"I am going to take you in," I ventured, confidently, to the horizontal flesh I used to know as my beloved. "Non negotiable." I persisted. "Fight me over it and I'll call your mother." I kept backing myself up. He was quiet. He didn't argue, surprisingly. This was stranger still. Whether it was that he was so tired of feeling so lousy, or whether it was the mother threat, we'll never know; but I do know that he crawled peacefully as a lamb into my car that morning and let me drive him - seat extended as far backwards as it would go – down to the clinic to see the doctor. Once there, he wanted to lie down on the floor, hoping to finally get comfortable, which was a tad random; but he was soon put into a little waiting room and able to re-extend himself and lie down to wait for the doc. A flu test later and a prescription for 'Tamiflu' and we were on our way. "It's just the flu?" I questioned the doctor closely. "Nothing terminal?" Despite his assurances to the fact, I had never seen such a violent flu bug and quietly resolved to get my flu shot this year and for every year thereafter.

After the first dose of "Tamiflu", Himself ate the first solid thing he had had in three days. By the evening he was up and ready for dinner. By the following day he was truly operating on all cylinders and headed back to work, nine pounds lighter no less.

And the moral of that story, ladies, is to drag your reluctant partners quickly to the doctor on the first day that they are ailing (and you are taking out the trash); not the third. "If you come in on the first day and get the 'Tamiflu', you will get over it so much more quickly," the clever doctor told us. A word to the wise; the flu season is so wretched this year, they are not kidding! And, we are not, truthfully, even in flu season yet!

If, like me, you found your plates had shifted this week and you witnessed yourself eyeing the long grass in the back of the house that needed some one to cut it, or the sentinel-soldier trash cans at the top of your driveway that needed some one to move them back down the driveway, hurry in with your beloveds to get their flu shots. Do not let it go, as I did, the three long days it took to get his lord and master into the doctor and for my life to resume somewhat of a normal pattern. It might be helpful to note – should any of you find yourselves in similar situations – that the trash cans do seem to have got a lot lighter in the decade plus since I last hauled any of those lumpy things around. Either that, or life has just given me the tools to deal with them.

**Lucy has not hauled the trash cans again from those days to this.**

# SOMETHING IS WRONG WITH MY NECK AND OTHER SAD STORIES

I have always been somewhat of a weekend warrior where exercise is concerned. Right before Thanksgiving, I felt the tire around my middle with both hands and resolved to do something about it before it turned into a double wide. Jumping on the treadmill, I was happily surprised by the fact that, even as old as I was, I could still jog for one rotation of the treadmill without stopping – a quarter mile, in fact – and sometimes even two. I was young, I was vivacious, I was an athlete once more and the tire would be just melting away before my very eyes right in time for turkey day with all the trimmings. I would find my abs again, my arms would be something to boast about, my thighs sleek. "Ask me if I have been on the treadmill today," I said to my husband defiantly. "In fact, ask me that every day from now on."

Her defiance was short lived. This new found athlete found a nerve she never knew she had when she stood up one morning, a day or so after this proclamation, and almost fell over, so extreme was the shooting pain which darted up and down her leg. She couldn't believe it.

"Oh yes," said a know-it-all friend, with confidence. "That is your sciatic nerve. At your age, you can't just be really out of shape and then, out of nowhere, start sprinting like an Olympian!" I glanced down at my tire in a conciliatory fashion. That was the end of my treadmill days, I can tell you. She now sits in the corner like a bad girl on time out, while she gathers dust and the odd jacket or two. She has been laid off; she is theoretically redundant. After that excursion down pain alley, it took some time to be able to put weight on that leg without nauseating twinges and I simply wasn't going to go there again. Maybe at my age, you just don't go there period.

Not a problem. There are other ways to exercise, I consoled myself. I love to swim, but it wasn't really swimming weather yet, so I had to come up with another plan to work on that still growing tire. I watched one of those skinny goddesses on the television talk about economic work outs at home - "Don't let the recession beat your work out routine! You don't need to go to the gym to get fit!" And I realized that she was right; I could work up quite a sweat in my own living room given the right motivation. Now to find that pesky motivation, wherever she was hiding! You'd think the swelling tire would be enough, but somehow it is tough to get all dressed up in your work out clothes to just jig around by yourself at home.

Luckily for me, motivation was just a DVD away. For Christmas, my husband had given me the full series of "The Office" which I just adore; so there I had my motivation and my quiet time all in one. Get dressed up to work out, pop a DVD in the player and jog away. I'd do jumping jacks, on the spot jogging, sit ups and all other kinds of wonderful exercises that you really prefer no one sees you actually attempt to do, so the bedroom is the best place for it. At the first bead of sweat, I really was very pleased with myself; I had found the golden key to my exercise solution, plus I was enjoying my show and getting a little stress relief all in one. What an all-round success story!

"Women over 40!" the golden goddess stressed. "When you are working out, don't forget your weight bearing exercise! It is so important to feed and work your bones, even if you feel as if your bones are plenty strong enough!" I pondered that thought. As the child of an osteoporosis sufferer, I certainly did not want to go there, despite the fact that I felt as if I had good bones; so I dusted off my 5lb hand weights and began a little regime with them, after my initial circuit of jogging and jacks. Now I was circuit training; what a champ! The weights made me feel good, they made me feel powerful. Maybe I too would one day have shoulders and arms like Michelle Obama!

Not long after I began my aggressive course of developing the most beautiful upper body yet to be seen in South County, not to mention dreamy triceps, biceps and any kind of 'ceps' that a human body might boast, I awoke in the middle of the night feeling paralyzed. Was I dreaming? I could not move at all. What on earth was wrong with my neck? I shuffled my heavy body out of bed sideways, my neck still in the horizontal plane mode, anxious not to try and move a muscle in that weight filled thing also known as my head. I had done something really foolish to my neck and this did not feel good. 2 pain killers later and I still couldn't turn my head without looking and maneuvering myself like a robot. Driving the car was ridiculous, putting on clothes painful, brushing my hair uncomfortable. I had never given my neck the slightest respect before then, but now I realized what a fundamental trunk she was for my tree to operate properly. You have a pain in your neck and you can think about little else, trust me.

I consoled myself with the likelihood that this would be a brief period of discomfort and soon I would wake up and be able to move and walk like a normal person again. In my mind, I promised the powers that be, if they could please just set me back to rights, I would not use the weights again, since they obviously did something really wretched to my upper regions and were quite evil. One week later, I was still contemplating all kinds of interesting manipulation from massage to acupuncture, not to mention amputation, and all the while waiting for this hell to subside; when miraculously, I awoke one morning and could turn my head like I had some oil in my parts again. What a happy morning that was! I downed a few anti-inflammatories, just in case some one was messing with me, but by mid-day, I had settled back into my regular routine of totally taking my neck for granted and moving around almost like an athlete. At least I could look behind when I was backing up the car – I had never really appreciated that before!

Now I am fully back and ready to get moving and working out again in the comfort of my own home, my small exercise goal has been reduced to just getting my heart rate up every day. More than that, I am not even going to challenge myself to attempt! Having gone through an experience of sciatica and near neck paralysis in the last few months, since I attempted to commence some kind of regular exercise regiment, I'm going to accept my limitations, not to mention my age, and step forward with caution, knowing all that I know I cannot do and all that can severely hurt me. In the meantime, the tire is still there, though marginally diminished. With all I now know, I'll take the tire over the sciatica or neck paralysis any time; trust me.

**Lucy is a former weekend warrior with the treadmill and the weights and fond swimmer.**

# THE RIVER FLOWS BACKWARDS

Every morning and evening during the winter time, I like to go to the place on my property I call "The Point", where I can admire the curves of the river and watch it flow what I call "backwards", (you stop and take a look for yourself. Doesn't it seem as if the Salinas River should truly be flowing in the opposite direction?) It is the point that I believe Steinbeck depicted in "Of Mice and Men' - "a few miles south of Soledad, the Salinas River drops in close to the hillside bank and runs deep and green;" and it is therefore not only a literary but also a magical position in our universe. This homage to our river gives my day symmetry and a shape; it helps me calm myself and pull myself back down to earth. It has become a part of daily life itself, which I count on to keep myself straight. Watch the light come up over water and watch the light go down over water; there's not anything much more basic than that.

Though habit is an essential, crucial part of all of our lives, breaking habit is almost doubly essential. We all need to take time away from our norm; that is a for sure. If you have children, you need to spend time away from them and them from you. If you have a job, it is imperative that you flee that humanely-disruptive environment as frequently as you can, in order to not become soured and disillusioned with the whole process; or, at least, that seems to be the standard in most modern work places. If you are married, a respite from your spouse can only put more fruit on the tree of your existence.

Every now and then when you are reaching out for a change, what you receive in return is an enormous gift. Recently I took some time away from the norm and what I took away with me was a huge slice of sweetness for the memory bank and the generations to come we still don't know.

I went horse riding with my daughter. Well, it wasn't quite as simple as that; it never is, is it. Friends of ours had kindly agreed to host the "2$^{nd}$ Annual Ladies trail ride" on their considerable property. This event coincided with my father's visit from England, strangely enough; so he got to witness a double whammy

- an incredibly beautiful part of our countryside inundated with all kinds of equestrian-obsessed women acting like cowgirls in the wild Wild West, all in one breath. He's from London; he doesn't get to see things like this except in movies. I felt honored for him. Not only did our generous friends allow this amazing event to transpire a second time, they made sure that my daughter and I both had steeds to mount for the fun ahead. Such a gift; such a gift!

The skies were aqua blue; the way they can be when you say to yourself," I want to put this in a box and keep it for a rainy day." Yeh, raindrops and roses and all those things nice. Up there on the mountain tops, close to the puff clouds, you could see the vistas for miles. Up there, it was cool, not too cool and the horses were fresh. We lined up for a group photograph, all 25 plus of us; and the joy of the moment was sealed for always. As I looked back at my little girl and watched the happiness sweeping and staying all over her little face, I knew that I had truly arrived. Though our horses were not exactly compatible for trotting along the path in unison, we were riding together in a larger sense. She knew, as a young one, I had had her passion for the horse; now we were enjoying it together and making it larger than either one had imagined. Some things you can just close your eyes and savor for always.

Though the river may always run backwards and some days be a little more backwards than others; be sure to reach out for those heavenly moments and hold them close, for they are rare. Seal the joy with a photo, a smile. Thank those around you for making it possible.

For Dad, who traveled all this way with a dodgy knee; we hope the view from the top was worth it. For our friends who made our magical day a reality, you know who you are. For Willie who lent the lovely Skunk and Jennifer Ray who made the heavenly smile shine through; may a million gratitudes shine down on all of you; and may your rivers always flow backwards.

**Lucy loves horses to this day.**

# THE SUN HAS GOT HER HAT ON

Yay, hip-hip-hooray! The sun is shining everyone; let's go out and play! She's got her hat on; it's going to be a good day; as the song sort of goes …

When our somber newscaster shared the news that, after the second wettest March- into- April in history, our forecast was that it was going to continue, well, wet; I almost packed my bags and headed back to Britsy, (only to quickly recall that it actually rains about 350 out of 365 days there, so the proverbial grass is definitely not greener over there!) The weather-casters love this kind of thing. Rain seems to be one of their favored things to predict day after day and they do it with a curl on their lips and a definite feeling of job security.

"We're on the storm watch," they say as if a mean hurricane is chasing all of us and, any minute, we will be forced to go below ground.

"Landslides cause mayhem! Road closures throughout the County, forcing evacuations! More on the storm watch after these very important messages …."

The severe narrative and deep frowns on the faces of our normally cheery casters reminds me somewhat of the voices from the Second World War radio broadcasts, when the bombers were certainly coming over to destroy people's lives, not just showering a little rain on their parade. Our storm-watchers guarantee that my mother-in-law stays glued to the television until said watch is over, just in case she misses anything; whether or not the watch continues for days, as it has in recent history. She never seems to care that they keep repeating themselves throughout the program; her loyal viewing must be good for the advertising ratings in any case.

And so it is; storm watch 2006, which started right after New Year's, took a major hiatus in February when our poppies actually thought that it was spring; then cascaded heavily down through the soggy days of March and into April which is where she pretty much has stayed.

Then, filled with soggy gloom: clay-choked mud on my shoes, flat, rain-kissed hair and a grey disposition, I arise, at last, to a peachy day; a day with clear blue skies and cream puffs floating around the lovely heavens. There's nothing like it when you have been living on the storm watch! I felt as if a huge weight had been lifted from my shoulders. Yesterday my neighbor was joking that we just might need my hubby's handsome yellow boat to find our way along Metz road into town; today we don't even need a window wiper! Yesterday, I had actually thought that that might be a viable prospect as the rain thrashed me sideways and the Salinas River bled her banks into the already-drenched fields. Today was different. Today, I practically whipped out my shorts and blasted the air-conditioning, as I sung my way into town, chewing on a piece of grass and dusting off my sunglasses against the glare. How brightly the yellow poppies smiled at me, how sweet, sweet the green grass of our homeland frolicked in the breeze and how lovely it was to be alive today, I thought!

All of a sudden, it doesn't seem so bad that the cat puked in the garage, I have no money in my bank and the escrow that I had been working on for 45 days fell crashing to its knees at the last hour. Sunshine can make you feel so deliciously alive, that elementary issues like mortgage payments, credit card explosions, (who knows what the heck I was thinking in Hangzou anyway; definitely not about how to pay a credit card), and work challenges can become almost irrelevant.

As I sat on my bench perusing the scene, admiring the soft – as- carpet, green mountains and ingesting, inhaling and just about any other "in" that you can do with sunshine, (Vitamin D is so very important and I've been a little deprived of late), I knew full well that there were many, many other things that I should be doing, but what I needed to do and what I deserved to do, I felt, was just to feel the sun on my skin, enjoy the blue sky in my sights and prepare to put it all in a box for the next anticipated rain day on our storm watch, which, if our experts predict correctly in all their euphoria, should be arriving just in time to take the icing off my super mood.

What's your cure for the rainy day blues? "Rainy days and Mondays always get me down" … kinda makes you feel like singing the blues, doesn't it …

**Lucy does love a good storm watch in Monterey County. They don't happen very often.**

# UNDER THE WEATHER

It's very hard calling in sick when you own the company, I've noticed. In the days when I worked for a large Fortune 500 company there was a strict protocol of how and when you called in to the office, if in fact you were dying and unable to be of service to them that day, (do not, under any circumstances, call in for anything less!) Now I'm self-employed and my own boss, as it were, I am never able to call in sick. Can't, in fact, remember the last time I did! I somehow drag myself out to work, pushed in part by the heavy burden of guilt and responsibility which drives us onwards and upwards in our careers and makes some people great bosses of themselves and others not so great.

Anyway, I was feeling under the weather that day; actually, if the truth were known, had been below par, as the British golfers would say, for several days, but there was always a perfectly wonderful reason to drag myself up and out into the working world. Since I wasn't exactly contagious and couldn't kill anyone, it wasn't as if anyone would notice I wasn't myself, except for maybe myself; so I kept on trucking, kept on pushing, until one day it wasn't working anymore. Then it stopped; I stopped; everything stopped. I realized I couldn't carry on as I had been doing.

"I'm not coming in today; I'm sick", I pronounced to the world. All of a sudden, people became a little nicer; concern was a bit more obvious in their tone and their demands. "You take care of yourself," they said. "Try and slow down a little. Let me know if there's anything you need help with." Boy, those words of kindness can really endorse the feeling you had all along; that you really needed to take the day off.

Now I had got permission from the boss to really take the day off from life, I started to enjoy things just a little more, even though I still felt somewhat lousy.

"And what would you like to do with this rare sick day," I asked myself, strangely euphoric by the stretch of free day which suddenly loomed before me like an empty playing field. "Oh, given the choice; absolutely nothing," I said to just myself. And so that is what I did. Except that it wasn't nothing; it was a whole lot of wonderful, beautiful, selfish things that I had been deprived off for way too long. I made myself some hot tea, I got back into bed in the middle of the day, (totally justifying it to myself; "isn't that what sick people do?") and I watched a movie I had rented only about a month ago and was determined to keep until I had watched it. (Heck, I now own stock in the darn thing!)

"Thank you for calling Lucy with Legacy Real Estate," so my voicemail went that day. (I changed it before I leaped back into bed). "I'm sorry I'm not available right now," which of course I wasn't. "Please leave a message, or, if it's a matter of urgency, please call my secretary", (she'll cover for me, she knows I'm under the weather), "and I'll call you back just as soon as I can", (or as soon as I'm not feeling how I'm feeling right now). And so it was conceded that I would take a day away from life.

I didn't step outside of the house once, I spent most of the day in my bed and I emerged from my day away with a renewed appreciation for time off, a hearty estimation of going back to bed in the middle of the day and a quest to try and do that very thing once a month, sick or not.

Sometimes our bodies tell us things that our brains refuse to. Listen to your body more than I do; I tell you. If it tells you to take the day off, it's better that you do and spare the world your interconnection with it for one day. You'll be so much better for it, and so, in all likelihood, will the world.

**Lucy seldom takes a 'sick day';**
**but when she does, she loves it.**

# TRAVEL TEACHES

# A SERIES OF SORRY AND UNFORTUNATE EVENTS

"Sorry seems to be the hardest word," or so the popular song goes; but you wouldn't think so, if you had been a voyeur on the Jensen family quest to reach the East Coast of England and start our vacation. 'Sorry' was spouting off all over the place.

Some times, however well you think you have micro-managed everything, planned to the every hour, printed off the every document, checked and re-checked; the Fates just go ahead and have a big old laugh at your expense. And this was our recent experience.

I had a big old wad of paper-proof in my possession for all the codes and dates and reservation numbers we were going to need for the coming days across the pond. I had crowned myself 'Queen of Detail' for what was supposed to be our well-earned bliss-trip of rest and relaxation. I even, on my father's good and punctilious advice, called to confirm, a day prior, that the rental car would arrive at our doorstep, as ordered, and it would arrive on time. "Yes, madam. All set for 8am", the rental dude confirmed. We were ready for phase one of our bliss-trip. We thought.

I was up early in order not to have to deal with the rental dude in my pajamas. I made my first cup of coffee and waited for him. Once he was 30 minutes late and my father already pacing, I made the call. "Oh – you will have to call the rental car company directly about that," the rental dude said quickly, anxious to get me off the phone. This was not a good sign and I was not then a bit surprised when the rental company informed me that, somehow, my reservation had been cancelled. "Well, not by me!" I said incredulously. "Sorry, madam," the young London lady told me. "The office is closed today because of the holiday. We can see what happened tomorrow."

Tomorrow? Tomorrow was a whole other universe. I had plans to be well into my bliss-trip in my house by the sea, well before the dawn of tomorrow. I had been told I could pick up my keys for the house by 4pm today! Tomorrow would just not do! "The only thing you can do at this point in time, madam, is to go to one of the airports and pick up a car there." One of the airports! And so my dream, that I thought I had planned down to the last specification, of having my ride delivered to my father's house on the dot of the pre-arranged delivery time, crashed cruelly down. "Sorry, madam," the young lady said lamely, as I found myself snarling ungraciously down the phone. And somehow 'sorry' now had a really annoying ring to it.

We found ourselves sitting in a taxi in London traffic waiting to get through the painful line of gridlock also known as the English traffic jam/road work system, rather easily found on any holiday on that small island. Luckily, we all had IPODS with us to cool our jets. The cab driver was chatty and cheerful too, and we realized at the time that, had we been in the know previously, we could have booked his car to take us the entire way to our East Coast beach house and pick us up again a week later for what our taxi-gridlock adventure and new car hire were going to cost us. Somehow our cabbie also got on the 'sorry' tack – a recurring theme for this day, notably Good Friday, (some religious folk might have a field day with that!)

"So this guy gets caught in customs trying to smuggle in some stuff to the country," the cabbie said in his strong Indian accent. "And the customs man he say, 'What do you have to say about this?' And the man, he say, 'I have to say I'm sorry'. And the customs man he say, 'sorry? What the heck sorry – what is that going to do for anything?" And our little cab driver dude just cracked up at this story, which got me thinking, as I perused the dirty houses lining the chock-a-block road we were stuck on, at what an overrated word 'sorry' actually was and how I would have to avoid using it whatsoever in the future, if I ever got to leave this sorry-ugly road amidst this sorry-ugly gridlock.

We finally make it to the designated airport. I comforted myself with the thought that, at least, we were headed in the right direction towards our fabulous beach house. We were off track, but we were closer than we were when we started our 'adventure' this morning.

We get to the rental car check and line up behind several Mr. Angrys. "No, madam! Sorry is not going to cut it," the gentleman's voice was rising and things were not going well at the check-in desk. His rental car had broken down, the tow company had taken the car and along with it, the keys to said car. He was here to get another one that worked. "Sir," the lady said emphatically. "The rules are that I cannot issue you with another car while we do not have the keys to the first car returned! I'm sorry, but those are the rules!"

"Stop saying you're sorry, when you are so obviously not!" The temper was flaring again. I couldn't help but wince at the sorry theme still pounding through the hours of our day. If I wasn't already so exhausted by it all, I would have laughed.

Finally it was my turn and I tried to describe to the nice young man at the desk the series of unfortunate events that had befallen us that day. "Gosh I'm really sorry," he said and I smiled meekly. "Yes, me too!" I said mildly, hoping to raise the level of success in our day with a dash of niceness on my part. "We really have been very inconvenienced, not to mention the additional expense and time .. I would appreciate it if we could receive the same rate we were given in the first place."

"Oh no, madam, sorry, that will not be possible. The only rate I can give you is the one I am authorized to give from the airport. You will have to take this up with the original rental company, sorry." Yes, that again. I was worn out, beaten up by the day already and just willing this young man to give me any darn car at any darn price. I couldn't have cared less at that point. I graciously retreated and signed the papers, trekking out into the rain with my crew and hoping upon hope that we would have no more unforeseen unfortunates that day and also that no one else would have to say sorry to us for anything. Since I would be driving on the wrong side of the road in the rain, I also hoped, for my part, I would not have to say sorry for anything either.

Thankfully, this was just one bizarre day in what turned out to be a blissfully restful and tranquil holiday by the beach with the perfect light, reasonable weather and best company possible.

Looking back at the contrast of that hellish start with the lovely tranquil days that followed made the trip even more memorable. Sometimes, no matter how you plan, the darndest things are going to happen to you; but along the way there are often some incredible views to be had and, sometimes, even a tale or two to be gathered.

**Lucy loves to go back to the East Coast of England where she spent her childhood.**

# A STREAM OF CONSCIOUSNESS IN CHINA

**SATURDAY IN MARCH** – It's minus-minus and the neon high buildings nod to the black of night. We are not used to any of this. Rickshaw bikes with back doors, whooshing through the chill, no lights. Grey alleys, dust, merging lanes of traffic, no right of way. Persistent, grey bicycles riding through the night on dark streets, grainy air. The people all look the same.

A brightly lit restaurant beckons – red and gold – tall, young Chinese girls, pretty in bright red, with heavy hooded eyes and black hair, greet us at the door. No English spoken or understood. Duck in many styles on the lazy Susan. Oily-glazed Peking duck with plum sauce, cucumber, bok choy and a light flour wrap. There's porcelain on the floor of the toilet, no bowl! The howls of the Westerners, wondering where they could go to comfortably pass waste. Not something we are used to either. The tour guide Alan apologizes for the cold as the Californians crease up and wonder why they had left their cashmeres at home.

Razzle-dazzle of marble and sparkle. 5 stars with a chandelier. Tall Chinese – how did they get so tall; the gentlemen in reception? The lights in the room are a mystery. How do you turn these things on? The mystery in the form of a credit card at the door and a push of a clock to arrive at your chosen destination; the simplicities of life become complex in a different culture. The shower too; it sprays all over without a semblance of a control system. Bed hard as a plank, but lying flat is so much better than not lying at all. The 16$^{th}$ floor is as high as the neon, almost kissing those ice grey clouds. We are in Beijing.

**SUNDAY IN MARCH** – The hotel room is luxurious, discounting the plank bed, (why no back ache?) and the luke warm water in the flask. Slept well thanks to warmth and melatonin, awaking at 5am to the dawn of a new adventure. Surprising mixture of vegetables and meats mixed with regular breakfast fare on the buffet in the morning. Searched for the illusive 'swimming pool' but never found it. Everything is run by the State – one thing is neatly linked to another, very uniform. We all knew it immediately; we knew it before, but it is still surprising. Private enterprise is the shabby shack down the side alley with all the bikes parked outside. We are in the government run operation and it is very slick.

Freezing! Cold, biting ice monsters sucking the moisture from your eyes. This is what Siberia feels like in the winter; we are there. Don't want to go there again. 'Beijing Olympics 2008' hats are purchased from the street vendors. They love our dollar bills; we had no idea! Why did I not check the weather a little more closely? Think of the many pairs of gloves looking at me from my house thousands of miles away. Temple Of Heaven; too cold for praying. Tai-chi keeps some warm, also floor painting with water. 1420 AD; inconceivable, ages ago. Jade factory – a little warmer. Thrown to the marketing machine which is modern-day China. My daughter is the year of the dog; she has a jade dog. I did not subscribe too well to the money machine. You pick up item, they give you slip of paper. You go to central cashier. You then try and find salesperson who gave you slip of paper to exchange another slip of paper for your item. Frightening. They all look alike. Who knows if I came home with what I actually paid for? After Jade, Ming tombs and cloisonné factory, followed by hot lunch with green bottles of liquor or jet fuel. Clever people! Show them how long it takes to make a miniscule little cloisonné something by hand, then jam them into the store where the factory-made items are copiously displayed and they will be pulling out the dollars as if there was no tomorrow. After all that retail activity, there's only one thing left to do; climb The Great Wall and the temp is still below freezing.

Up and up wide, wonky steps in heeled boots. We were supposed to be doing this tomorrow not today. Bitter, icy, dry eyes, sore lips; the climate of hell. Feet ache as they thaw. Giddy heights when you look down. Height got a little much. Mao said that you are not a hero until you've climbed The Great Wall. I am only a little bit of a hero, managing a slim portion of the large task. The lungs hurt. Went back down again, allowing the hearties in their trainers to keep on climbing. Couldn't find a hot tea for the life of me; plenty of ice cream though. Another meal around the lazy Susan. 3 bottles of wine – NOT CHINESE – chicken-head eating competition; not for me. Fore-go evening's acrobatic show, since Sandy had to speak at the US-China delegation back at the hotel. To my luxy room – finally – and a long bath of bubbles and hot tea.

**MONDAY IN MARCH** – Not so cold; good. Am woozy in cold weather; don't like it. Called Mike and Frou from Sandy's phone – how so? So good to talk to them; breaking back through the 'curtain' to the West felt naughty. Forbidden City – amazing Squares, ornate buildings, lovely reds. The Emperor and Empress; the quarters for the concubines. Huge moat around the palace to keep everyone in or out. Tian An Men Square across the way – impressive in size and bustle. Everyone curious about 1989. Lots of soldiers watching, keeping people moving; still. They don't want you to take photos of them. Lots of vendors pushing at you with postcards, hats etc. "Hello, one dollar!" they say, right in your face. Alan, our tour guide, tells us that much has changed in China since 1989 and the "incident" as they like to call it in Tian An Men Square. He lives and works in the city and likes the changes that have taken place in China over the past few years.

On we go, nearly dying ourselves in Tian An Men Square as we tried to cross the road. The cars do not stop for the pedestrians! We visited the medical museum where a group of white-coated doctors gave us a personal sales pitch on the benefits of Chinese medicine, its longevity etc. The doctors took time to feel pulses, ask questions, feel pressure points. Some people bought Chinese herbs, some had massages. Yang and Ying; the balance of condition. Everything in the world has an opposite side.

To the Hutong district, the area where the real people live; according to Alan. Small alley ways, high threshold steps – to keep out the bad spirits – bikes and more bikes, small courtyards of homes, old, dusty. Our ride on the rickshaws along the alleys and away from the street vendors who chased us along the canals, quite funny. Our rickshaw did not have any brakes and we kept crashing into the bike in front. A fine opportunity for some one to try and sell us another Rolex. We ate a traditional meal in a nice Chinese lady's house – dumplings and many indescribable things – lovely warmth and tea. We all hugged our hostess and left handsome tips. Crossing the roads in the bike-taxi – another fine Chinese experience. I closed my eyes and just hoped for a safe crossing.

To the 'Summer Palace' – how lovely this would be in spring! Howlingly cold at the moment! Huge lake, elegant architecture. You could just imagine the emperor and his concubines in one courtyard; the empress in another.

Off to a pearl factory – boy, we're moving fast! Another dollar opportunity, we're thinking, as they give us a number and a tag for our neck. A buffet dinner – they keep us well fed while we're spending our money. Alan said that Beijing is still a developing a city, China a developing country. Many of the ideas here are only 10 years old. "When you open the window," he said, "the sunshine comes in; but also the flies." He is very interested in how to put together a Chamber of Commerce in Beijing. He is a clever young man and could go far. Zonked; to bed. Our hotel is lovely, luxy and we don't really have any time to enjoy it. The tea is good, fragrant. The beds are hard. Talk of the bus Tuesday; the Americans rang up a $600 bar tab in the hotel; they must be happy to have us! Looking forward to seeing Mike and Frou again; Mike would have truly hated it, but Frou would have been a trooper.

**TUESDAY IN MARCH** – wake up call at 5am – off to Shanghai! Bye to Alan, sad. A great tour guide. He told us so many amazing stories about the history of the city as well as the evolving culture of today. He shared a photo of his baby "Travel" – he hasn't seen much of Travel these past few days. Last night he was delivering personalized name stamps to our rooms at 10.30pm. He maintains quite a schedule. Travel can be his only baby – they are just allowed the one. If you work for the government, as most do, and you have more than one child, then you can lose your job. This is inconceivable for us.

Late at night in the "Glamor Hotel", no expense spared for the Americans. A long, long day. Quiet flight to Shanghai. Ah – warmer climes at last. A relief not to be wearing a hat and gloves, plus 3 layers and a scarf! A new guide – Jack – a rookie – not so good, excitable, young. Our bus ride to Suzhou was relaxing though – lush, green, lots of little waterways, the Grand Canal – very busy with barges – and the Yangste River, (remember Ping?) Big city, but prettier than the slate grey Beijing – rather depressing in her coldness. The group is having fun together – each day a little warmer!

We visited the Leaning Pagoda on Tiger Hill – lovely gardens with blossom and bonsai, followed by the embroidery institute. More shopping! After every demonstration of fine craftsmanship comes the big marketing machine. I think the ladies in the group are about to rebel! They just want some plain shopping, none of this government organized stuff. Jack was getting a little stressed at the requests to allow us a few minutes of our own thing! We were able to rebel for about 10 mins in the small shops across from the institute, but then he panicked and rounded us all up onto the bus. He seemed afraid. We decided we needed to behave better and not stress him out. From there, things went a little better.

A group of us went out on walkabout before dinner and came across the shopping alley where the real locals shop. It was seething with bikes, cars and people. Tiny little markets spilled out onto the street, selling corn, snails, frogs, fish, chickens, rice, nuts – you name it. Quite the sight! A little unnerving with the hustle and bustle and everyone watching you and your strangeness.

**WEDNESDAY IN MARCH** – Up not too early in our 'Glamor Hotel', and we even stole a walk after breakfast. We loaded up and first stop was 'The Lingering Garden' which was the coldest garden we had visited in a while. Then it was onward to the silk factory where we watched the silk being woven and purchased yummy silk comforters. From there, they had us warmed up and took us to the silk and cashmere store – government owned, of course, but way superior to the other stores we had been let loose in. Could have done some serious damage there, but resisted all the temptation. Onto the canal in Suzhou and a barge ride. A bit like Venice? Real people living right on top of the water and we even got a chance to take a stroll down a local street. Off again to Hangzhou. Lots of small farming patches and shacks on the way. The dichotomy between peasant and rich man so apparent. Checked in and then out of the wrong hotel, young tour guide stressing. Off to the 'Knock Shop' around the corner. Super wow deals on the rip offs of Coach, Hermes, Louis Vuitton and more. Did not buy, but lots did!

**THURSDAY IN MARCH** – Off to West Lake in delightful sunshine, cream magnolias. (Must have husband grow!) Fishing boats, pagodas, truly lovely. Could have rented a room on this lake for 6 months and finally finished my book. The largest Buddha in China, the caves "lights from afar" and Chinese symbols on the cave walls. More cream magnolias. It came to me that I should plant one for Myrtle and she'd say 'lovely darling'. As I wear her pearls and earrings over here, it strikes me that that makes her so happy. People everywhere do stop and admire them – good ones or no.

At the Buddhist Temple with the smell of the incense steaming in the air, Mother came back and she was smiling. The largest Buddha in China smiled down on all of us also. The Chinese burn incense and make a prayer to send wishes up to Buddha. I inhaled the incense and sent up a wish that my family please now remain cancer free. If you write it down, maybe you can make it so too.

Beggars lined the street to the temple, most horribly disfigured and without various limbs or with growths on them. Jack explained that if families had too many mouths to feed years ago, they would deliberately amputate a child's limb and then send them out to beg. Couldn't get such an image of horror out of my mind. As we climb onto our bus, which is rapidly becoming our sanctuary, we are pursued on all sides by pushy vendors and beggars alike. Shanghai proved to be the worst of all.

We left Hanzhou Lake from there and visited the West Lake Dragon Tea City, an incredible tea plantation, boasting the best green tea in China. It was truly delicious and invigorating – we all bought some. This 'resort', as it is now called, has not been open to the public for very long. It is one of those spots that the Chinese held back for themselves and gradually have allowed in the West – and their money. Another Buddhist temple on our route had only been open to tourists for the past two years also. We felt a bit like Western pioneers. Buddhism seems like a civilized religion – more an attitude of mind than a religion. Anyone can aspire to be a Buddha – there is not just one and there are Buddhas on many levels.

Onward to the big city of Shanghai – about a three hour drive away. Two wingey passengers refuse to eat with the group; that got our guide going again. Our lunch was actually super with rice wine to accompany, but some people just like to dull the pleasure of others. These charmers had also been upset at the lack of windows in their room last night and complained about that too.

An interesting ride to Shanghai, though – lots of small farming communities; people out working their patches of land with old-fashioned instruments all the way along. Very hard-working and very determined people. Dinner in Shanghai, then a river boat cruise. Incredible neon light shows with ads and building displays. Spectacular architecture all reflected in the Yangste River. The other bank, a London-like street, then a container port – obviously a city of contradictions, before you even break the skin and discover what's beneath the surface. Certainly, a city that never stops and never sleeps. Late back to the hotel – everyone tired and stressing about whether we had rooms for the night or not, after the brouhaha from the night before. Not the greatest room, but a great shower and all clean, so what else is there that really matters? Bought red and gold pajamas for my babe.

**FRIDAY IN MARCH** – They think they have the formula down – take them to the factory, show the handcrafting involved in a $4000 carpet, try and sell them a $4000 carpet, then feed them, giving them plenty of time after the food to buy another $4000 carpet in addition. Like a well-oiled machine; it seems to work fairly well for them, but less well with our group as times goes by. Today we go to a silk carpet factory with a cashmere sweater shop and nobody bought a thing. We're on strike with the whole government-manipulated purchasing lark! But then this is a Chamber of Commerce sponsored trip and we are out there to examine business. We are certainly doing that! The afternoon in Shanghai they let us loose in the outdoor mall and Sandy and I went off the beaten track and found her an authentic Chinese hat. A hooker also tried to pick her up in the icecream shop. A nice dinner – just a few of us. Jack bought us some wine with our dinner and placed flowers in our rooms. He has become a lot of fun and loves to have political discussions with us. Everyone is ready to go home, but it has been a long, full-on, rich week that we will need to absorb over time. After dinner we overloaded the elevator; that made everyone chuckle. The maximum allowed weight was stated at 13 persons; so we realized that 13 Chinese equated to 6 Americans. Though with all the 'Kentucky Fried Chickens' popping up all over the place, that scale will probably tip some in the other direction shortly.

Heading out to the airport and our way home, we visited another mineral factory for the jade buying opportunity. I sipped delicious lychee tea to nurse my slightly sore throat and aching ear. What a fascinating and contradictory place to visit over the course of several days. My eyes were wide open when I left.

**Lucy went along with the Soledad Chamber of Commerce on an organized trip to China.**

# ALIEN IS AS ALIEN DOES

I got there late, as they say, but I did get there in the end. Having resided in this fair land for over 17 years now as a "resident alien", (if you saw my photo I.D., you'd know why they call us that), I finally came to the conclusion that I needed to set about applying for dual nationality. Yes, folks, it **is** possible to be both American and English at the same time; strange though that may seem. I can never truly get rid of my Britishness; that's an intrinsic part of me: my wacky ways; strange humor; (or humour, if you're really a Brit and can spell correctly); my odd habits and peculiar turns of the vernacular. Born a Brit, always a Brit, that's just how it is; and these days the kind British don't even require you to choose to be one nationality over another! That's so very nice of them, because, though I have no plan to live on the chilly wet shores of Blighty again, I would find it hard to completely renounce my homeland. Call it kooky if you like; but you'd have to walk in my shoes to know how deep the roots go. Just visit an event at the Swiss Rifle Club in Gonzales and you get the feeling that you can take Switzerland away from the Swiss, but ... you get the drift. Renouncing the place where my people are from; turning my back somehow on my family and friends is a tough stance to adopt; even if I would not really be doing any of those things.

I worry when I forget the words "we" use for certain things, when the American terminology now comes to me so much more easily than the English; I hate it when I find myself slurring my language like everyone else around me; or when people ask me if I'm an Australian; (piece of trivia for you; Londoners who have lived in the U.S. for any period of time sound like Aussies, trust me. The first white settlers in Australia were convicts sent over to Never-Never Land from London; hence the accent). But I like to live here not there; so I started to think I should embrace that choice whole-heartedly and give myself permission to vote, to work for the government, (no danger there), and to learn the words of the pledge of allegiance properly and not just lip-synch. But it's still a big deal for me, whether I'm renouncing the home country or not. Get over it! I hear you say. Walk in my shoes, I reply.

When I was traveling back through 'Immigration' at the airport, (and those guys have got a little bit more nosey in recent days, I can tell you ..."where have you been, with whom and for how long ..?" right after they scan your eyeball); the immigration officer examined the ancient terrorist-looking photo of me on my green card and asked me if I was ever going to become a citizen. No one had ever asked me that before; and it came as a bit of a surprise. "Well, yes," I stuttered, (thinking to myself "and actually, it's none of **your** business!") "Probably should do that one of these days, shouldn't I! Ha, ha!" I laughed nervously. He let me go, I'm glad to say, with just a look of caution. But he did make me think of all the reasons why I should now be traveling on a blue passport, as well, or instead of, a red one.

So what is the procedure, I hear you ask, of becoming "naturalized"? There's a lot more to it than just paying your dues to society through the honorable greenback and swearing allegiance to that famous flag. Scanning through the multitudes of documents now cramming up my computer in that regard, I'd have to reply that it is **quite** a process. It may take a decade or so to complete even if I get started right away! In this day and age of the Department of Homeland Security and the mega paranoia which rules our land, the powers that be are, not surprisingly, very skeptical about persons wanting to get their hands on that powerful blue book, the American passport; so they want to put you through the mill and make sure you've earned it. Luckily I fulfill some of the criteria already:-

1. Have been in the country over 5 years. Check. 2. Have been married to an American for over 5 years. Oh yeh. 3. Have not ever been convicted of a felony. Praise the lord no! And so it goes on. Then we get to the part about "knowledge of American history" and I start to get the cold sweats. Back in the land of Britsy, we weren't too keen on American history; it became a sore subject right after we got our butts whooped and were swiftly sent home right around 1776; so, it goes without saying that we weren't really taught American history from about 1775.5 onwards. Hence, I know almost nothing about American history except that, thanks to John Wayne movies, the cowboys were never very nice to the Indians, and also, thanks to the good ol' right to bear arms, the presidents never seemed to stay alive for very long. Other than that; my mind is an open book! I can see that particular endeavor

may take some time, (in my other language that would be "endeavour", and I still try to write that sometimes; see! I'm a long way from getting this down!)

But if; or rather when I accomplish this dual national lark; I shall be at the voting podium in my red, whites and blues, (goes for both countries; no conflict there.) I shall no longer have to steal my husband's vote or bully him into submission. I shall have my own chad all for my own-some. I shall be able to, hopefully, chose my line at the airport immigration and proudly show off my pledges of allegiance to either Super Power number 1, (that would be the US of A – blue passport), or her smaller step-sister, (little England – red passport). I shall not have to worry about some super-alien estate tax on my ga-billions when I get old, (be warned, you rich aliens, there are different rules for you!) and I shall die a proud Brit-Merican, knowing what terrific fun I had with it all; and, oh yes, I would have had it all.

P.S. I did finally become a proud Dual-National in November 2005, leading the pledge of allegiance after the swearing in at the San Jose ceremony in my mother's sparkly "Old Glory" hat, which had been purchased in England, no less.

**Lucy is a proud Brit-Merican.**

# FINDING PEACE IN ALL THE RIGHT PLACES

Vacations are taken to give the body and mind welcome respite from the day to day trappings of regular life; the stresses of work, the tedium of household necessities and the tire of what is normal and expected in the structure of our daily routine. We steal time away for ourselves and our families, when we break our routines in this way. Vacations are supposed to be relaxing, but then I seldom practice what I preach.

Most of the time when I take a vacation, I travel to England to see the family, visit my father, extract as many minutes as I can with my busy friends and other members of my busy family. I seldom rest, as you are supposed to, and just watch the world move around me from someplace else. I zoom around, trying to fit as many people and experiences into the limited time allotment that I have for my allowance away from real life. I seldom return home in a complete zone of relaxation; but I do return mostly more exhilarated by all the colors and trials I have experienced during my travels, inspired to write down the more amusing exchanges between my relatives and totally and completely ready to be back home again in my own arena, where the silence is mine, the ground familiar and the bed the best ever.

This year was no exception. In addition to our usual annual course across the Atlantic from America to England, my daughter and I also deviated off the beaten track and traveled on the train with my father and sisters to France - in celebration of my father's 80$^{th}$ birthday. (Such an adventure deserves its own story, which is gradually evolving in my brain to spew out at a later date.) From there, we swiftly turned around the contents of our suitcases and journeyed onwards to the Isle of Man with my middle sister and her partner; another tale of its own. Back again to the hub of London Town, we changed again and prepared ourselves for our annual pilgrimage to the East Coast of England and the small town which I have always considered my original home, the place I can return to and say to myself, 'boy it's nice to be home."

Though I left my native country twenty plus years ago, this place is one I can honestly say I can still find my peace amidst the hullabaloo of my modern American life of self employment, mortgages, raising children and trying, most days, to be all things to all people. When I arrive there, in my place of origin, despite all my adventures in the days before in other places, I feel my vacation begin. It is a place that our family "sold" and left probably close to a quarter century ago; the cottage, that we had owned for decades, damp and abandoned before she was put up for sale and lost for always, still a private source of sadness to me. However, though the bricks and mortar were lost, the soul of the town was never lost to me. She remained a bright light in my memory, a safe haven I could always visit in my mind, a port I could make a point to visit when I needed grounding, space or peace.

We spent every weekend and holiday there, from when I was first born to when I was a teenager, and memories like that become engrained in a person, part of their core. That could be the definition of home or roots; I don't know for sure. But I do know how I feel when I enter my town and all the images of my happy childhood come rushing back to me.

Familiarity breeds content, I have learned over the years, in some special cases. Traveling to my town, I come over the hill and see the curve of the river, the thorn of the briar and the green, green mounds of the golf course. As we swing around past the church and down the hill, the sea peek tells me if the waves are rough today and how high is the tide. I can't wait to run down to the shore line and see when the tide will be low and the beach-combing on the pebbled shore the best. I am always on the quest to find that perfect cornelian, or, in my wildest dreams, the type of amber lump that my grandfather gleaned by chance, so many moons ago. The bustle of the high street reminds me that the bread and cakes are freshly baked and sell out quickly, the fish shop opens for business at noon. There are signs out on the street for local events and one day only shoe sales. The book shop is open and a new flick is showing at the old cinema. These store fronts have been in place for as long as I can remember and I can remember quite far back; as surprisingly old as I am these days. I drive into town year after year and the comfort I get from these old haunts covers me like a blanket and makes many unrelated things right.

How many places can you return to after all those years and still run into several people who still remember you and your family? My daughter and I chased after a lady we recognized and reminded her who we were. She had known me from when I was about 3. We hugged and visited for a while. Another remembered my 40 year old sister as a baby with a bad hip and asked after her. I saw many familiar faces there; some who would need several days to catch up with and others who we were able to walk and talk with for half an hour and catch up on our shared experience.

I got up early with pleasure in the morning, drank my first cup of coffee on the window seat over looking the beach and delighted as the sparkly sun strip accompanied me on my quest along the beach, as I walked and sought gems in the shingle. I said good morning to the early bathers, as they eased themselves into the chilly waters and remembered that that was us too, many years ago. I thought of Mum and the way her formerly powerful body would swim the crawl stroke out to sea; her energy in the early morning and her ambition that we all join her for the morning dip in the summer sea. We strolled along the marshy area where, years before, our Labrador had wallowed in the muddy holes in search of river rats. We slipped down the banks to the carcass of the former house boat, the landmark that had been burned decades back, when rats had eaten its bowels and made it unsafe. We had watched her burn in ceremonial fashion a mere 4 decades ago and now we find bones of her former being waiting for us in the mud – metal, mud-covered ore rotting away, to be rescued and given a home in the memory bank. The ore came home with me to its final resting place.

I had only two nights and one and a half days back in my original home after a long and busy vacation, when I gave myself little time to breathe, let alone be tranquil. It was only really there in my place that the rest came to me and the peace, too, which followed. Though it was a race against the clock to do all I needed to do in that place to fill myself up again and restore the peace of childhood once more; the longest day of the year gave us plenty of light to accomplish much and plenty of hope too for a long and nourishing tomorrow with all the pieces still intact, the memories preserved in time and the treats all ready and lined up for the next visit.

Sometimes, on your vacation, all you really need to do is to go home again and revisit all you hold inside your heart and carry along the way. You don't need to go to far off places and eat snails. You don't need to speed along the highway of new experiences and seek rare and unusual gifts that you think you are missing. All the gifts you need are the ones that give you peace and bathe your soul in a rich and delightful light. With those, you have everything you'd ever need.

**Lucy is a fond visitor down memory lane.**

# FORGETTING SECOND NATURE

I am very afraid of heights. That small fact from way back when had completely slipped my mind during the planning of our trip to Lake Tahoe, just a few thousand feet up in some places, more in others. Though I had completely forgotten that mini factoid before our trip; it certainly came back to me in a flash.

This did not happen as we were climbing the mountain road in our old VW Bus, which was literally crying out for mercy at 5,000 feet, (in the form of an oil leak); or even as we stepped out for photo ops over the ice-laden winter wonderland in April and gazed up at the majestic peaks above; no this remembrance slammed back in the brain as we proceeded to crawl up the slope at 'Heavenly' in a "Gondola". (For those of you not in the ski-bunny mode, this is a wobbling cart on a cable which will take you up to ungodly heights). As we whizzed upwards towards a place I prefer to only see from an airplane, all of a sudden I remembered my phobia of heights as clear as a bell. My stomach started wobbling, my head felt heavy and not well placed on my head at all. A feeling of sick nausea threatened to overcome me. These were my first key clues as to a sense of displacement– my systems of balance, ever sensitive, alerted me to the fact that all was not well, and it was about to get worse.

As I looked down into the cavernous valley where, only 5 minutes ago, my feet had been standing firmly on dry land, I felt completely sick; just like a sailor who suffers from sea-sickness might feel as he leaves the safe port for the wide ocean wave. My palms began to sweat and my memory bank proceeded to work on overtime. I was back on the high beam at junior high, which I had bravely ascended only to make the mistake of looking down to the cruel wooden floors way below. After much humiliating yelling from my unsympathetic gym mistress, I had to be rescued from the beam by a cavalier class-mate - to the total amusement of my peers and the embarrassment of myself.

I was also drawn back to the memory of my mother and how she couldn't be on the edge of anything high without feeling nauseous. She would never have been caught dead on an ascending gondola; that was for sure. My boat trip from Athens in Greece to Crete came back to mind, when the rolling ocean for 12 long hours had made me just want to jump overboard and end it all. There was also that time – my first and last adventure as a ski bunny with all the gear and none of the skill – when I panicked, as I saw a crevice coming close to me and managed to fall over – not down the crevice – but still securing myself a dislocated hip and a ride down the mountain on a blood wagon. Somehow my clammy palms took me back to all of those strange and long gone places, as my family and I took a sedate gondola cruise up the placid side of 'Heavenly' and down again.

"I wonder, if I throw a complete fit, maybe they will let me just walk down the mountain, or – even better - slide down on my bottom," I'm thinking to just myself. "Maybe they can bring in the Heavenly mountain rescue chopper for phobic cases like me," I ponder and then swing back to earth with the realization that that would be a most expensive way to career myself off the mountain side and not at all popular with the husband.

My entire family – including my hardy mother-in-law - had fits of giggles at my torment, and my son pronounced me "weak", as I stolidly sat with my back positioned to the swiftly declining mountainside and created happy thoughts, eye to eye with the snow, reassuring myself that the snow was actually really close to my feet and that if the cable car really did do a nose dive crash to the hillside, how totally survivable that would be.

At 40 plus, I'm still just a big ol' baby; I realize that now; and I'm likely to remain so. I also realize that our childhood fears are never too far away and the phobias we had then we probably carry throughout our entire lives; they may just be hiding a tad beneath a slightly thickened skin.

Thanks to my mother-in-law who let me tightly clutch her poor arm both up and down the mountain, I survived the ordeal relatively unscathed. I am also a little more bathed in self-knowledge after our escapade. I informed my daughter that she had definitely witnessed my last mountain adventure ever, and to just put that in her memory bank for years to come when she could use a giggle, because it would never – I repeat never – happen again.

**Lucy is a former mountaineer/Heavenly survivor.**
**I have the shirt to prove it.**

# HITTING THE ROAD

Even though we live in Paradise, which of course we do; every now and then even we need to break away from heaven and remind ourselves of just how lucky we are to live where we do. Every one needs a little time away once in a while to regroup, refinish or just breath; even if it means going to Fresno, which, let's face it is no Carmel, Monterey or even Soledad.

If I go away for a day, my own personal leashes – my cell phone and email – can only follow me partially and for me, that is quite a blessing. Being self-employed you live under a kind of self-inflicted incarceration; once in a while it's important to break out and run away as if your life depended on it.

On the pretence of visiting her mother; though we really were indeed visiting her mother, my friend and I packed up the car and headed for the central valley. It's never been an area that's really grabbed me as such with enticements such as its famous "Tully fog", or blistering windless summers. It's never exactly been a target destination on my 'places to visit before I die' list; but I was offered a day away from life, and I was in dire need of that, no matter where we went, so off I went.

We have fabulous mountains here in our neck of the woods, which embrace every movement of our lives. You realize that especially, when you venture forth to areas which have to survive without mountains. Though we take for granted the pink blush of the Gabilans at sunset or the dour face of the Lucia's at the end of the day and the snow kiss they receive early morning to remind you it's still winter; as soon as they go away and the ground is flat for hundreds of miles, as far as the eye can see, you can miss them like a long lost sister. I found that instantly, as the mountains became but a memory in the rear view mirror; and I resolved to appreciate them more when I got to see them once again.

We also don't leave our old vehicles in the back of our yards the way they seem to in the central valley. There, the old clunkers abandon their families, but their families don't abandon them. They stop and die at the back of the yard, or even on the side of the yard, and then get dragged to the back; and there they stay, rotting and rusting for the next generation or light-yeared generations away to have to deal with them. Definitely eye sore, not eye candy. I'm glad we don't do that; at least not at almost every homestead you pass on your way to somewhere else.

They certainly do eat well over yonder; I can tell you that! We dined handsomely at what must surely be the most famous Basque restaurant in Los Banos – the half light of the dining room making you wonder whether you were truly feasting with the spirits of travelers of yore still passing though – and were treated to authentic country cooking from the old country. Definitely a pit stop to revisit, should I ever find myself on the way to the central valley again and in need of enough food for a week in one sitting.

What can be surprising on your road trip to somewhere else is that the people there like their home as much as you like yours. What are the odds of that? It's just as well they don't all love Soledad the way I do; or we'd be in a right pickle. Elsewhere, they have villages with friendly neighbors and welcoming restaurants close by; their streets are clean and loved just like ours; it's a pleasure to behold. They don't seem to notice their lack of mountains and don't noticeably dread the heavy weight of summer just a few short months away. They seem to like it there; they really do and that's good.

And so a short road trip away from home and back again can give you a bird's eye view of the world and a hearty re-appreciation of your own. Most of the world outside your door equally views their lot with their glass half full, no matter how few mountains they have. They make the best of what they have with what they have to work with and that is a commendable adage in anyone's existence. It's all about the people anyway; about ma and pa and showing your family members that you care about them and that they are only just a short drive away and closer still to your heart.

Should you also be needing a day away from life, think about where you could go to make the largest difference to some one else. It'll be just what you need and, for sure, they'll need it too.

**Lucy loves to travel – even to the Central Valley!**

# LIVE YOUR LIFE

With the uncovering of another terrible terrorist plot to kill thousands of innocent people in the skies over our strange world, I find myself feasting on inevitable anxiety. My first reaction is that I am never going to put myself and my family in that situation ever again, where they could possibly fall victim to such a horror i.e. I will never visit my original homeland again, (since I have absolutely no stomach for the ocean). My second response - a little more realistic, perhaps – is that I fly back and forth over the pond about twice a year. I've done that now for many years and I shall continue to do so. To do anything less is to acquiesce to the monsters who perpetrate these disgusting crimes and to give them the ultimate winning prize; relinquishing our freedom to live our lives as we choose.

I call it the 2nd world war mentality – may as well change that to the 3rd world war. During the 2nd world war in England, as in many other places, I'm sure; the British stoicism was at its very best. With Winston Churchill as their leader, I've heard that the British stubbornness manifested itself as an admirable resilience to stand tall and live their lives as best they could in such trying times. True, when the bombers were flying over London – the Brits were not stupid, they went down into the bomb shelters, mostly in underground train stations. Other than that, they got on with it, the best they could.

The week after September 11th, 2001, when many people elected not to fly the scary skies at all, my father – ever frugal – and having notably lived through the 2nd world war, kept his reservation from London to San Francisco and enjoyed a very peaceful, almost empty flight, with no lines and the best of service. "Probably the safest time in the history of flight," he quipped, tongue in cheek, as ever.

I would be lying if I now board a plane with the same girlish exuberance as I did years ago. Short of finding the "people watching" at the airports still pretty interesting, I no longer enjoy the "exoticism" of flying. I'm always a little anxious when we take off and relieved when we land. I secretly make sure that all my affairs are in order when I'm going up in the air; the bills are paid, the husband reminded of the location of all the documents he might need in my absence and so on. If I go down, I'll go down with everything in its neat and tidy place, and I'll go down having had a heck of a ride. But like it or not, the passion I hold dear of going to new and fascinating places, the love I have of seeing old friends and family in the old and familiar places still heavily override the real fear I have that something will happen to me while I'm traveling, or make me even remotely likely to only travel on land or over the sea. I will put myself into therapy before I allow that kind of irrational fear to take over my free world.

"I'm a bit afraid of flying," my friend confided to me as we were getting ready to travel to London together.

"You're much more likely to die in a car crash," I assured her and it's statistically true.

"It's just still amazing to me how the plane gets up in the air and stays there," she continued, as we cruised along at 35,000 feet and she sucked on her second vodka.

On the second leg of our flight, from London to the Isle of Man, we had been up in the air only about ten minutes when we hit a large bird. The noise was like a loud "clonk"; not something you really want to hear when you're way, way off the ground. This was followed by a theatrical gasp-in-unison from the passengers. The captain comes on the mike to tell us calmly that, yes, a bird had flown into our engine and, yes, they suspected damage to the engine and, yes, we would be turning the plane around and hoping to land again within 10 minutes. The word "hoping" really bothered me at the time, but I didn't tell my friend. That was a long ten minutes, I can tell you. My friend and I both sat watching that the remaining engines and wings remained in place, as best we could, until we had safely touched down. Then we had more vodka.

Things happen and you do hope to land safely, as captains all around the world are trained to ensure. We must continue to live our lives, as we will; traveling if we get the opportunity and wrapping up our anxieties in cotton as best we can. We are free people living in a free country. It's important that we exercise our rights as citizens of the civilized world and do not allow others, with less free aspirations for us, to dictate the quality of our existence.

**Lucy is still a fairly frequent flyer.**

# MY OWN PERSONAL DUST BOWL

Before I moved to America, my points of reference were pretty much limited to television shows such as 'Dallas' and 'Dynasty'. Obviously everyone in America had swimming pools and huge horse ranches, not to mention perfect hair, because that was what they wanted us to think. If you are given an opportunity to move to this place of plenty, you obviously do. The worldly goods must just fall in your lap the minute you step off the plane, that's all you can figure at the beginning of your relationship with that huge land mass. Everyone wanted to move to the United States, there had to be a really simple reason why. I just hadn't grasped it yet.

I got my Green Card in an 'Immigration Lottery'; no kidding, the only darn thing I've ever won of any value and I had no idea just how valuable this thing was at the time. I wasn't a brain surgeon or even a millionaire, but somehow the Department of Immigration and Naturalization picked little ol' me to be one of their newest legal aliens, way back in the late 80's, when the powers that be decided they had too many of one population and needed to filter in a few more of the other to balance things out appropriately. I came in under the "other" category. I passed the aids test, gave out pertinent information about my great grandparents and their various occupations – i.e coal mining and tavern keeper – sold a few possessions, packed a few others in a case with not much money to my name and took off on a jet plane for what I imagined would be a few months of hanging out on ranches and swimming in pools. That was until I found my own personal dustbowl.

I never tire of reading Steinbeck's 'Grapes of Wrath'. Now my brain is more mature, I can read and re-read this epic work and find new and startling observations about human nature every time within its timeless pages. It reads like something that could still happen in our own world of the Salinas Valley, just as it did back then. The journey of the Joads, so filled with hope, as they left what they knew in the mid-West dust bowl and traveled bravely west to the land of plenty, as they imagined it. They had the golden vision I had also imagined of the world before me across the Atlantic. Anytime you travel to somewhere unfamiliar, encountering people you don't know and situations you never dreamed of, you will touch skin with the tougher side of the world. The Joads found that out very quickly and so did I.

Europeans have a strange fascination with places abroad that seem European in style or manner. We were no different. My traveling companion and I had a thirst to see New Orleans way back when, when we landed in Washington D.C.; and the more we stayed around that marshy, swampy oddity, the more we found only an impulse to keep on moving and seeing.

Three months on from our first naïve steps on American soil and with fresh stamps in our passports, we were on the road again in an old converted black Chevy van – with the added special feature of a multi-colored Led Zeppelin angel on the side. Soon we were cruising down the old Highway 1 with a one-track mission towards New Orleans, Louisiana, the big Easy, the place where we might find our home for a while, and we hoped it would be easy.

In Key West Florida at the very bottom of the Highway 1, I got quite sick. (Hadn't counted on that in the travel plans at all, let alone the budget!) It seemed as if I couldn't keep the mosquitoes off me in high summer July, and my fever raged. (Should have stayed with the nice kind man who offered us shelter and the possibility of work in Fort Lauderdale, but we knew best!) High on the raised opinion of our own good fortune at the time, we passed on that option - a sign post in the road that might have led us down a kinder path – and we kept on obstinately moving towards the jewel in the eye of our storm. Not heeding the warning of the nice narcotics law enforcement gentleman who visited us with his dog in the middle of the night and told us in no uncertain terms that we were out of our obviously drug-crazed minds and there was no work to be had in New Orleans, we found her. The eye of our storm was right there in the midst of her own personal dust bowl.

New Orleans, Louisiana. The bottom had fallen out of the oil industry and many, many people were out of work when we pulled into town, at this point needing to find work and money very quickly. Store fronts were shuttered, many of them, streets a little shabby and sordid on that steamy August afternoon, when we arrived, fresh-faced at the end of our journey, with renewed optimism in our quest. We looked around for signs of help being wanted, but they were sadly missing. In the French Quarter we chatted to locals in the Blacksmiths pub at the end of Bourbon Street, hoping for some kind of a break, but it wasn't to be found. It felt a bit like the end of the world, not just the end of Bourbon Street. "If you want to stay alive, you'd better get out of Nawlins, "a local Cajun glumly noted, as he sipped on the remnants of a warm beer. "She become the murder capital of the country." (Now there's a tourist recommendation for you!) A street person stops us in the street as we are down to our last few dollars and, in the irony of the moment, we realize that the breaks are not going to be found right there at that time. We had better take the message we had been ignoring as truth and step away while we still could.

In Baton Rouge – the Louisiana Capitol - our dustbowl continued. We couldn't get a break. If you live in your vehicle in the 'civilized world', you are officially homeless and with that stigma attached to your back, people do not want to hire you. Regardless of how clean you keep yourself, from hoses in trucking yards to brushing teeth in Burger King Restaurants, you are of no fixed abode in the eyes of the job application and therefore an undesirable. Every human being should know how that feels. This 'unfortunate' situation gives you a humanity of experience, however, which you will take with you through life – if you manage to find your way through it and over to the other side. You are only as good as the roof over your head, not on your back – you learn that quickly when you have no key to your own door. Here I was silver-spooned, University of London grad, lost in America with an old Chevy van to live in and not much else. No one in that place could care less. You learn that quickly when you are of no fixed abode and with no great possibility of things altering from that low vista anytime soon.

We tried to get work with a traveling crew, removing asbestos from buildings, figuring that that stuff could kill you and no one else would want the work. No fixed abode? Ironically the placements had all instantly been filled as soon as that was mentioned, and there was suddenly no work available. We wised up and 'stole' an address to get a waitressing job for me and a loading trucks job for the companion. I actually ended up with two waitressing jobs shortly after this, which felt like manna from heaven, and some times I sneaked a few leftovers from plates because I was hungry. I'd count out my tips in the evening to see if dinner was a possibility that night. On the nights I worked through to the 2.30am breakfast buffet when the bars turned out and appeared bleary eyed at 7am, I'd sometimes sneak a rasher of bacon or two into my pocket for later. In the dustbowl of America, many go hungry and I have known that feeling. It's not one you forget. It's one that later makes you put your hand in your pocket for the local food bank when your stomach and your heart are full.

I read about the Joads and those like them and it makes me ache all over again. They had bad luck, poor judgment at times, misfortune, hunger and despair – they knew all of those things and I knew them too during my early dust bowl days in this country. You move forward with the best intentions, looking for an honest way to make a living and put one step in front of another, and, sadly, some times that is just not enough.

Now things are a little better for me and I seldom go hungry unless I am too busy working to remember to eat; and not because there is nothing for me to eat and no money to buy it. However, some things never leave you. I am still only as good as the next job I have, the promise of the next few dollars around the corner. I am still frugal with food, insisting on coveting the leftovers which drives my family to distraction. I still clip coupons which mostly I lose and, two decades on, I still worry about being homeless again.

I have never forgotten where I came from in my early days as a pioneer of sorts, making my own uncertain way across this sometimes unforgiving country. I remember clearly the people who helped me and those who most certainly did not. I recall, crystal clear, the feelings of fear and despair and I will certainly never forget those of hunger. And now during tough times for our nation, I look at folks suffering through their own personal dustbowls of experience, and hope that they too will find their way through to the other side, where the sun is bright, the road clear and the food plentiful. We should all know both sides of that coin. It makes us better members of the human race.

**Lucy is a forever immigrant. She will never forget where she came from.**

# OUR WEEKEND AWAY

Sometimes you just have to go away to appreciate all you have at home; it's a cliché, maybe, but still it is true. Sometimes you just need to go away, period. You need to be in a different place, see different people, eat different food, sleep in a different bed - good or bad – and travel the highways and byways of our nation and beyond to feel somehow refreshed, invigorated, strengthened by the experiences you taste, the emotions you experience, the change in geography. Change is good for the mind and the soul, no one doubts that. But in our regular lives of working and raising children, we mostly forget that a change can be just around the corner of opportunity; a new vista just a glance away, if we open our arms wide and embrace what comes along, if we're lucky.

"Want to go to Oregon for the weekend?" my friend asked. "I have to go to an automotive show up there." It had been a particularly foul week in my working realm. She could have offered just about any place on the planet, short of Chualar, for just about any darn reason in the hemisphere and I would have jumped at it; at that moment in time. I recognized the signs of needing a modification in my daily routine; I needed to make this trip happen regardless of any obvious obstacles along the way.

We were going on an adventure and I was ready to leave by 6am for our 8.50am flight out of San Jose. 6.30 am and I was still ready but not yet quite riding to the airport. We eventually took off and proceeded to chatterbox our way past our airport exit, turning around and wasting valuable time as we amazed ourselves that we had actually missed a well signposted exit that we had glided through many, many times before. At the long term car park, there was a shift change in progress and several elderly people who needed extra time to board and un-board the shuttle bus. The minutes were accelerating and we should have already been boarding; we knew that much. San Jose has an unseemly construction site aura to its construction site and the shuttle buses drop the shuttled to a spot a ways away from the check in lounge; fine when you are early, lousy when you are not.

"Sorry," the nice lady said in a very matter-of-fact way as we panted before her at the check in desk. "That flight is closed." Closed? In all my many years of traveling, I had never actually missed a flight. There had been that one to Amsterdam that I made just by the skin of my teeth and the fateful trip to the South of France when they had literally closed the plane door behind me; but missed entirely? This was a new experience.

Judging by the sweat on my friend's brow, this had never happened to her before either. "Oh no," she said calmly, still in a state of shock. "When is the next flight?" (I had visions of there being no more flights that day and our adventure culminating, beginning and ending, at the check in desk of the San Jose airport, before we turned swiftly around and headed back home again.) "The next flight is 5pm," the lady advised, then paused as we choked a little, "unless you want to fly up to Seattle and change planes there for Portland. That one leaves in an hour." Now that was a better option. I'd never actually been to Seattle. Good coffee I knew of and of course the home of Microsoft, also lots of rain – that might be a fun side bar!

For those of you who have never had the opportunity to dine in Seattle airport, let me tell you that it has a super fish restaurant right there that boasts the best halibut known to man. No soggy corn dogs for us! Both my friend and I enjoyed the lunch so much we swore that it was worth missing our direct flight to Portland to have had this particular culinary experience. We had also sat behind the famous Jack LaLanne the entire duration of the flight, (yes, and I already own his juice maker!) Never mind that this icon is 90 plus and on his way to a speaking engagement with his wife, there was some entertainment value there also, as a lady passed him by in the aircraft, recognized his dark clothed self and proceeded to enquire whether the lady sitting next to him was his wife or his mistress. Stuff like that you just can't make up! We later looked him up on the internet and read all about what he had done for health and exercise back in the days when smoking was fashionable and seat belts not even a concept. Here he was still getting around at close to one hundred years old. Ah traveling! You just couldn't find that quality of entertainment in little Soledad for love nor money. I bought my daughter a 'Seattle' t-shirt, so that I could say that I had been there and done that, and we jumped onboard for the next leg.

We arrived in Portland well in advance of our evening engagement and noted our room had a super view of the construction site and freeway below. That gave us a giggle. All we had to do to enjoy the spectacular view of the beautiful flowing Columbia River and her bridges was to go around the other side of the building where most of the guests were staying; but we knew that was just the way our day was going. We still appreciated that our side of the building was the quiet one, ultimately, and the beds were really comfortable. Sometimes it is not the destination, but the laughs you can have along the way. We realized that on our journey from Soledad to Portland via Seattle.

When you are in a foreign city, whether it is Portland or Beijing, the smallest things can throw you. The light rail down town, for instance, was food for contemplation. Ah, the yellow line – and where does she go? Do you need to really validate your ticket in order not to be ejected from the train car, or is that for people traveling with a bicycle, of which there were many? Down town Portland! Do not go there hungry. You will wander through Nordstroms - one and two - and other large metropolitan stores, you will cross the main square, you will get a waft of something edible somewhere; but you will not find anywhere to serve you food. Finally we ventured into the tourist office and enquired, before we died of hunger. "Oh there is a good restaurant three blocks up, two across." It sounded like a long way away, but we were off, salivating as we strolled. They were still closed. "Specials of the day," we read the board outside the restaurant, (the next best thing to eating when you are hungry), "pork chops, pork loin, pork special today only!" A lot of pork! We glanced across at the street at the local paper headlines "Swine flu concerns grow". Hmm. Pork chops, swine flu, pork specials." This tickled our joint funny bone, as we ordered our third day of halibut and pondered the fate of the pork chop over the next few days. We also looked up in the fancy-smancy restaurant and witnessed a large raw pig leg hanging from the kitchen rack. This struck us as one of the more bizarre incidents in our weekend's travels and certainly did nothing for our wish to consume pork – swine flu pandemic or not. We caught the yellow line back to the hotel and the rest of the day and our trip home was fairly by the good traveler's guide book.

Take a trip somewhere anywhere, beyond Chualar for sure, but somewhere different. It can sharpen your senses, give your taste buds a rise, (love that halibut), and certainly tickle your funny bone in more place than one. You might chance to go somewhere you had had no intention of visiting on that particular trip and enter alley ways down memory lane that you never thought you'd see again. It might even be the recipe for a good, long life. Just ask Jack Lalanne and his wife of 45 years!

**Lucy is a fond traveler. She's been to a lot of places; just ask her!**

# PRESERVING THE PAST

My friend and I have just returned from the most delightful stay down in Long Beach, CA; an adventure which gave a new meaning to "traveling on business" and, I'm afraid, set a new precedent for the quality of our abodes in future travels. We had traveled down to Southern Cal. to attend the annual California REALTOR meetings; but had no idea that our "free time" would be so immensely pleasurable in such a way. Normally we are spendthrift and stay in the cheapest budget motel out of sheer necessity; this time we went all out and gave ourselves a gift.

It came about that I had been living under a misguided notion that my grandmother had sailed on the Queen Mary way back when in the early thirties; and this misconception urged me on to make the booking. Once I came to realize that the ship was not only a museum but also a hotel, I realized that I could walk the same corridors, as my granny had moons ago, and what an unusual and wonderful experience that would be. I wanted to imagine my lovely Myrt gliding around the decks in her elegant fashion all those years past.

After I made our booking, my father quickly corrected me. "No, Lu, she sailed on the Queen Elizabeth", he said in his inimitable way, "not the Queen Mary." But it was too late. We had paid for our room and we were staying on the Queen Mary. Gladly, that was that.

It is quite clear that, back in the 1960's, the city of Long Beach needed a focal point; a tourist destination, and seized on the opportunity to acquire the ship, when she seemed destined only for the scrap yard after a long and noble career as not only a pleasure boat, but also a troop carrier during the war.

"If the Americans had not purchased her," a rather fruity English voice said on one of the recorded programs you could listen to onboard, "then she would have surely disappeared into scrap long ago." Looking at her now and how loved and revered she is makes you anxious that icons from the past be preserved more than is sometimes the custom. A ship that carried a total of 765,429 military personnel, not to mention all the civilians, over her long and illustrious sea-faring career, deserves a little love and tenderness at the very least.

The Queen Mary is a resounding nod to the 1930's. Her ballrooms, bars, corridors, decks, life boats, even her cabins, cabin cupboards, safety rails, port holes and faucets have been preserved; not to the point where you can't use them; but that if you respect them, they will last. My friend and I delighted in strolling around the decks and getting ourselves completely lost in this vast time warp. It was such a hoot! Everywhere we went there were old photos of the ship with life bustling all over her; troops being taken overseas from the port of Southampton in England, war brides and children being brought over to America and her eventual return to her eternal resting ground in Long Beach after a long, proud life. She is quite a touching shrine for the many years which came before many of us and, as I strolled on her decks, I felt the voices of time past resounding in her corridors. That came as no surprise, since, over the years, there have been many strange and unusual occurrences and sightings documented aboard. From wet footprints padding along the deck from a now dry pool to a lady sitting on one of the outdoor benches in 1930's attire to a piano playing by itself. History has been preserved in a very rich and lasting way aboard that lovely ship, rich with souls still loving her to this day.

I cannot wait to return to her lovely self in 2 years time when our conference will yet again be situated in Long Beach; and I already know that we won't be going the budget route. Oh no ma'am; we'll be staying in her Majesty's quarters once more.

Spending time on such a regal slice of history made me reflect on our own footprints that we make in the sand of our lives. What do we do to record the years that pass us by so quickly? How do we document our children growing up, our lives evolving? Years ago, I used to write a diary and document my daily life; exciting or not. I seldom find the time to do that these days. I do take lots of pictures, many of which sit idly in dark boxes, waiting for the magic day when I will have the necessary 8 free hours to put them into some kind of attractive order. I think back to my grandmother and her colorful life; her life through the war, her three husbands, the plane she actually flew herself to Le Touquet, their boat moored in Majorca. I have a few pictures of her; but little actual documentation. Equally, if I don't write down what I think I know about my mother, her story will simply evaporate when I eventually do; because I know more about her than just about anyone left on the planet.

We have a duty to record noteworthy things for future generations of our families. They may not have the historical significance of the Great Queen Mary; but they are a small time marker in our rapidly sweeping lives; something to be preserved for the next generation to wonder over and be glad that we did, whilst all the time filling in the blanks.

**Lucy is a now fond visitor of the wonderful ship 'The Queen Mary'. May she ever be docked close by.**

# THE OTHER WINE COUNTRY

My husband and I went on an adventure recently to 'Wine Country' – that expanse of rolling hills, white barns and tasting room after tasting room – in the areas of Petaluma, Sonoma and Napa. We were on a mission to examine what they do up there that draws so many people and, of course, to do a little tasting on the way.

We had been up in those parts two years ago; and little has fundamentally changed since then. There are still lots and lots of tasting rooms – about 300, in fact - acre upon acre of vineyards and lots of traveling folks with expendable income to keep the area rich and lush, both with green-backs and industry. One thing that had changed, however, were the wine tasting fees. Coming from Monterey Wine Country, we were a little surprised, when we were there the last time, to note that a $5 tasting fee was not out of the ordinary, (though reimbursed with wine purchase). On this occasion, the fees had risen to a non-slender $10 fee on the whole, with no reimbursement for purchase; plus a limitation on varietals for tasting at that price-point. The $10 fee was for the less good wines. If you wanted to taste the executive list, that came with a steeper $15 or $20 price tag. Going to 5-6 tasting rooms over the course of an afternoon could run into some serious money! With the increased fee, the friendliness hadn't increased much either and, in some respects, it was rather a disappointing experience.

You felt that the tourist had become such a common occurrence in those parts that it had developed into an annoyance. Drivers raced up the rear end of our rather slow VW Bus, as we cruised along the highways and byways, enjoying the views; and tried to push us to go faster, (we couldn't, if we wanted to). Hosts at the tasting rooms were mostly unfriendly, without even a look in the eye, as they poured us a drop of local nectar, swiftly throwing out the wine banter, ("blackcurrant influences with chocolate hue, fruit forward; blah, blah"), in a hurry to move on to the next taster; and hurriedly took our $10 without even a smile or a curiosity about where we were from. Even local tasting here in our County encourages for some friendly banter and some value for your money. The wine tasting public expects it and our tasting rooms deliver. The bottle prices too were alarming up there, when you consider the excellent value we receive from our Monterey County wineries. We were examining price sheets with $80 bottle prices, no problem. And are the wines up there any better? I would certainly not say so.

And so, as our own wine industry in the "other wine country" grows and our home wine tourism increases accordingly, I think we all have a responsibility to examine what is attractive in business and what is not. Would we like 300 tasting rooms in our growing region? I think that we would not. (Napa is becoming more and more like the wine outlets of California – "Got wine?" - But without an outlet price tag). We might well like a few more tasting rooms than we currently have, but that segment is definitely growing by degrees and recognizing the concept that if we build them, they will come. We definitely enjoy tourists in our area, as the Napa area has over the years and should continue to; but we need to make sure that in welcoming the tourist dollars here, we treat the visitors as we would be treated ourselves. There are some tasting rooms in the Napa area in which I shall not care to re-enter; good wine or not. I can be treated like pond scum in my own house, thanks very much; I do not plan to pay for the favor.

We returned home from the other wine country, having learned very much how not to be in the wine tasting arenas; as well how not to behave in the varied arenas of life.

**Lucy is a big supporter of her local wineries.**

# THE ROUGH GUIDE TO CHINA

<u>2006 American Business Delegation to China, Soledad-Mission Chamber of Commerce</u>.

When you're accustomed to one particular route on your travels, a change in destination can come as quite a shock to the system; not just where you're going, but how you're going to get there.

Loading up on a 6am bus from Soledad for a 2pm flight from 'Frisco seemed a bit excessive to all of us; especially on the first ring of our dark and rainy 5am wake-up call; but with different rules and regulations, visas etc to be examined, it was possible – I rationalized – that we might need the extra time.

In line at 8am before a still closed check-in counter, the traveling troop began to wonder if they had been the target of a bad joke. Several hours later, when check-in actually began, you could only conclude that the Chinese viewed the Americans as notoriously tardy; hence the reason for the ridiculous start.

The Air China planes are quite a bit older than the ones I am used to on the Frisco/London transatlantic run; not comforting. You do not have your own personal movie screen with all the latest videos you'd been hoping to catch up on. You do have a video from a distance of a pretty Chinese woman showing you how to perform "seat aerobics" in a 2x2 space. In fact, I felt as if I had more leg room on this older plan than on the flashy modern ones; but that could just have been me stealing space from the neighbor. If the lady behind me was to tell me one more time to put my seat in the upright position … They're not too worried about safety videos on these flights or guiding you to your nearest exit with your inflatable yellow device on your person. They are probably more practical than us Westerners in their estimation that if you goin' down over Siberia, baby, you goin' down forever; and putting your mouth on the inflatable mouthpiece is, in all probability, not going to help you into the next world.

As we crossed the International Date Line, I had a noble feeling of history being witnessed within the confines of my own family. The air hostess was to toast this honor with a nice cold glass of water being poured first over me and then the lady across the aisle from me. Behind me, I could still hear the lady whining… "Could you put your seat up a little more?" As I catapulted into the row in front, I smiled to myself. I was on my way to the Orient; I'd crossed the date line and I'd had my first ever in-seat, in-flight shower. Doesn't get much better than that, now, does it; and we hadn't even arrived. Ah, traveling; it can test the best of us.

<u>A CRASH COURSE TO TRAVELING LONG HAUL TO CHINA AND SURVIVING THE WEEK</u>:-

1. Leave home sleep-deprived, so that you can fold yourself up like a piece of origami on the plane and pass out. Alternatively, stock up on "Melatonin" from the drug store and impose sleep that way; you'll need it.
2. Take lots of water along with you. Soy sauce will make you thirsty; as will many of the less-identifiable foods that you will be served on your adventure.
3. Be sure to take off your shoes as soon as you get on the plane. Your feet will need the blood circulating during the fourteen hours spent in a tiny cramped space and you do not want your limbs swelling up like sausages just in time for vacation.
4. Take along a book you want to finish in one sitting; you'll be able to do it on the plane if you fail to follow 1.) Make it a big book.
5. Bring along your own wine to have with dinner. The Chinese wine is terrible and they know it. Their beer is much better.
6. Bring along your own toothbrush and toothpaste; they do not supply these items on the plane, unlike other long-haul carriers. You will also need to do a lot of brushing while you are over there in order not to smell consistently like a Chinese restaurant.
7. Bring a soft squishy neck-pillow and eye shades if you plan to capture any shut-eye. Sleeping without either will be impossible in your allotted 2x2 space.
8. Adopt the mentality that being comfortable is so last year; this is traveling. Don't worry that your hotel bed has no give to it; none of the other passengers' beds do either. Do

not try and change your room to find another more flexible mattress; you will be wasting your time.

9. Take along plenty of $1 bills and keep them sealed in a tight pocket; you will need them. The Chinese vendors like them better than their own currency on the whole and the term "hello; one dollar!" will forever take on a new meaning after your trip. Bring along comfortable running shoes to run away from the "Rolex Watch" vendors; again, you'll need them.
10. Be prepared to barter; they expect it, which is why the average item is marked up 100%.
11. Just in case you have any whiners on your tour, bring along some ear plugs and some "Don't Worry Be Happy" hats for the rest of the group; they'll need them. Alternatively, encourage the whiners to go on their very own special VIP tour just for them; much better for everybody.
12. Go prepared to hand out numbers for each member of the group, so that you can do an ez-attendance roster, to prevent your tour guide from losing his mind every five minutes.
13. Be warned that paper products are extremely rare in China, so if you forget everything else I've told you; try not to forget that a roll of toilet paper, preferably Charmin, and some tissues and napkins for back-up, will make you a lot of friends. It could also make you quite rich, if you begin to charge for these items, which our group seriously considered. Before you leave, get your leg muscles in shape for the peculiar squatting positions required over the Chinese body waste systems.
14. Bring along an empty suitcase or two, and a ripe supply of cash. Contrary to popular misconception, China is not especially cheap especially when they know the Americans are coming. If you don't heed this advice, you'll be buying extra suitcases while you're over there and borrowing cash from your friends.
15. Do not stress if the overload buzzer starts flashing while you and your fellow travelers are in the Chinese elevator. 13 Chinese people equals 6 Americans; and it will probably always be that way.

16. Take along your sense of humor; no matter whatever else you leave behind. Again; you'll need it.

    We are so much creatures of habit; and that is never more apparent than when we go away from home for a little while. Take away our toilet paper, our white porcelain bowls, our regular food, our cozy beds and we become dysfunctional, distracted, and child-like even. Our bodies fight against a change in diet, time, culture; even though we go of our own free will and with open mind.

    Positively speaking, in venturing forth to pastures new, we become more appreciative of all we left behind, we bond comfortingly with our fellow traveler and, on arrival in an unfamiliar land, we quietly anticipate our return home with the deepest of pleasures.

    Whilst we are away from our own sanctuary, we laugh deeply and think a lot. Our eyes stay open wide to the world and all she has to offer to us, during the very short time that we are with her. We learn a little and we grow as beings; at least that was our experience.

**Lucy survived her crash course to China and is always ready to contemplate the next adventure.**

# THE THIN LINE

There are many thin lines to be crossed in life; many crossroads where you wonder; I want to take this route, but what would happen if I went against my gut and took the other? There have been definite crossroads in my life; moments of lucidity when I somehow sensed I had the ability to change the course of my life as I knew it. Doesn't mean I did it, but I certainly sensed it. How many of us wonder if we were to cross that thick double yellow line on that blind curve and lived to tell the story, how that might increase our confidence or something for the day ahead. Many of us face danger every time we step outside the door; we just don't know it. From earthquakes to auto malfunctions to drunk drivers to aneurysms; the threats in our daily lives are endless. And that's discounting any kind of possible trips to the city or adventures in airplanes!

This week I faced danger of a different kind, way out of my comfort zone. It was an escapade I was not sure I would be able to return from. I went and showed property in Carmel Valley. Not to be mean to this particular area at all. I'm sure if you have a nice pad close to the Bernadus Lodge, or your family owns several acres located close enough to be able to walk to Wills Saloon for your good steak and glass of red, then you might get a little defensive about this particular part of the world. But me – I'm just a visitor to the area from across the valley in Soledad, for heavens sakes – and I trust that there are many, many people in the local region of Carmel Valley who cruise around these peaks and valleys as if there is no tomorrow and certainly no sheer cliffs to fall off. However, this was not my particular experience.

My clients wanted to see properties in Carmel Valley. This was my axe to bear. I had not shown property over there before. Not entirely trusting my navigational device, Martha-the-Mouth, as you should, since she is a machine, a computer and much more geographically sound than I, I studied the area as sincerely as I could, printed out my mounds of paper directions and set off into battle. I learned a lot that day. I learned that shared driveways do not always have all of the addresses on the outside of the entrance/exit as they should in a perfect world. I learned that land is quite coveted in these parts and an almost million dollar mansion may well be perched on a sheer crevice in order to save space. I also learned that homes can be built on blind curves with a sheer cliff at the back of the curve and no one thinks twice about it; unless, like me, you are backing out of this sheer driveway towards this sheer cliff and wondering whether this might possibly be the end of life as you know it. One house we visited – the one that was occupied by two large barking dogs and no one else in sight, no less – was located in just such a way. I said a mild prayer, as I backed out onto the blind curve with no other place to go, and cast my mind briefly over the earlier concept of the crossing of dual yellows in the corner of my imagination. This felt a bit like that concept, but with the helpless aspect thrown in - since there was no other way to get out.

Once I made it back to the relative civilization of South County and roads I knew and areas I could navigate without nervous tension or "Martha-the-Mouth" guiding me through life, I realized how far out of my comfort zone I had been forcing myself the entire day. My hands were sweaty, my make up smeared and my car a war zone of discarded papers and drained water bottles. I was exhausted. And to think I used to be quite the adventurer! I have distinct memories of taking the international bus alone from London to Athens, via the Yugoslavia that was. In Athens I made my young way precariously across town to the port and caught the ferry to the island of Crete – a mere 12 hour boat ride away. I was robbed on the boat as I slept and horribly sea sick the rest of the way, but I made it. I was young, I was foolish, I was alone. I was not in my comfortable car traversing my way across the hills and dales of Carmel Valley, a neighboring locale to my own home town. And how far we move away from our comfort zones, as we age and we dig ourselves into our own little comfortable ruts with our own daily movements and habits. The deeper we dig, the less courageous we become, it seems to me.

Looking back, I see a distinctly thin line etched in my past between bravery and foolishness that I no longer possess. It has evaporated over time. Now I am all cowardliness lined with an edge of experience and quite a lot of pessimism, because of some really terrible experiences, I imagine. Now if I was to board the bus for Athens, it would be with a group of people I knew and could save me from certain abduction and robbery. If I boarded the boat to Crete, it could only be that I was on a death wish, (I no longer do boats in any shape or form); and recently, if I jumped in the car and said I was off to show property in Carmel Valley, it was that my sense of humor needed a little sharpening; or that I needed to swing by Bernadus to visit for a while, and I just happened to be in the neighborhood - or that, again, I was just on a death wish to see how many blind curves I could back around before somebody came to meet me on the corner, or how absolutely close to the sheer edge I could get before it was no longer a joke and some body would certainly wake me up from the nightmare. The thin lines we traverse through life are made to test us. Or even to make us dig deeper into our comfort zones and to mostly refuse to leave the house.

**Lucy is a former adventurer.**

# THE HOLIDAYS

# A DAY OUT IN THE COUNTRY

Sometimes we need to be reminded of just what lovely countryside we enjoy here in this valley. As I gazed at the rushing Arroyo Seco river, rampaging down stream through craggy rock and cliff, leaving almost a beach on the bank in its sea-green wake and a million amazing rocks as its spoils, it came to me that snapshots such as this should be treasured and put away; so close to home geographically speaking and yet so very far away from so much of our everyday life. The life in the woods next to the river tranquil and the lush fertile soil boasting citrus groves and deep green lawn; yet the quiet fencing a dead giveaway that the life beyond the fence lived to get inside the fence. You could just imagine the deer peeking in at dusk with big eyes gazing at the flowering borders, the pigs snorting at the so near and yet so far opportunity to pillage and rout.

And so it was last Easter Sunday. We received an invitation to travel just a skip away to Arroyo Seco for Easter dinner and we came away again a few short hours later with so many lovely photographs in our minds.

"Call us when you get to the river," they said; and I was taken back to Laura Ingalls Wilder and at least one of her books, I'm sure, where Ma, Pa, Laura and the baby had problems – to say the least - crossing the river in their covered wagon. When we saw the power of the river, we knew that our covered wagon, the VW van, was definitely no match for it; so we waited patiently, just as we were instructed. A river is quite a good intruder deterrent, for sure; there's just no getting across a force of that magnitude. Fortunately some big 4x4 trucks are intended just for this very thing – if you believe the commercials on television – and, once rescued, we cruised over the torrents, me glancing down nervously, as the water moved vigorously around us, ready to eat us up, like a big bad bear.

For those of you who had big outdoor Easter egg hunts planned in the local area, you already know that we had some pretty good rain on Easter Sunday; but that didn't bother us a bit. The barbecue stayed lit, which was a good thing, and we enjoyed some delicious tri-tip and chicken in the rain; again something I've never done. It had a flavor to it I can't quite describe; but serve to say that everything tastes good outdoors and this was no exception. I had forgotten how tasty food is when you camp and this is sort of how it felt. The chocolate strawberries with raindrops were the icing on the cake, as it were, and who would know that a Hahn Cabernet could get even better with a drop of rain added to it.

Then came the Easter egg hunt! I had been so busy prior to the Easter Sunday that I had completely forgotten to buy any eggs or consider any hunt, I am ashamed to say. Watching all the little and big kids rushing around with their Easter baskets or, alternatively, plastic bags, I was taken back to when my child was a tiny munchkin in her pretty Easter dress and bonnet with long curly hair, rushing around the garden trying to find the tiny chocolate eggs and almost toppling over with the weight of her enormous basket. In those days it was all about the chocolate. This year, she was on a quest to find the golden egg which was full of money; how things change, but then not really at all! I helped her just a little, though my two eggs certainly did not take her over the edge on the prize front and we didn't find the golden one. 30 years of not egg-hunting has really rusted up my skills. The balloon man made some super butterflies, dogs and horse balloons, to name just a few, to the delight of the crowd; it was a great celebration.

It was all a lovely, lovely sight; we brought in the launch of spring through the sprinkle of the rain drops and all was well with the world that day. Holidays should be memorable like that. We should take the time to feast, enjoy, relax, but also exercise our memories in all the treasures that come back to mind; at the sight of a tiny baby racing around after colored eggs or that pretty little thing in her Easter bonnet; or, now, our new memory of the taste of tri-tip and chocolate covered strawberries in the rain. Life is short; don't forget to take the snapshots and hold on tight to the memories.

**Lucy is a fond collector of memories. Just ask her family.**

# BROWN PAPER PACKAGES TIED UP WITH LOVE

I have felt so fortunate, recently, to live where I do. It is not often we allow a whoosh of well-being and contentment to drench over us like a wave; but I was lucky enough to be embraced by one of those out of body experiences this week, and, treat such as it was, I took the time to really feast on it.

I was asked to be a Judge of the Snow Queen's contest here in Soledad. "Oh, another night we have to attend an event", I grouched to my business partner, as we compared our black-inked schedules in dismay. "When on earth am I supposed to have time to shop, (let alone wrap the darn things), prepare for a trip, attend all those holiday luncheons, make all those meetings, let alone sell real estate. Need I say more?" She shushed me with an assurance, that it would be tremendous fun, which of course it was. She is very wise and I need to learn to shut my mouth; more.

As Judges, we did not have to sit with curly wigs on our heads, luckily for everyone in the general vicinity; but we did have to be sequestered in a nice, comfortable, candle-lit room with one chair placed in the center of it for the lucky interviewee. Can you imagine anything more nerve-wracking? The poor children – ranging in age from 4 to 15 – had to suffer a form of interrogation in that chair on topics from 'Most Favorite Person in the World', to 'What do you look for in a friend?'

In retrospect, I was incredibly surprised and humbled by the experience. After the event, I concluded, intelligently, that most children really rock. I can only assume it must be us adults who totally pollute the Innocent on their ladder to adulthood. Hence, as near adults, they become more and more like us and generally less charming, but that is a whole other subject.

You would imagine so close to Christmas Eve and all, with media ads invading each breathing second from every direction, that most children would have a healthy obsession, about this time of year, for stuff and more stuff under the tree. However, if you were to ask your child what he or she would most like in the whole world, you might be pleasurably surprised, as I was by the Soledad

Snow Angels, (or at least the ones which were not so nervous they could get a word out). We did get a few material answers, but on the whole, their responses warmed the heart. One little girl wracked the judges' sensibilities with her simple little answer that told of a whole world of hurt.

"If you could have one wish, what would it be?" she was asked. (Don't forget this child is 4 years old). Without blinking, she responded that she would "like my Mommy to go back to my Daddy". All we could do was wipe away a tear and move on quickly to the next question.

Saturday, I was again in the judges' chair, feeling even more weighed by the responsibility, knowing that the contest to be Queen for a year was drawing to a close. For this portion of the competition, the ladies were required to be in formal attire and present a simple little speech about themselves. I was astounded, that little 3rd graders in our society are already talking about college prep classes and a degree in medicine. Wise to the fact that they had probably been well prepped by anxious parents; I still thought this a pretty precious exercise in basic life preparation, not to mention public speaking. Just imagine how well these little people will perform on their first job interview or sound on their college application! Makes me almost want to sign up my own little precious for next year's Queenly bootcamp!

There was one little rebel Queen who had no intention of even giving out her name, let alone speaking publicly. As a Judge, I was not allowed to smile, but I really wanted to. I let myself smile when she was awarded her crown at the parade, surprising us all. Surprises are always nice, even when you're a judge and you think you know the way that things are going!

From my proud position of Judge, I was then put right back in my proper place, where I belong, and behind the Chamber of Commerce booth as a corn dog seller. From my selling stance, (luckily for me, I was the banker in the deal, whereas my Buddy for the afternoon got the taxing task of actually baking the dogs in the dog oven), I was able to accomplish my favorite hobby in the whole world of people watching and feasting on the crowds. What a super, peaceful community we have, Soledad. Families browsed the stalls and enjoyed our world-famous corn dogs, among other taste treats. Soledadians cheered the fine long parade of renowned citizens, fire trucks, cheerleaders and more. Christmas music played and all seemed well with our world in Soledad. Truly a case of peace on earth and good will to all mankind; if only for a night.

The parade was a seeming fiesta, a rightful culmination of all the Queens' hard work and a salutation to their efforts, (not to mention the grueling labors of their parents). On stage, the Queens received more gifts, awards and flowers than they could ever carry alone; and even those who did not win the largest crown, (which our token rebel Queen claimed was "too heavy" for her head and promptly removed), were made to feel extremely special, which of course they are.

Too all our Queens, wherever you are and wherever you may reign, you rock. You taught me things this week I didn't know and certainly didn't expect to learn from you. You reminded me how smart you all are and how we must never underestimate you. You made me laugh and reminded me how proud I am to be here. Thank you all for all those surprise gifts. You are brown paper packages wrapped up with love. See you next year.

**Lucy enjoyed being a judge of Queens.**
**May we all feel like a Queen, crowned for the night.**

**Lucy was proud to have the privilege to be**
**a Queens' Judge in Soledad.**

# CHRISTMAS IS BUT A SALE DAY AWAY

You really do have to feel for the retailers in this day and age. No sooner is "Back to School" on the shelves, but it becomes immediately obsolete. You can very swiftly spot Halloween shoving its way through with all its goblins and candy. You do have to wonder what on earth they do with all that neglected merchandise which no one has the time to buy, before the onslaught of the next retail "event". On the heels of the witches and goblins and half price trick-a-treatin' comes a quick Veteran's Day, a quiet turkey or two, then ka-boom, hallelujah; deck the halls, baby, Santa's on his way! I'm always amazed at the world-wide Santa build up; the huge crescendo of excitement and anticipation created from about June onwards; so that by the time you edge towards the real holy night, you're completely sick of the whole thing. Or is that just me?

Lost, as usual, in a big box store in the middle of a massive heat wave, taking refuge from the cruel heats outside, and edging as close to the refrigerated aisle as possible, I eye-spy a large fake Christmas tree. "Now that is just ridiculous," I say to just myself. "It's only the middle of summer!" But the retailers apparently know more than I do, because, as I was having these very un-festive thoughts, I noticed a lady studying said yuletide item with interest and, before I knew it, she had hauled this seven foot creation into her shopping cart and she was on her ho-ho way. I later caught her singing "Hark the herald", as she sweated at the check- out.

Being a little late with my back to school shopping this year; i.e. doing my school shopping after they had actually gone back to school, I am qualified to talk on this matter. If you dare to commence this children-back-in-the-classroom exercise anytime after the beginning of August, the shelves are stripped; there is not a piece of appropriate school clothing nor even a pen to be had within the boundaries of the western hemisphere; I guarantee it. Looks as if a plague of pen-sucking locusts has invaded our territory and gone home satiated! However, if you'd like a fake Christmas tree, you can probably still get one of those in August.

But don't hang around; 'cos there's lots of eager beavers out there; those annoying people who will get in line for half- price wrapping paper on the day after Christmas – they're out there now and they're hungry. Time is of the essence! Seems to me as if the Christmas collectible crowd is on a mission to get Christmas under their belts and taken care of prontissimo! These people live to stockpile. Far be it from me to over anticipate that I will still be alive to witness next December in all her mystery, let alone many to come! Those red and green bargain hunters have been looking out for Christmas sales since the birth of Christmas and, if there's a deal to be had, they're gonna be there! They'll be the ones sleeping in line after turkey day for that $10 television or the limited edition brand new gaming kit for little Johnny who's already bored of his limited edition gaming kit from last year. They'll be the ones sweeping the discount shelves the day after the holiday, when no one else in their right mind can even look at anything red or green. Those are the people who can definitely shop in those year-round Christmas shops. It's a simple philosophy; they know it's coming; so why wait? And so, why am I so scathing, you may ask? Because I'm probably just a little jealous! I'd love to be that organized. Every year I know I should plan a little earlier, shop a little smarter; in short not get caught with my pants down on Christmas Eve. It must be a genetic fault, that's all I can think of; a terminal incapacity to get it in gear in time to be able to sit back and enjoy it all when the time is right, like other civilized people seem to be able to do.

In Europe we "do" Christmas so much better than you guys. Sorry and all that; we just do. First of all, the majority of Europe closes down for a good 10 days over Christmas and New Year; it's just what you do. Always have, probably always will. There are a lot of reasons for this. Firstly, there are multitudes of parties you need to attend and mulled wine to drink at this time of year; copious boxes of chocolates to eat and goodies to share. Way too much goodwill going around for anyone to get any work done! So they just don't bother; they take the time off; they feast and they enjoy. The weather is also seasonally diabolical; so it's a darn good time to slouch around at home, hum a few ho ho's and eat a lot of chocolate. Secondly, the day after Christmas is a national holiday in most parts of Europe. Boxing Day is a big day; it's a day that you eat the leftovers from your huge turkey dinner on

Christmas day. You get to sleep in and play with all your toys. It's a joyous day without the Christmas carols or ho ho, 'cos all that stuff has, thankfully, already gone away. It's a family day, when you can stop and breathe and count your blessings. Everything is closed and quiet out in the commercial and retail world. Here in the land of too much of everything, your Boxing Day is a regular work day, where, if you're lucky, you get to leave work during your half an hour lunch break and buy all your festive labels at 50% off, in time for this time next year in 363 days. You just don't get enough rest here; I'm convinced of it. Way too much buying and planning for the next Hallmark holiday, and not enough of doing nothing or reading a book!

So, if you've learned nothing else about this anti-early-Christmas banter, know this. I love Christmas; but if I were governor, I'd change a few things too. My valuable opinion is that the build up to that magical time should begin directly after Thanksgiving and no sooner. It should become unconstitutional, if not illegal, to start ho-ho-ing any time earlier! I'd love to have all my pressies wrapped and gone by the week before Christmas, but I can't and I must forgive myself for that immediately. Another thing - shopping for holiday wrap the day after holy day is just flat wrong. Eating and drinking a lot over the days between Christmas and New Year is a custom that should be an obligation for all merry men to indulge in. It should be mandated; "work your rear ends off the rest of the year; deal with all the budget cuts and lack of sleep. But feast, my good people; feast you must, on the last week of the year!" Oh, and don't forget to throw a Boxing Day in there for good measure.

**Lucy will always be British where the Christmas season is concerned.**

# GETTING IN THE SPIRIT

If you are feeling less than cheery about the upcoming holiday season and you need to find a reason for the season, get out of yourself and go do something for some one else. That is a sure cure for the blues; I guarantee it.

SAP's toy drive in Soledad, (for the newcomers to the area, that would be Soledad Auto Parts), has been an inspiration and a joy to many in Soledad for many years now; and some of it comes all the way from Sacramento. "Some years I forget to even get a tree for the house," quipped owner Sandy Vosti. "We get so busy with the toy drive; that the rest of it gets away from us." But, tree or not, Sandy knows how to keep Christmas firmly entrenched in her heart.

Every year, Sandy, her husband John, the crew of SAP, the members of the Apostolic church and many other kind people deliver around 1,000 toys to the needy children of Soledad. "With that many chimneys to go down, we have to do some pre-delivering," joked Sandy, "but the gifts are in boxes and the parents can always hide them and save them for Christmas Day itself; so it's okay if they get them early. There are too many presents to do all in one night. Every year I think to myself ... maybe I'll let some one else do it this year; but every year I find another reason to do it again."

The procedure is simple; go to SAP after Thanksgiving and register a child who may not get much of anything if you don't. Sandy explained that every year there seems to be more and more children who need a gift of cheer; but that the community is always so generous and helps her out, it always works out in the end. "At least these days, the Apostolic church sings the carols," she said. "The first year, my guys from the auto parts had to sing; and there are still dogs howling around town because of it!"

The toy drive began years ago as an "All Pro" sponsored "Toys for Tots" effort, which Sandy and her crew seized by the horns and ran with. The parts warehouse in Sacramento still supports SAP every year with their toy collections, as do many of the farmers, customers and vendors at the store, as well as the generous people of South County.

The community of Soledad has no doubt that the SAP toy drive will continue to go the extra mile as long as they can to put the smiles on the less fortunate children among us; and so, what are *you* going to do, for your part, to warm the heart of some else? You could just start out simple with your giving and give Sandy a few bucks or a nice toy for the toy drive. Either way; she'll reciprocate with a smile as big as your heart and you'll feel better for it.

Are you going to sponsor a family through the Salvation Army? That is always so rewarding and fills such a tremendous need. My daughter and I have done that in years past and enjoyed making cards for the little faces, we can see in our minds, smiling on Christmas morning and unwrapping the gifts we feel sure they'd like. Just a quick call to the Salvation Army and they'll be thrilled to hear from you. If you can't see your way to doing a whole family, how about a "Christmas Angel"; again, another worthy program sponsored by the Salvation Army. Make a child happy this holiday season and save a soul; perhaps your own. Maybe you can volunteer in a homeless center and see how appreciative the people are who have nothing and who come in out of the cold for a hot meal and a smile. Give them a smile and word of encouragement; shake them by the hand. A little piece of humanity costs nothing. Perhaps you could donate coats and jackets to our local school districts for their needy kids. Just ask a teacher and they will tell you the need is there.

In years past, I have taken my daughter out caroling to rest homes and hospitals. The nostalgic tears and smiles of the people have made the cold bodies and the tired minds of the carolers want to sing all night. Sometimes, the people sing along, sometimes, they cry and shake their heads; always they clap and ask for more. Where could *you* go and sing to some one else?

We have also cleaned out my daughter's closet and my own many times prior to the holidays and retrieved all kinds of clothing, coats, dolls and toys that we volunteer to live without. We make sure everything is clean and nice and then we take it to shelters or half way houses, where there are women and children in tough situations who need just about anything you can spare. Giving up possessions is not an easy thing to ask a young child to do; but it gives them a reason for the season, teaches them how lucky they are and how not everyone in the world is blessed with such great fortune. It gives them values they will take onward in their lives, and hopefully, share with their children.

I also make sure my daughter rings the bell with me for the Salvation Army every holiday season. Cold or not, we don our Santa hats and we jingle with a smile, thanking everyone who spares even a penny for the kettle. It is good; it is right; it puts Christmas in our hearts. In recent years, we have even taken along our dogs to entertain the crowd and a little holiday music. Try and walk past a barking, dancing kettle if you dare!

Whether you are religious or not, find a way to take yourself out of yourself, as it were, this time of year, and give back to the world around you. What you will find is that life gives it right back and you will have the warmest heart and the toastiest toes you could ever dream of to take you through to the next year.

**Lucy loves to get in the spirit every year.**

# IT'S BEGINNING TO LOOK A LOT LIKE 'STRESSMUS'

I love the holiday season; always have. Just put a "Carpenter's at Christmas' song on the stereo and I can start singing along in my own little world, swathed in rich memories of yester-year; our Christmas by the sea in a little fisherman's cottage in England; the fire burning in the hearth, wrapping presents with Mother on Christmas Eve and feeling the magic riding on the chill in the air. I can do all of that at the first note of "Chestnuts roasting on an open fire"; just test me.

But this year, sadly, I'm already looking forward to January and her cool empty days. My problem, and I doubt I'm alone, is that I'm riding on overload, driven by a heavy calendar, multiple slots of obligations filling up every day and, look out, I'm wavering dangerously on the edge of over-promising and under-delivering; not an attractive place to be for some one who prides herself on running a tight ship, as it were.

My front room is sagging under the weight of wrapping paper and semi-wrapped gifts; half-completed projects, stocking stuffers and lists clutter the floor and any spare surface. My office/spare room is inches high with dust. Books and papers are falling off the bed; projects are yellow with the waiting to be filed, stories have become dog-eared in their aching to be written. (And this is the room where my father will be staying when he arrives from England in 10 days; ah me.) There are Christmas parties to bake for and attend, school concerts to clap at, plays to see, (bought the tickets ions ago when I had no clue of how much I wouldn't feel like going at the time); and not to mention work! Now, who has time for that?

All of these things can mound up and give you a fleeting respite at night and a ticky-stress-eye during the day. Your poor disposition mounts with the rising stress. The multiple lists you write yourself are always out of date and that's if you don't lose them first. My husband laughs at the fact that I will call myself at home to leave messages to just myself; but really people, what do you do at such a time? If I don't call myself and leave ludicrous, multiple messages on the machine, (it's really sad when you say goodbye to just yourself); then the few things I am capable of remembering right now, with my phone-calling support system, will be lost amidst the piles and the crud I'm calling call my life!

In this wave-machine powered stress pool I find myself, I realize I'm in deepest need of, above all, some time to myself. I'm yearning, aching, bleeding for a day of nothing; a day when the calendar shows a big blank, a day when I might just turn over in the morning and sleep a little longer, a day when I could perhaps watch a movie, a day when I might possibly be able to clean my filthy house or even read a book! I'm looking at my diary and saying that is just never going to happen ever again; ever. I am doomed to a life of overflow and spilling over the edge and down the sides of my own personal reality. Somebody say it isn't so, please. Stop the bleeding!

Always the bright spark; my sister has advised me to just say no. "Take the day off," she counseled, "before you have to anyway. Call in sick, why doncha?" "I can't call in sick if I'm not sick," I retort. "Anything that is not absolutely vital; i.e. work or child-related; don't do it," she said, always the insistent coach. "Go through your December obligations and start liberating yourself a little. Free up your calendar, otherwise you will go mad." She's absolutely right; I will go mad, if I haven't gone there already. Just put one more present in front of me for me to wrap and I will probably be extremely rude, (as poor husband discovered one evening as he found me neck-deep in wrap and wondered if I could manage to wrap just one more present; the one gift that he had actually found time to purchase this holiday season …). Just give me another project to work on, or another engagement to attend and it will not be pretty; I guarantee it. This particular Brit will be going off the deep end, headed solidly for the lunatic asylum in a straight-jacket; or at least that's how it feels.

"What are you stressing over?" asks husband, helpfully, as he sits and chills, watching something low-key on the television. "It will all soon be over." Before I ate his head and put it on a spit to cook, I took the time to consider what he had just said and remarked, to just myself, on oh what a smart fellow I had married and how equally smart I was to do it. The man was astute; he was so incredibly right! Why kill yourself with the stress – (and oh boy, stress will kill you in the blink of an eye if you let it) - when all this mammoth season of festivities and intense jubilation will be over in the blink of an eye! Stress can even damage your D.N.A. or, at least, I think that's what I heard of late, which cannot be a good thing; so it should be banished from our existence, put out with the garbage, in short, obliterated. (Better make a note to self on my New Year's Resolutions to no longer allow it in my life).

But never fear, even if I don't get much of a handle on the stress and I do end up stressing and yelling my way through the silly season; before we can say, "after Christmas sales", we'll be wallowing in the January greys, we'll be planning our summer vacations in the sun and we'll be left wondering where the big Christmas hoopla all went and why we made such a big fuss over it.

**Lucy loves Christmas. These days she makes sure she enjoys it too.**

# JOURNEY DOWN MEMORY LANE

With the arrival of my child's 12$^{th}$ birthday, I find myself in somber mood. How can she be almost a teenager, when I am still stuck back there at her birth, my mother close by and arguing with the doctors about my condition, myself indolent in drug-induced haze? I recall so clearly the warm blankets of the after surgery cocoon; the enormous sweeping relief that the surging pain was all over; that tiny little suckling thing with long finger nails and luscious black hair. Truly seems like yesterday!

All those twelve years forward with significant people in my world having moved on to St Elsewhere, I find myself in major bittersweet mode, as the nostalgic in me would still like to hold my baby in my arms and feed her a bottle and hold her tiny little hands, but the rational in me reminds me that those days are severely gone and lost to the earth. Her day of celebration of another year older is my commiseration for all the years now under her belt. Here we have birthday cake, cards, presents, parties and celebrations implanted heavily in my house and my world; and there we have it; my mind swinging way back down memory lane to where it all began and who was there to greet it.

No matter how old we are, we are all always too young to lose our mothers. With the arrival of another of my child's birthdays, at the door of this milestone event, I am yet again greeted by the ghost of birthdays past. How about her 2$^{nd}$ birthday when my family came over from England – my mother and grandmother both now gone – to enjoy and to celebrate with my family over here? What about the one when we went over to London and celebrated it all there? That was memorable too. My parents' house surging with laughter and merriment; the house which now sits empty except for my father who lives on his lonesome in his 3 story home once filled with the chatter and laughter of a large family. The bitter and the sweet; they collide in the middle and make something new, that's for sure.

I'm a great celebrator; in fact, my husband thinks that I hold the crown for remembering milestones and lifting them up high where everyone can see them. I love to celebrate birthdays, anniversaries, the holidays; you name it – I'm all over it. In August I start salivating over the Christmas buying season and working on my lists. I get a great frisson of pleasure when, around Labor Day, I see all the sparkly decorations start popping up in the shops. I know it's way too early; but I love it anyway. I can see myself already dusting off my copy of the Carpenters Christmas songs and blasting them in the sanctuary of my decorated living room; soon, very soon. In order not to send all around me completely potty, I never allow myself the self-indulgence of Christmas music before Thanksgiving; but the self control this commands is admittedly difficult for me, I have to concede; and it's a tremendous relief when I can just have at it. I love the sparkle and twinkle; just love it.

But, at the same time, you cannot be a great celebrator of things that make life rich and fun, without at the same time finding yourself in nostalgic and sometimes sad places. I find England at Christmas very difficult; now that my mother is no longer there to celebrate with us. I cannot throw away an envelope, let alone card that my mother or grandmother wrote to me. I have collected all my daughter's birthday cards and kept them over the years; (12 sets of cards, not to mention her shower cards, birth congrats and so on can really eat up some storage!) I can't ever see myself being able to throw that stuff away. It's invaluable; it's our family history and some. It's all part of the deep pattern of enrichment that we gather throughout our lives to look back on and savor as we grow old, hopefully, and have a long solid journey of life to look back on.

My daughter had another birthday, not to mention my own, and strange how it is that I'm okay with my turning another year older and less okay with her. The hands of time move on regardless of what any of us feel about them; our journey towards uncertain destiny always at a crossroads where we wonder what's around the next corner and who will be there to greet us.

**Lucy has always been nostalgic.**

# MY WISH LIST

Having given up resolutions years ago, I now compile a mild wish list for the coming festive season and the New Year just around the corner. Since the list is only in my mind and has no written evidence, I don't even have to make it so; it's just a pact between me, myself and I in the bizarre confines of my own space. I can still wish for world peace and freedom for all, but that is a utopia, a dream world beyond our reach. No, what I try to do is contemplate a small step towards improving myself and my place in the world in the coming months, not to mention making concentrated efforts to avoid any negative impacts I may make upon others. Some years I fare better than others – just ask my family.

But in looking forward, I think it also important to look back and see what we have learned in this whirlwind, also known as our lives, in the year behind us now almost a memory. I'll share my gleaned wisdom with you this time - for fun - imagining that you too might want to play this game at home in the private sanctuary of your own little world:-

1. Though I find the sequence of "Anti-Walmart" Christmas cards in my personal mail box wildly annoying this year, and a huge waste of paper not to mention postage, since few people send cards anymore unless they are the e-kind; at one point this holiday season these cards were the only ones I had, so I laughed and strung them up anyway. (I did not cuss and throw them in the recycle – yay me!) I have learned tolerance for others' forced opinions this year – now that is growth and maturity!
2. No one ever needs to know what you really think of them. I really did learn that this year and it's far better that way; trust me. When you live in a small community, it's much better to have everyone believe that you are their friend. This requires a huge degree of care and self control at all times – definitely not possible for anyone younger than 21

- but for us old horses, even British ones, we can learn, honestly!

3. Savings accounts do matter. It is better to have a few beans in the bank than that razzle-dazzle big screen you've been salivating over. I have really been reminded of that this year in a big, big way. I have known people employed for 25-30 years i.e. a lifetime, who have received their marching orders from their long-standing companies these past few weeks and are now wondering how to make their life work for them and what to do with the rest of it. In real estate, we tell people they should plan on having 6-9 months living payments in reserve; I'm now increasing that recommendation to 1 year minimum. You just never know what's going to happen, especially in this crazy rollercoaster world we've all been living in of late. Stock market up, stock market down. Homes selling, lenders making home buying near impossible! Government going into world of finance and automotive. It's quite a different world from this time last year. "Never know what's going to happen next!" does have to be tattooed on all of our foreheads once the last minute of the year kisses us gratefully goodbye.
4. Life is fragile. I already knew that – of course I did, as old as I am; but sometimes we are reminded of this tender fact in no uncertain terms, like the freight train rolling down the hill with no brakes; that death is just a paused breath away and we have no idea who won't be dining at the holiday table this year. We've lost our share as a family this year and who knows, there again, what the tomorrow will bring.
5. We never stop learning. Just when you think you've got it all figured out and the formula is one that works, life will teach you humility in the form of "you know nothing; now eat crow!" In my particular profession, the rules are changing by the minute and you can never assume that you have the latest info or the most complete set of rules. I try to stay ahead, I really do. I attend my classes and I try to pay attention, but I am constantly humbled all the same. Yeh, I did snort when some one told me not so long ago that they'd wait for the homes in Soledad to be under

$200,000 before they'd consider buying; well, now those smarty pants pushed the envelope there and then some. What did I ever know? Apparently not a darn thing.

6. There are not many constants in this life except for the love of my dogs. They love me when I feed them, they love me when I put them out into the cold of the early morn; they love me when I put them into their snuggly beds at night. No matter how ugly or old I really am, I am always beautiful to them, especially when I have a can opener in my hand. Constants like that are so endearing!

And so what would my wish list for the coming year be like, if I was to put one down in indelible ink? It would be that we could have a few more constants in our daily lives, like the love of my dogs. I would hope that people could have a bit more security, less fear, less stress. I would truly wish that for all of us. I would also like to lose 20lbs and not eat chocolate or drink wine, when I get stressed out. (Maybe that means I also need a new profession?). I would hope also that we all have less of a roller coaster ride than in recent years and more semblance of normalcy, if that even exists any more. I would hope that the homeless find homes and the hopeless hope, but maybe I'm moving towards that utopia thing again. I would hope that we can still be sitting with the loved ones we have today at our dinner tables. I would also hope that those dreadful anti-Walmart cards go away and are replaced by more of the nice surprises in my mail box, such as the nice photo card greeting from an old friend now living in Indiana, and a sweet snow scene from some one I thought had written me off the list a while back.

Whatever you believe in, happy season of it to all! May your quiet wish list for the year be as close to happening as possible.

**Lucy loves Christmas; lists and all.**

# RELIGIOUS OR NOT

You could never say that I was a particularly religious person; spiritual yes, religious no. Those who know me will know that I discuss neither religion nor politics. It's much better that way for everyone. I do however confess to love the Christmas season. I adore the spiritual mood in the air, the romanticism of loved ones coming together after times apart, the season of giving to all. In my turn, I do try to show seasonal spirit myself this time of year. I think about charity, about people who have greater needs than me. I try to give where I can and make up for other times of the year when serious charitable thoughts may pass me by a bit – full summer for instance. You don't worry so much about people shivering out in the night time chill when it's 100 degrees in the shade and everyone's sleeping with the windows open. This time of year when the temp is dipping to the 30's, you do stop and think more about others. Do I really need 10 jackets in my closet which I may or may not need in the next few months? How about those jeans I think I may fit back into one day when I start to take my fitness regime a little more seriously? What about those blankets napping in the deepest darks of the laundry closet? Do I need those more than that other person over there, who doesn't even have one warm covering to their name? I think this is a good time, religious or not, that we all take a good look at what we have and look yonder to those poor souls out there in the elements. What would one of our spare jackets mean to them? It might be the only one they would have and they would most certainly love it and give it a good home.

Another important part of giving to those less fortunate is the important role of the Salvation Army in all of our communities. "Caring has no season", they say. "Need has no season" also, and it's true. The Salvation Army works all year round for all people, regardless of the season. I have always had a lot of time for that organization. Years ago in Louisiana, when I was fresh to this country and immensely poor, a neighbor knocked at the door to my trailer with a large basket donation from the Salvation Army. It shocked me at the time, since I had not realized that other complete strangers recognized or cared that I was needy – and I was far too proud at the time to accept their kindness and their caring, needy or not; but it was the beginning of a life long love affair from my soul to their organization. They are a quietly pervasive organization that somehow makes it happen all the time. They rescue people from the depths of despair – from homelessness and hunger, the most basic of human needs. They nobly pick people up from where they have fallen and help them get back onto the horse of the living.

If I do nothing else every year, I will make a donation to the Salvation Army and I will ring the bell for their fundraising efforts in the hope that others will too. It is one of my annual learning curves. I enjoy watching the approaching folks as I ring the bell and play my holiday music to get their attention. I like to watch the smile of the children as they endeavor to remind their older relatives to look at the bell, smile at the lady, donate a penny or two. I like to guess in my mind who considers the organization a worthwhile cause and who simply can't be bothered. They glance in their pocket book and then they glance away, their thoughts already elsewhere. The glossy vehicles with the wealthier looking folks are the ones less likely to see you; it's a great exercise in the human condition I can tell you.

My first bout of bell-ringing this year was on the coldest night of the year. "At least my shift is only an hour," I told myself after a long day at work. I had a scarf, gloves and some warming Christmas music to while away those sixty minutes. Twenty minutes after the supposed end of my shift and I was still there waiting for my replacement to show up. My warmed human spirit had gone the way of my chilled toes and I was a bit peeved to tell the truth. What is worse than not bothering to sign up to bell ring in the first place, is to sign up and to flake, so that others feel less than cheery towards man kind. As I hopped around on my chilled toes and tried to entertain warm thoughts of hot soup and my toes thawing out by the log fire at some point that night, a young lady pulled her car up into the disabled parking spot in front of me. "A bit cold tonight?" she ventured as she made her way into the store. "You have no idea," I grouched, still angry that my shift replacement was cozy by the fire while I was ringing her bell. The lady said a few kind words and then climbed back into her vehicle. She pulled her car out of the space, then pulled forward, stopped and got out again. It wasn't easy for her to get in and out of her car I could see that – I thought she had maybe forgotten something at the drug store. "Can I maybe go and get you something hot to drink?" she asked. I wasn't cold anymore; she had warmed my heart up again. "That's so sweet of you," I replied, "but my shift is nearly over" – a white lie, not truly knowing if and when I would be relieved of my bell duty. I just couldn't imagine this lady parking up someplace else and struggling to get out of her vehicle just to get me – a complete able-bodied, if cold-toed stranger – something warm to drink. Besides I wasn't cold anymore. We waved and she left. I felt good. That was what it was all about – warm human exchange. More than that you can't ask for!

If you can spare even a dollar this year, please give to the Salvation Army. They provide to all of our communities in more quiet ways than you can imagine. Also, if you have a bell-ringing shift, please make sure you show up. If you can't, you need to send a replacement and keep the chain of good cheer moving right along. For those of us who are volunteering to do this, we hate to have our good feelings towards mankind charred by less than charitable thoughts towards our fellow man, the no show in our bell-ringing chain of duty. Happy Holidays to all, and especially that nice lady with the warm heart, who reminded me that the spirit of Christmas is still alive and well in our community.

**Lucy happily rings the bell every year**
**for the Salvation Army.**

# REMEMBERING CHRISTMAS PAST

The Christmas Eve after my mother died, I left the family party, went to bed and cried. It was the first Christmas Eve I had ever been without her and, with that huge, searing gap in my world, the night had lost its magic and its sparkle for me. The sentiment of the season created only a huge well of grief and suffering that made my entire body throb, as if shards of glass were keeping the wounds open and raw. I couldn't listen to my lovely Christmas music; I couldn't bear to take my mind back to years passed; I could hardly stand to shop and wrap; except that it was expected of me, so I went through the motions. I longed to have it all over with, so that I could wrap myself up in cotton and try to no longer feel that way.

That year has set me up for, inevitably, more of the same down the road, I'm sure; times when the pain is so raw that you could cut it with a knife, times when just the sound of "I'll be home for Christmas" makes you feel as if you were truly dying inside. Having experienced feeling that way even one time has made me since a lot more sensitive to those around me who have suffered painful loss in the past year and would be enduring the first holiday season without some one precious nearby.

Six years down the road I can think back to that Christmas Eve and marvel at how far I have come in my own journey away from raw pain and towards a condition of serenity and acceptance. It's a long trip. I can now think back to our Christmases by the sea in our fisherman's cottage without hurting all over. I allow myself to venture back in time to photos in my memory of the young family all together. My grandma was there too and my friend's mother from across the street. Our dear friends and neighbors – also now gone – are part of the picture too. I can find myself tiptoeing through Christmases past with the delicate tread of some one who's come a long way since then, but still wants to hold close all that was once so precious. I recall those times long ago. We were all there back then, not one of us missing. We'd come in from the roar of the beach, away from the black walls of water, our eyes stinging from the salt water, our noses red from the sharp whip of the wind. We'd hunker down near our tiny fireplace and feast on the twinkle of the tree, then maybe visit Father Christmas in the high street and ache with anticipation for the night to come, or go to a carol service at the local church or visit friends also humming with the season. "This time tomorrow." I'd tell myself in the land of Christmas past. "Father Christmas will have been. I'll already have opened my stocking. I'll already have that feeling that it's all over, the magic is gone for another year." In those days, I seemed to have a talent for looking forward with remorse, which I'm happy to say, with the passing of the years, has passed also.

"Boxing Day" – for those of you not in the know, the day after Christmas, also a National Holiday in England – helps with the passing of the holiday blues. It is the bridge, the day between Christmas day and the rest of your life, when you can still celebrate, but in a more chilled way. You can take stock, look back with calm and serenity and take in all that has just occurred. Boxing Day in my house is an institution, a necessity. With all the hype and lift of the drum roll towards Christmas we need a Boxing Day in our lives; a day of contemplation and reflection, a day to play with your toys and eat leftovers. We need to walk that bridge in order not to fall off the other one and tumble cascading into the sea of the year past and the threat or promise of the year to come.

Life is but a bridge between the very known and the lost and the very unknown and the things still to lose. In order not to drive ourselves to the edge of desperation and despair, we need to be able to examine the photo albums of our past lives and give them a passing grade. We need to be able to look at our people lost and say gone, but not forgotten; here, but in another room. We need to be able to tread forward to an unknown, indiscriminate future with some anticipation and in hope that all will, ultimately, be well in the larger scheme of things. I can honestly say that I am there now; I arrived. I can now look back on my childhood in the cottage, my crisp, fresh memories of Christmas past in the tapestry of my existence and feel at peace with the world. This is how it is, this is what it is. There is nothing more to be said or done about it. Merry Christmas and May peace and loving memories live on in your heart.

**Lucy has always loved Christmas time.**

# SANTA COMES IN DIFFERENT PACKAGES

Once upon a time in a little village in a big country there lived a fairly young girl with a big heart. She lived a good life, worked hard and created a better world for those around her, wherever she was able. She loved animals and people alike and always had a smile on her face for everyone, no matter what. Despite her constant cheeriness, she couldn't help feeling sad and sorry for the many around her who were not so fortunate. The holidays would come around and she would wonder about the local families in her neighborhood who struggled year round to just put the bare necessities on their tables; let alone provide any luxuries and surprises for their children over the festive season.

With that in mind, she decided to make a difference where she could and put together a toy drive for the needy children in her village; a labor of love for families she had never met, children she might never know, that they could themselves know an act of anonymous love at the peak of giving time all around the world. What greater gift to the planet could one person make? Give a gift to, perhaps, change a life. Not everyone gets to do that; few even wonder how.

Ever since the evolution of the toy drive, the elves and the carpenters around this fairly young girl labor the last quarter of every year, as they have for many holiday seasons, to create a Christmas in the hearts of children who have already known too much in the way of too few gifts in their young lives. The hard-working crew gathers together money, toys, books, bears, cars and dolls over the weeks and months prior to the special night. Many of their friends also get involved and get to feel the infectious spirit in the air. Many of them pass it along like a contagious disease.

In the village, they fill storage sheds and sleighs to the brim, in anticipation of the smiles they hope to see on young faces. They gather notes to Santa from young minds the village over and try to fit the toy to the child; try to make it magic for them, at least for one night. They deliver boxes to grateful families that they could hide the gifts themselves and wrap them up for Christmas Eve and something to put under the tree; they make sure that everyone who needs something has something special to unwrap on Christmas morning; they change worlds one present at a time.

As the big night approaches, the elves are already weary of map reading and prepping; worn to a frazzle from fighting the malls and filling the Santa wishes for so many; yet they are high on life and brimming with anticipation of the happiness that will coat the heavens over their village that night. Their homes are packed to the max with toys from all over; gifts to them from others also, that they may pass along to the unknown young among them. The true meaning of re-gifting; a contagious and spontaneous urge to make a little something right, build a bright star in some one else's dark of night.

The special night arrives. The presents are moved to the sleigh and, noisily, the convoy moves through the village; singing carols to the skies and raining goodwill down on all men.

Young children fall out of doorways with mouths open wide; babies unable to blink, for fear of missing something, cling on to their mothers, as plush flies without ceremony from the sleigh, and lands in their arms; the true meaning of manna from heaven. The lights of the sleigh reflect on the fairy lights of the homes it visits and, beneath the glimmer, all are one. Santa touches the babies as he touches the parents' hearts. Elves deliver boxes to the homes; and all around the spirit of Christmas infiltrates the air.

"We need to find a child who needs a bike," hollers the fairly young Santa girl riding at the helm of the sleigh. Her elves had been working through the night to make the bike completely perfect for some lucky child who would cross their path that night. The bike was riding without a name attached to it; but it would be leaving the sleigh that night, that much was certain. A young boy called Ruben rushed over, as the sleigh drew up in his part of the village. He was carrying his baby brother in his arms; his little friend beside him was riding a bike with one wheel larger than the other, but it was still a bike. "Do you have a bike of your own?" asked the fairly young Santa girl. Ruben shook his head. "Would you like a bike?" she asked. Ruben became immediately speechless and nodded deeply; his big brown eyes round as deep chocolate pools. Handing the baby brother to a nearby elf, Ruben leapt on his bike. It fitted him perfectly; the elves had done well. He raced down the path to show his parents, mouth wide in the largest grin of his young life. “Mama,” he cried. “Mama; Santa is here.”

For those of you struggling to still believe in the spirit of Christmas, look inside yourself and see what you can find, then look outside of yourself and see where you can go with it. For those of you doubting in the existence of Santa Claus, look around your village and you may find that there is more than one in your midst. For the children of Soledad, there is definitely one who comes to mind; she is a fairly young girl who lives in the village with a big heart and sometimes even bigger hats. Her name is Sandy or Sandty-Claus, at this time of year; and her spirit will live on for always within the many hearts she touches. It was estimated that, every year, around 1,000 toys are delivered to the children of Soledad.

**Lucy loves to collect books for the toy drive every year.**

# SHARING A FAVORITE PRESENT

My daughter's favorite present for Christmas was my IPOD, and I say that most sincerely. Right after we had purchased her gifts, none of which contained the 'POD' word, she announced to the world that the thing she most wanted for Christmas was an IPOD. It was the only thing she wanted; and the thing that would make her most happy and most content, (until she came upon the next thing that she couldn't stand to live without.) That's what happens when you are almost 13. Compulsive must-haves hit you in the head like a disease and take over every organ of your being.

"I didn't get her an IPOD", my husband confessed to me, during one of those rare, husband-wife come-to-Jesus meetings. "I got you one." A sick feeling came over me, almost as if he had told me, "I don't love you anymore. I love the neighbor." I could pre-imagine Christmas Day, as my darling baby suffered and stressed, probably with real tears, as I unpack the present that she wanted more than anything in the world and get to claim it as my own.

"Why don't you just give it to her?" I said nonchalantly. I had lived thus far without an IPOD; I was sure that it wouldn't break my heart to live without it a while longer.

"Why don't you just tell her that you'll share it with her?" he broached cautiously. And so, an unusual concept was born in our house; the idea that you could share a coveted present with a tween and nobody would get hurt.

The first day of its arrival in our house, I never even got to touch it. The Pod went from the wrapping – from which said tween extracted it – to her hot little hands; and then to the download station in my office, at my computer, with my credit card. Some present! It then had lots of rump-de-bump music put on it and I almost said goodbye to it forever. It then proceeded to travel away on a sleepover without permission, and I had to wonder if it would go the same way as the cell phone – lost and abandoned forever in the ice cream shop – but, to my surprise, it reappeared in all its white and silver glory to live to see another day in our house.

"See Mum; if you tell me which songs you want from your CD's, I can put them on the IPOD for you," the co-owner said helpfully; and so began a new relationship with my Christmas present and my daughter's most coveted Christmas present in the whole wide world. Leave it to a tween to teach you things you thought you didn't want to know!

The POD then got inadvertently left behind at home one day and I practically fell in love. Me and the POD and lots of classic songs from the 1980's and who knows when started going on long walks with the dogs. We looked at the river, the sky and the mountains. We watched the jack rabbit skirt through the vines and we laughed as the dog tried to find the scent and failed miserably. We admired the curve of the road and the line of the ridge top – all things we had never noted before from that particular angle in life with those particular tunes. We sang and we skipped just a little; me and the POD; and all because we could. As the sky darkened over the valley, we looked at the clock, we grabbed the POD and the walking shoes, and off we went again; again, all because we could, and all because it was now so much more fun than it had been before. Music can take you to places you thought you'd forgotten or left behind, somewhere on your journey.

And so the shared Christmas present is really quite a hit. It's almost always where I want it and how I want it to be. Most of the time it has the songs I want to listen to at my very finger-tips and, if not, some one very smart aged 12 knows how to get them there in no time at all. If you had told me a month ago, this small thing was possible – me working an IPOD and my daughter sharing a Christmas present, I'd have said "Get outta here!" Miracles are possible; even just very tiny ones and it's so lovely when they unfold before your very eyes.

**Lucy was later given back that very same IPOD as a gift she got to keep to herself.**

# AFTER THE HOLIDAYS

# RESOLVE TO KEEP RESOLVED

Many years ago I gave up trying to make New Year's resolutions. Most of the time, the resolve would involve attempting to lose the pesky 10 pounds, which had somehow found its way onto my already lumpy regions, through festive hours spent grazing and chowing as if there were no tomorrow.

I would then commence starvation proceedings on January 2nd, (still far too many goodies around on the 1st to take it seriously at that point and ridiculous lines into the gym a mile long). January 3rd, in strict diet mode and aspiring to very shortly drag myself into those jeans which had quickly become agony over the feasting season, I would then forbid myself to be tempted by all the things I had indulged in so freely during the previous month. Warning: inside we are all children. Forbidding yourself to have something/anything is like carte blanche to start immediately cheating on the regime, craving forbidden fruits at night and skidding through drive-through windows undercover, ordering the double extra-chunky-melty ooze-burger, (with the diet coke on the side), and procrastinating standing on the scale for another week at least to avoid the inevitable ensuing depression.

If it wasn't so sadly darn normal, this type of behavior would send health and fitness analysts into a frenzy of excitement, embracing another fool to be drawn into their pool of candidates for the life of ping-pong dieting, guaranteed to keep their industry afloat forever. However, I look around and I do think that it's pretty normal.

The Doctor Pills of the day thrive on writing yet another book on the "Weight Loss Phenomena", "The Obesity Crisis" or, my own personal favorite, "Living Fat Free", as they fill up their coffers on the miseries of millions and invite Bill and Belle from Tennessee onto their show to illustrate how they manage cheat on themselves in the weight loss race of life; how they lose the required 100 pounds with the help of top-level trainers and pantry monitors, not to mention the cameras installed on the wall over the refrigerator; then blow it all in one holiday season and end up crying for more help on national TV. There's a lot of money in fat and that is a for sure. Just like cancer and other big disease money makers – in my completely unqualified and biased opinion - they do not want us to figure out the formula for healthy living and a long life free of the stresses of yo-yo binge-stressing. And yes, I do know that the formula is diet and exercise, duh. Oh and some intake moderation on the side, with a regime of five miles jogging a week thrown in, cabbage soup for supper and definitely no chocolate or potato chips, no matter what your hormones tell you and definitely not together.

Few people seem to avoid the plague in our too-much-of-everything society; most people are "holics" in one way or another. We all seem to live with the excess gene under our roofs; whether it be for shopping, food, booze, gambling, tobacco and the list goes on and on.

My friend is an exercise-aholic, which is an interesting one. What this creates is a person who is completely self-obsessed much of the time. (May that be 'cos she just loves her body so much these days that she can't stop gloating over it, or that she hasn't exercised enough in any given week, so she beats herself up over it). It does seem that, discounting her gorgeous bod, this latest obsession cannot be that good for her mind or her popularity stakes. When she was young, she used to be a chunky food-aholic, which made her fit much more in with the rest of us. Now she is a lithe athlete, who can literally eat whatever she wants, run 10 miles and never gain an ounce; that just leaves the likes of me gawking and jealous. The last I heard she was going to climb Mount Shasta, which definitely makes her most interesting; though, as her good friend, I know that the grit which drives her at the base of it all is her fear that, if she stops all this manic-compulsive behavior, she'll be fat again.

My meager resolve this year is to do what I started last year, but just improve upon it. That may sound lame to the likes of you who have a fool-proof plan to lose 100 pounds or climb Mount Shasta, but for me it's probably about the most honest and realistic aspiration I can have at this juncture in middle age. Write things down, they say and then they become real. So we'll try and go with that:-

1. Read more books and keep a log of the good ones; write a quick note or two to that effect and share more of them with more friends.
2. Finally throw away, before New Year's Day, all the remnants of holiday food evil which are still sitting there on the shelves smiling at me.
3. Give away all the remaining size 8 clothes in my closet, even if I really like them and imagine my daughter may one day wear them for a fancy dress party. You'll never get there, girl; let it go.
4. Reorganize my computer files and throw away all the garbage, including any horrid pictures of myself.
5. Put my photos in albums as soon as I have processed them. This has been a pledge now for the past ga-zillion years and I have still not accomplished it; but it will remain on the list, because, as they say, if you write things down, they have a better chance of becoming real.
6. Go to the gym more than I have been doing and work a little harder when I am there. Just 'cos I hate doing push ups does not mean I should allow myself to lie on my back and gaze up at the ceiling, while others are toiling and working their booties. Learn some self-discipline, woncha?
7. Do not wait to do the laundry until we have all run out of socks.
8. Have more patience and a little less tongue. Be kinder, cooler, smarter. (Number 8 is just a dream).
9. Oh, and last but not least: at least lose the pounds I put on over the holiday season and try not to snack between meals. I mean, I learned that when I was like a tiny baby – don't you think I should have got it by now?

**Lucy knows that a perfect shape comes through diet and exercise. She just doesn't do it all the time.**

# THE LAST BITE

And so with the last bite of the creamy Christmas cheesecake, the ultimate morsel of chocolate and definitely the final crumb of ginger cake, you wave sorrowfully goodbye to the deluge of feasting that you promised yourself you would avoid this year; as you do every year. In the back of your mind, you have been listening to the skinny diet gurus wax lyrical about the feasting period, and that makes you even madder:-

"It's very manageable, if you do everything in moderation," they banter on in their skinny way. "If you go a little over one day during the festive season, with the Bailey's liqueur and cream puffs, then you cut back the next day; over-compensate, if you were, for your over-indulgence." Yeh, blah, blah; yadder, yadder; I get that whole concept, but why do I never, ever do it?

Thanksgiving was well over a month ago and our entire family has been off the wagon ever since. All that yummy gravy, mashed potato and pie somehow held caution hostage and threw any good intents we might have had prior to the wind. Since then, over a month down the long road of bingeing, it has been one thing after another; from office pot lucks and parties, to visitors with boxes of chocolates and guests bearing pie. It's really more than one over-indulged American family can take. I have a feeling somehow, though, looking around, that we're not alone.

With the end of Boxing Day and the last catered event at the house, our family just took their own destiny in their hands and threw away the last of the ice cream and the chocolate and vowed to live a more holistic existence from now on; at least until next Thanksgiving. As the last slice of cheesecake hit the trash can, husband could be heard whining, "But what are we going to have for dessert?" Over-eating becomes a habit which can easily transcend into a way of life if you don't watch it; and 7 long weeks from the largest feast of the year and several extra pounds later, we are all still suffering from it. Husband has put on 11lbs and counting; and who's crying now?

But we're remorseful now at least, which we weren't yesterday, and that's a step in the right direction. With the symbolic slinging of the delicious cheesecake into the trash, we have made a statement, taken a stand against the constant barrage of food advertising and enticements to become larger than we ever needed or wanted to be.

"Don't ever let me look like that, mom," my daughter will plea as she sees a person larger than herself in line at the fast food stand; and she'll then, without blinking, proceed to order her extra large fries with juicy burger and think nothing of it. But for now, our entire family is attending dietary boot-camp. We're all on board, and that has to make it easier to get things a little under control. The chocolates are gone, as are the cookies. On the shopping list this week is the lean chicken breast with the broccoli and yoghurt. No more the creamy sauces and the buttery breads. We're in nutritional detoxification and are moving back steadily towards our vegetable soups and salads; fruits, yoghurts and teas. No more the copious glasses of rich red wine in the afternoon and port late at night; we will be in rehabilitation for the entire month of January, maybe even beyond; until we learn some sort of self control and dietary responsibility. (Or, at least, until we're back to the weight we were pre-Thanksgiving, and that wasn't exactly optimum!)

So what happens at this time of year; you do have to wonder! Seemingly sane human beings become voracious addicts in their quest for the next creamy chocolate or slice of pie; that much we know. But what triggers this manic behavior? Happiness and merriment are transported from one family to another through the food chain; that much is clear. Meals are part of our celebrating and some of us just simply do not know when to say no; or to stop when are bodies are squealing that they're full and do we really have to continue to do that to them. That is why the gyms get full up at this time of year and the new memberships go on overdrive. So many of us over-exceed ourselves in our quest to enjoy, be happy and do things quite other than what we normally do; and remorse is the end result.

I am envious of people who can decline that additional dessert, or not go for the second helping of what was so obviously a delicious main course that they may not taste again for a very long time. I have no self control and I possess the appetite of an ox. Armed with that kind of self-knowledge, it is no wonder that I am now packing my gym bag for the months ahead and waddling around my life wondering what happened all those 7 weeks ago when caution was thrown to the wind and gluttony moved into my body.

Maybe if I am really hard on myself this year, next year will not be such a problem. In the meantime; let this be a word of caution to you all to stop the bleeding now, admit where you slipped up and, whatever else you do, throw that completely yummy piece of cheesecake immediately into the trash.

May remorse fill the sails of your ship and help guide you into safer waters.

Lucy

# WINTER OCCUPATIONS

Head thick with cold and nose red and sore with wiping, I gazed out at the constant grey and drizzle outside my window and from there to the soothing glow of the scarlet embers in my fireplace. For a while I am transported in time and place to my childhood in England; where the Januarys were always just so.

After the holiday season was over, all the sparkly lights would come down; there would be no more wrinkling of wrapping paper or gasps of excitement. No one talked about parties anymore or present- giving and the chocolate box was empty of all the good stuff and not even just metaphorically speaking. People always got ill and took to their beds and January would lie like a wet blanket around the necks of most who suffered her. “Everybody hates January, darling”, my mother would say to me just about every beginning of every year we had together; when I was ill in bed with bronchitis or sobbing with depression at the desolation I was feeling, which always seemed to be quite a lot that time of year.

There was the memorable January, when everyone in the family, except for mother and I, got horribly ill with the flu immediately after Christmas and stopped eating. Ever the thrifty product of a family growing up during war-time, mother cooked up every describable turkey dish in her repertoire to try and rid us of the holiday bird without actually throwing it away. I’m not sure if it was the 10$^{th}$ day of turkey – or if it just felt like it – that she made a turkey curry which almost killed me from food poisoning. I don’t know who felt more wretched about the whole thing; me losing the walls of my stomach, or her having inflicted it upon me. The memory of this has survived in our family archives to this day, (okay, in retrospect, it was pretty funny); and my contribution to the whole thing is that I will never be able to eat left-overs after more than 2 days of being “left over”. Just as well. Thanks, ma.

Ah, the cold gloomy greys of January, when the light never seems to really come up and the rain never seems to stop. That’s sort of how it felt the past few days when I was rudely afflicted by some nasty bug or other that an infectious person had graciously given to me, leaving me feverish and snarling at the used damp hankies and the wasted days in the snivel I call my life. As I began to recover somewhat from this rude invasion and not lie comatose at 5.30 in the afternoon, I came to realize that sometimes your body tells you what you need, and when you don't listen to it, it makes you mind.

As I gazed into my beautiful fire, I was giving myself the opportunity to stop and think, which I don't always allow when I'm up and healthy and game for the next round. I let my mind wander back to Januarys past; to my childhood and my mother and the laughs we had over her devilled turkey. I thought back to the cuddles I had been able to indulge in when I was feeling down and her reassurances that January would soon be over and everything would be better. I could go to all of those places just by snuggling up next to the fire and allowing it to happen. That was probably the beginning of my recovery in a lot of ways.

Then there was the trip down memory lane in the form of the famous Monopoly game, a truly great wet weather/nasty bug game. Not only can you play it indoors, you can truly play it for days on end. I had not touched a board for decades, but it is so like riding a bike. My daughter gleefully creamed my husband on her first 4 hour marathon hike around the property board. Discounting the fact that her mother is in property herself and had maybe played the odd game throughout her long-ish life, the little minx set off on her 2nd victory run a little quickly. Horrified, when she realized that not only had I played the odd game in my time, but that I was quite good at it and way more ruthless than her father, we began a delicious war which consumed much of a very wet grey slushy Sunday afternoon in January and seeped into Monday evening as well. Take your mind back to indoor games that you may have enjoyed and dust them off; it can be such a fun way to interact with your family, brings back some memories too on a damp post holiday afternoon. There's no way you can feel depressed when you're slaughtering somebody at Monopoly with the fire blazing in the hearth!

But in California we should truly be rejoicing; not for the nasty bugs that many of us are suffering, but for the fact that the winter has driven us indoors to the interiors of homes which many of us just barely glance at much of the year! Look at the bright side of things! Our men are not kicking dirt out on the ranches where they'd like to be, or spooling a reel in some distant lake or other; they are right here where we like them to be in the kingdom of "honey do". I can almost feel a list coming on! There are surely indoor painting projects to complete, pictures to hang, lights to fix, rooms to reorganize. Then, of course, there is the garage to tidy once again and shelving to hang. We can keep them so entirely busy, they'd never have time to be depressed about the weather.

We are so fortunate to live in the best climate in the world and I believe that most sincerely, despite our recent deluge. Our sunshine is something we take so entirely for granted that, after 2 weeks of what I will call the English greys and a "fair bit of rain", (to coin some good British understatement), we are all crying for the yellow stuff, begging for our hills to once again be corn-colored and aching for the Soledad wind to come howling down the valley and remind us, that yes, we're lucky, oh so lucky, to live where we do.

**Lucy has learned to love the Californian winter, which always seems to be brief.**